Heavenly Realms and Earthly Realities in Late Antique Religions

Heaven held a special place in the late antique imagination. A poignant sense of the relevance of heavenly realms for earthly life can be found not only in Judaism and Christianity but also in Graeco-Roman religious, philosophical, scientific, and "magical" traditions. The preoccupation with otherworldly realities transcends social, regional, and creedal boundaries. The topic of heaven thus serves as an ideal focus for an interdisciplinary approach to understanding this formative era in Western history. Drawing on the expertise of scholars of Classics, Ancient History, Biblical Studies, Jewish Studies, and Patristics, this volume explores the different functions of heavenly imagery in different texts and traditions in order to map the patterns of unity and diversity within the religious landscape of Late Antiquity.

Ra'anan S. Boustan is Assistant Professor in the Department of Classical and Near Eastern Studies at the University of Minnesota. A scholar of early Judaism, he has published studies on early Jewish mysticism, the relationship between Jews and Christians in Late Antiquity, and the role of gender and sexuality within Judaism, among other topics.

Annette Yoshiko Reed is Assistant Professor in the Department of Religious Studies at McMaster University. Her research spans the fields of Biblical Studies, Jewish Studies, and Patristics, and her publications include *The Ways that Never Parted: Jews and Christians in Late Antiquity and the Early Middle Ages* (coedited with Adam H. Becker).

HEAVENLY REALMS

AND

EARTHLY REALITIES

IN

LATE ANTIQUE RELIGIONS

Edited by

RA'ANAN S. BOUSTAN
University of Minnesota

ANNETTE YOSHIKO REED
McMaster University

CAMBRIDGE
UNIVERSITY PRESS

PUBLISHED BY THE PRESS SYNDICATE OF THE UNIVERSITY OF CAMBRIDGE
The Pitt Building, Trumpington Street, Cambridge, United Kingdom

CAMBRIDGE UNIVERSITY PRESS
The Edinburgh Building, Cambridge CB2 2RU, UK
40 West 20th Street, New York, NY 10011-4211, USA
477 Williamstown Road, Port Melbourne, VIC 3207, Australia
Ruiz de Alarcón 13, 28014 Madrid, Spain
Dock House, The Waterfront, Cape Town 8001, South Africa

http://www.cambridge.org

First published 2004

Printed in the United States of America

Typefaces ITC Legacy 10/13.5 pt. and Diotima   *System* LaTeX 2$_\varepsilon$ [TB]

A catalog record for this book is available from the British Library.

Library of Congress Cataloging in Publication Data available

ISBN 0 521 83102 4 hardback

Contents

Contents

Preface

The present volume is the product of a unique sort of collaborative effort aimed at bringing together relatively unseasoned scholars – that is, graduate students – and their more experienced counterparts in an environment conducive to interdisciplinary research. In 2000, when the editors were both still in the midst of our doctoral studies in the Religions of Late Antiquity subfield of the Department of Religion at Princeton University, Prof. Peter Schäfer approached us for ideas about innovative ways to enrich graduate-student training and to foster further collaboration between faculty and students in our subfield, with the support of funds generously granted for this purpose by Prof. John F. Wilson, then Dean of Princeton's Graduate School. This dovetailed with a growing sense on the part of the students in our subfield that we would benefit from having a formal yet supportive forum at which to share our ongoing research. Excited discussions soon yielded a plan for an event with a twofold structure: (1) a semester-long workshop on a theme of special relevance to the study of Late Antiquity, at which students would present papers and receive feedback from Princeton students and faculty, culminating in (2) a public colloquium that would feature reworked versions of these papers, alongside presentations from the faculty members of the workshop and invited scholars from other institutions.

To enhance this project's benefits for graduate-student training, it was determined that the responsibility for organizing both elements of this event, as well as for choosing the topic, the title, and the scholars to invite to the colloquium, would fall to us. Working under the guidance of Prof. Schäfer, we decided that the distinctively late antique fascination with the otherworldly realms presented a suitably variegated and widespread phenomenon for our project, intersecting the diverse areas of interest represented in our subfield while also opening the way for a profitably interdisciplinary vista onto the religious landscape of Late Antiquity. Accordingly, we chose a title that reflected our interest in the relationship between images of heaven and the social, cultural, and historical contexts that shaped them: "In Heaven as It Is on Earth: Imagined Realms and Earthly Realities in Late Antique Religions."

From September to December 2000, the faculty and doctoral students in our subfield met biweekly to discuss student papers on this theme. As we had hoped, these meetings served to foster a productive setting of continued, informal dialogue and to encourage the exchange of research between members of our subfield with expertise in different religious traditions and geographical areas, even as they fulfilled the aim of providing students with feedback toward revising their papers for presentation at the culminating colloquium. At this event, held at Princeton on January 14–15, 2001, we were joined by scholars from other universities, from a range of intersecting fields – Classics, Religious Studies, Ancient History, Jewish Studies, Patristics – who shared the products of their ongoing research on images of heaven.

The success of this event surpassed our expectations. The individual papers were of high quality, the dialogue that they sparked was unusually spirited, and even the participants expressed their surprise at the powerful perspective on late antique religion that emerged from the cumulative effect of the diverse presentations. Despite our different disciplines and fields of specialization, we found ourselves confronted by many of the same interpretative issues and methodological problems; not only were we pleased to discover many intriguing parallels and patterns within different late antique religions, but our interdisciplinary dialogue also allowed us to share the products of our individual attempts to forge heuristic new approaches to studying Late Antiquity. The present volume aims to capture the spirit of this event and to build upon its insights. We here include many of the papers presented at the 2001 colloquium, which have been revised and expanded to reflect our discussions there, together with six additional contributions solicited especially for this publication.[1]

Space does not permit a complete list of all those, at Princeton and beyond, who contributed to the success of the workshop and colloquium and who helped to make this volume possible. We would be remiss, however, not to express our deepest debt of gratitude to Prof. Schäfer, without whom

---

[1] The success of this project also opened the way for another workshop and colloquium in 2001–2002 – the second of what we hope are many, many more to come – which tackled the topic of early Jewish–Christian relations. Proceedings have recently been published by Mohr Siebeck: A. H. Becker and A. Y. Reed, eds., *The Ways that Never Parted: Jews and Christians in Late Antiquity and the Early Middle Ages* (TSAJ 95; Tübingen, 2003).

none of this could have happened. From our initial brainstorming sessions about the workshop and colloquium until the completion of this volume, he has shown an intuitive understanding of how to guide this project with a sure hand, while at the same time ensuring that it continued to be shaped primarily by those it was intended to serve, us graduate students. His selfless mentoring has been a rare gift, from which we both have profited more than words can say.

We would like to express our appreciation to Profs. Peter Brown, Fritz Graf, Martha Himmelfarb, and Elaine Pagels for participating in the workshop and chairing sessions at the colloquium. We are, in addition, profoundly grateful to Dr. Beatrice Rehl at Cambridge University Press for her keen advice on the shape, scope, and focus of this book during every stage of its growth, and for her kindness and patience in shepherding us through the publication process. The volume also benefited from the extensive and incisive comments offered by the anonymous readers who reviewed the manuscript. To Lily Vuong and Jennifer Sanders, we offer thanks for their herculean indexing efforts. And, last but not least, we offer our warmest thanks to the contributors to this volume for their unflagging patience and enthusiasm.

Ra'anan S. Boustan
Cambridge, Massachusetts

Annette Yoshiko Reed
Hamilton, Ontario

Abbreviations of primary sources, journal titles, and names of book series within this volume follow P. H. Alexander, J. F. Kutsko, J. D. Ernst, S. A. Decker–Lucke, and D. L. Petersen, eds., *The SBL Handbook of Style: For Ancient Near Eastern, Biblical, and Early Christian Studies* (Peabody, Mass., 1999), and S. Hornblower and A. Spawforth, eds., *Oxford Classical Dictionary*, 3rd ed. (Oxford, 1996).

Contributors

ADAM H. BECKER is Assistant Professor/Faculty Fellow in the Religious Studies Program at New York University. He completed his dissertation, a study of Christian institutions of learning in late antique and early Islamic Mesopotamia, in the Department of Religion at Princeton University in 2003. His publications include *The Ways That Never Parted: Jews and Christians in Late Antiquity and the Early Middle Ages* (2003), coedited with Annette Y. Reed.

RA'ANAN S. BOUSTAN (né Abusch) is Assistant Professor in the Department of Classical and Near Eastern Studies at the University of Minnesota. His dissertation, written in the Department of Religion at Princeton University, explores the literary and ideological relationships between Jewish mystical and martyrological literatures.

JAN N. BREMMER is Professor of History and Science of Religion at the Rijksuniversiteit Groningen. He is the author of *The Early Greek Concept of the Soul* (1983), *Greek Religion* (1994), and *The Rise and Fall of the Afterlife* (2002).

KIRSTI B. COPELAND teaches at Santa Clara University. She has held numerous fellowships, including the Woodrow Wilson Fellowship, the Whiting Dissertation Fellowship, and the Lady Davis Fellowship. She wrote her dissertation, "Mapping the Apocalypse of Paul: Geography, Genre and History" (2001), in the Religion Department at Princeton University. She is currently producing a volume of translations of Coptic Apocrypha for the University of Pennsylvania Press.

RADCLIFFE G. EDMONDS III is Assistant Professor of Greek, Latin, and Ancient History at Bryn Mawr College. His research interests include

mythology, religion, and Platonic philosophy, with particular focus on the
marginal categories of magic and Orphism within Greek religion.

SUSANNA ELM is Professor of History and Religion at the University of Cali-
fornia at Berkeley. She is the author of *Virgins of God: The Making of Asceticism
in Late Antiquity* (1994) and coeditor with E. Rebillard of *Orthodoxie, Christianisme, Histoire-Orthodoxy, Christianity, History* (2000). She is currently finishing
a manuscript on Gregory of Nazianzus, tentatively titled "Sons of Hellenism,
Fathers of the Church: Gregory of Nazianzus, Julian, Themistius, and the
Christianization of the Late Roman Elites."

CHRISTOPHER A. FARAONE is Professor in the Department of Classics and
the Committee on the Ancient Mediterranean World at the University of
Chicago. He is coeditor with T. Carpenter of *Masks of Dionysus* (1993) and
author of *Ancient Greek Love Magic* (1999), as well as a number of articles on
early Greek poetry, religion, and magic.

FRITZ GRAF is Professor of Greek and Latin at the Ohio State University where
he is also director of epigraphy at the Center for Epigraphical and Palaeo-
graphical Studies. His main research interests lie with Greek and Roman
religion, increasingly with their development in later antiquity and with the
contribution epigraphy can make to the field.

MARTHA HIMMELFARB is Professor of Religion at Princeton University and
chair of the Department of Religion. Her books include *Ascent to Heaven in
Jewish and Christian Apocalypses* (1993), which treats the heavenly Temple and
its relationship to the earthly.

SARAH ILES JOHNSTON is Professor of Greek and Latin and an Affiliate of the
Religious Studies Program at the Ohio State University. She specializes in
Mediterranean religions, particularly of Late Antiquity, with an emphasis on
practices that are often collected under the term "magic." She is the author
of *Restless Dead* (1999), *Hekate Soteira* (1990), and various articles, as well as
the coeditor of *Medea* (1996).

JOHN W. MARSHALL is Assistant Professor in the Department for the Study
of Religion at the University of Toronto. He is the author of *Parables of War:
Reading John's Jewish Apocalypse* (2001).

Contributors

ANNETTE YOSHIKO REED is Assistant Professor in the Department of Religious Studies at McMaster University. She received her Ph.D. from Princeton University in 2002 with a dissertation on the fallen angels. Her publications include *The Ways that Never Parted: Jews and Christians in Late Antiquity and the Early Middle Ages* (2003), coedited with Adam H. Becker.

PETER SCHÄFER is the Ronald O. Perelman Professor of Jewish Studies and Professor of Religion at Princeton University. His most recent book is *Mirror of His Beauty: Feminine Images of God from the Bible to the Early Kabbala* (2002).

GOTTFRIED SCHIMANOWSKI is a researcher at the Institutum Judaicum Delitzschianum. His publications include *Weisheit und Messias: Die jüdischen Voraussetzungen der urchristlichen Präexistenzchristologie* (1985) and *Die himmlische Liturgie in der Apokalypse des Johannes: Die frühjüdische Traditionen in Offenbarung 4–5 unter Einschluß der Hekhalotliteratur* (2002).

KATHARINA VOLK is Assistant Professor of Classics at Columbia University. She has published *The Poetics of Latin Didactic: Lucretius, Vergil, Ovid, Manilius* (2002) and is currently working on a monograph on the Roman astrological poet Manilius.

Introduction: "In Heaven as It Is on Earth"

Ra'anan S. Boustan and Annette Yoshiko Reed

The conquests of Alexander of Macedon radically expanded the horizons of the eastern Mediterranean and Near East, inaugurating an era paradoxically marked by the increased interpenetration of different cultures and the cultivation of self-conscious particularism within these same cultures. Although Alexander's empire soon fragmented, the scope of his conquests sketched the boundaries of a new world. In the following centuries, Hellenistic, Roman, Sassanian, and Byzantine rulers would attempt to conquer and administer parts of this domain, and members of subject nations would circulate through it with increased ease, distributing economic goods and religious knowledge along its trade routes.

Cross-cultural contact was hardly unprecedented. New, however, was the emergence of a common cultural landscape and the growing sense – whether positive or negative – of living in a single *oikoumene*. Scholars have traditionally focused on the "hellenization" of conquered nations, but the "orientalization" of Graeco–Roman society was no less significant in shaping the culture of Late Antiquity.[1] Moreover, both trends continued to be characterized by the dynamic interplay between acculturation and anxiety about acculturation. Among conquered nations, we find zealous attempts to guard ancient traditions against perceived threats of contamination, alongside enthusiastic efforts to embrace a cosmopolitan identity, with all the economic benefits and social status that came with it.[2] In turn, the "alien wisdom" of

---

[1] Here we use the term *Late Antiquity* in its very broadest sense, to encompass the period between the conquests of Alexander the Great and the rise of Islam. In research on the political and social history of the eastern Mediterranean world, the term is often used to denote only the late Roman Empire (i.e., 250–800 C.E.). With regard to the topics discussed in this volume, however, texts, genres, ideas, and motifs in these centuries cannot be understood apart from formative developments in the Hellenistic age and the early Roman Empire.

[2] This dynamic has been studied – and debated – most intensely in the context of Judaism, particularly after the publication of M. Hengel's classic *Judentum und Hellenismus: Studien zu*

1

Egyptians, Babylonians, Persians, and Jews attracted many Greek and Roman thinkers, and their fascination with the foreign facilitated innovations in religion, philosophy, science, and "magic," thereby birthing traditions with uniquely late antique pedigrees.[3]

If late antique culture is best characterized as a unity predicated on diversity and actualized in dynamic hybridity,[4] how can we describe its salient features? The present volume attempts to chart the religious landscape of this culture by following a single vital theme across social, regional, and credal boundaries: the fascination with heavenly realms. Our evidence suggests that the idea of heaven held a special place in the late antique imagination, shaped by a sharp sense of the relevance of otherworldly realities for earthly existence. Such concerns can be found not only in Jewish and Christian texts, but also in the literature of Graeco-Roman religions, the astrological and astronomical sciences, and the magical traditions that flowered during this era. Examples are as plentiful as our sources are diverse.

Perhaps the most striking development is the new sense of the possibility of movement between earth and heaven. In different literary discourses in a range of geographical, cultural, and religious milieus, we find descriptions of heaven from those who claim to have visited that realm. Heaven is not simply the distant abode of deities and souls of the dead, barred from invasion by human bodies, eyes, and minds. Rather, it is a locale frequented by patriarchs and prophets of the distant past and, in many cases, by martyrs, mystics, and magicians of the present age. Even when the essential inaccessibility of heaven is affirmed, our texts reveal heavenly secrets in surprisingly concrete terms; common topics of speculation include the topography of the starry heavens, the architecture of celestial structures, the identity and function of myriad angelic hosts, and the character of heavenly liturgies, rituals, and supernal objects such as tablets, scrolls, and books. The world above remains

---

ihrer Begegnung unter besonderer Berücksichtigung Palästinas bis zur Mitte des 2. Jh. v. Chr. (Tübingen, 1969). For a broader perspective see, e.g., A. Bulloch, E. Gruen, A. A. Long, and A. Stewart, eds., *Images and Ideologies: Self-Definition in the Hellenistic World* (Berkeley, 1993).

[3] We do, of course, find Near Eastern influences in Greek culture long before the Hellenistic era. It remains, however, that Alexander's conquests catalyzed a new type of contact; see the seminal discussion in A. Momigliano, *Alien Wisdom: The Limits of Hellenization* (Cambridge, 1971).

[4] The generative tension between religious diversity and cultural unity is well described by G. Bowersock, P. Brown, and O. Grabar, eds., *Late Antiquity: A Guide to the Postclassical World* (Cambridge, 1999), xi: "Whether they liked each other or not, they remained not only 'Christians,' 'Jews,' and 'pagans,' 'orthodox' and 'heretics,' 'clergy' and 'laity': they breathed the same heavy air of a common civilization – that of late antiquity."

shrouded in mystery, but more and more this mystery is cited for the sake of its revelation to those deemed chosen, pure, initiated, or wise.

As the limits of human knowledge expand to encompass exact knowledge about the world above, we also find an increased confidence in the human capacity to understand the influence of heavenly realities on earthly life. The widespread practice of astrology, for instance, simultaneously affirms the sway of the stars on the fate of humankind and empowers its practitioners to interpret their signs. The intimate relationship between heaven and earth similarly finds expression in the belief that our own realm swarms with otherworldly beings, whether angels, demons, or spirits of the dead. Whereas modern science conditions a sense of awe at the endless expanse of emptiness that stretches above us, late antique literature hints at a poignantly personalized view of heaven, charged with meaning for the individual and his or her community.

Scholars generally agree that Late Antiquity is marked by an intensification of interest in heaven. What is less clear, however, is how to explain this fascination with the space above and beyond this world. One of the most influential theories interprets the turn toward the otherworldly as a symptom of the alienation experienced by the rootless individual adrift in the vast imperial structures of the Hellenistic, Roman, Sassanian, and Byzantine worlds. Echoing the traditional characterization of the "postclassical" period as a trajectory of deterioration from "classical" ideals, this model assumes that people had once experienced the world as a coherent cosmic order, governed by enduring patterns of existence through which individual and society could maintain their harmonious relationship; after the conquests of Alexander the Great and the rise of the Roman Empire, however, imperial subjects increasingly saw themselves as living in an anonymous, cruel, and despotic system of capriciously imposed limitations and boundaries. In response, the disenfranchised individual could do nothing but "strive to return to the world-beyond-this-world which is his home, to the god-beyond-the-god-of-this-world which is the true god, to awaken that part of himself which is from the beyond and to strip off his body which belongs to this world."[5]

---

[5]   J. Z. Smith, *Map Is Not Territory: Studies in the History of Religion* (Chicago, 1978), 163–4. This emphasis on the collective religious experience of the post-Alexandrine age is particularly strong in H. Jonas, *Gnostic Religion: The Message of the Alien God and the Beginnings of Christianity*, 3d ed. (Boston, 2001) and E. R. Dodds, *Pagan and Christian in an Age of Anxiety: Some Aspects of Religious Experience from Marcus Aurelius to Constantine* (Cambridge, 1963).

This portrait of a society riddled with anxiety has a certain intuitive appeal, no doubt because it resonates with modern concerns about individuality and alienation. One might question, however, its heurism as an historical model. Instead of allowing for multiple impulses and causes, it reduces all interest in otherworldly realities to an escapist effort to cope with a collective cultural malaise.[6] By contrast, it is striking how often late antique authors use images of heaven to articulate their abiding commitment to this-worldly life and worship. Whereas some authors appear to project their earthly ideals into the skies above, poignantly evoking a sense of alienation from their mundane milieus, others construct radical images of heaven in order to critique their contemporaries on earth, undermining traditional structures of authority through appeals to a higher reality. Some sources do seem to be shaped by a yearning to abandon earthly thoughts entirely and participate in heavenly worship. But others tantalizingly suggest that the premundane or eschatological unity between earth and heaven can be actualized in the present, through religious rituals, magical practices, and/or liturgical performance.

No single attitude or disposition captures the disparate, often contradictory, aims of this literature. By positing a uniform narrative of disillusionment and alienation, we risk effacing the variety of conceptual valences and strategic aims found in our sources. Although the preoccupation with celestial realms transcends the boundaries between religious traditions, heavenly imagery serves different functions in different texts, communities, and cultures. As such, any attempt to survey this vast body of material must confront the paradoxical tension between cultural specificity and cultural hybridity so typical of an age in which a traditionalist impulse frequently served as the very ground of innovation.[7] To map the late antique discourse about heaven, we must thus base our search for cross-cultural commonalities in careful analyses of the specific religious traditions, literary genres, and social worlds in which they are expressed.

We now find ourselves at an apt moment in the history of scholarship to take up this challenge because of converging developments in research on Judaism, Christianity, and Graeco–Roman religions. Our understanding of the imagined heavens of Late Antiquity has been immeasurably enriched by recent developments in the study of the "pagan" religions and cultures of this period. Since its inception under the sway of nineteenth-century

---

[6]   P. Brown, *The Making of Late Antiquity* (Cambridge, Mass., 1978), 1–11.
[7]   A. Cameron, "Remaking the Past," in *Late Antiquity*, 1–20.

Introduction: "In Heaven as It Is on Earth"

Rationalism, the field of Classics had consistently disregarded the religious components of Greek and Roman life, privileging the philosophical and political works that modern western democracy claims as its heritage, while internalizing the theological dismissal of "paganism" as a primitive form of religiosity superceded by Judaeo–Christian monotheism. A new generation of classicists, however, has made startling progress in recovering the vitality of the Graeco-Roman religious tradition. Contrary to the traditional model of conflict and supercession, Greek and Roman forms of religious piety and ritual practice continued to flourish in a common sociocultural environment with Judaism and Christianity.[8] The acknowledgement of the continued vitality of "paganism" has opened the way for fresh insights into the complex social and linguistic interactions that generated the hybrid forms characteristic of religious thought and practice in Late Antiquity. Most notable are the rituals and beliefs gathered under the rubric "magic," which typically blurred cultural boundaries through the eclectic combination of elements from various traditions. The wealth of new research on this topic,[9] so sorely neglected by earlier scholarship, has simultaneously helped to stimulate academic interest in ancient astrology,[10] further illuminating the complex and multivalent conception of the heavens in the late antique imagination.

The past fifty years have also seen a paradigm shift in research on late antique Judaism and Christianity, spurred by the rediscovery of texts such as the Dead Sea Scrolls and Nag Hammadi Library and by the progressive integration of the study of these religions into the secular, academic discourse on human history, society, and culture more broadly. Shedding the theological biases that shaped past scholarship, scholars have increasingly sought to locate both Judaism and Christianity within the Graeco-Roman cultural context(s) of Late Antiquity. Likewise, the traditional bias for now-canonical literature – the Hebrew Bible, New Testament, classical rabbinic literature, writings of the church fathers – has gradually given way to more inclusive

---

[8] P. Chuvin, *A Chronicle of the Last Pagans*, trans. B. A. Archer (Cambridge, Mass., 1990); R. L. Fox, *Pagans and Christians* (New York, 1987); R. MacMullen, *Paganism in the Roman Empire* (New Haven, Conn., 1981), esp. 62–72; G. Fowden, "Bishops and Temples in the Eastern Roman Empire 320–425," *JTS* 29 (1978): 53–78.

[9] See most notably F. Graf, *Magic in the Ancient World*, trans. F. Philip (Revealing Antiquity 10; Cambridge, Mass., 1997); C. A. Faraone, *Ancient Greek Love Magic* (Cambridge, Mass., 1999); M. Dickie, *Magic and Magicians in the Greco-Roman World* (London, 2001); R. Ritner, *The Mechanics of Ancient Egyptian Magical Practice* (Chicago, 1993).

[10] For example, T. Barton, *Power and Knowledge: Astrology, Physiognomics, and Medicine Under the Roman Empire* (Ann Arbor, Mich., 1994).

5

approaches, which also encompass "apocryphal," "pseudepigraphical," and even "magical" and "mystical" literature.

In the process, it has become more and more evident that the history of Judaism and Christianity in Late Antiquity is not merely the story of the triumph of the "Great Church" over "pagans" and "heretics," the "Parting of the Ways" between Christianity and Judaism, and the rabbis' establishment of a new, normative Judaism, isolated from the world at large. Rather, the social, cultural, and geographical spread of Jewish and Christian communities in the late antique world was matched by a previously unimagined range of belief and practice that we are only now beginning to recover. Moreover, contrary to the conventional narratives about credal self-segregation and interreligious conflict, it seems that Jews and Christians alike forged their religious identities and community boundaries through a dynamic process of dialogue and debate, which engaged differences within and between the two traditions, no less than the "pagan" cultures around them.[11]

Among the many fruits of these developments is a richer understanding of how images of heaven functioned in the literature and lives of late antique Jews and Christians. The Dead Sea Scrolls, for instance, have provided exciting new evidence for the development of Jewish traditions about heaven and its hosts, ranging from the *Songs of the Sabbath Sacrifice*'s description of the angelic liturgy in heaven to the *War Scroll*'s vision of angelic participation in the eschatological battle on earth.[12] The discoveries at Qumran have simultaneously drawn attention to so-called "Apocrypha" and "Pseudepigrapha," which contain a wealth of ouranological and angelological traditions. Perhaps most notable is the apocalyptic literature, which served as a literary nexus for Jewish and Christian speculation about the heavens, influencing mystical, magical, and even martyrological traditions in both religions.[13] Research on these texts once privileged the historical and eschatological

[11] See D. Boyarin, *Dying for God: Martyrdom and the Making of Christianity and Judaism* (Stanford, Calif., 1999) and, most recently, A. H. Becker and A. Y. Reed, eds., *The Ways That Never Parted: Jews and Christians in Late Antiquity and the Early Middle Ages* (TSAJ 95; Tübingen, 2003).

[12] On the Dead Sea Scrolls' importance for the history of Jewish liturgy and mysticism, see, e.g., Elisabeth Hamacher, "Die Sabbatopferlieder im Streit um Ursprung und Anfänge der Jüdischen Mystik," *JSJ* 27 (1996): 119–54; M. D. Swartz, "The Dead Sea Scrolls and Later Jewish Magic and Mysticism," *DSD* 8 (2001): 182–93.

[13] On the reception of apocalyptic literature in Late Antiquity, see esp. J. VanderKam and W. Adler, eds., *Jewish Apocalyptic Heritage in Early Christianity* (Assen, 1996); I. Gruenwald, *Apocalyptic and Merkavah Mysticism* (AGAJU, 14; Leiden, 1980).

concerns that dominate the only two canonical apocalypses, the book of Daniel and Revelation. Yet, the discovery of fragments of 1 Enoch at Qumran exposed the special significance of two noncanonical writings therein, the *Astronomical Book* (1 Enoch 72–82) and *Book of the Watchers* (1 Enoch 1–36), for the early history of the genre. Now known to predate Daniel by some decades, these apocalypses conceive of heavenly secrets in a primarily spatial, rather than temporal, sense: In place of the eschatological timetables traditionally associated with apocalypses and apocalypticism, we here find an interest in topics like the gates of the winds, the paths of the sun, the prisons of the stars, and the supernal Temple, thus demonstrating the importance of ouranography and cosmology within the development of the apocalyptic literature.[14]

Although scholars had traditionally studied these and other noncanonical texts as part of the Jewish heritage of early Christianity and dismissed their relevance for our understanding of the allegedly this-worldly religion of the rabbis, recent research has revealed that many prerabbinic Jewish traditions – including those about the heavenly realms – enjoyed lively *Nachleben* in talmudic and post-talmudic Judaism.[15] At the same time, the study of early Jewish mysticism, which has flowered in the years since Peter Schäfer's 1981 publication of the Hekhalot literature,[16] has helped to illumine the wide range of ideological and theological perspectives still encompassed within late antique Judaism, even long after the rabbinic movement had more or less successfully extended its hegemony over most of Jewish life. Some scholars situate the Hekhalot literature in "mainstream" rabbinic circles, suggesting that the rabbinic movement was itself more diverse than previously imagined; others cite these writings to argue that the rabbis were unable (or unwilling) to police the boundaries of Jewish religious expression.[17] In

[14] For example, J. J. Collins, *The Apocalyptic Imagination: An Introduction to Jewish Apocalyptic Literature* 2d rev. ed. (Grand Rapids, Mich., 1998); M. Himmelfarb, *Ascent to Heaven in Jewish and Christian Apocalypses* (New York, 1993); M. E. Stone, "The Book of Enoch and Judaism in the Third Century B.C.E.," *CBQ* 40 (1978): 479–92; C. Rowland, *The Open Heaven: A Study of Apocalyptic in Judaism and Early Christianity* (London, 1982).

[15] For rabbinic innovations on early Jewish angelology, for instance, see P. Schäfer, *Rivalität zwischen Engeln und Menschen: Untersuchungen zur rabbinischen Engelvorstellung* (SJ 8; Berlin, 1975).

[16] P. Schäfer, ed., *Synopse zur Hekhalot-Literatur* (Tübingen, 1981).

[17] Recent attempts to situate the Hekhalot literature vis-à-vis rabbinic culture include D. Halperin, *The Faces of the Chariot* (Tübingen, 1988); M. D. Swartz, *Scholastic Magic: Ritual and*

either case, this literature has served to shed doubt on the monolithic portrait of post-70 Judaism painted in the classical rabbinic literature.[18]

The discovery and publication of the Nag Hammadi Library has had a similar impact on the study of early Christianity. The research of an entire generation of scholars has been shaped by the challenge of integrating both canonical and noncanonical materials in its account of developing Christianity, thereby transcending the simplistic dichotomy of "orthodoxy" and "heresy."[19] Our understanding of the specific sociological, regional, and literary trends within late antique Christianity has also been enriched by the research framework articulated by scholars such as Helmut Koester and James Robinson, who have stressed the tensions among multiple, often competing, "trajectories."[20] Whereas earlier treatments of church history tended to draw a straight line of evolution from apostolic age to the Holy Roman Empire, recent scholars have succeeded in tracing the numerous ideological and intertextual strands that weave their way throughout late antique Christianity, even broadening the project to embrace questions concerning the place of gender and ethnicity in the construction of Christian identity.[21]

Here, too, a more inclusive approach to our sources yields a plethora of traditions about otherworldly realms. New research on the texts in the Nag Hammadi Library and so-called New Testament Apocrypha has allowed scholars to situate the images of heaven in the New Testament and patristic literature within a broader continuum that encompasses noncanonical gospels, acts, martyrologies, apocalypses, and so on. The acknowledgement of the diversity within late antique Christianity has also facilitated research into the interaction between Christians and their contemporaries, both Jewish and "pagan." Once we begin to read the Christian rhetoric of supercessionism as rhetoric, we are able to see the degree to which Christian authors

---

Revelation in Early Jewish Mysticism (Princeton, N.J., 1996); J. R. Davila, *Descenders to the Chariot: The People Behind the Hekhalot Literature* (SJSJ 70; Leiden, 2001).

[18] So, too, with the extensive material and artistic remains of ancient synagogue life; see L. I. Levine, *The Ancient Synagogue: The First Thousand Years* (New Haven, Conn., 2000), and the ample bibliography cited there.

[19] See, e.g., H. Koester, "Apocryphal and Canonical Gospels," *HTR* 73 (1980): 105–30, and the essays in R. Williams, ed., *The Making of Orthodoxy* (Cambridge, 1989).

[20] J. M. Robinson and H. Koester, *Trajectories Through Early Christianity* (Philadelphia, 1971).

[21] For example, E. A. Clark, *Ascetic Piety and Women's Faith* (Lewiston, N.Y., 1986); P. Brown, *The Body and Society: Men, Women and Sexual Renunciation in Early Christianity* (New York, 1988); S. Elm, *Virgins of God* (Oxford, 1994); D. K. Buell, *Making Christians: Clement of Alexandria and the Rhetoric of Legitimacy* (Princeton, N.J., 1999); M. Kuefler, *The Manly Eunuch: Masculinity, Gender Ambiguity, and Christian Ideology in Late Antiquity* (Chicago, 2001).

strove to delineate a unique religious identity by distinguishing their own ritual practices, literary traditions, and communal institutions from the (often uncomfortably similar) forms in Judaism and Graeco–Roman culture. This, for instance, is clear in the constant refashioning and redeployment of Jewish and "pagan" images of heaven, which exemplifies the interplay between a resolute drive to unity and an enduring multiplicity in late antique Christianity.

These scholarly developments take on particular significance for those who wish to recover a more comprehensive understanding of the religious history of Late Antiquity. The study of the diverse religious phenomena of the postclassical world owes much to the work of Peter Brown.[22] Like E. R. Dodds before him, Brown recognizes the distinctive characteristics of late antique society, which made it so seminal for the history of Mediterranean and Near Eastern civilizations – as well as for the modern Western culture that they birthed. Brown, however, rejects Dodds' naive quest to reduce distinct social and intellectual movements to one determinative *Zeitgeist*. Paradoxically, in constructing a historiographic framework that transcends traditional disciplinary boundaries, Brown offers an expansive perspective on late antique society that calls attention to the generative tension between cultural commonality and local variation. His work has shown how the creation of a cosmopolitan intellectual *koine* was uniquely predicated on regional, social, and linguistic specificity. In Brown's account, the innovations that constituted the shared culture of Late Antiquity did not merely radiate out from its imperial center; rather, every periphery constituted a center with a distinctive social and cultural logic of its own.[23] Accordingly, this new approach to the "postclassical" world has paved the way for dialogue among specialists in quite diverse aspects of late antique religion.

The present volume is a product of such dialogue. Although no single book could cover all the relevant literature, we here attempt to provide a sampling of late antique literature that reflects the dazzling variety both within and between religious traditions. To emphasize the recurring themes, cross-cultural

---

[22] Although the study of religion in the late Roman Empire had never been fully neglected, its emergence as a major area of growth, at least within English language scholarship, can be traced directly to the appearance of Brown's *The World of Late Antiquity, AD 150–750* (New York, 1971) and the detailed social–historical account of late Roman life in A. H. M. Jones, *The Later Roman Empire: A Social Economic and Administrative Survey*, 3 vols. (Oxford, 1964).

[23] See esp. Brown's account of the complex negotiations between imperial power and local elites in *Power and Persuasion in Late Antiquity: Towards a Christian Empire* (Madison, Wisc., 1992).

motifs, and shared notions of the sacred in texts from different religious traditions, we have adopted a thematic arrangement that highlights the various ways in which late antique authors conceptualized the relationship between heaven and earth.

We begin with traditions that articulate the possibility of movement across the two realms. The articles in the first section, "Between Earth and Heaven," survey the range of attitudes toward the humans, angels, and souls that traverse this boundary, focusing on three themes: liminality, transgression, and transformation. In "The Bridge and the Ladder: Narrow Passages in Late Antique Visions," Fritz Graf challenges the pervasive tendency to harmonize the diverse images used to describe the passage from earth to heaven. In their quest for a single, unified history of the notion of the otherworldly journey, many scholars have simply smoothed over the fundamental structural difference between the vertical ladder and the horizontal bridge. By contrast, Graf's culturally and historically specific analysis succeeds in illuminating the process whereby each image gave rise to novel symbolic idioms within the Latin Christian literary tradition.

The ladders and bridges of Graf's article resonate intriguingly with a related metaphor from the scientific study of the stars, as analyzed in the next piece: "'Heavenly Steps': Manilius 4.119–121 and Its Background." Here, Katharina Volk argues that the description of the heavenly staircase in the Latin didactic poetry of Manilius draws on astrological motifs similar to those found in other contexts, such as the Hermetic corpus and Mithraism. When this Roman astrologer describes the heavenly heights that he himself climbs in his capacity as poet, he forges a parallel with the arc of the zodiac, thereby legitimating his authority with appeal to the cosmic order that binds together celestial and earthly realities.

In "Heavenly Ascent, Angelic Descent, and the Transmission of Knowledge in 1 Enoch 6–16," Annette Yoshiko Reed explores the transgression of the boundaries between heaven and earth by considering the epistemological ramifications of the descent of the fallen angels in the *Book of the Watchers*. Reed suggests that the redacted form of this early Jewish apocalypse cautions its readers against overzealous speculation into heavenly secrets by juxtaposing the fallen angels' corrupting teachings of humankind with Enoch's reception of divine wisdom after his ascent to heaven. As with the sources considered by Graf and Volk, this work presupposes the possibility of passage, both from earth to heaven and from heaven to earth. Here, however, the transgression of boundaries functions to underline the essential distinction between the two realms.

The next two contributions address the issue of transformation – first of humans on earth and then of souls in heaven. In "'Connecting Heaven and Earth': The Function of the Hymns in Revelation 4–5," Gottfried Schimanowski shows how the hymnic material in this New Testament apocalypse functions to unite earthly and heavenly communities in liturgical praise. His analysis focuses on the interrelation of these five hymns and their place in the apocalypse as a whole, exploring the role of heavenly worship in Revelation's unfolding drama of eschatological salvation. By progressively collapsing the gap separating heaven from earth and simultaneously bridging the past, the present, and the future, these hymns offer the earthly community a proleptic experience of worship in heaven, providing the reader/hearer with a foretaste – and a consoling promise – of an age in which evil will be defeated and the entire creation will be unified in praise of its creator.

In "Working Overtime in the Afterlife; or, No Rest for the Virtuous," Sarah Iles Johnston analyzes passages from the *Chaldean Oracles* and theurgic sources, which propose that the souls of the virtuous dead can choose to become guardian angels for the living. At the death of their bodies, these souls once traveled the path to heaven, but now they must turn their attention back to earth. Boundaries are articulated here to assert the meaningful interchange between earthly and heavenly spheres.

In our second section, titled "Institutionalizing Heaven," we turn to examine traditions about the structure and contents of heaven that draw on earthly models, thereby blurring the eschatological hope "On earth as it is in heaven!" (Matt 6:10) with the projection of earthly *realia* into the imagined realms above. In the process, we survey the most important earthly models for late antique ouranography: the Temple, the court, the city, the garden, and the school.

We begin with the Temple, the earthly institution most often associated with heaven in the ancient Near Eastern and biblical precedents. In "Earthly Sacrifice and Heavenly Incense: The Law of the Priesthood in *Aramaic Levi* and *Jubilees*," Martha Himmelfarb elucidates the complex relationship between early Jewish attitudes toward the Second Temple and contemporary images of the heavenly Temple by analyzing the representations of cultic practice in two Second Temple Jewish texts, *Aramaic Levi* and *Jubilees*. Many early Jewish and Christian texts betray a reticence about introducing blood sacrifice into the heavenly Temple; several of them imagine the heavenly cult as involving the bloodless medium of incense. Himmelfarb argues that this preference for aroma over blood not only determined the form of the heavenly cult, but also influenced the prescription for earthly sacrifice in *Jubilees* - thereby showing that, in certain cases, it is the heavenly reality that shapes the earthly.

In "Who's on the Throne? Revelation in the Long Year," John W. Marshall explores the radical appropriation and reconceptualization of imperial ideology in the Book of Revelation. Marshall offers an innovative interpretation of Revelation, read as a Jewish response to the Judaean war and simultaneous crisis of succession that gripped Rome in the "long year" of 69 C.E. His attention to the political valences of the text leads him to juxtapose its speculative discourse with passages concerning the political import of heavenly signs and portents in the writings of Graeco-Roman historians such as Tacitus, Suetonius, and Dio Cassius. He thus explores how this apocalypse engaged the ruling elite of the empire in impassioned conversation concerning the unfolding drama of imperial succession, achieving a complex combination of resistance, contrast, and inversion in its vision of heaven as the throne room and Temple of the true *Pantocrator*.

In "The Earthly Monastery and the Transformation of the Heavenly City in Late Antique Egypt," Kirsti B. Copeland considers the development of early Christian notions of the heavenly city from biblical and early Jewish traditions about the heavenly Temple and heavenly Jerusalem. Whereas the heavenly Jerusalem was once described as the idealized version of its earthly counterpart, Copeland proposes that Christians in late antique Egypt increasingly disassociated the two, adopting a new earthly model for the imagined city in heaven, namely the monastery. This development, Copeland argues, is most starkly evinced by the *Apocalypse of Paul*, a fourth-century Egyptian work that draws on earlier Jewish traditions about the heavenly Jerusalem to depict the heavenly city as a monastery teeming with monks.

In "Contextualizing Heaven in Third-Century North Africa," Jan N. Bremmer begins from the important insight that New Testament literature, apart from Revelation, is surprisingly reticent about providing descriptions of heaven. Bremmer then considers the ways in which these gaps are filled in the *Passion of Saints Marian and Jacob*, a third-century martyrology from North Africa. To conceptualize the heaven to which the martyr ascends, this text draws on both earthly models and traditional images from the Hebrew Bible and early Jewish literature, as evident in its descriptions of the heavenly tribunal and the heavenly garden. As with Copeland's consideration of

Egyptian Christianity, Bremmer's article demonstrates the degree to which late antique Christian images of heaven were rooted in early Jewish traditions but simultaneously shaped by the literary, geographical, and social circumstances of specific Christian communities.

The next contribution, Adam H. Becker's "Bringing the Heavenly Academy Down to Earth: Approaches to the Imagery of Divine Pedagogy in the East Syrian Tradition," analyzes the image of heaven as a classroom in the formation of East Syrian Christian scholasticism. In the process, Becker demonstrates the methodological value of combining diachronic, synchronic, and comparative approaches to late antique religious literature. After locating this concept of divine pedagogy within earlier Syriac tradition, he considers its connections with contemporaneous developments in East Syrian scholastic institutions. He then explores its relationship to the Babylonian Jewish traditions about the heavenly *beit-midrash*, exploring their continuities and discontinuities in terms of the relationship between Jews and Christians in late antique Mesopotamia.

Whereas the previous section analyzed images of heaven that bear a discernible relationship to familiar, earthly institutions, our final section considers how some late antique authors chose instead to generate meaning through the deconstruction, fragmentation, and inversion of traditional views of the world above. Titled "Tradition and Innovation," this section begins with an article that undermines the widespread assumption that the "breakdown" of such models represents a late development – rather than a deliberate strategy that could be utilized by a variety of writers at different times. In "Angels in the Architecture: Temple Art and the Poetics of Praise in the *Songs of the Sabbath Sacrifice*," Raʿanan S. Boustan argues that this cycle of Sabbath hymns found at Qumran follows a carefully constructed narrative arc as it moves methodically from conventional accounts of the angelic liturgy to startling descriptions of the Temple art and architecture singing the praises of God. At the same time, by portraying the angels in material terms, as images carved or woven into the Temple's walls and furnishings, the work further collapses the boundary between angelic beings and architectural elements in what might best be termed the "angelification" of the celestial Temple. The cycle's studied juxtaposition of the animate and inanimate spheres reveals the generative relationship that existed between Second Temple angelology and the plastic arts of the Jerusalem cult.

Our next two contributors take up the themes of inversion and conflation. In "The Collapse of Celestial and Chthonic Realms in a Late Antique

'Apollonian Invocation' (*PGM* I 262–347)," Christopher Faraone discusses a series of invocations to Apollo in the Greek Magical Papyri that ask the god for prophetic inspiration. Although most of these spells imagine Apollo as a celestial or solar deity and his divine inspiration as heaven sent, one recipe from *PGM* I borrows the language and accoutrements of traditional Greek necromantic ritual as well. In conflating the celestial and chthonic realms, this unusual text departs from traditional "pagan" views of the cosmos, in which these spheres were viewed as strictly incompatible.

This conflation of the heavens and the underworld has an interesting counterpart in the Jewish cosmological treatise *Seder Rabbah di-Bereshit*, the subject of Peter Schäfer's contribution: "In Heaven as It Is in Hell: The Cosmology of *Seder Rabbah di-Bereshit*." In this fascinating and little-studied text, the contents of the seven heavens are said to have exact equivalents in the worlds and underworlds beneath. This shocking projection of "what is above" into "what is below," although heavily dependent on classical rabbinic sources, represents a radical departure from earlier Jewish cosmology, which is far more concerned with the heavens than with the earth and the netherworld. The text uses its unconventional cosmology to celebrate the divine order that permeates the entire cosmos – from the heights of heaven down to the deepest hell.

With Radcliffe Edmonds' "The Faces of the Moon: Cosmology, Genesis, and the *Mithras Liturgy*," we shift from the rhetorical power of inversion to the generative potential of absence and, in the process, further locate the late antique discussion of heaven within a broader cosmological context. Edmonds considers the absence of the moon in the cosmology of the *Mithras Liturgy* and contextualizes its approach to the heavens by mapping the locations of the moon in "gnostic," magical, and philosophical cosmological systems. He proposes that the appearance of the moon's face – by turns benevolent and malevolent – is closely related to the conception of the genesis and incarnation of souls in these sources, as well as of the physical world more generally.

Just as speculation about the cosmos and reflection about the fate of the human soul are inextricably interwoven within the *Mithras Liturgy*, so the following article explores how similar philosophical concerns inform Christian baptismal theology. In "'O Paradoxical Fusion!': Gregory of Nazianzus on Baptism and Cosmology (*Orations* 38–40)," Susanna Elm considers Gregory's innovative conception of baptism as the actualization of a "paradoxical fusion" between human and divine. Elm argues that Gregory eschewed the commonplace articulation of "conversion" as an abrupt transformation realized in a single moment of illumination and instead described religious change in processual terms. She recovers the wide-ranging significance of Gregory's understanding of baptism by showing how his approach was forged in response to competing philosophies of embodiment in fourth-century Constantinople.

This volume, when taken as a whole, aims to provide a cumulative rendering of late antique speculation concerning heaven, sketching a "family portrait" of late antique religions that showcases the resemblances among them as well as the individuality of each. In this manner, we hope to show that the appeal to heaven in late antique literature cannot be reduced to the simple projection of earthly realities into the empty skies or to the escapist dream of a distant realm free from earthly troubles. Nor does our evidence allow us to write a single "history" of heaven, tracing a unilinear trajectory of development from concrete to abstract notions of the world above or from the construction of traditional images to their deconstruction.[24] The reality is much more complex but also much more interesting, owing in large part to the generative power of the underlying paradox: The late antique discourse about heaven is no less about life on earth.

---

[24] That the diversity of the data frustrates any easy synthesis or simple generalization is clear from the shortcomings of generalist surveys, such as J. E. Wright's *The Early History of Heaven* (New York, 2000); see reviews by D. Frankfurter (*Shofar* 20 [2002]: 163–6) and A. Y. Reed (*Koinonia* 8 [2001]: 63–5). The benefits of a more variegated and nuanced approach are evident, e.g., in J. N. Bremmer, *The Early Greek Concept of the Soul* (Princeton, N.J., 1983) and *The Rise and Fall of the Afterlife* (New York, 2002).

PART ONE

BETWEEN EARTH AND HEAVEN

The Bridge and the Ladder: Narrow Passages in Late Antique Visions

Fritz Graf

The topic of this symposium and book, "in heaven as it is on earth," is provocative and paradoxical. We assume that the Beyond - be it heaven, hell, or outer space - is a place different from ours. In narrations, this difference is objectified as a physical boundary between the here and there; when traveling from here to there, we must cross this boundary.

Historians of the ancient Mediterranean are familiar especially with one boundary that, in countless narrations, delimits the Beyond from our world: a river.[1] From Mesopotamia to Dante, through Homer and Virgil, any visitor to the other world either has to cross the river or, as Odysseus does exceptionally, to stop on our side and somehow call the souls over here. And, from Mesopotamia to Dante, if one needed to cross the river, one had to persuade a ferryman, Urshanabi in the epos of Gilgamesh, Humut-tabal in a Neo-Assyrian vision, or Charon in Greece and Rome or in Dante. The obvious alternative to a ferryman, a bridge, does not appear before the late sixth century C.E., at least inside our cultural area, although bridges are much older in our world. This is surprising and needs an explanation.

An obvious answer would be this: In the cultures of the ancient Mediterranean world, the Beyond is never on exactly the same level as we are. The world of the dead - Hades, Orcus, hell - is somehow below, as heaven is above. Thus, communication with those below by means of a hole in the ground would be an obvious alternative to somehow walking down, but it is rare and, more importantly, the hole is not a manhole. One does not physically descend through it, with the exception of the oracle of Trophonios;

---

[1] There is no comprehensive account of this narrative theme; for the ancient Near East, see esp. D. O. Etzard, "Die Mythologie der Sumerer und Akkader," s.v. "Unterweltsfluss," in *Wörterbuch der Mythologie* (Stuttgart, 1965), 1:132; for the Greeks, C. Sourvinou-Inwood, *"Reading" Greek Death: To the End of the Classical Period* (Oxford, 1995), 303–61.

but there we deal with ritual, not with narrative, that is, with an entirely different symbolic system.[2] One calls up the spirits from below through a hole in the ground, as the Sumerian Gilgamesh did when calling up Enkidu[3] or as Odysseus did in the Homeric "Nekyia." Heaven being above, on the other hand, one has to ascend, at least from our side. Gods come down and move up again; in the Mesopotamian narrative of Nergal and Ereshkigal, they use "the long stairway of heaven," whereas the angels in Jacob's dream use a ladder.[4] Greek gods simply fly, as do angels, at least outside the Jacob story. Mortals are unable to fly; they have to be lifted up, as are Elijah in the fiery chariot, Ganymede by the eagle, or Paul and many other Christian visionaries by an angel. As far as I can see, only rarely does a human climb a staircase or ladder up to heaven. Relevant material from Greek and Roman paganism is collected in Katharina Volk's contribution in this volume; with the exception of the Mithraic ladder, there is not much.[5] A rare gem is preserved in the story about the Thracian priest-king Kosingas: When his subjects began to question his leadership, this shrewd barbarian built a huge ladder and threatened to ascend to Hera (the main goddess of the Thracians, as at least the Greek storyteller makes us believe) and to complain about his recalcitrant subjects, which brought them back in line.[6]

But this seemingly obvious answer has not been obvious to scholars. Mircea Eliade's book on *Shamanism* contains two lengthy chapters on the bridge and on the ladder as shamanistic ascension devices; he traces both images all over the world, to the tune of "The myth of the ascent to the sky by a ladder is also known in Africa, Oceania, and North Africa."[7] For the ancient world, his main guide was Franz Cumont's 1949 masterpiece, *Lux Perpetua*; here, the master had already given an impressive list of instances.[8] In 1973, the Austrian medievalist and folklorist Peter Dinzelbacher published

---

[2] See Pausanias 9.39.4–14; Philostratus, *Vita Apolloni* 8.19; P. Bonnechère and M. Bonnechère, "Trophonios à Lébadée: Histoire d'un oracle," *Études Classiques* 57 (1989): 289–302; P. Bonnechère, *Trophonios de Lébadée* (Leiden, 2003).

[3] Gilgamesh, tablet XII, line 242; A. George, ed., *The Epic of Gilgamesh* (London, 1999), 187.

[4] Nergal: S. Dalley, *Myths from Mesopotamia: Creation, the Flood, Gilgamesh and Others* (Oxford, 1989), 163–77; Jacob: Gen 28:10–18.

[5] For the ladder in Mithraic initiations, see Celsus in Origen, *Cels.* 6.22; R. Merkelbach, *Mithras* (Koenigstein, 1984), 78–80.

[6] Polyaenus, *Stratagemata* 7.23.

[7] M. Eliade, *Le chamanisme et les techniques archaïques de l'extase* (Paris, 1951); the citation is from the (revised and enlarged) Eng. ed.: *Shamanism: Archaic Techniques of Ecstasy*, trans. W. R. Trask (London, 1964), 480.

[8] F. Cumont, *Lux perpetua* (Paris, 1949), 282–3.

his *Die Jenseitsbrücke im Mittelalter*, the most comprehensive account to date, which also comprises "the equivalent of the bridge," the ladder.[9] All scholarly work suffers from two defects (especially, but not only, Eliade's). All the learned accounts (Cumont's the least) lump together all the bridges and ladders they can find and regard them as equivalent means of crossing from here to there, although to a practical mind the fact that the bridge is a horizontal contraption and the ladder a vertical one would at least have deserved some comment. Furthermore, all scholars assume that all these images somehow belong genetically together, which induces or rather seduces them to contemplate channels of diffusion. For Eliade, bridge and ladder both originated in the shamanistic ascent ritual, which explains why he never reflected on their practical difference. This panshamanistic universal comparativism was deflated long ago.[10] Dinzelbacher less fleetingly (but with a more than polite nod in the direction of Eliade) traces a development of the motifs from ancient Iran and India to Europe. He was immediately contradicted by Eliade's pupil Ioan Culianu, who suggested a different diffusion[11]; this debate demonstrates how problematical global comparativist constructions are. In what follows, I try to keep bridge and ladder apart, and I confine my discussion to the smaller world of western Late Antiquity.

This means that, to understand what is going on when these two images appear in the course of Latin Christian writings on travels to the Beyond, we have to look at the specific texts in which the images appear, at their aims and their forms – this is always advisable, but is especially rewarding with ancient Christian literature. Unlike its pagan companion, Christian literature in the imperial age was struggling to find the genres and forms in which it could express itself; this original struggle constitutes a large part of the excitement and delight for a literary scholar who deals with these texts. It will be apparent soon that, of the four texts I look into more closely, only one really conforms to traditional genres.

---

[9] P. Dinzelbacher, *Die Jenseitsbrücke im Mittelalter* (Dissertationen der Universität Wien 104; Vienna, 1973); also idem, "Seelenbrücke und Brückenbau im mittelalterlichen England," *Numen* 31 (1984): 242–87 and idem,"Il ponte come lugo sacro nella realtà e nell'immaginario," in *Luoghi sacri e spazi della santità*, ed. S. Boesch Gajano and L. Scaraffia (Messina, 1990), 51-60. For the ladder alone, see also C. Heck, *L'Échelle céleste dans l'art du Moyen Âge: Une image de la quête du ciel* (Paris, 1997). I owe this last reference to Katharina Volk.

[10] See J. N. Bremmer, *The Early Greek Concept of the Soul* (Princeton, N.J., 1983), 24–53; idem, *The Rise and Fall of the Afterlife* (London, 2001), 27–40, with ample bibliography.

[11] I. P. Culianu, "Pons Subtilis: Storia e significato di un simbolo," *Aevum* 53 (1979): 301–12.

The Bridges

In late antique Christian texts, the bridge in or to the Beyond appears for the first time in two Latin texts dated to the late sixth century – one by Gregory, the bishop of Tours, the other by Gregory the Great, bishop of Rome.

In Book IV of his *History of the Franks*, written shortly after 573 C.E., Gregory of Tours narrates the dream [*visio*] of an exceptionally holy abbot, Sunniulf of Randan (near Clermont-Ferrand).[12] Sunniulf, despite his holiness, had one shortcoming: He was too lenient toward his monks – until one night God sent him a dream. He dreamed that he was led to a fiery river (the text does not tell by whom). From its shore, a large crowd, "like bees streaming to a bee-hive," was entering it, and others were already standing in it, "some up to their belts, other to their shoulders, others again up to their chin"; all complained that they were being burnt. A very narrow bridge was leading over the river where, at a distance, the visionary could see a large white house or palace. Sunniulf was told that only persons who during their lifetime had been severe leaders of their flock could walk safely over this bridge; he who was too lenient a leader was precipitated into the fiery river. With this, Sunniulf woke up and, from that day on, became a model of severity.

The story is tailor-made for its immediate purpose: to educate the pious but all too lenient dreamer or, rather, in the agenda of the bishop of Tours, to teach a lesson in authority to any religious leader. The right measure of discipline in a Christian community was a much debated topic; monastic rules emphasized the rule of one and the obedience of all the others.[13] In the

---

[12] Gregory of Tours, *Historia Francorum* 4.33 (Sunniulf):

> [D]uctum se per visum ad quoddam flumen igneum, in quo ab una parte litoris concurrentes populi ceu apes ad alvearia mergebantur, et erant alii usque ad cingulum, alii vero usque ad ascellas, nonnulli usque ad mentum, clamantes cum fletu se vehementer aduri. erat enim et pons super fluvium positus ita angustus, ut vix unius vestigii latitudinem recipere possit. apparebat autem et in alia parte litoris domus magna, extrinsecus dealbata. tunc his qui cum eo erant, quid sibi haec velint interrogat. at illi dixerunt: "de hoc enim ponte praecipitabitur, qui ad distringendum commissum gregem fuerit repertus ignavus; qui vero strenuus fuerit, sine periculo transit et inducitur laetus in domum quam conspicis ultra." haec audiens a somno excutitur, multo deinceps monachis severior apparens.

[13] *Regula Sanctum Patrum* 1.10–18, comp. 2.1 (*fratrum insignia virtutum habitationis vel oboedentiae ... praevenerunt*; "The most visible virtues of the brothers, collective living and obedience, have been treated first"); *Regula S. Macharii* 2; *Regula Benedicti* 1.2 (general); 5 (on obedience); 23–30 (on punishment). The texts are collected in S. Prioco, ed., *La regola di San Benedetto e le Regole dei Padri* (Milan, 1995).

Dialogues of Gregory the Great, we are confronted with a vision in which we meet "Peter, the head of Church Personnel" [*ecclesiasticae familiae maiorem*] in chains deep down in hell: He had found pleasure in meting out harsh punishment instead of regarding it as a hard necessity only.[14] The bridge that leads to a paradisiac place – the white house, a shiny palace, is one way of picturing it, besides the more common image of a flowery meadow – is not only a means of river crossing; it is a test instrument that spots the flawed religious leaders. The fiery river is a place of punishment, but presumably also of general purification; the great majority of souls [*concurrentes populi*] is immersed there, not just specific sinners.

This short vision, as all late antique and medieval visions of hell and Paradise, manipulates a long narrative tradition; this is especially obvious in the one image that is not functional in its didactic purpose. The image of the souls who stand in the fiery river, some up to their belts, some to their shoulders, some up to their chin, recalls an image in the *Apocalypse of Paul*, a text whose core dates to the late fourth century.[15] In this vision, which exploits Paul's own confession of ascent experiences (2 Cor 12:2–5), the archangel Michael first leads Paul to a "large river" that separates the worlds and that his guide calls Oceanus. Close by, he sees "a terrible place" without light, Cocytus, and "three other rivers," the Virgilian underworld rivers "Stix, Flegeton, and Acheron."[16] He then is led to a fiery river (whether or not this is Flegeton, as its name and tradition would suggest, seems unclear)[17] and sees a group of sinners, "some in it up to their knees, others to the navel, others to the lips, others again up to their eyebrows."[18] Michael explains that these are four different groups of sinners; here, the fire is a punishment that will last forever.

---

[14] Gregory the Great, *Dialogi* 4.37.11.

[15] I follow the Vienna text, cod. 362f. (14th c.), ed. by T. Silverstein in *Visio sancti Pauli: The History of the Apocalypse in Latin, Together with Nine Texts* (SD 4; London, 1935), 153–5. For the date, see K. Copeland in this volume, esp. n. 1.

[16] In Virgil, *Aen.* 6.295, Acheron is the main river to cross, with Charon and his boat; it flows into Cocytus (v. 297), which is the overflow of the Stygian swamp (v. 323); Phlegeton, as Virgil calls it consistently and not, as others, Pyriphlegeton (Homer, *Od.* 10.513 etc.), finally, belongs to Tartarus (v. 551), but can double as a synonym for Underworld (*Aen.* 6.265). The rivers, of course, go back to Homer, *Od.* 10.513–514.

[17] The Latin tradition is aware of the Greek etymology, see [Virgil], *Culex* 272, although Ovid can treat it as a sort of (powerful) water, *Met.* 5.544.

[18] Chap. 3: "Et vidit ibi multos homines diversos in flumine ignito: alii usque ad genua, alii usque ad umbilicum, alii usque ad labia, alii usque ad supercilia erant mersi."

Compared with the clear spatial information in the *Apocalypse of Paul* (with the exception of the possible identification of the fiery river with Flegeton, as one would expect given its name),[19] the sketchy account of Sunniulf's dream leaves the location of the fiery river unclear: Is it the river that separates the worlds, or is it somewhere in the otherworld? The Christian historian is interested, not in eschatological details, but in moralistic teaching, as his comment on another vision makes abundantly clear.[20] Salvius, the visionary bishop of Albi, suffered an apparent death; he ascended through the cosmos like another Ciceronian Scipio ("so that I meant to see under my feet not only this sordid earth, but also the sun, the moon, the clouds, and the stars": Scipio ascends until he sees earth and all the planets below him),[21] and he was brought into God's palace. The historian comments on all this with a citation from that most moralistic of ancient historians, Sallust, in his preface to the *Catilinian Conjuration*: "When one writes about the virtue and fame of good men, everybody accepts willingly what he thinks he himself might easily perform; what goes beyond, is received as fiction and lie."[22] Gregory is not telling a fictional tale; he is relating history: Salvius personally informed him, and the two Gallic bishops must have known each other.[23] And Gregory is telling a Sallustian tale that has to do with "the virtue and fame of good men," examples for posterity.

Nonetheless, this does not call for consistency in the imagery of the after-life: Expressed in term of literary traditions, one vision's layout of the Beyond conforms more to the philosophical mind of Cicero, the other more to the poetry of Virgil and his underworld rivers. In Greek and Roman accounts, the fiery river has the speaking name Pyriphlegeton, and it is inside the underworld, as it is in Paul's vision; in Virgil, whom Gregory certainly knew well, it receives the waters of Acheron and flows around the dark fortress of Tartarus in the innermost part of the underworld.[24] Another Virgilian echo, though, connects it with the boundary between the worlds. The image of the

---

[19] I doubt the identification, despite what seems to be the editors' consensus.
[20] Gregory, *Hist.* 7.1.
[21] Gregory, *Hist.* 7.1: "ita ut non solum hunc squalidum saeculum, verum etiam solem et lunam, nubes et sidera sub pedibus habere putarem"; compare Cicero, *Rep.* 6.15–17, with Cicero's insight into the smallness of the earth; Salvius shares this feeling. Less certain seems the echo of the vision in Rev 12:1.
[22] Sallust, *Cat.* 3; the moralistic intention is obvious.
[23] See the story of Salvius' prophetic gaze, narrated in *Hist.* 5.50.
[24] Virgil, *Aen.* 6.547–551.

souls streaming to the river bank, like bees to a beehive, recalls the scene in which Virgil's Aeneas approached Acheron, the boundary river between the upper world and the underworld. Here, he saw a large crowd that was assembling in front of Charon's jetty "like leaves, falling in autumn, or like birds, flocking together before winter to set out for their travel to warmer weather"; Dante was so impressed with the image that he repeated part of it.[25] Whether this means that Gregory regarded the fiery river as the boundary between the two worlds or simply used an impressive image for his narration is open to debate; what counts more, anyway, is the certain Virgilian influence in a Christian eschatological vision.[26]

The second text comes from the *Dialogues* of Gregory the Great, written not long after he was elected pope in 590 C.E.; the *Dialogues* are one of these open forms in which Christian writers tried out their art. Book IV collects miscellaneous stories about the afterlife and is a mine of eschatological visions; only one, however, features the bridge. It is the vision of a Roman soldier who nearly died in the Great Plague of 590.[27] However, like the other Gregory's holy abbott Salvius (or Plato's Er), he was only apparently dead. An apparent death (i.e., a near-death experience) had been an obvious vehicle for eschatological visions since Plato. In the corpus of the relevant Christian texts, it appears for the first time in Jerome's famous autobiographical dream; it then becomes standard fare in medieval

---

[25] Virgil, *Aen.* 6.305–312: "huc omnis turba ad ripas effusa ruebat..., quam multa in silvis autumni frigore primo lapsa cadunt folia, aut ad terram gurgite ab alto quam multae glomeratur aves, ubi frigidus annus trans pontum fugat et terris immitit apricis." Dante, *Inferno*, Canto 3.112–117: "Come d'autunno si levan le foglie l'una appresso de l'altra, fin che'l ramo vede a la terra tutte le sue spoglie, similmente il mal seme d'Adamo gittansi di quel lito ad una ad una, per cenni come augel per suo richiamo." The Virgilian verse has its own tradition; see E. Norden, ed., *P. Virgilius Maro Aeneis Buch VI*, 2nd ed. (Leipzig, 1915), 223–4; Virgil already used this image in the Orpheus story in *Georgics* 4.473–74.

[26] For this complex, see P. Courcelle, "Les pères de l'église devant les enfers virgiliens," *Archives d'histoire doctrinale et littéraire du Moyen Age* 22 (1955): 5–74.

[27] Gregory, *Dial.* 4.37.7–12 (In Rome, a soldier lies as dead for a while, then returns to life and tells his story):

[8] Aiebat enim sicut tunc res eadem multis innotuit, quia pons erat, sub quo niger atque caligosus foetoris intolerabilis nebulam exhalans fluvius decurrebat. transacto autem ponte amoena erant prata atque virentia, odoriferis herbarum floribus exornata, in quibus albatorum hominum conventicula esse videbantur. tantusque in loco eodem odor suavitatis inerat, ut ipsa suavitatis fragrantia illic deambulantes habitantesque satiaret. [9 describes houses on the other side of the bridge] [10] haec vero erat in praedicto ponte probatio, ut quisquis per eum iniustorum vellet transire, in tenebroso foetentique fluvio laberetur, iusti vero, quibus culpa non obsisteret, securo per eum gressu ac libero ad loca amoena pervenirent.

visions.[28] The first thing the soldier saw was a bridge over a dark and smelly river that led to a beautiful meadow full of flowers, peopled by persons in white dress and containing many houses, some in the meadow, some on its slope toward the river.

Again, the didactic purpose of the vision is clear, and Gregory insists on it. It is an image, not historical truth, he says, and illustrates this with Matt 7:14, from the Sermon on the Mount: "Enter by the narrow gate. Wide is the gate and broad the road that leads to destruction, and many enter that way; narrow is the gate and constricted the road that leads to life, and those who find them are few."[29] This explains (much easier than in the historian Gregory of Tours) why the several visions that the book presents need not be coherent. They do not teach otherworldly geography, and we are not confronted with an article of strict faith: Gregory uses them not very differently from the way Plato does.

This time, the location of river and bridge is clear: the bridge marks the transition between this world and Paradise, with the dark river as the boundary in between. The function of the bridge is explicitly one of *probatio*, a test. Every soul must cross it, but only the just succeed; all others fall and are then attacked by "black men" who try to pull them into the river, while "white men" from above try to help them. This is the usual fight for any soul between the devils and the angels. Thus, like the fiery river in Sunniulf's dream, the black river becomes more than just a boundary; it is a place, ultimately, of punishment.

In a way, this bridge could be regarded as the equivalent of a ferryman: a boat could cross such a river, however slimy and smelly it was. But a closer look at the Christian story shows the vital difference. In the Christian text, we deal with more than just a crossing; the passing over the bridge is a thrilling test of human virtue. When, in Christiane Sourvinou-Inwood's words, with the Homeric (or Virgilian) Acheron, "the division between the upper world and Hades is definite but not dramatic," this division has now become high moralistic drama.[30] In comparison, any narration about Charon is much less dramatic, even one in which he is a cranky old man, as in Virgil or Dante; he

[28] Jerome, *Epist.* 22.30; for the motif see M. P. Ciccarese, *Visioni dell'Aldilà in Occidente* (Milan, 1987), 86–7, and for near-death experience as a source of eschatological information, see Bremmer, *Afterlife*, 87–102.

[29] Cited in Gregory, *Dial.* 4.38.3: "per pontem quippe ad amoena loca transire iustos aspexit, quia angusta porta et arcta via est, quae ducit ad vitam, et pauci sunt qui inveniunt eam."

[30] Sourvinou-Inwood, *"Reading" Greek Death*, 63.

might first refuse to let the living board his vessel, yelling at them all the while, but he can always be persuaded in the end to take them aboard. Now the passage has become much more crucial and much more difficult: Can the human soul, sinful by its very form of existence, overcome this handicap? Can it pass directly to Paradise and, if not, how will it be punished and purified? Every time a soul goes from here to there, its fate is disputed between angels and devils; the visionary ascetic, Saint Anthony, saw dramatic air battles every time a hermit died. Gregory's soldier sees the same battle going on around the bridge.[31]

At the same time, though, the boundary between here and there has changed. From Homer's Odysseus to Virgil's Aeneas (and, in the wake of Virgil's Aeneas, Dante's *persona*), humans simply walked from here to there, with but a river to cross; or, in those visions in which the soul is carried upward through the cosmos, the visions of Cicero's Scipio, or Paul, or Gregory's Salvius, there is another contiguity, insofar as the soul ascends in an unbroken course through God's Creation. Now, in the more recent Christian visions, the spatial or essential contiguity seems broken. Somehow, the soul is transported to the river that forms the boundary of the Beyond; somehow, the familiar earth ceases and, after a blank space, river and Paradise appear (even in Dante, this blank space makes itself vaguely felt). That is, our world and the world beyond are much too different to share simple contiguity. Only the medieval romances see things differently. There, the heroic knights chance upon a strange river with an even stranger bridge that they must cross: Lancelot had to choose between a submerged bridge and a bridge in the shape of a narrow and sharp sword[32]; Amphiaraus in the *Roman de Thèbes* arrived at a bridge that led him safely over Acheron.[33] In secular fiction, even Amphiaraus' Hades, not to mention Lancelot's land of Gorre, are just other places of high adventure.

Another vision, written about a century after Gregory's *Dialogues*, shows further developments. It is the vision of another person who was apparently dead, a monk in the monastery of Wenlock (Shropshire); Boniface, monk at Wessex, reports it in a letter, written presumably in 717 C.E., and he heard it from both the abbess of Wenlock and from the visionary whom Boniface

---

[31] Athanasius, *Vit. Ant.* 65; see A. Recheis, *Engel, Tod und Seelenreise: Das Wirken der Geister beim Heimgang des Menschen in der Lehre der alexandrinischen und kappadokischen Väter* (Rome, 1958), 144–5.

[32] C. de Troyes, *Lancelot ou le chevalier de la charrette*; see Dinzelbacher, *Die Jenseitsbrücke*, 107–11.

[33] Dinzelbacher, *Die Jenseitsbrücke*, 61–2.

personally interviewed.[34] As soon as his soul left the body, the visionary narrated, the angels lifted him up high over the earth, and he looked down on an earth engulfed in flames; the flaming wall marks the boundary between the earth and the world of the Beyond. He, too, sees angels and devils fighting for each individual soul; then, he is brought to a tribunal at which both his sins and his virtues confront him in person and accuse or defend him (Prudentius' *Psychomachia* being the obvious, although perhaps distant, source of inspiration). He is released and offered a guided tour – first through the place of punishment, then over to Paradise. After Paradise, he sees the heavenly Jerusalem; the two are separated by a fiery river. A plank serves as a bridge, but only the very pure pass without problems; all others fall into the fire and stay there for a certain time, immersed to different depths (the echoes of Gregory of Tours and the *Apocalypse of Paul* are obvious). But, in the end, they all will leave the fire again, shining with purity, and enter the heavenly Jerusalem.

In this vision, the borderline between here and there has become even more dramatic. This dramatization emphasizes both the incompatibility of the two worlds and the danger of border crossing. Contiguity has become very precarious. Heaven and hell are outside of this world and somehow above it. The soul has to ascend; there is no longer a river to form the border. That is not to say that there is no river, but it has moved to the center and forms the borderline between Paradise and the ultimate goal, the heavenly Jerusalem; despite this rarefied location, it is still fiery, a descendant of the Virgilian Phlegethon. However, through this shift in imaginary space, the fiery river loses all functions of punishment: Its fire serves as the final means of purification that makes the soul fit to enter the heavenly Jerusalem. The narrow bridge retains its role as a test mechanism, but it is now the test of

---

[34] Bonifatius, *Epistula* 10 (MGH epist. III, Merov. et Carol. Aevi 1.252):

> [Letter to Eadburg about the] visiones de illo redivivo qui nuper in monasterio Milbruge abatissae mortuus est et revixit. [When the visionary arrived in the other world,] igneum piceumque flumen, bulliens et ardens, mirae formidins et teterrimae visionis cernebat, super quod lignum pontis vice positum erat. ad quod sanctae gloriosaeque animae ab illo secedentes conventu [i.e. the *beati* in paradise] properabant, desiderio alterius ripae transire cupientes. et quaedam non titubantes constanter transiebant, quaedam vero labefactae de ligno cadebant in Tartareum flumen; et aliae tinguebantur pene, quasi toto corpore mersae, aliae autem ex parte quadam, veluti usque ad genua, quaedam usque ad corpus medium, quaedam vero usque ad ascellas. et tamen unaquaeque cadentium multo clarior speciosiorque de flumine in alteram ascendebat ripam, quam prius in piceum bulliens cecidisset flumen. et unus ex beatis angelis de illis cadentibus animabus dixit: "Hae sunt animae, quae post exitum mortalis vitae, quibusdam levibus vitiis non omnino ad purum abolitis, aliqua pia miserentis Dei castigatione indigebant, ut Deo dignae offerantur." Et citra id flumen speculatur muros fulgentes clarissimi splendoris.

ultimate purity, no more the basic separation of a few pure and many impure souls.

It is this location in the interior of the other world that will become highly popular in medieval visions of the Beyond. Ordinarily, this bridge is part of an entire array of infernal tests, tribulations, and punishments. The most intriguing description is found in the rather fantastic, but highly popular, *Vision of Tnugdal*, written in 1147/8 by an Irish monk in Regensburg. The narrator, the Irishman Tnugdal, a great sinner, sees, again in apparent death, not one but two bridges. The first is a simple plank, one mile long, over the terrible "Valley of the Arrogant" [*vallis superborum*]. The second crosses over a lake full of devils and is two miles long, one palm wide, and studded with iron nails. Souls, of course, are barefoot and, to make things worse, they had to carry over this bridge whatever they stole during their lifetime. Tnugdal happened to have stolen a rather stubborn cow, which leads to some infernal slapstick ("when the soul managed to stand upright, the cow fell down, and when the cow stood upright, the soul was falling").[35]

This is a far cry from Eliade's cosmic bridge that gave the shaman a way to cross into the other world, so far away that any diffusion model seems doubtful. This does not mean that we are entirely forbidden to ask from where more or less simultaneously the two Gregorys got the new image. In its first occurrence, in Gregory of Tours, it is treated so cursorily that one suspects a longer, oral tradition behind it that was alive in late antique France; and there seem to be Irish parallels that could be understood as Celtic antecedents.[36] This is no more hypothetical than any other answer.

The Ladder

The ladder, as we saw, was regarded by scholars from Cumont to Dinzelbacher, as the functional equivalent of the bridge, despite their different spatial orientations and despite the different contexts in which it appears. The ladder as a means of ascension occurs in widely different eschatological accounts, in eastern and western ascetic writings, in western saint's Lives, and, close to the beginning of Christian Latinity, in the prison diary of Perpetua, who was to be executed in 203 C.E. in the arena of Carthage.

---

[35] For the Latin text, see A. Wagner, ed., *Visio Tnugdali Lateinisch und Altdeutsch* (Erlangen, 1882); Eng. trans. by Jean-Michael Picard, *The Vision of Tnugdal: Translated from Latin* (Dublin, 1989); see also N. F. Palmer, ed., *Visio Tnugdali: The German and Dutch Translations and Their Circulation in the Later Middle Ages* (Munich, 1982).

[36] Dinzelbacher, *Die Jenseitsbrücke*, 124–5.

The ladder is an obvious image for the direct ascent up to heaven and one resonant with biblical imagery: It was a ladder Jacob saw in his dream, "which rested on the ground with its top reaching to heaven, and messengers of God were going up and down on it" (Gen 28:11). Christian exegesis of this passage, from Tertullian onward, saw it as an image for the Christian's ascent to God. Still, the ladder must be climbed, which requires some effort and initiative: Thus, the ladder became, in later antiquity both in eastern and western Christianity, an allegory for the determined ascetic's ascent through the many steps of an ascetic life. It prompted complex systems of ladders in which each rung symbolized one specific step in the ascetic life, with up to fourteen (Honorius of Autun) or thirty rungs (John Klimakos); as an easy image, it was also an easy didactic and mnemotecnic tool. As an image for the ascetic life, it comes close to the narrow and dangerous bridge, as the ascetic life is always endangered and thus is a test; around the ladder, as around the bridge in Gregory the Great, angels and demons fight for the ascending human. On the other hand, if the ladder was well built, it turned into quite a comfortable instrument: in medieval saint's Lives, often enough, it is nothing more than an easy shortcut for holy men and women, whereas ordinary humans have to suffer trial and punishment – this is why many holy abbots and founders of religious orders, like Dominic, were thought to have ascended a ladder that brought them directly up to God.[37]

Another ascetic image of Late Antiquity, before the images hardened into the conventional signs that they became later on, signifies this comfortable way out in a clearer fashion. The second book of Gregory's *Dialogues* is devoted to Benedict, the founder of western monasticism, whom Gregory shaped into a superior ascetic, Italy's answer to Egypt's Anthony and Gaul's Martin. After narratting Benedict's death, Gregory reports a vision that two monks had simultaneously in two different places, shortly after the death of Benedict; the identity of the vision guarantees its veracity. Both saw "a road, decked with tapestries and well illuminated with many lamps that led straight east from his monastery towards the sky." At its end, a venerable figure explained to them that this was the way Benedict took up to the sky.[38]

---

[37] See Dinzelbacher, *Die Jenseitsbrücke*, 143–44. Romuald, founder of the Camaldulensians, or Dominic, founder of the Dominicans; but also individual monasteries with holy abbots.
[38] Gregory, *Dial.* 2.37.3.

It is a triumphal way or the way an emperor used to walk when visiting a city: Here, it is prepared for the most successful ascetic of his age, bringing him up to heaven.[39]

This leaves us with the first and most spectacular image, Perpetua's ladder, which many writers understood as the starting point of these Christian ladders.[40] The text is well known. While the small group of Christians around Perpetua are waiting in prison for their trial, Perpetua, prompted by her brother, asks God for information: Will she be executed, or will she be freed? God answers in a dream. Perpetua thus makes use of a dream oracle, as did many of her pagan contemporaries; the Greek Magical Papyri contain many rituals and prayers to provoke such a dream in private space. In her sleep, Perpetua sees a long but narrow bronze ladder (rather than a staircase, although *scala* technically means both; but the thing is too narrow and too steep for a flight of stairs) that connects earth and heaven. It is spiked on its sides with all sorts of sharp iron weapons and instruments of torture that threaten to hurt any careless climber ("swords, spears, hooks, daggers, and spikes; so that, if anyone tried to climb up carelessly ... he would be mangled and his flesh would adhere to the weapons")[41]: One had to look up to see where to place one's hands and shoulders. Its foot is guarded by a large dragon that attacks potential climbers. Nevertheless, Saturus, her teacher, climbs up first, seemingly without effort, and he calls her up too. She begins to climb, cowing the dragon by uttering the name of Jesus and

---

[39] There might also be an echo of Jesus' entry into Jerusalem; Mark 11:8.

[40] *Passio Perpetua* 4.3 (ed. A. A. R. Bastiaensen, *Atti e Passioni dei Martiri* [Milan, 1987]:

> video scalam aeream mirae magnitudinis pertingentem usque ad caelum, et angustam per quam nonnisi singuli ascendere possent, et in lateribus scalae omne genus ferramentorum infixum – erant ibi gladii, lanceae, hami, machaerae, veruta –, ut si quis neglegenter aut non sursum adtendens ascenderet, laniaretur et carnes eius inhaererent ferramentis. [4] et erat sub ipsa scala draco cubans mirae magnitudinis, qui ascendentibus insidias praestabat et exterrebat, ne ascenderent. [5] ascendit autem Saturus prior, qui postea se propter nos ultro tradiderat, quia ipse nos aedificaverat; et tunc cum adducti sumus, praesens non fuerat. [6] et pervenit in caput scalae et convertit se et dixit mihi: "Perpetua, sustineo te, sed vide ne te mordeat draco ille." et dixi ego: "non me nocebit, in nomine Iesu Christi." [7] et desub ipsa scala, quasi timens me, lente eiecit caput. et quasi primum gradum calcarem, calcavi illi caput ascendi. [8] et vidi spatium immensum horti.

> See i.a. P. C. Miller, *Dreams in Late Antiquity: Studies in the Imagination of a Culture* (Princeton, N.J., 1994); G. G. Stroumsa, "Dreams and Visions in Early Christian Discourse," in *Dream Cultures: Explorations in the Comparative History of Dreaming*, ed. D. Shulman and G. G. Stroumsa (New York, 1999), 189–212.

[41] *Perpetua* 4.3; the translation is from H. Musurillo, *The Acts of the Christian Martyrs* (Oxford, 1972), 111.

31

firmly stepping on its head; on top, she arrives in a large garden where she meets God who welcomes her and feeds her some milk.

God's answer to Perpetua's question is easily understood; its symbolism is obvious and resonates with biblical imagery. She will suffer martyrdom, but martyrdom will bring her immediately close to God. The way up is not easy and can hurt one's flesh, and there is always the human temptation to give in and renounce; Saturus explicitly warns her not to be bitten by the snake. But, once she has made up her mind, success is certain.

Commentators usually point to Jacob's dream as the immediate inspiration; given that already Tertullian, Perpetua's contemporary and perhaps the editor of her diary, read the Genesis passage in such a light, this makes sense.[42] Commentators also connect Jacob's ladder with Egyptian, Near Eastern, or even shamanistic ladders, about which I feel less comfortable.[43] But even compared with Jacob's ladder, Perpetua's ladder has vital differences that we should not overlook. Jacob's ladder is the connection that God and his angels use to announce to Jacob the future of Israel; Jacob is the passive, sleeping receiver of a divine message, and he reacts only afterwards, by consecrating the stone upon which he slept and calling the place beth-el [House of God]: God has reached down, and his creature recognizes its earthly consequences. For Perpetua, God reaches down only by sending her a dream; the ladder he shows her is an invitation and provokes her decision to go up actively to heaven – a narrow, difficult, and dangerous way that she has to choose and then to climb, with the potential of failure ever present. Becoming a martyr and thus entering Paradise is the result of human decision and toil.

Thus, the ladder is a potentially powerful symbol of martyrdom; the iron instruments at its side are instruments of torture and execution. It is all the more surprising that it found no following: No other martyr texts take up the image. The later ascetics, in some respects the followers of the martyrs, do so, but they do it in a different context. Given these differences and Tertullian's interpretation of Jacob's dream, there is no need to look for Perpetua's vision as an inspiration to the later ascetics: Gen 28:11 is enough. Perpetua's strange ladder is unique, in a way her very own private dream symbol.

---

[42] Tertullian, *Marc.* 3.24.9–10.

[43] On Egyptian ladders and staircases, see S. Curto, "Il simbolo della scala dall'Egitto Antico al Copto e all'Arabo," *Aegyptus* 78 (1998): 3–14.

Conclusions

Graeco-Roman travels to the Beyond somehow looked at the road from here to there as being basically horizontal (with the exception of the spectacular ascensions to the sky). Even when they were called *katabaseis* or *descensus*, the stories never emphasized the way down. Odysseus sails over the Okeanos and enters the first realm of the underworld; Aeneas walks more or less straight into it; and Virgil, in a beautiful image, compares Aeneas' journey to a walk through the woods at night, when there is no moon in the sky: This underlines the nondramatic and not very disruptive nature of death of which Christiane Sourvinou-Inwood has spoken. Crossing a body of water in a boat is the most horizontal way of traveling imaginable. The few instances of a clear way down do not contradict this: In Gilgamesh XII, in which communication uses a hole in the ground, death is seen as deeply troubling; and when Ovid's Orpheus descends [*descendit*] and later climbs back a steep path [*adclivis et arduus*], we again deal with a death that was much more disruptive than was ordinarily the case.[44] The Christian imagery, on the other hand, underlines verticality from the very beginning. A ladder is a vertical contraption; as for the bridge, all the images exploit more the possibility and, indeed, likelihood of a vertical fall from the bridge than that of a horizontal passage. This importance of the vertical movement might again explain why the bridge was moved away from the borderline and no longer functioned as an entry into the other world; with the exception of the saints who used a ladder, there was no longer any easy or unspectacular way from here to there.

---

[44] Ovid, *Metam.* 10.13: *est ausus descendere.* 53–54: *adclivis…trames…arduus*; Virgil, however, avoids indications of descending and mounting, *Georgics* 4.467–502.

33

2

"Heavenly Steps": Manilius 4.119–121
and Its Background

Katharina Volk

Astrology, a "science" now wholly discredited, but one that enjoyed enormous prestige from antiquity up to the Enlightenment, is predicated on the idea that heaven and earth are not two separate entities, but are intrinsically connected. Everything that happens in the upper reaches of the sky, every change in the alignment of heavenly bodies, will have an effect on the terrestrial realm, including, crucially, the lives and fates of human beings. There is thus a continuum between the high and the low, an unbroken chain of cause and effect, but also a strict hierarchy: The stars above are all-powerful and eternal, whereas the men and women below are mortal and subject to a fate that they themselves cannot control.

Developed in Babylon and refined by the Hellenistic Greeks, astrology became popular in Rome toward the end of the Republic. In the second decade of the first century C.E., Marcus Manilius, a Latin author about whose life we know nothing, wrote a lengthy didactic poem titled *Astronomica*, which – owing to the serendipities of textual transmission – now happens to be the earliest extant complete treatment of astrological thought and method.[1]

This paper is a complement to my discussion of Manilius' poem in *The Poetics of Latin Didactic: Lucretius, Vergil, Ovid, Manilius* (Oxford, 2002) and "Pious and Impious Approaches to Cosmology in Manilius," *Materiali e discussioni per l'analisi dei testi classici* 47 (2001): 85–117, to which I refer the reader for a more detailed treatment of some of the general issues raised in what follows. I would like to express my thanks to the editors for inviting me to contribute to this volume, to Fritz Graf for letting me see an advance copy of his article on heavenly bridges and ladders, and to the Fondation Hardt pour l'Étude de l'Antiquité Classique (Vandœuvres, Switzerland) for providing a genial atmosphere for Manilian research during my stay in the summer of 2001. A version of this paper was presented at the 133rd Annual Meeting of the American Philological Association, Philadelphia, Pa., January 2002.

[1] On ancient astrology, its history and underlying beliefs, see A. Bouché-Leclercq, *L'Astrologie grecque* (Paris, 1899); F. Boll, C. Bezold, and W. Gundel, *Sternglaube und Sterndeutung: Die Geschichte und das Wesen der Astrologie*, 5th ed. (Darmstadt, 1966); and T. Barton, *Ancient Astrology* (London, 1994), as well as F. H. Cramer, *Astrology in Roman Law and Politics* (Philadelphia, 1954),

"Heavenly Steps": Manilius 4.119–121 and Its Background

Manilius did not shy away from the more technical aspects of his topic: As his famous editor A. E. Housman dryly remarked, he had an "eminent aptitude for doing sums in verse."[2] At the same time, however, the Roman poet delighted in the mystical elements of the subject matter, creating in his verse the sublime vision of a universe in which everything is interconnected and in which there exists the possibility of an intimate communion between heaven and earth.

In language informed by Stoic philosophy, Manilius identifies the universe or heaven [*mundus*] with god, whom he also calls reason [*ratio*, the equivalent of Greek λόγος], and maintains that it is through the medium of the stars that the divinity controls what happens on earth:

> hic igitur deus et ratio, quae cuncta gubernat,
> ducit ab aetheriis terrena animalia signis,
> quae, quamquam longo, cogit, summota recessu,
> sentiri tamen, ut uitas ac fata ministrent
> gentibus ac proprios per singula corpora mores. (2.82–86)

This god and all-controlling reason, then, derives earthly beings from the heavenly signs; though the stars are remote at a far distance, he compels recognition of their influences, in that they give to the peoples of the world their lives and destinies and to each man his own character.[3]

The communication between heaven and earth is not, however, entirely one-sided. While the *mundus* (also called nature, *natura*) exerts its influences on human beings, it at the same time invites them to direct their attention upward and contemplate the workings of heaven. Man is called upon and able to understand the cosmos because he is a microcosm himself and has a

specifically on astrology in the Roman period; ancient astrological writings are surveyed by W. Gundel and H. G. Gundel, *Astrologumena: Die astrologische Literatur in der Antike und ihre Geschichte* (Wiesbaden, 1966). There is no good general treatment of Manilius; the *Loeb* edition (G. P. Goold, *Manilius, Astronomica*, 2nd ed. [Cambridge. Mass., 1992]) and its introduction provide the best starting point for the interested reader, who may additionally wish to consult F.-F. Lühr, "Ratio und Fatum: Dichtung und Lehre bei Manilius" (Ph.D. diss., Frankfurt, 1969); W. Hübner, "Manilius als Astrologe und Dichter," *ANRW* 2.32.1:126–320; C. Salemme, *Introduzione agli* Astronomica *di Manilio* (Naples, 1983); M. Neuburg, "Hitch Your Wagon to a Star: Manilius and His Two Addressees," in *Mega Nepios: Il destinatario nell'epos didascalico/The Addressee in Didactic Epic*, ed. A. Schiesaro, P. Mitsis, and J. S. Clay (Pisa, 1993 = *Materiali e discussioni per l'analisi dei testi classici* 31), 243–82.

2   See A. S. F. Gow, *A. E. Housman: A Sketch Together with a List of His Writings and Indexes to His Classical Papers* (Cambridge, 1936), 13.

3   I quote Manilius from G. P. Goold's *Teubner* text (*M. Manilii Astronomica*, 2nd ed. [Stuttgart, 1998]); the translations are adapted from the same scholar's Loeb edition.

share of the divine, and because the universe actively wishes to reveal itself
to him. For how else could we encompass the wonders of the heavens in our
narrow minds,

> ni sanctos animis oculos natura dedisset
> cognatamque sibi mentem uertisset ad ipsam
> et tantum dictasset opus, caeloque ueniret
> quod uocat in caelum sacra ad commercia rerum? (2.122–125)

> . . . if nature had not endowed our minds with divine vision, had not turned to
> herself a kindred intelligence, and had not prescribed so great a science, and if
> there did not come from heaven a power that calls us heavenward to a sacred
> exchange with nature?

If all human beings are thus invited into heaven to a "sacred exchange"
(*sacra . . . commercia*, 2.125), it is, in Manilius' scheme of things, especially the
poet himself to whom the *mundus* is willing to lay open its secrets (see esp.
1.11–12) and in whose astrological song it takes pleasure (*et gaudente sui
mundo per carmina uatis*, "heaven rejoices in the song of its bard," 2.142). This
interaction between poet and universe is a central motif of the *Astronomica*,
and there is one poetic image in particular that Manilius uses to express his
participation in the divine: Again and again, the poet presents himself as
physically advancing into the realm of heaven, ascending to the stars, and
thus becoming himself part of the cosmic events he describes in his poem.

The image of the heavenly journey in Manilius has attracted a certain
amount of scholarly attention.[4] It is obvious that the poet's use of this trope
is influenced by a number of different traditions. When he describes his
own activity as *ire per ipsum / aera et immenso spatiantem uiuere caelo* ("to traverse the very air and spend my life touring the boundless skies," 1.13–14),
he is employing a fairly conventional metaphor by which the intellectual
efforts of astronomers and cosmologists could figuratively be described as
οὐρανοβατεῖν [sky-walking].[5] In addition, his repeated description of his

---

[4] See, among others, Lühr, "Ratio und Fatum," 19–23, 43–52, 73–82; Salemme, *Introduzione*,
38–9; M. Scarsi, "Metafora e ideologia negli *Astronomica* di Manilio," *Analysis* 1 (1987): 93–
126, here 101–14; L. Landolfi, "OYPANOBATEIN: Manilio, il volo e la poesia. Alcune pre-
cisazioni," *Prometheus* 25 (1999): 151–65. I discuss the motif in greater detail in *Poetics of Latin
Didactic*, 225–34 and "Pious and Impious Approaches," 86–92.

[5] See R. M. Jones, "Posidonius and the Flight of the Mind Through the Universe," *CP* 21
(1926): 97–113; L. Delatte, "*Caelum ipsum petimus stultitia* . . . (Contribution à l'étude de l'ode
I,3 d'Horace)," *Ant Class* 4 (1935): 325–35.

movement through heaven as a chariot ride (2.58–59, 136–144; 5.1–11) is indebted to the widespread concept of the poet's journey – that is, the comparison of poetic composition to travel, especially on a ship (cf. 2.59) or in a chariot.[6] And finally, his insistence on the divine nature of the universe turns the poet's described movement into a spiritual ascent (a cross-cultural concept known from Judaism and Christianity, but also found in, for example, Platonism and Hermeticism), whose ultimate goal is the transcendence of human nature and the union with god[7]: *impendendus homo est, deus esse ut possit in ipso* ("man must expend his very self before god can dwell in him," 4.407).

As hinted in this brief discussion, Manilius is a poet notable for his eclecticism, his ability to combine a number of different discourses – science, poetry, and mysticism – to create startling (and sometimes difficult) imagery, which he employs to illustrate the tenets of his astrological worldview. In the following discussion, I take a closer look at one specific example of the heavenly journey metaphor in the *Astronomica*, a short passage that some scholars have regarded as inauthentic, but one that I hope to show fits in well with Manilius' poetic practice. In the proem to Book 4 (4.1–118), the poet celebrates the absolute rule of Fate (whose agents are the stars) before turning to a detailed discussion of zodiacal influences (4.122–293). The three lines in between mark the transition:

> quod quoniam docui, superest nunc ordine certo
> caelestis fabricare gradus, qui ducere flexo
> tramite pendentem ualeant ad sidera uatem. (4.119–121)

Since I have taught this, it remains for me to build heavenly steps in a certain order, which are able to lead the suspended poet to the stars on a curved path.

---

[6] On the poetic journey metaphor in antiquity, see O. Becker, *Das Bild des Weges und verwandte Vorstellungen im frühgriechischen Denken* (Berlin, 1937); M. Durante, "Epea pteroenta: La parola come 'cammino' in immagini greche e vediche," *RAL* 13 (1958): 3–14; M. Asper, *Onomata allotria: Zur Genese, Struktur und Funktion poetologischer Metaphern bei Kallimachos* (Stuttgart, 1997), 21–107; R. Nünlist, *Poetologische Bildersprache in der frühgriechischen Dichtung* (Stuttgart, 1998), 228–83.

[7] The literature on spiritual ascent in various cultural, religious, and philosophical contexts is too large to be listed here. For an introduction, as well as copious bibliography, see the articles "Flügel (Flug) der Seele," "Jenseitsfahrt I (Himmelfahrt)," and "Jenseitsreise" in *Reallexikon für Antike und Christentum*; see also A. F. Segal, "Heavenly Ascent in Hellenistic Judaism, Early Christianity and their Environment," *ANRW* 2.23.2:1333–94 for a comparativist perspective on classical, Jewish, and Christian ideas of ascent.

In his edition, A. E. Housman brackets these lines, providing two reasons for doing so.[8] First, he maintains that *quod quoniam docui* ("since I have taught this," 4.119) makes no sense because "*in toto hoc prooemio nihil sane poeta docuit*" ("in this entire proem, the poet has taught nothing at all"). Second, he asserts that the lines interrupt the close connection between the preceding proem and the following announcement of the poet's new topic, which is again introduced by *nunc* (*nunc tibi signorum mores... reddam*; "now I shall tell you... the dispositions imparted by the signs," 4.122–123), something he feels is impossible after the *nunc* of 4.119.

As for Housman's first argument, a number of critics have pointed out that his insistence that Manilius has not "taught" anything in the proem amounts to little more than pedantry, for there is no reason why the poet's exposition of the fateful workings of the universe could not be termed "teaching," especially given that the *Astronomica* is a "didactic" poem and that *quoniam docui* is a "didactic" formula made famous by Lucretius and employed by Manilius also at 3.560.[9] Housman's second reason for athetesis carries somewhat more weight: It is definitely true that if the lines were not there, they would not be missed, and one may indeed feel that the repetition of *nunc* is somewhat infelicitous. Still, given that the lines *are* there (they are not suspect on textual grounds), one may well accept the explanation, as some commentators have, that, after his lengthy and sublime proem, Manilius takes some time to introduce his readers to the new topic, inserting a more general transitory passage (the three lines under discussion) before the actual announcement in 4.122–123 of the treatment of the zodiac.[10]

---

[8] See A. E. Housman, *M. Manilii Astronomicon liber quartus* (London, 1920), *ad loc*. In declaring the lines spurious, Housman follows Richard Bentley, *M. Manilii Astronomicon* (London, 1739) and is, in turn, followed by Goold in his *Teubner* and *Loeb*, as well as by W. Fels, *Marcus Manilius: Astronomica* (Stuttgart, 1990).

[9] See Lühr, "Ratio und Fatum," 136, and esp. D. Liuzzi, *M. Manilio: Astronomica, Libro IV* (Galatina, 1994), *ad loc*. Funnily enough, Richard Bentley, who was the first to cast doubt on the three lines, and whom Housman explicitly follows, complained not that Manilius had not *taught* anything in the proem to Book 4, but that he had taught nothing *new* ("*nihil novi hic docuit*," *ad* 4.119) – as the topic of Fate makes a number of previous appearances. This argument is specious: In 4.119, Manilius does not say that he has taught anything new, and it is quite unfair to hold the poet to a claim of novelty that he never made.

[10] See T. Breiter, *M. Manilii Astronomica*, 2 vols. (Leipzig, 1907–1908), *ad* 4.119–121, and Lühr, "Ratio und Fatum," 137, n. 2. E. Flores, "Aspetti della traduzione manoscritta e della recostruzione testuale in Manilio," in *Manilio fra poesia e scienza: Atti del convegno Lecce, 14–16 maggio 1992*, ed. D. Liuzzi (Galatina, 1993), 9–19, here 19 (see also the same scholar's *apparatus criticus* in S. Feraboli, E. Flores, and R. Scarcia, *Manilio: Il poema degli astri [Astronomica]*, 2 vols. [Milan, 2001], 2:88) believes that Manilius first wrote 4.119–121 to serve as a transition

Ultimately, though, the question of the lines' authenticity hinges on their interpretation. Does the passage actually make sense, and make sense where it is placed? Housman did not think so, remarking sarcastically, "*secuntur deinde caelestes gradus miro consilio fabricati, quibus uates, non discipulus, flexo tramite, non recto, ad sidera ducatur*" ("there follow the celestial steps built for the strange purpose of guiding the poet, not the student, on a winding, not straight, path to the stars"). Clearly, the famous editor found the imagery of the verses bizarre. By contrast, I believe that a careful examination of the diction of the passage will reveal much about Manilius' poetic method, as well as about the intellectual traditions on which he is drawing, and will ultimately lead to the conclusion that the three lines are indeed authentic.

The poet's wish to reach the stars is not merely another example of the metaphor of the heavenly journey, but an instance of the more specific idea that the achievement of fame, especially poetic fame, equals a rising to the stars.[11] In particular, Manilius' diction may be inspired by the famous ending of Horace's first ode, where the poet tells Maecenas,

> quodsi me lyricis uatibus inseres,
> sublimi feriam sidera uertice. (*Carm.* 1.1.35–36)

If you place me among the lyric poets, I shall touch the stars with the top of my head.

The fact that Manilius likewise refers to himself as a *uates* (poet) about to reach the *sidera* (stars) makes this parallel especially attractive.

What, however, of the "heavenly steps"? Some interpreters have compared a passage in Book 2 of the *Astronomica*, in which Manilius explains his didactic method (2.750–787)[12]: The teacher must proceed step by step, providing the student first with basic information and moving on to more complex topics only once the simpler facts have been mastered. The poet compares this process, in two elaborate similes, both to the slow progress of children who

---

between proem and main text, but later replaced these lines with 4.122–123: By mistake (as a result of the supposedly premature death of the poet, who was thus unable to provide a final revision), both passages survived and entered into the manuscript tradition. This theory has the advantage of vindicating Manilian authorship while also acknowledging a certain redundancy in 4.119–123; its flaw, of course, is that it is based entirely on speculation.

[11] See Delatte, "*Caelum ipsum*," 315–16, n. 3, as well as R. G. M. Nisbet and M. Hubbard, *A Commentary on Horace, Odes, Book 1* (Oxford, 1970), *ad* Horace, *Carm.* 1.1.36 (quoted immediately following in the text).

[12] See Lühr, "Ration und Fatum," 137, as well as J. van Wageningen, *Commentarius in M. Manilii Astronomica* (Amsterdam, 1921 = *Verhandel. Nederl. Akad. van Wet. Afd. Letterk.* 22.4), *ad* 4.120.

learn to read (they first master individual letters, then syllables, then words, then sentences, and are finally able to read poetic texts, 2.755–764) and to the building of a city (in which the raw materials, such as wood and stone, have to be procured first, before the actual building can start, 2.772–783). He also describes his approach in more general terms:

> quoque deus regnat reuocanti numen in artem,
> per partes ducenda fides et singula rerum
> sunt gradibus tradenda suis, ut, cum omnia certa
> notitia steterint, proprios reuocentur ad usus. (2.768–771)

As I summon to my art the power by which god rules, I must by degrees win credence and assign each matter to its correct step, so that, when all the parts have been grasped with sure understanding, they may be applied to their proper uses.

Expounding his complicated subject matter, the poet takes one step [*gradus*] after the other, and it is quite possible that in our passage in Book 4, too, the "heavenly steps" are meant to evoke the teacher's commitment to "gradual" pedagogy.

Still, this cannot be the whole explanation of 4.119–121. As Housman correctly points out, it is not the student, but the teacher, who will avail himself of the *caelestes gradus*; moreover, aside from the phrase *quod quoniam docui*, the three lines betray little interest in didacticism but concentrate entirely on the anticipated achievement of the poet [*uates*], whose intention it is to reach the stars. In this context, I suggest understanding the *gradus* in a much more concrete way, as the rungs on a ladder or the steps of a stair, an interpretation first proposed by Karl Kerényi.[13] Kerényi argues that Manilius' image is indebted in particular to Hermetic ideas, quoting as a parallel the use of βαθμός [step] in the *Corpus Hermeticum* XIII 9, where Hermes Trismegistos describes to his son Tat the different elements of the process of regeneration: ὁ βαθμὸς οὗτος, ὦ τέκνον, δικαιοσύνης ἐστὶν ἕδρασμα ("this step, my son, is the seat of justice").[14]

---

[13] See K. Kerényi, "De teletis Mercurialibus observationes II.," *EPhK* 47 (1923): 150–64, here 156. Lühr, "Ratio und Fatum," 137, n. 1, quotes Kerényi but is skeptical of his idea.

[14] It is not clear, though, whether βαθμός here really does have the strong meaning "step" or is simply a dead metaphor: After all, the passage in question (unlike others in the Hermetic Corpus) does not mention the initiate's actual "ascent." Generally speaking, it is controversial whether the image of the stair or ladder plays a role in Hermetic ideas of purification; cf. B. P. Copenhaver, *Hermetica: The Greek* Corpus Hermeticum *and the Latin* Asclepius *in a New English Translation* (Cambridge, 1992), 189 (*ad CH* XIII 9), with references.

However, I do not think it necessary to posit a specifically Hermetic origin for Manilius' steps, as the stair or ladder that bridges the gap between heaven and earth is a cross-cultural motif.[15] Its most famous and influential instance is Jacob's ladder in Gen 28:11–17, but the image is also found elsewhere in the ancient Near East – for example, in Egyptian funerary ritual and in the *Book of the Dead*.[16] Although the Greeks for the most part appear not to have used the ladder as a symbol of spiritual or eschatological ascent,[17] ladders are occasionally mentioned as quite practical instruments for gaining access to the upper reaches of the sky: According to Pindar (fr. 162 Maehler), the giants used a ladder in their attack on the heavenly gods, and Polyainus 7.22 tells the story of the Thracian leader Kosingas, who threatened to climb to heaven on a series of ladders to complain to Hera about his unruly subjects.

In the Roman world, by contrast, the metaphor of the ladder proliferates in the first few centuries C.E. with the spread of "eastern" cults and religions, including Christianity. Thus, for example, miniature ladders have been found in Roman tombs, where they had been placed with the purpose of ensuring a safe passage to the afterlife, a custom presumably taken over from the Egyptians[18]; in Mithraism, a mystery cult first attested in the Roman Empire toward the end of the first century C.E., but one that may have arisen earlier,[19] the ladder came to play a central role and was crucially connected to cosmology since the seven steps of Mithraic initiation were identified with a purifying ascent via the spheres of the seven planets; and finally, beginning

---

[15] See F. Graf in this volume, as well as F. Cumont, *Lux perpetua* (Paris, 1949), 282–3; M. Eliade, *Shamanism: Ancient Techniques of Ecstasy*, trans. W. R. Trask (New York, 1964), 487–90; P. Dinzelbacher, *Die Jenseitsbrücke im Mittelalter* (Vienna, 1973), 141–58; C. Heck, *L'Échelle céleste dans l'art du Moyen Âge: Une image de la quête du ciel* (Paris, 1997), 9–28; my examples of individual occurrences of the motif are gleaned from these works. Note that, in this paper, I am not interested in tracing the origin and diffusion of the image of the ladder (see Graf's paper for a rejection of Eliade's claim that all ladder symbolism has its origin in shamanistic ascent ritual), just in ascertaining that Manilius could have known it and in explaining the use he makes of it.

[16] See Spells 98, 149, and 153A in R. O. Faulkner, *The Egyptian Book of the Dead* (London, 1985), as well as E. A. Wallis Budge, *The Book of the Dead: The Hieroglyphic Transcript and Translation into English of the Papyrus of Ani*, repr. ed. (New York, 1996), index s.v. "ladder."

[17] Although see Heck, *Échelle céleste*, 22, for possible ladder imagery in mystery cult and in Plato.

[18] See Cumont, *Lux perpetua*, 282.

[19] On the earliest evidence for the cult of Mithras in the Roman empire, see M. Clauss, *The Roman Cult of Mithras: The God and His Mysteries*, trans. R. Gordon (New York, 2000), 21–2. The origin and early history of (Roman, as opposed to Iranian) Mithraism are controversial; if there is any truth to Plutarch's claim (*Pomp.* 24) that the Cilician pirates subdued by Pompey in 66 B.C.E. practiced some form of the cult, its spread through the Roman world might have begun before the time of Manilius.

with St. Perpetua's dream (*Passion of Perpetua* 4), the ladder became a common Christian symbol for the soul's ascent to god.[20] On the whole, it seems that, even though in Manilius' time and place the image of the ladder was by no means as ordinary as it was to become in Late Antiquity, there would have been enough contexts in which the poet could have encountered the motif, from Greek literature to (proto-)Hermetic treatises to contemporary religious practice – not to mention the possibility that the image may well have appeared in one of Manilius' (now lost) astrological sources, some of which may have been of Near Eastern origin.

One peculiar feature of Manilius' ladder is the fact that the poet intends to build (*fabricare*, 4.120) it himself. What this means, of course, is that the "steps" are ultimately a metaphor for the poet's work – or, at any rate, the part of his work on which he is embarking at this moment and that our three lines serve to introduce. The poet's verses are the "steps" that will "lead him to the stars," an expression that can be understood in three ways: First, Manilius' poetry figuratively takes him into the celestial realm in that the stars are, after all, his subject matter; second, the reaching of the stars stands for the poetic fame to which the work will conduct its poet; and third, there is a spiritual aspect to Manilius' poetic activity, which – as expressed in the mystical image of the ladder – will help its author lift himself up to the divine. Presenting the composition of poetry as "building," Manilius makes original use of the very old metaphor of the poet as craftsman, found in Archaic Greek poetry, but also, for example, in Vedic texts and, therefore, believed to be of Indo-European origin.[21] Just as (to take a famous example) Pindar at the beginning of *Olympian* 6 (1–3) declares that he is about to build a "splendid palace" (θαητὸν μέγαρον, 2), so too does Manilius in our passage announce that he will build "heavenly steps," likewise referring self-consciously to his own poetry.

There is, however, something odd about the poet's *gradus*. Manilius maintains that they will lead him to the stars *flexo tramite* (4.120–121), "on a curved

---

[20] On Perpetua, see Graf's contribution in this volume, which stresses the unique features of her vision's ladder symbolism and thus calls into question the assumption that the *Passion of Perpetua* served as a kind of "blueprint" for later Christian uses of the motif of the heavenly ladder. See also J. N. Bremmer in this volume.

[21] On the poetic craft metaphor, see M. Durante, "Ricerche sulla preistoria della lingua poetica greca: La terminologia relativa alla creazione poetica," *RAL* 15 (1960): 231–49; R. Schmitt, *Dichtung und Dichtersprache in indogermanischer Zeit* (Wiesbaden, 1967), 295–301; and Nünlist, *Poetologische Bildersprache*, 83–125.

path," an expression derided by Housman, as we have seen. Ladders are not usually curved and, although staircases can be, it remains to be explained why the poet does not expect his route to the stars to be a straight one. Some interpreters believe that Manilius is alluding to the inherent difficulty of his astrological subject matter: Jacob van Wageningen, for example, explains that *"in astrologia nullae viae sunt directae, sed plerumque tortuosae"* ("in astrology, no paths are direct, but [they are] mostly twisted").[22] I do not see, though, how the mere word *flexo* can be supposed to conjure up the idea of difficulty, especially since the passage, unlike others in the *Astronomica*, appears to be indicative of the poet's optimism regarding his work (it will lead him to the stars) and the notion of "tortuousness" is not elsewhere applied to Manilius' approach.

I suggest that the poet imagines his *trames flexus* as a quite concrete route, an actual path across the heavens. In the language of astronomy, a "path" is often a celestial orbit or circle,[23] and I believe that this is true for Manilius' *trames* [path] also – which would, of course, make sense because a circle is by definition *flexus* [curved]. As for the specific orbit along which the poet envisions himself as moving, Manilius must here be referring to the zodiac: After all, his detailed treatment of the zodiacal signs begins immediately following our passage and, for the next 170 lines, the poet is indeed mentally proceeding along the zodiac, treating each sign in turn, from Aries to Pisces. Manilius himself calls the zodiac an *inflexus orbis* (curved circle, 1.675), and the use of *trames* specifically in the context of the zodiac is found also in Seneca (*secat obliquo tramite zonas*, "it [the zodiac] cuts through the zones with a slanting path"; *Thy.* 845).[24]

If the poet's celestial journey is thus imagined as following the zodiac, a further way of understanding *gradus* suggests itself. As we have seen, the word, which originally refers to the steps a person takes while walking,

---

[22] Van Wageningen, *Commentarius, ad* 4.120; see also Lühr, "Ratio und Fatum," 136, n. 3, and A. Reeh, "Interpretationen zu den Astronomica des Manilius mit besonderer Berück-sichtigung der philosophischen Partien" (Ph.D. diss., Marburg, 1973), 120.

[23] See A. Le Bœuffle, *Astronomie, astrologie: Lexique latin* (Paris, 1987), s.v. "semita."

[24] Note in passing that, in another metapoetic passage (2.138–40), Manilius appears to be saying that his celestial journey will *not* follow the path of the zodiac (as I argue in "Manilius' Solitary Chariot-Ride [*Astronomica* 2.138–40]," *CQ* 53 (2003): 628–33); on Manilius' general tendency to self-contradiction, its implications, and possible reasons, see *Poetics of Latin Didactic*, index s.v. "Manilius: 'have-one's-cake-and-eat-it-too' principle" and "Pious and Impious Approaches," esp. 113–14, as well as the end of this paper.

often denotes the steps of a stair or the rungs on a ladder. However, *gradus* also comes to mean degree (of a circle) in a mathematical and astronomical sense,[25] in a semantic development that André Le Bœuffle describes as follows:

> Chaque degré franchi par le soleil sur l'ecliptique était assimilé à un pas, GRADVS.... Mais le terme, perdant peu à peu toute expressivité, deviendra tardivement la désignation habituelle du degré.[26]

The idea that the 360 degrees of the zodiac are actually "steps" that the sun and other planets have to climb in their orbit around the earth is found in the following description of Manilius' older contemporary Vitruvius:

> Per ea signa contrario cursu luna, stella Mercuri, Veneris, ipse sol itemque Martis et Iouis et Saturni ut per graduum ascensionem percurrentes...ab occidenti ad orientem in mundo peruagantur. (9.1.5)

> Through these signs (i.e., those of the zodiac), the moon, Mercury, Venus, the sun itself, Mars, Jupiter, and Saturn proceed as though through a rising staircase of degrees...and wander through the universe from West to East.

As this passage shows, the metaphor degree = step was still felt to be alive in Manilius' time and, indeed, *gradus*, although used in this technical sense (compare Man. 1.581, 3.268, and 445), had not yet become the standard term for degree (which at this point was still *pars*).[27]

The "heavenly steps" on their "curved path" are thus both the work (cf. *fabricare*) that will make its poet famous and raise him to a higher state of being (lead him to the stars) and, on a more technical level, the degrees of the zodiac that his poetry treats. In its complexity, the image is an example of Manilius' overall tendency to blend the realms of his song and his subject matter and to describe his poetic activity with the same terms he uses to describe the workings of the universe. The very metaphor of the celestial journey implies such a blurring of boundaries: Instead of keeping a distance from his topic, the poet places himself in the realm of heaven. This procedure is entirely consonant with the idea of a "sacred exchange" to

---

[25] I am indebted to Roger Beck for first pointing out this meaning of *gradus* to me.

[26] See Le Bœuffle, *Astronomie, astrologie*, s.v. "pars."

[27] Cf., e.g., Manilius' extended treatment of the *partes damnandae*, or "injurious degrees," of the individual signs of the zodiac in 4.408–502.

which, as we have seen, heaven is thought to invite the earth, and the poet in particular.

In our three lines, the intimate connection between Manilius' poetry and the heavenly phenomena he treats is brought out by the expression *ordine certo* ("in a certain order," 4.119). On the level of the image, of course, anybody building a ladder or staircase had better arrange the steps in an orderly fashion. On the level of metapoetics (the steps = Manilius' poetry), the poet announces that he will treat his subject in a clear order – certainly a virtue in a didactic poet. And, on the level of astronomical *realia* (the steps = the degrees of the zodiac), the "certain order" is clearly the orderly succession of the 360 zodiacal degrees all around the ecliptic. However, the poetic order and the astronomical order are ultimately the same because, in treating the zodiac, Manilius is, indeed, following the natural series of signs. His reference to the "certain order" (an expression that the poet uses elsewhere in the *Astronomica* to similar effect: 1.256, 2.690, and 3.157) thus serves to highlight the fact that his poem has the same structure as the universe it describes.[28]

If my interpretation is correct, lines 4.119–121 lead coherently from Manilius' exposition of the rule of Fate to his discussion of the zodiac by reflecting on the relationship between heaven and earth and, specifically, on the role of the poet in mediating between the two. On his celestial steps, the *uates* finds himself *pendentem* (suspended, lit. hanging, 4.121), a term so startling that in a number of manuscripts it has been changed to the colorless *prudentem* [careful]; however, the word is a perfect expression of the liminal status of the poet who is forever suspended between what is above and what is below, forever traveling the great staircase that serves as a conduit between heaven and earth.[29]

To conclude, I have argued that lines 4.119–121 of the *Astronomica*, far from being inauthentic, fit in well with the poet's use of heavenly journey imagery elsewhere in the poem and serve to underline the poet's mission as a mediator between heaven and earth. The passage is also typical of Manilius' eclecticism, his method of combining images and concepts from different backgrounds. In his "mix-and-match" approach, the poet does not always proceed with strict logic: In 4.119–121, the idea of the ladder that leads up to

---

[28] Cf., my discussion in *Poetics of Latin Didactic*, 233–40.

[29] On the meaning of *pendere* in the *Astronomica*, see also Hübner, "Manilius als Astrologe und Dichter," 128 and n. 4, 194–5.

the stars is not really compatible with that of the "curved path," especially if the *trames flexus* is indeed the zodiac, as I have suggested. While we can choose to find the resulting image overdone or even absurd, we may also come to appreciate it as the poet's original effort to invest with due sublimity a work that, after all, deals with nothing less than the most profound mysteries of the universe and the all-encompassing rule of Fate.

3

Heavenly Ascent, Angelic Descent, and the Transmission of Knowledge in 1 Enoch 6–16

Annette Yoshiko Reed

Secrets in Heaven, Knowledge on Earth

One of the most salient features of 1 Enoch is Enoch's reception of special knowledge through heavenly ascent and angelic revelations. The exact scope of this knowledge varies among the five originally independent writings within this collection. In our earliest Enochic pseudepigraphon, the *Astronomical Book* (Chaps. 72–82; third century B.C.E.), the revelations to Enoch focus on calendrical and cosmological matters. The *Book of the Watchers* (1–36), composed slightly later, similarly uses Enoch to impart information about ouranography and geography. In that apocalypse, however, cosmological wisdom has been increasingly integrated with eschatological and ethical exhortations. A further shift away from "scientific" concerns is evident in the two subdocuments from the mid-second century B.C.E., the *Epistle of Enoch* (91–108) and the *Book of Dreams* (83–90). Like the only canonical Jewish apocalypse, the Book of Daniel (also from the mid-second century), these works equate heavenly secrets with ethical pronouncements, historical predictions, and eschatological prophecies.[1]

I am grateful to my Princeton mentors and colleagues for reading multiple forms of this piece on multiple occasions. In addition, I would like to express my appreciation to John J. Collins for his insights and critiques of my argument. Warm thanks, as well, to my favorite interlocutor, my wise and sweet Dove C. Sussman.

[1] See further O. Neugebaur, "The 'Astronomical Chapters' of the Ethiopic Book of Enoch (72 to 82)," in Matthew Black, ed., *The Book of Enoch or 1 Enoch: A New English Edition* (PVTG 3; Leiden, 1985), 386–414; J. VanderKam, *Enoch and the Growth of the Apocalyptic Tradition* (Washington, DC, 1984), 110–14; G. Nickelsburg, "The Nature and Function of Revelation in 1 Enoch, Jubilees, and Some Qumranic Documents," in *Pseudepigraphic Perspectives: The Apocrypha and Pseudepigrapha in Light of the Dead Sea Scrolls*, ed. E. G. Chazon and M. E. Stone (Leiden, 1999), 96–9. Note that I here omit the *Similitudes* (Chaps. 37–71) from my survey because of its later date.

Before the manuscript discoveries at Qumran exposed the early dating of the *Astronomical Book* and the *Book of the Watchers*, scholars had privileged Daniel as the paradigmatic apocalypse and thus stressed the importance of historical and eschatological concerns for the genre as a whole. The evidence of the two earlier Enochic apocalypses has not only demonstrated the priority of speculative wisdom in the apocalyptic conceptualization of revealed knowledge, it also has prompted further research into the literary strategies, epistemological concerns, and social settings that shaped the early Jewish apocalyptic literature. From "historical apocalypses" such as Daniel, for instance, one might be tempted to dismiss apocalyptic pseudepigraphy as merely a tactic to ensure the historical accuracy of *ex eventu* prophecies. Yet, the evidence of "speculative apocalypses" such as the *Astronomical Book* and the *Book of the Watchers* leads us to reconsider the literary practice of pseudepigraphy within the broader context of apocalyptic epistemology.[2]

Alongside their shared appeal to the authority of Enoch, the writings collected in 1 Enoch share a set of attitudes and approaches toward the manner by which humankind can properly gain access to divine secrets. A special concern with knowledge is reflected in the projection of many different types of wisdom into heaven, encompassing both spatial and temporal planes of existence. No less striking is the strategy of secrecy, by which knowledge is veiled for the purpose of being uncovered. Implicit is the claim that salvific truth derives from secrets in heaven revealed on earth, whose veracity is vouchsafed by the righteousness of the one who rises to receive them and descends to proclaim them to his progeny.

Within these writings, references to Enoch's visions of heaven – whether achieved in dreams or by physical ascent – function as narrative occasions for the revelation of special knowledge to their readers. The trope of pseudepigraphy thus serves a self-referential function that fundamentally informs the truth-claims that the texts themselves pose to their audience.[3] Just as the narrative structure of these apocalypses justifies the veracity of the knowledge received by Enoch by emphasizing its heavenly origin, so their stress

[2] Contrary to Nickelsburg's theories about the Enochic testament at the core of 1 Enoch, as outlined most recently in his new Hermeneia commentary (*1 Enoch 1: A Commentary on the Book of 1 Enoch 1–36; 81–108* [Minneapolis, 2001]), I here approach the *Book of the Watchers* as an apocalypse; see further A. Y. Reed, "The Textual Identity, Literary History, and Social Setting of 1 Enoch: Reflections on George Nickelsburg's New Commentary on 1 Enoch 1–36; 81–108," *ARG* 5 (2003): 283–90.

[3] J. J. Collins, "The Apocalyptic Technique: Setting and Function in the *Book of Watchers*," *CBQ* 44 (1982): 97.

on Enoch's role as scribe and on his transmission of writings to his progeny tacitly attests the authenticity of the texts themselves, as true records of the mysteries revealed to the antediluvian patriarch.[4] Beyond the unquestionable significance of the prominence given to scribes and writings, the texts' self-conscious approach to their own reception-history is significant to note: The pseudonymous appeal to Enoch enables these pseudepigrapha to propose a heavenly etiology for the human reception of divinely authenticated calendrical, eschatological, cosmological, and ethical wisdom, while simultaneously asserting trustworthy continuity in the transmission of this knowledge to the present day – even across the radical historical disjuncture of the Flood.

In light of these powerful claims to reveal hidden truths, we might be surprised to discover that one of the two earliest Enochic writings, the *Book of the Watchers* (henceforth *BW*), includes a strikingly negative counterpart to the apocalyptic revelation of heavenly secrets. Even before recounting Enoch's reception of special knowledge, this text dedicates six chapters to the Watchers (6–11), which describe their descent to earth and its disastrous results. Consistent with the references to the "sons of God" in Gen 6:1–4, *BW* depicts the fallen angels as seducing human women and fathering the Giants/*Nefilim*. In *BW*, however, they play an even greater role in the antediluvian deterioration of life on earth: By revealing secret and forbidden knowledge, the Watchers are said to have caused "all manner of wickedness" to be adopted by humankind, thereby facilitating the proliferation of human sin that led to the Flood.

Both the notion of wayward angelic pedagogues and the specific topics of their instruction recall the ambivalent culture-heroes of Graeco–Roman mythology (e.g., Prometheus, Idaean Dactyls), whose teachings combine seemingly beneficial civilized arts with more socially marginal "magical" practices.[5] Whatever the significance of these phenomenological affinities,[6]

---

[4] For example, 76:14; 79:1; 83:1; 85:1–2; 91:1–3; 92:1; 93:3; 94:1; 104:11–13.

[5] For example, [Aeschylus], *Prom.* 446–504; Hesiod, *Op.* 42–105; Diodorus 5.64.4–5; Pliny, *Nat.* 7.61.

[6] For different views, see G. Nickelsburg, "Apocalyptic and Myth in 1 Enoch 6–11," *JBL* 96 (1977): esp. 399, 403; D. Suter, "Fallen Angel, Fallen Priest: The Problem of Family Purity in 1 Enoch 6–16," *HUCA* 50 (1979): esp. 115; F. Graf, "Mythical Production: Aspects of Myth and Technology in Antiquity," in *From Myth to Reason? Studies in the Development of Greek Thought*, ed. R. Buxton (New York, 1999), 322–8; and my discussion in "What the Fallen Angels Taught: The Reception-History of the *Book of the Watchers* in Judaism and Christianity" (Ph.D. diss., Princeton University, 2002), 56–8.

this tradition cannot be easily reconciled with the overwhelmingly positive stance toward knowledge that characterizes most early Jewish apocalypses. The corrupting teachings of the fallen angels imply an ambivalent attitude toward human learning that is, as Martha Himmelfarb notes, "quite isolated in the apocalyptic literature."[7]

To explore the significance of this tradition for our understanding of the different approaches to knowledge in 1 Enoch, this inquiry analyzes the motif of illicit angelic instruction within BW. After locating this motif within the text-history of this apocalypse, I consider its literary function within the redacted form of BW. My analysis suggests that the account of angelic descent in 1 Enoch 6–16 reflects two distinct attitudes toward human learning: (1) an "antispeculative" perspective in 1 Enoch 6–11, which appeals to the teachings of the Watchers to highlight the corrupting power of knowledge, and (2) a more nuanced approach in 1 Enoch 12–16, which uses the contrast between the fallen angels and Enoch to explore the relationship between secrets in heaven and knowledge on earth. When combined into the redacted whole of BW, the result is a poignant reflection on the power of knowledge, both to corrupt humankind and to save us.

Asael, the Instruction Motif, and the Text-History of the
Book of the Watchers

In light of the complex text-history of BW, one cannot address the motif of illicit angelic instruction without considering the relationship between different literary strata. Although BW seems to have circulated as a self-contained document by the second century B.C.E., most scholars concur that it originated as a composite text, integrating several distinct units into the narrative framework of an apocalypse. Five sections can be readily distinguished: 1–5, 6–11, 12–16, 17–19, and 20–36. Within BW, the references to illicit angelic instruction cluster in the two sections that most concern the Watchers, namely, the account of their descent in 6–11 and the account of Enoch's commission to rebuke them in 12–16.

Most scholarship on the Enochic myth of angelic descent has focused on 1 Enoch 6–11.[8] This section contains no reference to Enoch himself, and its

---

[7]   M. Himmelfarb, *Ascent to Heaven in Jewish and Christian Apocalypses* (New York, 1993), 78; also VanderKam, *Enoch and the Growth*, 126.

[8]   For the history of scholarship: E. J. C. Tigchelaar, *Prophets of Old and the Day of the End: Zechariah, the Book of the Watchers, and Apocalyptic* (Leiden, 1996), 168–72.

third-person narrative form differs notably from the pseudonymous first-person and second-person addresses in the rest of the apocalypse. These factors have led scholars to propose that Chapters 6–11 represent one of the earliest strata in *BW*, whether a "literary unit of distinct origin" or an extract from "an independent midrashic source."[9] Insofar as 1 Enoch 6–11 appears to integrate multiple versions of the angelic descent myth, much research has been dedicated to reconstructing the underlying traditions by isolating different strata within the text.[10]

Characteristic is the theory of George Nickelsburg. Observing that 1 Enoch 6–11 contains verses that depict the angel Shemiḥazah as the chief of the Watchers together with verses that depict the angel Asael as their leader, Nickelsburg identifies the earliest stratum with those sections that concern Shemiḥazah.[11] The Shemiḥazah material, he suggests, presents a midrashic elaboration of Genesis 6–9 that expands on the descent of the "sons of God," their cohabitation with the "daughters of men," and the birth of the Giants.[12] In his view, the references to Asael and his teachings derive from an "independent myth about the rebellion of a single angelic figure" and reflect later editorial activity.[13]

Central to Nickelsburg's reconstruction is his contrast between what he sees as two distinct approaches to the origins of antediluvian sin and suffering: Whereas the Shemiḥazah material focuses on the Watchers' sexual sins and the violence caused by their progeny, the Asael material posits the revelation of forbidden knowledge as the cause for the deterioration of earthly life before the Flood.[14] Despite this convenient division of labor, however, 1 Enoch 6–11 includes several verses that link Shemiḥazah and his hosts to illicit pedagogy. Nickelsburg accounts for this apparent inconsistency by positing two other strata of additions to the Shemiḥazah material, which

---

[9] G. Nickelsburg, "Reflections Upon Reflections: A Response to John Collins' 'Methodological Issues in the Study of 1 Enoch,'" *SBLSP* 17 (1978): 1:311; D. Dimant, "1 Enoch 6–11: A Methodological Perspective," *SBLSP* 17 (1978): 1:323.

[10] Esp. R. H. Charles, *Book of Enoch* (Oxford, 1912), 13; Nickelsburg, "Apocalyptic and Myth," 384–86; Dimant, "1 Enoch 6–11," 323–4, 329; P. Hanson, "Rebellion in Heaven, Azazel, and Euhemeristic Heroes in 1 Enoch 6–11," *JBL* 96 (1977): 195–233.

[11] That is, 6:1–8; 7:2–6; 8:4–9:11; 10:1–3; 10:11–11:2; Nickelsburg, *1 Enoch 1*, 165. Contrast Dimant, "1 Enoch 6–11," 324, 326, 333.

[12] Nickelsburg, *1 Enoch 1*, 166–8. Also Dimant, "1 Enoch 6–11," 324–26; Hanson, "Rebellion in Heaven," 197–220.

[13] Nickelsburg, *1 Enoch 1*, 171.

[14] Nickelsburg, *1 Enoch 1*, 171. Also Dimant, "1 Enoch 6–11," 326–7; Hanson, "Rebellion in Heaven," 220–6.

preceded the "interpolation" of the Asael material. According to his reconstruction, redactors first expanded the Shemihazah material by adding verses
about teaching (i.e., 7:1de; 9:8cd) and later elaborated on the specific topics
of their instruction (i.e., 8:3). Nickelsburg thus sees the references to Asael
(8:1–3; 9:6; 10:4–8) as reflecting the final stage in the redactional growth of
1 Enoch 6–11.

Although other theories differ in their details, it proves significant for
our purposes that most scholars, like Nickelsburg, dismiss the Asael material as a later accretion to the original core of the narrative.[15] By contrast,
John J. Collins has highlighted the importance of this material within the
redacted form of BW. Although acknowledging the composite character of
this apocalypse, he critiques the tendency of previous research to focus on
the derivation of the traditions within 1 Enoch 6–11.[16] Whereas this focus
has led scholars to address "breaks in the continuity, inconsistency in the
explanation of evil and duplications of angelic functions" by atomizing the
text into hypothetical sources, Collins suggests that our understanding of
BW might suffer from the imposition of "a modern ideal of clarity or consistency."[17] In his view, "we cannot purposefully discuss the meaning and
function of the Shemihazah story apart from the Asael material" and, furthermore, "the fact that these distinct traditions are allowed to stand in
some degree of tension is already significant for our understanding of the
function of this book."[18] When approached from this perspective, the motif
of illicit angelic instruction takes on a new importance, inasmuch as the
Asael traditions appear to have "significantly influenced the final shape of
the book."[19]

Consistent with his concern to explore the form and function of BW as
a redacted whole, Collins also calls attention to the next section, 1 Enoch
12–16. Whereas Chapters 6–11 contain no reference to Enoch, this section
describes the sins of the Watchers within the context of Enoch's commission
to rebuke them. By drawing on the trope of prophetic rebuke, 1 Enoch 12–16
combines traditions about the fallen Watchers (cf. Gen 6:1–4) with traditions

---

[15] For example, Dimant, "1 Enoch 6–11," esp. 324, 326, 333; Hanson, "Rebellion in Heaven,"
220–6.

[16] Collins, "Apocalyptic Technique," 94–5.

[17] J. Collins, "Methodological Issues in the Study of 1 Enoch: Reflections on the Articles of
P. D. Hanson and G. W. Nickelsburg," SBLSP 17 (1978): 315–16; also Tigchelaar, Prophets of
Old, 172–3.

[18] Collins, "Methodological Issues," 316; idem, "Apocalyptic Technique," 97.

[19] Collins, "Apocalyptic Technique," 102.

about the elevation of Enoch (cf. Gen 5:18–24). This function has led Collins to suggest that "as transitional chapters, they provide a key to the way in which the parts of the book are connected."[20]

Building on Collins' insights, I here use an analysis of 1 Enoch 12–16 to explore the literary and epistemological significance of the motif of illicit angelic instruction within the redacted whole of *BW*. In a recent article, Carol Newsom similarly turns her focus away from Chapters 6–11 to consider 12–16 and 17–19, taking up Collins' challenge of combining the source-critical insights of scholars such as Nickelsburg and Devora Dimant with a literary analysis of the redacted form of this apocalypse.[21] Newsom argues that the motif of illicit angelic instruction represents a later accretion, not only to 1 Enoch 6–11, but also to the next section, 12–16; in her view, the original form of 1 Enoch 12–16 interprets a version of 1 Enoch 6–11 that did not yet contain this theme.[22]

Newsom's hypothesis necessitates numerous textual emendations. For instance, she dismisses Enoch's rebuke to Asael for teaching unrighteousness in 13:1–2 as an "intrusion," on the grounds that it is a doublet of his rebuke to the other Watchers in 13:3 and in no way fulfills the archangelic commission of Enoch in 12:4–6. Similarly, she questions the originality of 16:2–3, God's instruction to Enoch to reprimand the fallen angels for revealing secret things. Citing the "redundancy" of 16:1 with 15:2 and the alleged absence of previous references to the angelic transmission of "secrets" in 1 Enoch 12–16 (i.e., if one follows Newsom in similarly excising 13:1–2), she concludes that these verses too are "redactionally suspect."[23]

Instead of identifying allegedly redundant verse as doublets and trimming the text accordingly, my reading highlights the patterns of repetition and elaboration in 1 Enoch 12–16. Whereas the exuberant polysemy of 1 Enoch 6–11 reflects the redactional combination of numerous conflicting traditions, I suggest that 1 Enoch 12–16 results from careful literary construction. In this, the motif of illicit angelic instruction plays a pivotal role, facilitating what is arguably the main purpose of this section: to combine traditions about the fallen angels with traditions about Enoch.

Whatever the origin of the traditions about illicit angelic instruction in 1 Enoch 6–11, the references to the Watchers' teachings in 1 Enoch 12–16

---

[20] Collins, "Apocalyptic Technique," 96–7.
[21] Newsom, "Development," 310–29, esp. 315.
[22] Newsom, "Development," 319.
[23] Newsom, "Development," 317.

probably did not result from later editorial activity and, at the very least, cannot be excised without substantial violence to the meaning of this transitional section. Rather, I argue that 1 Enoch 12–16 addresses the skeptical attitude toward knowledge in 1 Enoch 6–11 by juxtaposing the illicit revelations of the fallen angels with the elevation of Enoch. Consequently, these transitional chapters may attest continued reflection in the scribal circles that composed, redacted, and transmitted *BW* – not only about the Watchers' pedagogical transgressions, but also about the dangers of overzealous, human speculation into secrets from heaven.

Attitudes Toward Knowledge and Secrecy in 1 Enoch 6–11

Before analyzing the manner in which 1 Enoch 12–16 adapts and transforms themes from 1 Enoch 6–11, we should first consider the treatment of the teachings of the Watchers in the earlier section. 1 Enoch 6–11 begins with a paraphrase of Gen 6:1–2 (6:1–2) and describes the Watchers swearing an oath to descend to the earth to beget children with the daughters of men (6:3–6; cf. Gen 6:2a). After listing their names (6:7–8), it turns to recount their sexual defilement with human women, the instruction of their wives in magical arts, and the birth of the Giants from this impure union (7:1–2; cf. Gen 6:2b, 4). The great violence of the Giants is then described (7:3–5; cf. Gen 6:11), culminating in the outcry of the earth against them (7:6). The next chapter, 1 Enoch 8, lists a group of nine Watchers and identifies the specific types of knowledge taught by each (8:1–3), similarly concluding with the violence of the Giants and the human outcry against them (8:4). Following a description of the archangelic response to this outcry, there is yet another summary of the sins of the fallen Watchers, framed as the archangels' retelling of these events in a petition to God (9:6–10).

Within 1 Enoch 6–11, the topics of the Watchers' instruction are described in several different ways, which appear to reflect attempts at categorizing the teachings and explaining the exact reasons for their impropriety. Within the archangels' petition, for instance, Asael and Shemiḥazah are both described as teaching "sins" (ἁμαρτία; ἀδικία; 9:6a; 9:8b). Yet, the archangels also denounce Asael and other Watchers for revealing "secrets" (μυστήρια; 9:6b; 10:7; see 8:3h). Whereas the former forefronts the effects of their teachings on human behavior, the latter points to the act of instruction itself, emphasizing the Watchers' transgression of proper epistemological boundaries through their revelation of mysteries to humankind.

These themes resonate with the specific topics of instruction that 1 Enoch 6–11 associates with the Watchers. In 8:1–2, metalworking and cosmetics are attributed to Asael. This passage appeals to these civilized arts to emphasize the corrupting potential of knowledge: Asael's instruction in metalworking leads men to forge weapons and fight among themselves, paralleling the bloodshed caused by the Giants in 7:3–5. Likewise, after this Watcher reveals knowledge about feminine adornments, the artificial beautification of women causes promiscuity to proliferate among humankind, paralleling the Watchers' own lust and sexual defilement in 7:1.[24] In each case, the motif of illicit angelic instruction allows for an explanation of the antediluvian deterioration of earthly life that shifts the blame away from the Watchers, positing instead the shared culpability of corrupting angels and corrupted humans.

Whereas the teachings of Asael highlight the corrupting power of the knowledge that shaped human civilization, the other topics of illicit angelic instruction in 1 Enoch 6–11 invoke categories of forbidden wisdom. The human discovery of spells and sorcery, practices explicitly prohibited in the Torah (Deut 18:9–14), is attributed to the teachings of Shemiḥazah, Hermoni, and other Watchers. Just as 7:1 recounts how the Watchers taught their wives "sorcery (חרשה; 4QEnᵃ III 15), spells, and the cutting of roots and herbs," so 8:3a–b depicts Shemiḥazah transmitting knowledge about "spell-binding ([ו]חבר; 4QEnᵃ IV 1) and the cutting of roots" and Hermoni teaching about the "loosening of spells ([חרש למ]שרא; 4QEnᵇ III 2), magic, sorcery, and sophistry ([כ]שפו וחטמו ותוש[יו]; 4QEnᵃ IV 2)." Although *BW* describes these skills as wrongly obtained by humankind, its appeal to the fallen angels simultaneously allows for the assertion of their (albeit tainted) origin in heaven – thereby suggesting that the efficaciousness of spells and sorcery was never in doubt.

The mantic teachings described in 8:3c–g signal the broader epistemological significance of the instruction motif. Here, six angels are listed, with names that correspond to the natural phenomena whose auguries (נחשי;

<hr />

[24] If we follow Nickelsburg in reconstructing 8:2 from Syncellus' Greek version, then *BW* posits a causal connection between Asael's teachings about jewelry and cosmetics and the lust-motivated descent of Shemiḥazah and his hosts: The latter were drawn to earth by their lust for the artificially enhanced beauty of human women. See Nickelsburg, "Apocalyptic and Myth," 397–8; also 1 Enoch 86:1–2. If so, then the theme of corrupting knowledge becomes all the more striking, insofar as the mastery of forbidden arts prompts the downfall of both humans and angels.

4QEn[b] III 3; also 4QEn[a] IV 3) they reveal to humankind. The "auguries of lightning" are taught by Baraq'el (ברקאל = lightning of God); "auguries of the stars" by Kokhav'el (כוכבא[ל] = star of God); the "auguries of fireballs" by Ziq'el (זיקאל = fireball/storm of God); the "auguries of earth" by Ar'teqif (ארע[תקף] = the earth is mighty); the "auguries of the sun" by Shimshi'el (שמשי[אל] = sun of God); and the "auguries of the moon" by Sahri'el (שהריאל = moon of God).

As with spellbinding and sorcery, the practice of divination is explicitly prohibited in the Torah (Deut 18:10–12; see also Isa 44:25–26; 47:12–13; 46:9–11), such that *BW*'s association of this art with wayward "culture-heroes" invokes the dangers of ill-gotten wisdom. This topic of illicit angelic instruction, however, proves especially illuminating for our consideration of the attitudes toward knowledge in 1 Enoch 6–11. Not only does the implied critique of divination raise questions about this tradition's relationship to the positive presentation of mantic wisdom within other early Jewish apocalypses, but also the specific modes of divination listed in 8:3c–g evoke a common apocalyptic conceptualization of heavenly secrets: cosmological and, particularly celestial, phenomena.[25]

The inclusion of knowledge about the sun, moon, earth, stars, lightning, and fireballs among the teachings of the fallen Watchers presents a striking contrast to the elevated status of cosmological wisdom in other parts of *BW*, as well as the earlier Enochic apocalypse. In the *Astronomical Book*, the revelations to Enoch concern the sun, moon, stars, earth, winds, and seasons, focusing on calendrical cycles. A similar correlation of the cosmic order with the proper patterns of human life can be found in 1 Enoch 2–5, the nature poem in the first section of *BW*. Here, Enoch exhorts the reader to "observe" and "consider" the "works of heaven" – the heavenly luminaries (2:1), the earth (2:2), and the weather fluctuations in the progression of seasons (2:3–5:1a) – because the orderliness of their cycles attests to God's act of creation (5:1b) and provides humans with models for ethical steadfastness (see also 1 Enoch 41; cf. 80:2–8). The descriptions of Enoch's tours of heaven and earth in 1 Enoch 17–19 and 20–36 exhibit similar concerns, including an interest in meteorological and celestial phenomena (esp. 36).

---

[25] On the former, VanderKam, *Enoch and the Growth*, 52–75; on the latter, M. E. Stone, "Lists of Revealed Things in the Apocalyptic Literature" in *Magnalia Dei: The Mighty Acts of God: Essays on the Bible and Archaeology in Memory of G. Ernest Wright*, ed. F. M. Cross, W. Lemke, and P. D. Miller (Garden City, N.J., 1976), 426–41; C. Rowland, *The Open Heaven: A Study of Apocalyptic in Judaism and Early Christianity* (London, 1982), 120–2.

In those sections of *BW*, the association of cosmology and revealed wisdom is used to praise God and to encourage human righteousness.[26] By contrast, a very different attitude toward cosmological wisdom is communicated by the image of the fallen angels improperly instructing humanity about the sun, moon, earth, stars, lightning, and fireballs in 1 Enoch 6–11. As Himmelfarb observes,

> [The] knowledge of the very phenomena that are signs of faithfulness in the introduction to the *Book of the Watchers* (i.e., 1–5; esp. 2:1–5:4) and cause for praise of God in the tour to the ends of the earth (i.e., 17–36) here contributes to the corruption of humanity.[27]

In the subsequent discussion we see how this tension functions to generate very interesting levels of meaning within 1 Enoch 12–16 and the redacted whole of *BW*. When we consider 1 Enoch 6–11 as an originally independent unit, however, the association of these mysteries with the teachings of fallen angels raises an intriguing possibility: This tradition may have once been used to critique the same kinds of cosmological speculation and mantic wisdom that would later come to predominate in the redacted form of *BW*.

Here, it proves significant that 1 Enoch 6–11 inverts the conception of heavenly secrets as divine knowledge uncovered for salvific aims – a notion presupposed by the early Enochic pseudepigrapha in their transmission of secrets allegedly received by Enoch in heaven.[28] This is perhaps most evident in 8:3h, which concludes the list of the Watchers' teachings with the summary statement: "And they all began to reveal mysteries/secrets (4QEn[a] IV 5, 4QEn[b] III 5: לגליה רזין; Gr[Syn]: ἀνακαλύπτειν τὰ μυστήρια) to their wives." When applied to heavenly luminaries and meteorological phenomena, the language of secrecy [רז] and revelation [נגלה] simultaneously evokes and inverts the association of divine mysteries with cosmological wisdom in later Enochic books and other early Jewish apocalypses (e.g., 1 Enoch 41:3; Dan 2:16–19, 26–30, 47; 4:9).[29]

---

[26] Himmelfarb, *Ascent*, 72–4.

[27] Himmelfarb, *Ascent*, 77.

[28] As C. Molenberg notes, there is only one reference to the positive revelation of knowledge in Chaps. 6–11: God's instruction to Sariel to tell Noah about the coming Flood in 10:2–3 ("A Study of the Roles of Shemiḥazah and Asael in Enoch 6–11," *JJS* 35 [1984]: 140–1).

[29] In Daniel, for instance, the term רז denotes the hidden meanings of dreams, which God reveals [נגלה] to Daniel in visions (e.g., 2:16–19, 26–30, 47; 4:9). See further M. Bockmuehl, *Revelation and Mystery in Ancient Judaism and Pauline Christianity* (Tübingen, 1990), 31–40.

Moreover, 1 Enoch 6–11 deploys the rhetoric of secrecy in a wholly negative manner. Although this stance differs markedly from the rest of BW, other early Enochic pseudepigrapha, and apocalyptic literature more broadly, a similar skepticism toward the human quest for hidden knowledge can be found in the biblical and postbiblical Wisdom literature. Most notable are Qohelet and the Wisdom of ben Sira, the two products of the Wisdom tradition that are closest in date to BW. Consistent with the emphasis on the essential inscrutability of God and his creation in earlier Wisdom literature (e.g., Prov 30:1–4; Job 11:5–6; 28; 38–40; also Sir 11:4), these texts level explicit critiques against the apocalyptic claim to uncover the mysteries of heaven (Qoh 3:21; Sir 3:21–22; 34:1–8; 41:4).[30]

If 1 Enoch 6–11 reflects a similar attitude, only voiced in a different manner, how might we account for the integration of this tradition into Enochic materials whose attitude toward human knowledge and divine secrets are more classically "apocalyptic" (in both the generic and the literal sense of this term)? Most relevant, in this regard, is Michael E. Stone's analysis of the common topics and structures in the "lists of revealed things" found in the Wisdom literature and early Jewish apocalypses. Stone has demonstrated that the same formulaic lists were used to catalog topics of apocalyptic speculation and to stress the limits of human knowledge.[31] Such textual parallels may evince the close interchange and continued literary borrowing between circles that embraced speculative wisdom and those that emphasized the dangers inherent in the unrestrained search for knowledge.

Recent research has also suggested that the Wisdom literature and the earliest Jewish apocalypses both emerge from the literary activities of intensely scribal circles with priestly concerns.[32] If the articulation of the motif of illicit angelic instruction in 1 Enoch 6–11 does indeed reflect "antispeculative" leanings, then it is possible that this unit took form among writers and redactors whose stance toward cosmological inquiry was more similar to that of ben Sira than to that of the scribes responsible for the Astronomical Book and the other sections of BW. Indeed, the probable sociological commonalities

---

[30] R. Argall raises the intriguing possibility that ben Sira's critique of those who "seek after hidden things" is aimed at the very circles responsible for producing the early Enochic literature (1 Enoch and Sirach: A Comparative Literary and Conceptual Analysis of the Themes of Revelation, Creation, and Judgment [Atlanta, 1995], esp. 74–6, 250).

[31] Stone, "Lists," 435–9.

[32] J. Z. Smith, "Wisdom and Apocalyptic" in Visionaries and Their Apocalypses, ed. P. Hanson (IRT 4; Philadelphia, 1983), 101–20; Collins, "Wisdom, Apocalyptic," 165–86; Stone, "Lists," 414–52.

between such groups further allows for the possibility that 1 Enoch 6–11 was thenceforth adopted by scribes with more positive attitudes toward speculative wisdom.

The Instruction Motif and the Literary Structure of 1 Enoch 12–16

The difficult task of interweaving this antispeculative tradition with Enoch's ouranographical, geographical, and eschatological revelations is masterfully achieved by the transitional chapters of 1 Enoch 12–16. In contrast to 1 Enoch 6–11's narrative account of the descent of the angels, this section describes the sins of the Watchers in the context of Enoch's commission to rebuke them. Two key passages elaborate on the Watchers' transgressions: 12:4–13:3 and 15:2–16:4. Both describe the myth of angelic descent in the form of second-person rebukes framed by third-person instructions to rebuke. Although these passages are narratively distinct, their structural parallels expose the artful use of repetition, the careful modulation of speaker, and the special place of the instruction motif in 1 Enoch 12–16.

The pattern of repetition and elaboration that connects the two passages is signaled by the lexical parallels in the introductory verses of 12:4–13:3 and 15:2–16:4. Both begin with instructions to Enoch to go and speak to the Watchers, who are accused of "leaving the high heaven," corrupting/defiling themselves with women, and "acting like the children of earth" (12:4; 15:2–3). The first passage goes on to condemn the Watchers for bringing "great destruction on the earth" (12:4; cf. 7:3–5; 8:4; 9:3). The second passage expands on this theme; by equating the Giants with the evil spirits who continue to plague humankind (15:8; cf. 19:1), it extends the Watchers' destructiveness far beyond the antediluvian era. Then, the two passages each record a prophecy concerning the eventual destruction of the Giants, which is followed by a brief narrative transition.

At this point, the first passage shifts the subject of direct speech to Enoch, who rebukes Asael. The second inserts another statement to Enoch from God, echoing his instructions at 15:2 ("And now [say] to the Watchers, who were once in heaven, who sent you to intercede on their behalf"; 16:2). In each case, this transition occasions the introduction of the theme of secret knowledge. In the first passage, the accusations of illicit pedagogy are addressed solely to Asael, whereas the object of the second is unspecified and presumably more general. Both passages, however, emphasize the sin of revealing forbidden mysteries and the great punishment that will ensue.

The parallels between the two passages can be charted as follows:

1 Enoch 12:3–13:3	1 Enoch 15–16
12:3: Transition, introducing instruction of angels to Enoch	15:1–2: Transition, introducing instruction of God to Enoch
12:4: Description of the Watchers as 12:4a: descending from heaven 12:4b: taking human wives 12:4c–d: acting like humans, by taking wives	15:3: Rebuke of the Watchers for 15:3a: descending from heaven 15:3b–d: taking human wives 15:3e–f: acting like humans, by bearing sons
	15:4–7: Contrast of spiritual and fleshly
12:4e: Rebuke for the destructive result of these relations	15:8–12: Description of the destructive result of these relations: the activities of the evil spirits of the Giants
12:5–6: Predictions about the punishment of the Watchers, through the destruction of the Giants	16:1: Predictions about the destruction of the Giants
13:1a: Transition, introducing words of Enoch to Asael	16:2: Transition, introducing instruction of God to Enoch
13:1b–2: Predictions about the suffering of Asael ("You will have no peace…") because of his transmission of sinful knowledge	16:3: Rebuke of the transmission of secret knowledge 16:4: Predictions about the punishment of Watchers ("You will have no peace…")

The symmetry between 12:3–13:3 and 15–16 suggests that the use of repetition reflects a deliberate literary structure. This appears to be confirmed by the careful modulation of speaker and context within 1 Enoch 12–16, which ensures that the repetition of content does not result in any redundancy or contradiction on the level of the narrative itself. The first passage depicts the "Watchers of great Holy One" as summarizing the sins of the "Watchers of heaven who have left the highest heaven" in a manner that focuses on their sexual misdeeds and the violent results (12:3–6). Subsequently, Enoch himself presents a summary in his rebuke of Asael, focusing on the improper revelation of knowledge and its sinful results (13:1–2). In the second passage, both themes are combined in the dialogue attributed to God himself (15–16).

Rather appropriately, the angels are here concerned with the departure of their sinful brethren from the dwelling place and activities proper to their kind; Enoch is troubled by "all the deeds of godlessness, wrongdoing, and sin" that humanity learned from Asael; and God considers both aspects of this transgression. The angels cite the Giants' destruction of the earth (12:4), but they neglect to mention the negative results of the Watchers' fall for humankind. By contrast, Enoch appears wholly concerned with the effects of angelic descent on humankind; he paraphrases the angels' statements about the punishment of the fallen Watchers to Asael, but he does not mention their transgression of the physical boundaries and characteristic activities proper to angels. God, however, is portrayed as omniscient (cf. 9:5, 11), insofar as he alone considers both aspects. Furthermore, he is depicted as understanding the ramifications of these events on a much deeper level, exploring the implications of angelic descent for the proper order of the cosmos that he created (15:4–7); the ramifications of the birth of the Giants beyond the antediluvian era (15:9–12); and the shared culpability of angels, women, and men in bringing about this lamentable situation (16:3).

The variation of context thus ensures that the duplication of content is in no way redundant within the text's own narrative schema, even as repetition may still serve a stylistic function on the level of the text and its reader. Not only does this reading of 1 Enoch 12–16 throw doubt on Newsom's rejection of 13:1–2 as a later addition, it also suggests that 16:2 should not be dismissed as "both unexpected and redundant."[33] Rather, the treatment of the instruction motif in 13:1–2 and 16:3–4 is consistent with the pattern of repetition and elaboration that connects 12:3–13:3 and 15–16. Consequently, there is little reason to believe that the motif of illicit angelic instruction was a later accretion to 1 Enoch 12–16 or that this section was originally based on a version of 1 Enoch 6–11 that similarly lacked this motif.[34]

The Descent of the Watchers and the Elevation of Enoch

The instruction motif also serves a pivotal function within the literary structure of 1 Enoch 12–16 as a whole, helping to smooth the transition between the story of the fallen angels in 1 Enoch 6–11 and the accounts of Enoch's

---

[33] Newsom, "Development," 317, 319.

[34] Certain parallels between 1 Enoch 6–11 and 12–16 also suggest that the latter interpreted a version of the former that was similar in shape to our extant version. For instance, the sequence in the objects and topics of rebuke in the latter mirrors the progression in the corresponding narrative of Chaps. 7–8 and follows the groupings of fallen angels in the rebukes in Chap. 10. Moreover, if 12–16 were based solely on the Shemihazah stratum of 6–11, it would seem peculiar that Shemihazah himself is nowhere mentioned in these chapters.

tours of heaven and earth in 1 Enoch 17–19. In this transitional section, each rebuke of angelic sin is correlated with a different stage in Enoch's elevation. And, in each case, the motif of illicit angelic instruction serves as the pivot that joins the account of angelic transgression with the account of Enoch's progressive elevation:

Sins of the Watchers	Enoch's Elevation
[Accounts of angelic descent in 1 Enoch 6–11]	
	Stage 1: Physical ascent (cf. Gen 5:24) Enoch is "taken up" from earth (12:1–2)
Rebuke of Watchers for sexual sins and violent results (12:3–6)	
Rebuke of Asael for the transmission of *sinful* knowledge (13:1–2)	
	Stage 2: Angelic petition and divine commission
Fallen Watchers request that Enoch petition on their behalf (13:3–4)	
	In dreams and visions, God commissions Enoch to rebuke them (13:7–14:7); Enoch sees throne vision (14:8–24).
Rebuke of Watchers for sexual sins and violent results (15:1–12)	
Rebuke of Watchers for the transmission of *secret* knowledge (16:2–3)	
	[*Stage 3: Revelation of knowledge to Enoch* Account of Enoch's tours of heaven and earth in 1 Enoch 17–19]

Each statement about improper angelic instruction in 1 Enoch 12–16 corresponds thematically and inversely to the events subsequently related about Enoch. Just as 13:3–14:25 depicts Enoch as elevated from mere human to a potential intercessor for sinful angels and a prophet divinely commissioned to rebuke them, so the preceding verses (13:1–2) explore the motif of improper angelic instruction along the axis of sin and punishment.

The angelic instructions for rebuke in Chapter 12 had established the nature of rebuke as twofold, consisting of witnessing to past sin (12:4) and foretelling future punishment (12:5–6). In Enoch's rebuke of Asael for transmitting improper knowledge, the order is reversed. Enoch first describes the punishment to which Asael is fated (13:1) and then explicates the nature of his transgression (13:2). The latter is framed as an explanation for the inescapability of this fate:

> Nor shall forbearance, petition, or mercy be yours, because of the wrongs that you have taught, and because of all the deeds of godlessness, and the wrong-doing [Gr. ἀδικίας, Eth. gefʿ] and the sin [Gr. ἁμαρτίας, Eth. xaṭiʾat], which you showed to the children of men.

This suggests a link with human experience that is simultaneously causal and typological. The teachings of Asael caused wickedness to proliferate among humankind. Just as Asael cannot escape punishment, so his human students will be fairly punished for their "deeds of godlessness" and their "wrong-doing and sin." Hence, the motif of illicit angelic instruction here functions not only as an etiology of human sin but also as a means to stress the essential inescapability of divine punishment.

These themes are developed in the following passage (13:3–14:25), which recounts the second stage in Enoch's elevation. Corresponding to the focus on Asael's sin, resultant human wickedness, and Asael's punishment in 13:1–2, this passage explores Enoch's unique role within the divinely ordered arithmetic of sin and punishment. First, the heavenly angels request that Enoch rebuke the fallen angels (12:1–6), and then the Watchers appeal to him to petition on their behalf (13:3–4). Enoch's special status as a human who can mediate between different levels of heaven is heightened even further when God himself commissions him to "speak to the sons of heaven and rebuke them" (13:8; also 15:2; 16:2). Enoch subsequently learns that he was, in fact, "endowed, fashioned, and created to reprimand the Watchers" (14:3), and he is granted a vision of the heavenly Temple, God's throne, and God's glory (14:8–24).

The second description of illicit pedagogy (Chaps. 15–16) is similarly linked to the next stage in Enoch's elevation. Whereas 12:3–13:3 explored the implications of the improper teaching of Asael for human sinfulness, 15–16 address the teachings of a collective, anonymous group of angels and their ramifications for our understanding of proper and improper categories of knowledge. Correspondingly, we find a shift from the rhetoric of sin in 12:3–13:3 to the rhetoric of secrecy in 15–16,[35] accompanied by a subtle transition from the vocabulary of teaching and showing to the vocabulary of revealing and informing.[36]

The focus now turns from the corrupting results of illicit angelic instruction to the act of revealing forbidden knowledge. Whereas the rebuke of Asael's pedagogical transgressions in 13:2 had emphasized the human wickedness catalyzed by him, 16:3 suggests that the crux of the Watchers' sin lies in the impropriety of heavenly secrets for human consumption. This corresponds to the next description of Enoch's elevation: his reception of special knowledge during his tours of heaven and earth, beginning in Chapter 17. Just as the concern with the Watchers' corruption of humankind in 13:1–2 inversely paralleled Enoch's subsequent transformation from a righteous man to a special mediator in the divine arithmetic of sin and punishment (13:3–14:24, esp. 13:4, 6, 8–10; 14:3–4), so the focus on the Watchers' improper revelation of knowledge in Chapter 16 is directly followed by the proper revelation of heavenly secrets to Enoch.

In the final lines of 1 Enoch 12–16, God tells Enoch to proclaim to the Watchers:

"You were in heaven,
And there was no secret that was not revealed to you.
Unspeakable secrets you know,[37]
And these you made known to women, in the hardness of your heart.
And, by these secrets, females and mankind multiplied evils upon the earth . . .
You shall have no peace." (16:3–4)

On this dramatic note, this transitional section comes to a close. Just as the account of angelic descent in 1 Enoch 6–11 had begun with the Watchers' oath on Mount Hermon (6:6), so Enoch finds himself suddenly transported to a "place of storm-clouds and to a mountain whose summit reached heaven" (17:2). As *BW* turns to describe Enoch's otherworldly journeys, Enoch first learns the "places of the luminaries and the chambers of the stars and of the

---

[35] 13:2: Gr., ἀδίκημα, ἀσέβεια, ἀδικία, ἁμαρτία, Eth., *gef'*, *derfat*, *xaṭi'at*. 16:3: Gr., μυστήριον, Eth., *meṭir*, *xebu'*.

[36] 13:2: Gr., δείκνυμι, ὑποδείκνυμι, Eth., *mahara*, *'ar'aya*. 16:3: Gr., ἀνακαλύπτειν, μηνύειν, Eth., *takaštu*, *zēnawa*.

[37] Following Black, *Book of Enoch*, 155.

thunder-peals" (17:3), the positive counterparts to the celestial and meteo-rological divination taught by the Watchers (8:3). In this manner, *BW* shifts from the fallen angels to Enoch's tours of heaven and earth – and from the improper teachings of the Watchers to the divine revelations received by Enoch.

Crossing the Epistemological Boundaries Between Heaven and Earth

The literary juxtaposition of the descent of the Watchers with the elevation of Enoch in 1 Enoch 12–16 mirrors the interest in inversion in Chapters 15–16, the account of God's own denunciation of the Watchers. Inasmuch as this version of events is presented as the direct speech of the all-knowing God, it represents this section's "last word" on the angel story in 1 Enoch 6–11. In the redacted form of *BW*, both the exuberant polysemy of 1 Enoch 6–11 and the modulation of different voices in 1 Enoch 12–16 are thus resolved through appeal to an omniscient perspective.

Evoking the concern for the orderliness of God's creation in 1 Enoch 1–5, 17–19, and 20–36, the dialogue attributed to God in 15–16 interprets angelic descent in terms of the inversion of the ideal relationship between identity and activity that properly delineates the heavenly and earthly realms. In 15:3, God denounces the once-immortal Watchers for "act(ing) like children of the earth" by bearing Giants for sons. This rebuke occasions a contrast between the proper types of action for spiritual and earthly beings. Although sexual reproduction is an acceptable activity for "those who die and perish" (15:4–5), this only strengthens God's argument that it is categorically improper for "spirits that live forever and do not die for all generations" (15:6).[38]

Likewise, the birth of the Giants is here explored in terms of the improper mingling of "spirits and flesh" (15:8). Angels properly dwell in heaven, and humans properly dwell on earth (15:10), but the nature of the Giants is mixed. This confusion of categories brings terrible results: After their physical death, the demonic spirits of the Giants "come forth from their bodies" to plague humankind (15:9, 11–12; 16:1). According to God's statements in Chapter 16, the fallen angels' transmission of heavenly knowledge to earthly humans can also be understood as a contamination of distinct categories within his orderly creation. As inhabitants of heaven, the Watchers were privy to all the

---

[38] On the possible typological significance of this assertion, see Suter, "Fallen Angel," 122–4; Nickelsburg, *1 Enoch 1*, 54; Himmelfarb, *Ascent*, 20–3.

secrets of heaven; their revelation of this knowledge to the inhabitants of the earth, however, was categorically improper and thus morally destructive.

Although 1 Enoch 12–16 includes the interpretation of illicit angelic instruction as improper because of its corruption of humanity, this section privileges God's own concern with the proper epistemological boundaries between heaven and earth. On the narrative level of the redacted text, the implications are striking. The antispeculative tendencies in 1 Enoch 6–11 are not simply subsumed into the rest of *BW*. Rather, the interpretation of 1 Enoch 6–11 presented by 1 Enoch 12–16 treats this tension as generative. Heeding the warning against overzealous cosmological speculation in 1 Enoch 6–11, it presents a negative antediluvian paradigm for speculation into heavenly secrets, alongside the positive paradigm of Enoch.

For our understanding of the pseudepigraphy of *BW*, it is equally significant that 1 Enoch 12–16 achieves this synthesis by elaborating on Enoch's elevation. Within the redacted form of *BW*, the placement of 1 Enoch 12–16 before 1 Enoch 17–19 functions to link the revelations to Enoch to his predestined commission from God. Far from presenting the antediluvian patriarch as a model for any contemporary practice of "ascent-mysticism," *BW* stresses that its pseudonymous author has received and revealed heavenly secrets because of his unique status. Together with the juxtaposition between Enoch's special wisdom and the forbidden secrets revealed by the fallen angels, this assertion helps to attenuate the potentially radical epistemological ramifications of this man's access to knowledge through heavenly ascent, by contextualizing his reception of that knowledge within a broader consideration of the proper relationship between heaven and earth, angels and humans, sacred and forbidden knowledge.

4

"Connecting Heaven and Earth": The Function of the Hymns in Revelation 4–5

Gottfried Schimanowski

Although references to heavenly liturgy abound in late antique literature, we rarely find this liturgy described in full detail.[1] One important exception is Revelation 4–5, the most extended body of literature of this
kind. The five hymns in these chapters (4:8, 4:11, 5:9–10, 5:12, and 5:13) are
closely interlinked; they are first sung by heavenly beings and then intoned
by the entire earthly creation. As such, they present a frame of reference
for the readers and hearers of Revelation, drawing attention to a full heavenly worship containing several parts. Moreover, the heavenly liturgy plays
a dominating and definitive role in Revelation. Not only do these hymns
stand at the beginning of the vision section, functioning as an impressive
portal into the rest of the apocalypse, but they set the tone for the following
chapters (6–21), which allow its readers and hearers to glimpse further into
heavenly realities.[2]

This paper is based on my German publication, *Die himmlische Liturgie in der Apokalypse des
Johannes: Die frühjüdischen Traditionen in Offenbarung 4–5 unter Einschluß der Hekhalotliteratur*
(WUNT 2,154; Tübingen, 2002). I thank Martin Dorn (Münster) for his help in correcting
the paper and transforming the "Germanisms" into readable English!

[1] Cf. esp. 1 Enoch 39:10–14; *Qedusha de Sidra*; 2 Enoch 18, 19, 20–21; *Lad. Jac.* 2:7–22; 3 Enoch
1:12 (§2); 35:1–6 (§52); without trisagion: *T. Levi* 3:4–9, also 1 Enoch 14:17–23; *T. Ab.* 11; not
clear: *Apoc. Ab.* 18.

[2] Aside from commentaries, cf. the secondary literature, esp. K.-P. Jörns, *Das hymnische Evangelium: Untersuchungen zu Aufbau, Funktion und Herkunft der hymnischen Stücke in der Johannesof-
fenbarung* (StNT 5; Gütersloh, 1971); D. R. Carney, "'Worthy Is the Lamb': The Hymns in
Revelation," in *Christ the Lord*, ed. H. H. Rowdon (Leicester, 1982), 243–56; L. L. Thompson,
The Book of Revelation: Apocalypse and Empire (New York, 1990); R. Bauckham, *The Climax of
Prophecy: Studies on the Book of Revelation* (Edinburgh, 1993); J. P. Ruiz, "Revelation 4, 8–11; 5,
9–14: Hymns of the Heavenly Liturgy," *SBLSP* 34 (1995): 216–20; J. F. T. Cuadrado, "Apocalip-
sis 4–5: Díptico litúrgico de creación y redención," *Mayéutica* 22 (1996): 9–65; J. M. Ford, "The
Christological Function of the Hymns in the Apocalypse of John," *AUSS* 36 (1998): 207–29;
A. R. Nusca, "Heavenly Worship, Ecclesial Worship: A 'Liturgical Approach' to the Hymns

Because the hymns are closely related to their literary context, it is clear that they were not composed to describe only heavenly worship. Hence, we must further ask these questions: What is the nature of the hymns, and how should we understand their content and their function within John of Patmos' broader message? How are they connected, and what is their background? How does John relate them to the earthly struggle between the faithful community and the powers, among the gods, between the elected people and their enemies, between the divine and profane forces, between Good and Evil? Inasmuch as the trisagion in Isaiah 6 serves as the core of all subsequent descriptions of heavenly liturgy, it is evident that the trisagion of the living creatures in Rev 4:8 plays a fundamental role in this context, as well. However, what is its function in relation to the other four hymnic poems dedicated to God and his Lamb in the throne scene? Taken together, these hymns include cultic terms and expressions that point to a worship setting; they emphasize that all beings are involved in the adoration of God. But how do heaven and earth each participate in this worship? God, as the ruler and king of the whole creation (Chap. 4), seems to be the focal point of the entire scene, but how does this chapter relate to the Lamb (Chap. 5), and what is the origin and background of that vision?

A complete analysis of the rich connections between these hymns and the apocalypse as a whole would go well beyond the framework of an article.[3] Here, I thus focus on a few significant points. First, I consider the structure and content of Revelation 4–5, exploring the literary setting of the hymns and its significance for our understanding of their meaning. Then, I turn to examine the heavenly liturgy itself, as it is fully described in these important chapters. Finally, I consider the broader issues raised by Revelation 4–5, offering a more comprehensive analysis of the implications of the liturgy for Revelation's depiction of heaven and earth – and the connections between them.

Whereas most scholarly interpretations of these hymns have examined the constituent parts of Revelation 4–5 in isolation, here I show how the hymns are closely interlinked and how the liturgical action of the worship scene relates to the message of the apocalypse as a whole. It is at the initiative of God himself that the entire creation is called (Revelation 4) and brought to

of the Apocalypse of St. John" (Ph.D. diss., Rome, 1998), esp. 1–105. For full bibliography, see my *Die himmlische Liturgie*, passim.

[3] Cf. esp. the recent study of Nusca and my publication, 37–42.

his throne (5:13) through the salvation of the cross (5:9–10). Consequently, the rhetorical strategy of the text aims to create not only catharsis, but also transformation. In effect, salvation is brought directly to human beings from all corners of the earth through the worship and adoration of the creator.

The Structure and Content of Revelation 4–5

The temporal clause μετὰ ταῦτα in Rev 4:1 presupposes the first chapters of the book, especially the initial vision in 1:9–20.[4] The seer presents himself once more as the witness of heavenly realms and as a "brother" of the faithful congregations. He is called to leave earth and to receive a vision of heavenly realities, because these things are hidden to the naked eye and become visible only through "heavenly" invitation. Despite the temporal clause in 4:1, the two chapters – Revelation 4 and 5[5] – are tightly knit, and they form a coherent and comprehensive unit with the following structure:

1. Introduction of the Vision (4:1–2a)
2. The Throne Vision (4:2b–7)
3. The Heavenly Worship (4:8.9–11)
    A: The *Qedushah* of the Four Creatures (4:8)
    B: The Doxology of the Twenty-Four Elders (4:11)
4. The Book (5:1–5)
5. The Slaughtered Lamb (5:6–7)
6. The Acclamation (5:8–10)
    C: The Hymn of the Living Creatures and the Elders (5:9–10)
7. The Three Responses (5:11–12, 13, 14)
    D: The Hymn of the Multitude of Angels, Living Creatures, and Elders (5:12)
    E: The Hymn of Every Creature in Heaven and on Earth and under the Earth and in the Sea (5:13)
    F: Living Creatures (5:14): "Amen!"
    G: Elders (5:14) Fell Down and Worshiped

---

[4] Note the first-person singular spoken by the seer, the subsequent noise of the "trumpet," and other close connections between Revelation 1 and the following messages to the seven churches (4:1–2).

[5] Because these two chapters form a unit, the next transition occurs at 6:1: καὶ εἶδον ὅτε; against D. E. Aune, *Revelation 1–5* (WBC 52a; Dallas, 1997).

The seer first describes the throne of God as encircled by flashes of lightning, noises, and diverse groups of angels. He attends the heavenly worship and observes the four living creatures, the twenty-four elders, and – at the end – all the angels and finally the whole creation. They conclude the liturgy appropriately with the heavenly "Amen" of all creation (5:13). The worship culminates with the prostrate adoration of the elders. In the "inner" circle by the throne, the Lamb stands and receives the book out of the hand of God; God and the Lamb – and, therefore, by implication, God's redemption – are the addressees of the whole worship sequence.

The first part of the description of the throne room (4:2b–7) begins with the outer area and ends with the inner circle, which consists of the four living creatures in the midst of the throne shouting "Holy, holy, holy" (4:8). The last line of 4:8 thus draws on the commissioning scene in Isaiah 6 and the traditional trisagion (Isa 6:3), which emphasizes the holiness of God. However, it also includes an interesting and distinct predication of God, which is phrased in a manner characteristic of John of Patmos[6]:

Isa 6:3	Rev 4:8
Holy, holy, holy	Holy, holy, holy,
is the Lord of hosts	the Lord God the Almighty,
the whole earth is full of his glory.	*who was and is and is to come.*

The term παντοκράτωρ [Almighty] is itself striking, in light of its derivation from the Hellenistic Synagogue,[7] but it is the threefold phrase covering all past, present, and future time that expresses the seer's message: God, as the Lord of the universe, is not only near in his eschatological coming, but he also transcends creation. Correspondingly, he is the one "who lives forever and ever" (4:9, 10).[8] This fundamental theological statement about God's subsistence is emphasized in the first liturgical text (4:8), which is sung "without ceasing"[9] by the members of the throne's inner circle positioned

---

[6] See Rev 1:4, 7, 8; also 6:17; 11:18; 14:7, 15; 16:15; 18:10; 19:7 as opposed to 17:8; see subsequent discussion and the allusions to the subsistence of God.

[7] See Rev 1:8; 4:8; 11:17; 15:3; 16:7, 14; 19:6, 15; 21:22 and R. Feldmeier, "Almighty," in *Dictionary of Deities and Demons in the Bible*, ed. K. van der Toorn, B. Becking, and P. W. van der Horst (Leiden, 1995), 35–41, with emphasis on the language of the LXX.

[8] Contrast the beast ascending "from the bottomless pit" (ἐκ τῆς ἀβύσσου; 17:8); it "was, and is not" [ἦν καὶ οὐκ ἔστιν]!

[9] Rev 4:8: καὶ ἀνάπαυσιν οὐκ ἔχουσιν; contrast the negative formulation in 14:11.

next to the creator of the universe.[10] In that way the *Qedushah*, the first hymn of the living creatures, the "song *par excellence*,"[11] is depicted as professing God in his glory and omnipotence since the very beginning of creation.

The message is clear: God alone determines time and space, the cosmos and history; profane forces possess no real power. This message provides the necessary foundation for the author's subsequent description of conflicts, destruction, and catastrophes all over the world. Here at the beginning of the vision section of the book, Chapters 4–22, the reader is assured that, in every respect, God is "seated on the throne." This positive statement stresses God's greatness and sovereignty, even as he is depicted as wholly other and transcendent, a theme to which the author will return at the end of the apocalypse (esp. 21:5–8).[12] Beyond worshiping God in his sanctity, the first hymn ("Holy, holy, holy") – a refrain known by the earthly community as part of its liturgy – connects heaven and earth.[13] The earthly community gathered for worship "on the Lord's day" (1:10) joins the praise of the angels who are positioned close to God himself. The audience of Revelation knows, therefore, that the words of their song bridge these different realms.

Nevertheless, God in his holiness is separate and distant from his creation until the eschatological fulfillment of Revelation 19–22.[14] God cannot be described as precisely as other heavenly beings.[15] Only in the end will God and the Lamb end this radical separation (21:22–22:5). Until then, the *Qedushah* at the very beginning of the vision section of Revelation, including its antiphonies, connects these different spheres, the borders of which are opened for the seer and all of his brothers and sisters who hear and believe in this "revelation of Jesus Christ" (Ἀποκάλυψις Ἰησοῦ Χριστοῦ; 1:1).

The first ones to hear this "kernel of liturgy" are the other heavenly beings around the throne, who are mentioned briefly by the author after his description of the throne (4:4). As the text progresses, each react in their own way. It

---

[10] The position is stressed through the double description of 4:6: "*in the midst* and around the throne" [καὶ ἐν μέσῳ τοῦ θρόνου καὶ κύκλῳ τοῦ θρόνου].

[11] Thompson, *Book of Revelation*, 57.

[12] See the direct statement, uttered by God himself, 21:5–8, which is antecedent to the vision.

[13] Nusca, "Heavenly Worship," 254; cf. 257: "the liturgy served as the locus in which the eschatological mysteries being described by the seer came to be realized in the present experience of the worshipping community." This is a very important aspect in Qumran texts as well.

[14] The term ἄξιος is applied to the human believers only here and in the cry of the martyrs at 6:10; for Christ, see 3:17.

[15] Revelation 4 describes only the throne and the angelic world, not God himself. Through this description of what surrounds him, a "description" of God, a "picture" of him, is created. Cf. H. Kraft, *Die Offenbarung des Johannes* (HNT 16a; Tübingen, 1974), esp. 112.

is in response to the living creatures that the twenty-four elders (4:9–11) give their acclamation to God the creator. This is accompanied by several gestures of obedience and cultic adoration as part of the unceasing heavenly liturgy.[16] This liturgical action, together with their robes and thrones, alludes to the elders' royal and priestly authority and identity.[17] Because of their proximity and participation in the liturgy, they share in power and divine might, but their actions (leaving their thrones, falling "before the one who is seated on the throne," casting "their crowns before the throne") evoke a striking image of powerlessness, which poignantly resonates with the description of the Lamb in the next chapter.[18]

The elders' hymn of praise in Rev 4:11 (B in the preceding list) – not phrased in a nominal but in a long infinitival clause – is explicitly linked to the everlasting trisagion (see A: ὅταν with future):[19] God is always glorified as the one who lives "forever and ever" in 4:9 and 10.[20] But this text should not be heard in isolation: The content of their hymn corresponds directly to the preceding *Qedushah*. Other lexical and thematic connections include these:

1. the two predications of God: κύριος and θεός
2. the threefold doxological terms: δόξα, τιμή, and εὐχαριστία[21]
3. the emphasis on creation, which is part of the term παντοκράτωρ.

In effect, the other heavenly group now connects the well-known trisagion with the reasons for his holiness.

What is new in the second hymn is the address with the predicate adjective ἄξιος plus the verb εἰμί (in either third or second person) plus an

---

[16] For an analysis of their falling in prostration and the casting down of their "crowns," see G. M. Stevenson, "Conceptual Background to Golden Crown Imagery in the Apocalypse of John (4,4.10; 14,14)," *JBL* 114 (1995): 257–72, whose discussion yields much more material than just the Hellenistic imperial cultic background of the text.

[17] See Stevenson, "Crown Imagery," 270.

[18] Here, the sovereignty of God is expressed through adoration and worship. In 5:7, the power of God is expressed through the delivery of the book.

[19] This (difficult) construction occurs only here. See G. Mussies, *The Morphology of Koine Greek as Used in the Apocalypse of St. John* (NTS 27; Leiden, 1971), 3–11; S. Thompson, *The Apocalypse and Semitic Syntax* (SNTSMS 52; Cambridge, 1985), 45–7.

[20] A close connection, overlooked when 4:5–8 and 4:9–11 are separated (*pace* Jörns and others).

[21] The triadic character of the doxological terms corresponds to the triadic character of the trisagion; see Ruiz, "Hymns," 1995; but there is, at the same time, a binary character to the text: the predication of God (κύριος and θεός) and the double statement about creation. Nevertheless, the emphasis lies on the three parts. See also the rhyme ending with -ν.

infinitive (λαβεῖν) plus ascriptions.[22] This grammatical construction is the *crux interpretum* of the clause. Nevertheless, before God is praised because of his actions of salvation, he first must be recognized as heavenly ruler and creator. The term ἄξιος becomes a kind of leitmotiv for the rest of the section and functions as a bridge to the following chapter (see 5:2, 4, 9, 12).

Scholars have usually assumed its dependence on ruler proclamations of that age.[23] Such texts, however, are scant, and their form and content lack any clear connection to the songs of the throne scene. My research indicates that a better source for comparison may be the Hekhalot literature, in which "worthiness" is also a key theme. Although late in their written forms, these texts include important parallels in grammatical construction, hymnic form, and content.[24] One example is the end of Enoch's examination when he ascends to heaven in 3 Enoch 2:3 (§3).[25] There, the angels acclaim,[26] "This one is certainly worthy to behold the chariot [ראוי להסתכל במרכבה], as it is written ... [Ps 144:5]." In this and similar descriptions of the ascent to heaven, the human being is deemed worthy to enter the heavenly world. Any doubt or hesitation on the part of the heavenly entities is rejected, and the door between heaven and earth lies open. In Revelation, John similarly sees the glory, which only God and the Christ are worthy to receive. Yet, the Hekhalot literature goes a step further: These texts not only describe "worthiness," but they attribute it directly to a human being with a personal pronoun in the second person.

A fragment of a short account of a heavenly ascent should be mentioned at this point; here, the investigation of those who are worthy or unworthy

---

[22] Its occurrence in three different hymns (4:11; 5:9; 5:12) points to the widely accepted conclusion that the author is not dependent on earlier material (cf. the absence of *hapax legomena*) but uses the same vocabulary consistently throughout the whole book (see, e.g., Charles; but *pace* Cullmann, Läuchli, and others who assume a kind of given "*Gottesdienststruktur*" in the hymns of the book).

[23] Ever since E. Peterson (1926). See L. L. Thompson, *Revelation* (ANTC; Nashville, 1998), 58: "the ... elders collapse into one human spheres of politics and religion"; D. E. Aune, "The Influence of Roman Imperial Court Ceremonial on the Apocalypse of John," *BR* 28 (1983): 5–26 and *ad. loc.* in his commentary.

[24] See also recently M. Hengel, "Die Throngemeinschaft des Lammes mit Gott in der Johannesapokalypse," *ThBeitr* 96 (1996): 159–75 and J. Frey, "Die Bildersprache der Johannesapokalypse," *ZThK* 98 (2001): 161–85.

[25] All references to the Hekhalot literature follow P. Schäfer's *Synopse zur Hekhalot-Literatur*, 2 vols. (TSAJ 12/13; Tübingen, 1981).

[26] Cf. §346 (*Hekhalot Zutarti*): "For he is worthy to behold my glory [שהוא ראוי להסתכל בכבודי]"; here also in the third person (Rabbi Aqiva).

to enter the throne room begins with a question on the part of the "angel of examination" (§§258–259; *Hekhalot Rabbati*): "Aren't you unworthy to see the king and his throne [ואין אתה ראוי לראות במלך וכסאו]?" An entire section of the following "throne songs" proclaims God and his glory with "a new song" sung by all of his creatures.[27] This is much different from the case of the Merkavah mystic who is allowed to enter the transcendence and to come to the throne of God. The dangers and risks involved in this enterprise are still expressed, even as the texts differ theologically from Revelation.[28]

The hymn of the elders in Revelation ("You are *worthy*, our Lord and God, to receive glory and honor and power, for you *created all things*, and by your will *they existed* and *were created*"; B in the preceding list) contains a special emphasis on God's act of creation, which is the reason for their praise. The topic of creation, first mentioned here, becomes a theme that runs throughout the whole book.[29] It is no accident that the final hymn (5:13) emphasizes creation once again, with a crescendo sung by the characters in the scene – that is, by all creatures in the entire universe. This means that the "new creation" is the ultimate goal; the beginning and the end of all of God's actions have his creation as their purpose.[30] Over and against all past and future upheavals, troubles, conflicts, and judgments, the praise of creation is the eternal foundation throughout all ages. In this way, the elders prove the dignity of God in the act of creation.[31] Eschatological "glory, honor, and power" is the starting point leading to the beginning of God's creation; the very beginning and the end of the world [*Urzeit und Endzeit*] belong together.[32] Theologically, God's power of creation seems to be endangered, both inside and outside the addressed communities. By hearing and "seeing" the continuity of heavenly praise, however, the seer receives an open heart

---

[27] See also §§407, 408, 409 (*Hekhalot Zutarti*).

[28] For an indispensable and differentiated discussion regarding this question, see P. Schäfer, ed., *Übersetzung der Hekhalot-Literatur* (Tübingen, 1987), 2:239, and idem, *Der verborgene und offenbare Gott: Hauptthemen der frühen jüdischen Mystik* (Tübingen, 1981), 37.

[29] See J. Roloff, "Neuschöpfung in der Offenbarung des Johannes" in "Schöpfung und Neuschöpfung," *JBTh* 5 (1990): 119–38.

[30] Cf. the call of the angel to all inhabitants of the world, "to worship him, who has made heaven and earth, the sea and the water-springs" (14:7). This would be an "eternal gospel" [εὐαγγέλιον αἰώνιον].

[31] Cf. the oath of the angels in 10:6 and the call in 14:7.

[32] See esp. E. Lohmeyer, *Die Offenbarung des Johannes* 3rd ed. (HNT 16; Tübingen, 1970), ad loc. 50.

and eyes, which in turn see the unbroken power of God the creator. All who confess "our Lord and God" will also participate in this "reality."

After the description of the coming and the commissioning of the Lamb (5:1–5, 6–7), Revelation portrays the elders and living beings giving praise together (the "new song") to God's emissary, the Lamb (5:8–10), in the midst of the throne, at the heart of the heavenly world:

> *"You are worthy* to take the scroll and to open its seals, for you were slaughtered and by your blood you ransomed for God saints from every tribe and language and people and nation; you have made them to be a kingdom and priests serving our God, and they will reign on earth." (5:9–10; C in the preceding list)

We have already examined to the crucial term "worthiness."[33] Addressed in the second person, the first hymn to the Lamb (*"You are worthy* [ἄξιος εἶ] to take the scroll") is, formally understood, essentially a continuation of the forgoing hymn dedicated to God (4:11: *"You are worthy* [ἄξιος εἶ], our Lord and God"). In response to the creative act in that hymn, the "action of the Lamb" in the "new song" (ᾠδὴν καινήν; 5:9)[34] is described as redemptory for all believers.[35] The reference to a "new song," therefore, implies a clear eschatological perspective with a special qualification[36]: "By the blood of the Lamb," they are "ransomed for God," and as kings and priests[37] "they will reign on earth" (5:9–10). This perspective is made available to the whole human world, as this redemption is valid for those "from every tribe and language and people and nation" (5:9).

[33] Here, this term functions rhetorically as a response to the question as posed by the "mighty angel with a loud voice" in 5:2: "Who is worthy to open the scroll?" [τίς ἄξιος ἀνοῖξαι τὸ βιβλίον].

[34] "A new song" is used as an expression of praise exclusively for God's (eschatological) victory over his enemies in seven passages in the Hebrew Bible: Pss 33:3; 40:3; 96:1; 98:1; 144:9 (in combination with "playing the harp"!); 149:1; Isa 42:10. The "eschatological overtones" are stressed by H.-J. Kraus, *Theologie der Psalmen* (Neukirchen, 1979), 1:410; further Jörns, *Evangelium*, 48–9.

[35] With emphasis on Exod 15. See Carnegy, "Worthy Is the Lamb," 148–9, for an example of the further development in the portrayal of Christ.

[36] See subsequent discussion, *pace* Ford, "Christological Function," 217.

[37] A proleptic expression; the sovereignty remains a potentiality until 20:4; see R. H. Charles, *A Critical and Exegetical Commentary on the Revelation of St. John* (ICC; Edinburgh, 1920), 1:148. An eschatological dimension, therefore, is a constant presence in all three texts in which the reign [βασιλεία] of the faithful is mentioned: 20:4, 20:6, and 21:5 (cf. 1:6 and here).

This "new" (eschatologically oriented) hymn,[38] sung by the four creatures together with the elders, is accompanied by instruments (κιθάραν)[39] and the offering of "golden bowls" (φιάλας χρυσᾶς).[40] The interpretation of the song as "prayers" indicates once more the close relationship with the heavenly cult, but also with the worship of earthly believers.[41] The content of the song also emphasizes the theme of participation. By their act of worship, the heavenly beings respond to the act of salvation [Heilsgeschehen] that is symbolized in the Lamb. At this point the earthly worshipers are also involved through their prayers.[42]

Diametrically opposed to this heavenly worship and the adoration of the Lamb is the beast in Rev 13:11–17, which comes out of the earth.[43] It also receives worship, is wounded, and has power and authority. The parody in 13:4 emphasizes the adoration of people ("they *worshiped* [προσεκύνησαν] the dragon … and they *worshiped* the beast"), and the description of the "horns" in the presentation of the Lamb is also related to the description of the beast

---

[38] Regarding cosmological changes, see in particular 1:1, 3; 3:11; 22:6, 7, 10, 12. The core of these statements is the explanation given by the divine ruler of the universe as he sits upon the throne in 21:5. See M. Hengel, "Hymnus und Christologie" in *Wort in der Zeit: Neutestamentliche Studien: Festgabe für Karl Heinrich Rengstorf zum 75. Geburtstag*, ed. W. Haubeck and M. Bachmann (Leiden, 1980), 7; for rabbinical allusions, see K. E. Grötzinger, *Musik und Gesang in der Theologie der frühen jüdischen Literatur* (TSAJ 3; Tübingen, 1982), 15 and esp. the summary on 209. The "new song" refers to the new special things God creates; in the Hebrew Bible, see Pss 144:9; 147:7; 149:1. Rev 14:3 depends on Rev 5:9 (those who are allowed to learn the "new song").

[39] What does this mean? The "harp" occurs in different ways; see also 14:2 (in comparison); 15:2 (the expression "having the harps of God"). A climax is reached at this point, for the instruments are mentioned only here. Once more, the Hekhalot literature provides the best means of understanding Revelation: cf. *Hekhalot Rabbati* §161 (8, 4), which mentions three different instruments of the Ḥayyot, the Ofannim, and the Keruvim. Nothing is known about instruments accompanying the hymns in Christian worship in the first and second centuries. The first reference is in Clement of Alexandria, who permits the use of instruments during the meals (*Paed.* 2.4). Interestingly, Sir 40:21 places the beauty of the human voice above that of the flute and the harp.

[40] In contrast to other verses (Rev 15:7; 16:1, 2, 3, 4, 8, 10, 12, 17, etc.), the bowls here have a positive connotation; a thematic parallel is *T. Levi* 3:6: "(The archangels) present to the Lord a pleasing odor, a rational and bloodless oblation"; also Tob 12:15.

[41] This relationship is created through the (daily?) prayers and not through a kind of martyrdom. Martyrdom is first mentioned in the following chapters (6:9–11; 7:9–17) and in the final chapters (21:1–22:5).

[42] Cf. also the "weeping" of the seer in 5:4.

[43] The opposition against the Roman Empire is rightly emphasized by J. Marshall in this volume.

in Revelation 13.[44] In an inverted version of divine power, the power of the antagonists encompasses the entire world.[45] Nevertheless, it is clear that the enemies of the Lamb have less power, for the term "eyes" [ὀφθαλμοί] never occurs; that is, they do not have any omniscience or omnipresence, even if they bear the symbols "head" [κεφαλή], "horns" [κέρας], "feet" [πόδες], and "mouth" [στόμα].[46]

Therefore, the triumph of the Lamb, which is here described in the presentation and commissioning scene, must be recognized and made known prior to all the plagues and judgments. The emphasis lies on the victory of the slaughtered Lamb "on the cross" (="its blood") who is praised with the phrase "you ransomed for God [ἠγόρασας τῷ θεῷ] saints."[47] This can be seen in contrast to Revelation 14,[48] in which the metaphor "ransom" presupposes the change of sovereignty. They – those who come from all corners of the world – belong to God alone as his possession. They are obedient to him and to the Lamb[49] through the victory on the cross. Now the Lamb is able to open the seals, which will be the activity of the next chapter, Revelation 6.

A special emphasis is placed on the twofold antiphonies sung by all of the angels and the whole creation (5:11–13), which crowns the heavenly liturgy. The term "worthy" connects this hymn to the preceding hymn dedicated to the Lamb (5:9–10), and the term "slaughtered" refers back to the crucifixion of Christ. At the same time, however, the predications themselves point to the former praise of the creator himself (4:11).

In Rev 5:12, the second and last hymn dedicated to the Lamb (D in the preceding list), the Lamb is highlighted by means of *seven* predications (cf. 7:12). Their order also seems to suggest a special emphasis. It is no accident that the list of attributes begins with power [δύναμις], the final element of

---

[44] See the angelic interpretation in 17:14. However, in opposing apocalyptic expectations that the "Messiah" must conquer the unbelieving enemies, Revelation looks back to the crucifixion and victory of Christ. See W. Bousset, *Die Offenbarung des Johannes* (KEK 16; Göttingen, 1966), 258: eine *"Analogiebildung zu dem Tier"*!

[45] Rev 13:7 is surely an allusion to the power of the Romans.

[46] But there are expressions of power without any symbolic character; cf. power [δύναμις] and authority [ἐξουσία] in 13:2 and elsewhere.

[47] Remarkable in the Greek text is the climax in four segments: καὶ ἠγόρασας τῷ θεῷ ἐν τῷ αἵματί σου ἐκ πάσης φυλῆς | καὶ γλώσσης | καὶ λαοῦ | καὶ ἔθνους.

[48] Rev 14:3 mentions the (heavenly) song of the 144,000 "who have been redeemed from the earth."

[49] This idea is rightly stressed in H. Giesen, *Die Offenbarung des Johannes* (RNT; Regensburg, 1997), ad loc. 169.

the trisagion.[50] This means that the Lamb is the eschatological authority, linked exclusively with God, acting in full unity with him. His death on the cross brings salvation. His victory is the resurrection, which is explained to the seer by one of the elders at the beginning of the chapter (5:5). Thus, the hymn is itself a response to an act of salvation, as achieved by God (*actio dei*). Finally, honor and dignity are conceded to the Lamb by the entire heavenly world.[51] The liturgy, therefore, with its crescendo at the end, resembles a hymnic finale. It presents all of the angels "with full voice" [φωνῇ μεγάλῃ]; in response, praises "blared over."

However, we must go one step further. In contrast to the preceding hymns, this last binitarian one, dedicated to God and the Lamb, contains the climax of the scene and of the whole worship. At this point, after the heavenly beings have acclaimed the Lamb, the whole creation offers its exaltation in the form of a general doxology. That which was, in the second clause of the trisagion, the crucial point in the song of the "liturgical leaders" is now depicted in fulfillment: The communities in heaven and on earth are united in antiphonal liturgy. The boundaries between them are broken.

The last part of the hymnic praise is sung by the whole creation (Rev 5:13; E in the preceding list). Even the creatures of the sea share in this acclamation. The term "worthy" is missing, but the reference to eternal life once again alludes to the trisagion.[52] The list of actors contains an important chiastic construction.[53] None of the elements of creation are abandoned. The fourfold doxological praise is also linked to the preceding praise of the Lamb by the myriads of angels. The last of the seven predications, "blessing" [εὐχαριστία], here opens the group of four. The term "might" [κράτος] appears for the first time in the heavenly liturgy, but also points back to the blessing at the beginning of the book (1:6).[54] In this way, the whole creation takes over the extant heavenly praise, intones it autonomously, and completes the series of doxologies that began with the trisagion. Some scholars would limit the worshipers only to those "who are ransomed by the blood of

---

[50] "Honor" [τιμή] and "glory" [δόξα] are mentioned, too, albeit in the opposite order.

[51] In this way, the Lamb is understood as superior to all heavenly beings; see L. Stuckenbruck, *Angel Veneration and Christology: A Study in Early Judaism and in the Christology of the Apocalypse of John* (Tübingen, 1995).

[52] See also the naming of the seer with the verb "I heard" [ἤκουσα].

[53] With five elements: (1) "*in* heaven," ἐν τῷ (οὐρανῷ); (2) "*on* earth," ἐπὶ τῆς (γῆς); (3) "*under* the earth," ὑποκάτω τῆς (γῆς); (4) "*on/in* the sea," ἐπὶ τῆς (θαλάσσης); (5) "all that is *in* them," (τὰ) ἐν αὐτοῖς.

[54] The "eternity clause" also refers to this text; see also ναί ἀμήν in 1:7.

the Lamb," but that idea belongs to later texts and is not present here when the human world is mentioned for the first time.[55] Here, all humans may join the angelic praise of God.[56]

As a whole, the heavenly liturgy has a triadic structure (cf. the preceding list):

1. two hymns to God himself (Rev 4:8 [A], 11 [B])
2. two hymns to the Lamb alone (Rev 5:9b–10 [C], 12 [D])
3. the hymn of all creation to God and the Lamb together (Rev 5:13 [E]).

These final words of praise point once more to the earthly community, in which Revelation should be read on the "Lord's Day" (1:10; see also the preceding beatitude in 1:3). Blessings and protection seem to be laid "upon those who recite them, as well as those in whose presence they are recited."[57]

Just as the liturgical material in the throne vision began with the *Qedushah* (4:8), so the heavenly liturgy in Revelation 4–5 is rounded out with another well-known liturgical text[58] – the "Amen" (5:13). This formula has both a closing and a responsive function. The "singers" of the highest rank around the throne have the "first words" at the beginning of the vision. Now they have the "last word" and add to this *conclusio* an act of prostration.[59] It may be that the author has in mind the Temple worship[60] of the Second Temple in Jerusalem and here draws from personal experience. In any case, he is sure to have had experience of synagogue worship, even if we do not know much about it.[61] In this way, the "Amen" is an apt conclusion, not only to the

---

[55] *Pace* D. Peterson, *Engaging with God: A Biblical Theology of Worship* (Leicester, 1993), 273.

[56] This can also be seen in Qumran (see 1QH; *Songs*; other hymns such as the "Self-Glorification Hymns"). See B. Nitzan, "The Idea of Holiness in Qumran Prayer and Liturgy," in *Sapiential, Liturgical and Poetical Texts from Qumran*, ed. D. K. Falk (Leiden, 2000), 127–45.

[57] Nusca, "Heavenly Worship," 307.

[58] "Amen" and "Hallelujah" are part of the beginning of liturgy in temple worship. "Amen" in response to a prayer is testified for the first time in Neh 8:6 (with the prostration of the worshiping community). See references to rabbinical texts in S. T. Lachs, "Why Was the 'Amen' Response Interdicted in the Temple?" *JSJ* 19 (1988): 230–40. On the "fluid and reciprocal relationship between angelology and Temple art," see R. S. Boustan in this volume.

[59] Prostration (always on the part of the elders as their distinctive mark) occurs three times in the throne vision. First, in response to the trisagion (4:10); second, when the Lamb receives the scroll out of the hand of God; and, finally, here at the end together with the "Amen" of the living beings.

[60] The best examples of liturgical acts on the part of the Levites and the worshiping community are depicted in Sir 50:17–21, the brilliant portrayal of the high priest Simon.

[61] See I. Elbogen, *Der Jüdische Gottesdienst in seiner geschichtlichen Entwicklung* (1931; Hildesheim, 1995); I. Heinemann, *Prayer in the Talmud: Forms and Patterns* (StJ 9; Tübingen, 1977);

chapter, but also to the entire throne section (Rev 4–5): a complete heavenly liturgy in full detail.

The Heavenly Liturgy in a Fivefold Form

The heavenly liturgy fills out the seer's throne-vision in three sections containing five individual parts.[62] First, the ruler upon the throne is addressed with the praise of all existing creatures, which transcends all limitations of time and space; all that exists in heaven and on earth is included in unending worship. This infinite perspective becomes the presupposition and basis of the following scene with the Lamb and its mission.

The living creatures intone the acclamation of the creator upon his throne, his holiness, greatness, and omnipotence with the *Qedushah*. This first section, however, is rounded off with the second individual part (see the preceding list): the elders, standing in the other circle around the throne, respond to the living creatures with the first "worthy" acclamation, celebrating the uniqueness of the Creator. These important connections are overlooked when Rev 4:5–8 and 4:9–11 are divided and interpreted separately, or when the hymns are studied only with respect to the question of their relationship to early Christian worship.

In light of the emphasis on unending heavenly praise, one might suggest that the following scene with the Lamb is not a description of the moment of enthronement, but rather portrays a continuous act of redemption that is revealed, announced, and proclaimed in time and space for the entire world. In the context of the heavenly cult, it is observed through the eyes of the seer and disclosed to all the congregations step by step. In effect, all the hymns are a response to an *actio dei*.

Up to this point, it is only through John that the believers are able to participate in the heavenly liturgy, and they are, as a result, overwhelmed by these realities. Other humans can ascend to the throne room and the heavenly sphere only through the distance of the secondary perspective transmitted by the seer. Any quick approach to the transcendence is prevented. It is only at the initiative of God himself that one is called and brought close to his throne. This rhetorical strategy aims to effect not only catharsis but also

---

St. C. Reif, "The Early Liturgy of the Synagogue," in *Judaism and Hebrew Prayer: New Perspectives on Jewish Liturgical History* (Cambridge, 1993), 53–87.

[62] 1 Enoch 39 only in twofold form with a *trisagion* and respondent *berakhah* (Ezek 3:12).

transformation. Here, the knowledge of the comforting visions, together with the words of praise sung by all the heavenly beings, serves to create a virtual experience of worshiping God and Christ. Ultimately, these texts invite the congregations to stand with the Lamb against all eschatological opponents.

The interpretation of these texts indicates a strong reaction against the imperial cult and idolatrous worship in Asia Minor.[63] That can be seen particularly (1) in the contrast between the Lamb and the beasts (Chap. 13) and the modes of worshipping them, and (2) in the example of the term "power" [δύναμις] in 4:11 set against 11:15, 16–18 (the last trumpet). The throne vision thus helps the believers to stand firm in the eschatological struggle. Knowledge of the "one seated on the throne" and of his power and activity helps to unmask other claims to power in the world.

Space does not permit a comparison of the heavenly liturgy in Revelation and the heavenly worship at the beginning of the Enochic *Similitudes* (1 Enoch 37–71; esp. 37:2–3; 39:5–7, 10–14) nor an analysis of its relationship to the unending acclamation of the *Qedushah* in the early Jewish liturgy.[64] It suffices to note, by way of comparison, that the heavenly liturgy of Revelation is much more rich and extended. Nevertheless, common is the idea that heavenly liturgy sets the pattern for earthly adoration and not the other way around.[65] That is why, according to both texts, salvation must come from God and not from any other power on earth.

Connecting Heaven and Earth

As we have seen, the five hymns in Revelation 4–5 are closely interlinked. The author's intent is that all three "inner" hymns begin with the unusual ἄξιος εἶ. The first and the last hymns contain the dimension of time. Other terms such as δύναμις and εὐχαριστία present further links among the hymns. It

---

[63] Marshall (in this volume) situates the message of Revelation 2–3 against the struggles for rulership in "the Long Year," 70 C.E.; but I am not persuaded. Cf. D. E. Aune, *Revelation 6–16* (WBC 52b; Dallas, 1998), esp. 775–9 (Excursus 13E).

[64] See Schimanowski, *Die himmlische Liturgie*, 132–41.

[65] Cf. the structure of 7:10–12: (1) the acclamation intoned by the glorified righteous (see also 14:3 without any text and 15:3f as ἡ ᾠδὴ Μωϋσέως…καὶ ἡ ᾠδὴ τοῦ ἀρνίου); (2) the response of the whole heavenly world with an "Amen" at the beginning and at the end. And, with a different focus, 19:1–5, 6–9: (1) the victory song of the great multitude; (2) the proclamation of the perpetuity of the harlot's fate; (3) the response of the elders and living creatures with "Amen, Hallelujah"; (4) the last voice acclaiming God's omnipotence and kingship.

is obvious that, without exception, all hymns of the throne vision are part of the heavenly worship. Those who want to know them must have "a call." The hymns require worshipers to imagine the celestial array through John's witness. Their content anticipates universal worship, which will occur at the end of time and space. For this reason, the distance between heaven and earth is still emphasized. But now, through the liturgy, the earthly praises echo the heavenly songs and express in the context of worship the present aspect of eschatology.[66] Heavenly and earthly worshipers are unified. Believers are encouraged to remain loyal to their confession of faith. Only in this way are they prepared for the final conflict that will last until the coming of the victorious Lamb and the beginning of the new creation.[67]

This indicates the goal of the hymns in Revelation 4–5 – namely, to draw the earthly community into the heavenly praise of God, a liturgy that is closed with the "Amen" sung by the inner circle before the heavenly throne.[68] Nevertheless, Revelation 4 also shows that the heavenly world is separated from earthly situations; only the content of the hymns[69] refers to the human world and creation. To this extent, it is the last hymn in particular, sung by the whole creation (5:13; E in the preceding list), that anticipates the new creation that will be proclaimed in Chapters 21 and 22.

The participation of the earthly community in the heavenly liturgy is not mentioned *expressis verbis* in the text, but there are indications that Revelation 4–5 is meant to be understood in this way. Not only is there an atmosphere of worship right from the beginning of the book, but there is also a clear connection between John and the seven congregations in Asia Minor, as well as a promise to transform the believers into a kingdom and into priests (5:10) through the redemptive work of Christ. In addition, the five hymns are suitable for recitation in a liturgical setting. All this suggests that the liturgy of the throne scene serves to re-create the experience of a ritual of worship common to heaven and earth.

---

[66] This is emphasized in some Qumran texts, but differs from the *Songs of the Sabbath Sacrifice*. See E. G. Chazon, "Liturgical Communion with the Angels at Qumran," in *Sapiential, Liturgical and Poetical Texts from Qumran*, ed. D. K. Falk (Leiden, 2000), 95–105.

[67] See 1 Clem 34:6–8: After reciting the trisagion, the community is united in one voice of praise, but there is also an element of an eschatological perspective.

[68] This differs from the expression of reconciliation of "all existence, heavenly and earthly," 2 Enoch 19:3 (J); F. I. Anderson in *APOT* 1:132 translates: "and they (sc: the archangels) harmonize all existence."

[69] See 4:8–11: παντοκράτωρ and τὰ πάντα...ἦσαν καὶ ἐκτίσθησαν.

Summary

The throne scene, with its full liturgy, shows how the author aims not only to "strengthen and console" his sisters and brothers, but also to depict a proleptic experience of heavenly worship sung in unison by angels and humans. The eschatological tone increases in the following chapters, becoming a crescendo that leads into the last eschatological struggle.[70] The reader/hearer is assured that the boundaries between heaven and earth will be broken.[71] Until the end, however, the description of the heavenly Jerusalem and the visions are an experience that belong exclusively to the seer (and all who are willing to follow him). John leads his addressees "standing side-by-side with the heavenly ranks"[72] against all eschatological opponents. "Connecting heaven and earth," the seer functions as mediator by the grace of God and his Lamb.[73]

Not only are the hymns in Revelation 4–5 part of the heavenly topography, but they also bridge the past, present, and future as a reminder to all readers/hearers that God himself remains in full control over the world's destiny. John's hope is that the earthly community will come (back) to participate in his experience, not only at the level of moral exhortation,[74] but also by sharing the Lamb's glory and serving him through earthly worship. That is why Revelation not only records that the angels sing but actually presents the text – the very *words* – of their songs[75]: The earthly community is invited to take up this liturgy on its own. Revelation is not only a book of visions, but is also an oral book, which should be read *out loud* in the weekly worship – an important but often overlooked point. In this way, practicing the liturgy

---

[70] Marshall (in this volume) tries to play down the eschatological aspect of the final struggle, in favor of the political levels and the events of the fall of the Jerusalem Temple.

[71] This fits well with the new sensibility in late antique religious discourse of the possibility of movement between heaven and earth, as discussed in the introduction to this volume.

[72] C. Newsom, *Songs of the Sabbath Sacrifice: A Critical Edition* (HSS27; Atlanta, Ga., 1985), 17–18, 61–72.

[73] The right way to understand the structure of the entire book of Revelation is not to describe first and foremost the well-known judgments and destruction, but to outline of the worship of God and Christ – first presented in the heavenly liturgy of Chaps. 4–5 – as the key to the whole work.

[74] See the messages to the seven congregations in Asia Minor in Revelation 2–3 in the light of this broader understanding.

[75] Contrast the *Songs of the Sabbath Sacrifice*. The *words* of the angelic praise are *not* given in the text – thus expressing a greater distance between heaven and earth than Revelation!

joins earth with heaven and heaven with earth. The community worships and praises God in the face of eschatological challenges and struggles with profane forces. When the *actio dei* takes place in creation and in the act of redemption, then the eyes and hearts of the faithful are opened. Thus, the two chapters of worship (Revelation 4–5) point to the hopeful cry μαράνα θα (see 1 Cor 11:26; 16:22) at the end of the book (Rev 22:20: ἀμήν, ἔρχου κύριε Ἰησοῦ) and the intense hope of divine presence in the new Jerusalem where heaven is on earth and earth is "in heaven" (21:1–22:5) – and both take on a totally new form.

5

Working Overtime in the Afterlife; or, No Rest for the Virtuous

Sarah Iles Johnston

One of the most interesting things about eschatology is the fact that so many cultures have developed the idea of postmortem reward and punishment. It is not inevitable. In early Greek sources, for example, virtually everyone gets the same deal after death, whoever they were while alive and whatever they did.[1] Even more to the extreme, some strains of early Judaism preached that there was no afterlife at all. One simply died and that was the end of it.[2] But in many more cases, the afterlife becomes a place where one gets what one deserves. For instance, in the *Apocalypse of Paul*, it is the souls of only virgins who enter the City of Christ, the most desirable realm of the afterlife, whereas even the most virtuous of married souls receive only a lesser reward in the Land of Promise instead (*Apoc. Paul* 22). In contrast, according to some strains of ancient Greek eschatological belief, the souls of virgins are forced to wander unhappily between the worlds of the living and the dead forever, venting their frustrations by killing the babies of women who

I am grateful for the helpful suggestions made by several members of the audience after I delivered this talk at the conference and again after I delivered it as part of the 2001 Halstead Lecture at Drew University. I also thank John Finamore for his help.

[1] Homer, *Od.* 11, for example, suggests that the underworld is a dark, dull place where all souls – whoever they might have been while alive – collect as a group. The few possible exceptions are people such as Tantalus, who committed crimes against the gods and suffer great punishments as a result, or people such as Menelaus, who are taken away to a paradisiacal island instead – but it is highly questionable whether these people are really to be understood as "dead" in the normal sense. For discussion both of *Od.* 11 in general and of the problem of rewards and punishments in Homer, see S. I. Johnston, *Restless Dead: Encounters Between the Living and the Dead in Ancient Greece* (Berkeley, 1999), Chap. 1.

[2] J. Goldingay, "Death and the Afterlife in the Psalms," in *Judaism in Late Antiquity*, part 4, *Death, Life-After-Death, Resurrection and the World to Come in the Judaisms of Antiquity*, ed. A. J. Avery-Peck and J. Neusner (Leiden, 2000), 61–86; R. E. Friedman and S. D. Overton, "Death and Afterlife: The Biblical Silence," in ibid., 35–60; and R. E. Murphy, "Death and Afterlife in the Wisdom Literature," in ibid., 101–16.

managed to marry.[3] Obviously, you can tell a lot about what a culture values and admires and, conversely, what it devalues and condemns, by studying who gets rewarded in the afterlife and who gets punished.

Equally fascinating is the nature of the rewards and punishments themselves. The logic underlying some of them is quite transparent, to be sure. In the *Apocalypse of Peter*, mothers who exposed their infants exude breast milk that congeals, smells foul, and engenders tiny monsters that devour the mothers' flesh – the punishment fits the crime insofar as that which mothers should have used to nurture their infants becomes the instrument of their postmortem torture (*Apoc. Peter* E 8). In ancient Greece, those who had been initiated into certain mystery cults got to loll about after death in verdant meadows, surrounded by abundant food and drink.[4] The reward for having performed the right rituals while alive was release from having to do anything at all afterward.

The conference that gave rise to this volume gave me an opportunity to ask such questions about an eschatological variation that had been puzzling me for years: namely, the idea that the virtuous would be rewarded for the

[3] For the Greek belief, see Johnston, *Restless Dead*, Chaps. 5 and 6. Cf. Gilgamesh, tablet XII, particularly in the most complete, Sumerian version, as provided by A. George, *The Epic of Gilgamesh: A New Translation* (London, 1999), 141–5 and 175–95, which articulates the similar idea that the more children one leaves behind, the more good things – including bread and water – will be allowed to one after death. The eunuch and the childless man or woman fare very badly, in contrast. Cf. also *CH* II 17:

> Prudent people therefore regard the making of children as a duty in life to be taken most seriously and greatly revered, and should any human being pass away childless, they see it as the worst misfortune and irreverence. After death such a person suffers retribution from demons. This is his punishment: the soul of the childless one is sentenced to a body that has neither a man's nature nor a woman's – a thing accursed under the sun (trans. in B. P. Copenhaver, *Hermetica: The Greek Corpus Hermeticum and the Latin Asclepius in a New English Translation* [Cambridge, 1992], 12).

That this traditional Mediterranean eschatological idea still shows up in an esoteric system of the late Imperial period – an esoteric system, moreover, that encouraged rejection of the material body and its needs – both demonstrates the idea's tenacity and helps to underscore the uniqueness of the eschatological doctrine being examined in this essay, especially given that the Hermetic and theurgic systems were, in other ways, similar in doctrine, origin, and practices.

[4] Discussed at F. Graf, *Eleusis und die orphische Dichtung Athens in vorhellenisticher Zeit* (Religions-geschichtliche Versuche und Vorarbeiten 33; Berlin, 1974), 79–150, esp. 98–103; cf. also statements made in the Bacchic Gold Tablets: A4.6, P1 and 2.6–7 (numbering as in idem, "Dionysian and Orphic Eschatology: New Texts and Old Questions," in *Masks of Dionysus*, ed. T. Carpenter and C. A. Faraone [Ithaca, N.Y., 1993], 239–58); the newest tablet published by P. Chrysostomou, " Ἡ Θεσσαλικὴ Θεὰ Ἐν(ν)οδία Φεραία Θεά" (Ph.D. diss., University of Thessaloníki, 1991), 372; and the scene on the Toledo Vase as interpreted by S. I. Johnston and T. J. McNiven, "Dionysos and the Underworld in Toledo," *MH* 53 (1996): 25–36.

good works they had performed while alive by being given the chance to keep working after they were dead. In the context of today's pop culture, this may not seem too odd. The entertainment media are full of heavenly guardians who spend eternity doing nothing else but rescuing poor humans from the messes they stumble into. Television has offered us "Highway to Heaven" and, more recently, "Touched by an Angel," both of which are indebted, at least distantly, to Frank Kapra's classic film *It's a Wonderful Life* (1946).

But in the ancient Mediterranean, the idea was highly unusual. One of its very few expressions, and one of its earliest, comes from texts called the *Chaldaean Oracles*, dactylic-hexameter poems composed in Greek around 170 C.E., which served as sacred texts for theurgists.[5] By theurgists I mean, in this context, adherents of an esoteric brand of Neoplatonism that advocated combining ritual actions with contemplation and philosophical training. The *Oracles* are the first texts in which we find the word "theurgist" or its cognates,[6] and it was believed in antiquity that the founders of theurgy – a father and son named Julian the Chaldaean and Julian the Theurgist, respectively – had copied down the *Oracles* as they were delivered by the gods either directly or through the mouth of an entranced medium.[7] The *Oracles* were studied closely by later theurgists such as Iamblichus; by men like Proclus who, although we cannot be sure called themselves theurgists in name, believed that the *Oracles* contained important cosmological and soteriological truths that could be revealed through exegesis; and by men such as Michael Psellus, who, although Christian, wished to show whenever possible that a basic concord between paganism and Christianity could be found. The fact that we have any fragments of the *Oracles* at all is thanks to these men, who quoted them in their writings.[8] In the course of using the

---

[5] For discussions of the *Oracles*, their date, etc., see the introductions to E. Des Places, ed., trans., and comm., *Oracles chaldaïques avec un choix de commentaires anciens* (Paris, 1971) and R. Majercik, trans. and comm., *The Chaldean Oracles: Text, Translation and Commentary* (SGRR 5; Leiden, 1989).

[6] *CO* fr. 153 = Lydus, *de Mensibus* 2.10; 31, 19 W.

[7] S. I. Johnston, "Iulianos" [4] and "Iulianos" [5], *Der Neue Pauly Enzyklopädie der Antike* (Stuttgart, 1999), 6:9–10.

[8] On Iamblichus' debt to the *Oracles*, see particularly E. Des Places, ed., trans., and comm., *Jamblique: Les mystères d'Égypte* (Paris, 1966), 14–19; F. W. Cremer, *Die Chaldäischen Orakel und Jamblich de mysteriis* (Meisenheim am Glan, 1969); O. Geudtner, *Die Seelenlehre der Chaldischen Orakel* (Meisenheim am Glan, 1971). Also see a book that appeared only weeks before I completed this article and that I was not fully able to incorporate into these notes: J. F. Finamore and J. M. Dillon, eds., transs., and comms., *Iamblichus De Anima* (Philosophia Antiqua 92; Leiden, 2002). More generally on all of the *Oracles*' exegetes and their roles in

Oracles to support or clarify other arguments, these and other later writers also gave us information about theurgical practices and beliefs that we would not otherwise have; with care, we can use such comments to build a more complete picture of theurgy.

In the *Chaldaean Oracles*, the virtuous soul is said to be rewarded by becoming an angel after death.[9] But these angels then redescend to earth and reincarnate into new bodies[10] to do two things. First, by serving as teachers, they help others perfect their souls.[11] Second, by redescending into materiality, they participate in the demiurge's continual re-creation and reordering of the material world.[12] We will return to discussion of both of these duties,

transmitting and clarifying our fragments, see comments in the introductions to Des Places' and Majercik's editions.

[9] *CO* fr. 137 (= Proclus, *In Remp.* 2.154.17-19), discussing the theurgists: "Whoever is truly devoted to sacred causes, says [one of the Chaldaean Oracles] 'shines as an angel, living in power.'" Cf. also *CO* fr. 138 (= Olympiodorus, *In Phd.* 149 [64.2-5 N] W): "But Plato holds that the souls of the theurgists do not remain forever in the intelligible order but that they, too, descend into generation, concerning which [that is, the souls of the theurgists] [one of the Chaldaean Oracles] says 'in the angelic order.'" Other *Oracle* fragments that may allude to this idea are fr. 130 (= Proclus, *In Ti.* 3.266.19, 21-23), and fr. 153 (= Lydus, *de Mensibus* 2.10; 31.19). Similarly, Iamblichus speaks of purified human souls being assigned to the angelic realm: *Myst.* 2.6, 83.3 and cf. *Myst.* 2.2, 67.7-69.19, in which he states that the soul can rise to the angelic realm, although apparently, in this case, Iamblichus means while the soul is still attached to a living body, and that the ascent will be only temporary; *de Anima* 1.457.8-10, in which he says that blessed human souls ascend after death to the angelic realm; and *In Phd.* fr. 5 (= Olympiodorus, *In Phd.* 191.26 N. and 203.26 N.), in which he alludes to the idea. Cf. also Porphyry, *De regr.* fr. 294bF Smith (= fr. 6 Festugière = Augustine, *De civ. D.* 10.26), which mentions that the theurgists could become angels as well. For further discussion, see H. Lewy, *Chaldaean Oracles and Theurgy: Mysticism, Magic and Neoplatonism in the Later Roman Empire,* 2nd ed. by M. Tardieu (Paris, 1978), 212-26; P. Hadot, *Porphyre et Victorinus* (Paris, 1968), 1:392-95 with notes; A. Smith, *Porphyry's Place in the Neoplatonic Tradition: A Study in Post-Plotinian Neoplatonism* (The Hague, 1974), 36, 58-63, 132.

[10] *CO* fr. 138 and Olympiodorus' remarks on it (see previous note). Cf. Porphyry, *Philos. Orac. Haur.* fr. 325 Smith = 144-45 Wolff, which distinguishes between angels who stand eternally before God, those who are sent forth by him as ministers and messengers to humans, and those who perpetually bear his throne and sing his praises; and Porphyry, *De regr.* fr. 294bF Smith (= fr. 6 Festugière = Augustine, *De civ. D.* 10.26). Discussion at Lewy, *Chaldaean,* 9-14; Hadot, *Porphyre,* 392-95; Smith, *Porphyry's,* 132; Majercik, *Chaldean,* comm. *ad* fr. 138; J. Finamore, "The Rational Soul in Iamblichus' Philosophy," *Syllecta Classica* 8 (1997): 163-76, esp. 169-70 and 173-6.

[11] Proclus, *In Remp.* 2.153-155 in commenting on *CO* fr. 137; cf. Iamblichus, *De Anima* 1.380.7-9. Discussion at Lewy, *Chaldaean,* 223-25; Hadot, *Porphyre,* 394-95 with n. 3; Smith, *Porphyry's,* 59-63; J. Finamore, *Iamblichus and the Theory of the Vehicle of the Soul* (ACS 14; Chico, Ca., 1985), 96-114 (particularly good at contrasting Iamblichus' explanation of the reasons for the soul's descent with those of earlier thinkers); G. Shaw, *Theurgy and the Soul: The Neoplatonism of Iamblichus* (University Park, Penn., 1995), 144-5; and Finamore, "Rational," 173-76.

[12] Iamblichus, *De anima* 1.379.1-2, but see also subsequent discussion.

but for now, the important thing to note is that in the theurgic system the escape from materiality that the soul won by practicing virtue while alive brings only further opportunities to practice virtue back within the material world. To use an academic metaphor, it seems a lot like getting tenure. The assistant professor slaves away for six years to prove his or her worth and then, as an associate professor, is rewarded with new administrative assignments. Unlike the associate professor, however, the angelic soul is supposed not only to accept its new assignments, but to rejoice in them. Theurgists distinguished between ordinary souls, who were required to reincarnate because they were not yet perfected in their virtue, and the privileged angelic souls, who *had* been perfected but chose to reincarnate nonetheless.[13]

To interpret the eschatological variation on which I am focusing in this paper, I divide it in half temporarily: the first half discusses the belief that, after death, the souls of the virtuous could become angels; the second, the belief that, after death, the souls of the virtuous would go back to work.

Angelic Souls

Somewhat similar to the first belief is the Roman idea that emperors and other exceptional individuals could become not angels, but gods after death and, in a few cases, even before death. Earlier, Alexander the Great and other Hellenistic rulers occasionally had been declared gods as well,[14] and even earlier than this (fifth century B.C.E.), the philosopher Empedocles had claimed that he was a god; the claim suited Empedocles' larger arguments about how the individual soul suffered repeated incarnations as punishment for its misbehavior and his avowal that his own soul had at last won escape from this cycle. Empedocles' ideas about incarnation influenced later philosophical

---

[13] Iamblichus, *De anima* 1.380.6–25; Synesios, *Hymn* 1.573 ff (with Porphyry as probable source). See comments at Lewy, *Chaldaean*, 225; Hadot, *Porphyre*, 393–4; Smith, *Porphyry's*, 36–7, 59, 132; Majercik, *Chaldean Oracles*, comm. ad 138; Shaw, *Theurgy*, 144–6, 151; Finamore, "Rational," 169. For the relationship between Synesios and the *Chaldaean Oracles*, see W. Theiler, "Die Chaldäischen Orakel und die Hymnen des Synesios," *Schriften der Königsberger Gelehrten Gesellschaft* 18 (1942): 1–41; repr. in *Forschungen zum Neoplatonismus* (Berlin, 1966), 252–301.

[14] J. D. Mikalson, *Religion in Hellenistic Athens* (Berkeley, 1998); S. R. F. Price, *Rituals and Power: The Roman Imperial Cult in Asia Minor* (Cambridge, 1984); A. Small, ed., *Subject and Ruler: The Cult of the Ruling Power in Classical Antiquity: Papers Presented at a Conference Held in the University of Alberta on April 13–15, 1994, to Celebrate the 65th Anniversary of Duncan Fishwish* (*Journal of Roman Archaeology* Suppl. 17; Ann Arbor, 1996); ANRW 2.16.2; M. Beard, J. North, and S. R. F. Price, *Religions of Rome* 2 vols., (Cambridge, 1998), 1:206–10, 348–63.

and esoteric systems of thought, some of which influenced theurgy in turn, but they stood alone for their time; other people did not, as far as we know, claim to be gods. Among more ordinary people, we first find traces of this idea in the Gold Tablets from fourth-century B.C.E. Italy (the doctrines of which probably grew out of the same background as did Empedocles' ideas).[15] On the Tablets, the soul that has been initiated into the Bacchic mysteries while its body was alive is promised that it, too, will become a god after death.[16] Given theurgy's broader phenomenological debt to Greek mysteries,[17] it is possible that the ideology behind the Tablets helped to pave the way for the theurgic expectation that the virtuous became something more than mortals after death, although it has to be admitted that the statements on the Tablets are highly unusual even within the context of mystery cults. Most Graeco-Roman mysteries promised their initiates only the standard post-mortem reward of eating, drinking, and lolling about in meadows; the gods of the Gold Tablets enjoy these perquisites as well, to be sure, but they enjoy them in an exalted status.[18]

It is also important to note that there are significant functional differences between gods, as we see them in the systems I have just surveyed, and angels, particularly as we see them in theurgic thought and in Neoplatonic thought more generally. Like the Olympians, mortals who become gods generally are defined by their lack of obligation to do anything other than what they want to do. People may have hoped that some erstwhile mortals, such as the divinized Hellenistic and Roman rulers, would look down from their heavenly perches and support the nations over which they had formerly ruled, but there was no more guarantee of this than there was that Zeus would attend to any particular human request. Angels, in contrast, existed to serve, as we shall see – the very word "angel," meaning "messenger," already intimates this. Earlier Greek and Roman systems in which mortals become gods, in short, are appropriate parallels for our theurgic belief only broadly,

[15] Empedocles' claim to be a god: fr. 102 Wr. (112 D–K). On Empedocles in general, P. Kingsley, *Ancient Philosophy, Mystery, and Magic: Empedocles and Pythagorean Tradition* (Oxford, 1995). On Empedocles' relationship to the Gold Tablets, see esp. 256–72, 308–14.

[16] Tablets A1.8, A4.4 and cf. A5.4 from second-century C.E. Rome. On the question of their "Bacchic" nature, see Graf, "Dionysian," and Johnston and McNiven, "Dionysos."

[17] See Lewy, *Chaldaean*, index s.v. "mystery-religions, terminology" and S. I. Johnston, "Rising to the Occasion: Theurgic Ascent in its Cultural Milieu," in *Envisioning Magic: A Princeton Seminar and Symposium*, ed. P. Schäfer and H. G. Kippenberg (SHR 75; Leiden, 1996), 165–94, esp. 176–81.

[18] See n. 16 above.

insofar as they promise that some humans can win a higher status after death.

Somewhat better parallels are found in the esoteric writings attributed to Hermes, which date from approximately the same time as that of the *Chaldaean Oracles* and which partially share their Neoplatonic background. In the *Corpus Hermeticum* I 26, the soul of the blessed is said to rise through the cosmic realms to the Ogdoad, where it receives a new power that is proper to it [ἰδία δύναμις], sings hymns to God, and becomes able to listen to hymns sung by even higher Powers [Δύναμαι], which dwell above the Ogdoad. We are not told what such creatures are to be called (if anything), but both their position between ordinary humans and higher Powers and their obligation to praise God indicates that, like angels, they are medial entities with tasks to perform. Unlike theurgy, however, the *Hermetica* promise these angelic creatures that they will win something even better, eventually. They will rise higher yet, joining in song with the Powers to whom they used to listen and, ultimately, will become one with God [θεωθῆναι] as a reward for *gnosis*. Similarly, in the *Kore Kosmou* (*CH* XXIII 37–39), God promises that souls who manage to keep away from wrongdoing while incarnated will again "greet their home above" – that is, rise into the realm between the earth and the heavens that is proper to them. We learn from *CH* XXIV 4, which probably was a continuation of *CH* XXIII, that a soul who has behaved well while incarnated can even be transmuted into a god [ἀποθεοῦσθαι] after its final incarnation as an earthly king.

Jewish and Christian ascent literature of the last few centuries B.C.E. and the first few centuries C.E. offers similar parallels.[19] Men such as Zephaniah and Isaiah were carried up to heaven, where they became angels, in some cases, or at least creatures who were allowed to interact with angels, in other cases. Although the vast majority of these ascenders stayed in heaven only a short time and then returned to earth to resume the incarnate existence from which they had briefly departed, some achieved a permanent angelic

---

[19] A. F. Segal, "Heavenly Ascent in Hellenistic Judaism, Early Christianity, and their Environment," *ANRW* 2.23.2:1333–94, esp. 1341–5; P. Schäfer, *The Hidden and Manifest God: Some Major Themes in Early Jewish Mysticism* (Albany, 1992), 140, 150–5; M. Himmelfarb, *Ascent to Heaven in Jewish and Christian Apocalypses* (New York, 1993), 5, 95–8, 106–10; cf. Johnston, "Rising," for more specific discussion of how theurgic ascent differed from the kinds discussed by Segal, Schäfer, and Himmelfarb; Schäfer and Himmelfarb have convincingly argued that most of the texts they discuss were not intended as "manuals" – that is, that their readers would not attempt ascent themselves – but rather that the recitation of ascent stories served liturgical purposes.

status: Enoch became Metatron, for example, and Isaiah was promised –
during his temporary ascent – that, after he had died one day, he would
rejoin the angelic realm forever.[20] There are some indications that, perhaps
already by the second century B.C.E. and certainly by the first century C.E., it
was believed that angelic status after death would be afforded even to the
ordinary soul at the end of history, so long as it had practiced virtue.[21] Given
that theurgic angelology seems to have borrowed other traits from Jewish
and early Christian angelology, it is possible that these stories influenced
theurgy as well.[22]

Working Souls

In sum, the first half of our theurgic belief looks more or less at home in
the second-century Mediterranean world. By this time, humans – or at least
some humans – expected to win higher status for themselves after death,
or even before death in a few cases. The other half of our belief, however,
looks distinctly odder. The traditional reward for good behavior in the Greek
afterlife, as mentioned in the preceding section, was to eat and drink forever
in a meadow. In Judaism and early Christianity, too, the ordinary blessed soul
expected to dwell in a lovely place and enjoy itself.[23] When Christ said that
the righteous would be "like angels" in the afterlife (Matt 22:30; Luke 20:36),
he specifically meant that they would no longer be bound to the constraints
of the physical body; instead they would, like the angels themselves, serve as
constant messengers between heaven and earth or perform other heavenly
duties.[24]

Other possible parallels that come to mind for our theurgic belief are
distant. For example, the Greeks expected the souls of the dead to aid the
living, but typically, this applied only to one's own relatives, and the aid
offered was of a sort that was practical in everyday life: avenging injuries
and encouraging fecundity, for example. To take a classic example, Electra and Orestes pray to the ghost of their father Agamemnon to help them

[20] On Zephaniah and Isaiah, Himmelfarb, *Ascent*, 51–9; on Enoch, 37–46; and on such ascents more generally, *passim*.
[21] J. J. Collins, "The Afterlife in Apocalyptic Literature," in *Judaism in Late Antiquity*, 119–40.
[22] Lewy, *Chaldaean*, 9–15, 162–3; Hadot, *Porphyre*, 392–4.
[23] J. B. Russell, *A History of Heaven: The Singing Silence* (Princeton, N.J., 1997), 27–37, 54–65, 81.
[24] At Matt 20:30, Jesus says "for in the resurrection they neither marry nor are given in marriage, but are like angels in heaven," and at Luke 20:36, those who are worthy of resurrection are said to be "like angels" and to be "children of God."

avenge his murder. Nonliterary sources offer examples as well. In some Greek cities, for instance, families worshiped ancestral spirits called the Tritopatores, in hopes they would promote the conception of children. Even those dead who helped nonrelatives, such as the heroes, limited themselves to quotidian problems such as famine and war; they did not serve as spiritual guides. One might ask Heracles for help on the battlefield, for victory in an athletic competition, or to avert illnesses from one's household, but it would have been inconceivable to ask him for advice on how to purify one's soul.[25]

Another general parallel is provided by the Jewish and Christian ascenders whom I already mentioned, as well as by the (somewhat later) Hekhalot ascenders, for when these men return to earth after their ascents, they often carry important information that they deliver for the instruction of a chosen group or for the betterment of other mortals in general – in other words, they act as messengers from God, as *angeloi*.[26] There are also some earlier, Greek variations of this type of story, one of which – the Platonic myth of Er from the fourth century B.C.E. – is particularly interesting in the context of this paper.[27] While Er's body lay apparently dead for twelve days on a battlefield, his soul traveled into the afterlife and witnessed how other souls were judged and sent out into new lives again after experiencing either punishment or reward. Er was told by a divinity whom he met in the afterlife that he was to serve as a messenger – an *angelos* – on his return.[28] He was to preach the virtuous life that the living must embrace in order to reap rewards in the afterlife and in the after-afterlife – that is, in the new life that they would enter into after their next period of death was over. Proclus, in fact, argued that Er was a prototheurgist and used the theurgic belief that I am treating in this paper to explicate Er's story.[29]

---

[25] Electra and Orestes: Aeschylus, *Cho.*, esp. 123–51, 479–509 and cf. *Eum.* 598; Euripides, *Or.* 1225–1240. Further on this topic generally, see Johnston, *Restless*, esp. Chap. 2; the Tritopatores are discussed at 47–58. On Heracles, see discussion and notes at W. Burkert, *Greek Religion: Archaic and Classical*, trans. J. Raffan (Oxford, 1985), 210–11.

[26] For example, *Ascen. Isa.* esp. 1, 5, and 11:36–40; and *T. Levi* 2:10; discussion of the general topic throughout Himmelfarb, *Ascent*. On the Hekhalot tradition, Schäfer, *Hidden and Manifest God*. Two interesting variations of this idea are found in the Enoch tradition: (1) fallen angels bestow on mortals knowledge that is inappropriate and corrupting (discussed by A. Y. Reed in this volume), and (2) subsequently, Enoch himself ascends to gain knowledge with which he is supposed to rebuke the fallen angels after he has descended.

[27] Plato, *Resp.* 10.614b2–621b7.

[28] Plato, *Resp.* 10.614d1.

[29] Proclus, *In Remp.* 2.153–155, with reference to *CO* fr. 137.

The Hekhalot tradition also offers us angels in the more traditional Jewish sense of the concept – that is, not mortals who briefly visit the divine realm or the afterlife and return to earth as messengers, but creatures who properly reside in the divine realm all the time. These angels do have tasks to perform, however. Some mediate on behalf of humanity; some tend to the divine throne; some guard the boundaries of heavenly spheres against interlopers. But, most important, like the Hermetic Powers, they are charged with singing God's praises; indeed, according to one text, if they fail to do so in perfect harmony, they will be cast into rivers of fire.[30] This idea of an angelic duty to praise God may have made its way into theurgy as well, through Judaism, the *Hermetica*, or some other source. Porphyry quotes an oracle (perhaps a *Chaldaean Oracle*, as Hadot and Lewy suggested) that distinguishes among three types of angels. Those who remain permanently in God's presence singing his praises, those who are separated from him, and those who are sent forth by him into the world of mortals.[31] If the oracle is, in fact, theurgic, it is into this last group that the reincarnated theurgists fall.

As helpful as these parallels are in contextualizing the most general characteristic of the theurgic belief we are examining – the idea that virtuous entities dutifully fulfill their cosmic obligations – the parallels leave one important aspect untouched. Only in the theurgic variation are the virtuous required to *reincarnate* in order to serve God or to help the living. Dead souls, including heroes, stay dead. Holy men who journey in their souls while alive return to and reanimate the same bodies from which their souls had temporarily departed – and, one assumes, they eventually die a normal mortal death while in those bodies and reap a normal eschatological reward. Figures such as Enoch–Metatron, who pass back and forth between heaven and earth continually, do so *as angels*; they are not required to enter into mortal bodies once again. Angelic praise-singers, although apparently liable to bodily suffering akin to that of humans (the river of fire does burn them), need never depart from heaven so long as they perform their task correctly. The closest parallel to the theurgic belief (as Proclus already realized) is offered by Er, who could be said to "die" and then be "reborn." But even here, we are

---

[30] Schäfer, *Hidden and Manifest God*, esp. 27, which quotes *Hekhalot Rabbati* (MSS New York 8128 and Munich 22), §§185–186 on disharmonious angels being cast into fiery rivers.

[31] Porphyry, *Phil. Orac. Haur.* fr. 325 Smith = 144–145 Wolff. Cf. Lewy, *Chaldaean*, 9–10, Hadot, *Porphyre*, 393–5.

not on completely firm ground, for not only does the text insist that Er was never really dead, but when Er returns to the land of the living, like other holy men, he returns in his own identity to continue the life that he briefly left.

True reincarnation, in which a soul freed from one corporeal life is thrust again into a new corporeal life, was, in fact, viewed as highly distasteful in almost every ancient Mediterranean culture that believed in it and was to be avoided by the soul if at all possible; in the mystery cult that underlay the Gold Tablets, for example, the highest reward offered to the soul was that after leading enough virtuous lives he might one day "fly out of the heavy, difficult circle" forever. Passages from the *Hermetica* present incarnation as loathsome as well, as a punishment inflicted on souls (who were originally disincarnate) because they had audaciously compared themselves to God (*Kore Kosmou* = *CH* XXIII 17–39).[32] Indeed, in *CH* XXIV 4, we find almost an inversion of the theurgic idea that we are examining in this essay. Souls who have nearly perfected themselves are sent to earth one last time, incarnated as kings, so that by ruling over people in the flesh, they may be better prepared for their final, and permanent, postmortem reward: ascension into a disincarnate state that gives them a godlike power [τὴν τῶν θεῶν...ἐξουσίαν] over others. Pastoring people properly in the material world is represented as a final hurdle to escaping materiality altogether.[33] To serve God or one's fellow humans from the heavenly realms is one thing; to have to do so back within earthly chains would be another, and seemingly a far more distasteful and dishonorable matter.

---

[32] On metempsychosis in antiquity in general, see Burkert, *Religion*, 296–301; R. J. Zwi Werblowsky, "Transmigration," in *Death, Afterlife and the Soul*, ed. L. E. Sullivan (New York, 1987), 130–7; J. Bruce Long, "Reincarnation," in the same collection, 138–145. On metempsychosis in Orphic contexts, G. Casadio, "La Metempsicosi tra Orfeo e Pitagora," in *Orphisme et Orphée: En l'Honneur de Jean Rudhardt*, ed. P. Borgeaud (Geneva, 1991), 119–56; L. Brisson, "Damascius et l'Orphisme," in *Orphisme et Orphée*, 157–210. Aversion to incarnation in the *Hermetica* (in addition to the passages already cited): II 17; X 7–8 and 19–22; *Asclep.* 12; 25.8; and 26.2. A partial exception to the general rule that reincarnation was distasteful may be offered by the Pharisees, according to Josephus (*J.W.* 2.163). They claimed that, whereas the souls of the wicked were condemned to eternal punishment, the souls of the good "only would be sent into other bodies." Even here, however, reincarnation is not so much a positive boon as a less distasteful alternative.

[33] Cf. also *CH* I.26 (cited already in part), which tells the devotee to serve God by becoming a guide [καθοδηλός] to the worthy, so that "through you, humans might be saved by God." The passage as a whole, however, concerns proper behavior here and now, and there is no implication that the devotee must do this after death as well.

Platonic Influences

What, then, was the background from which the theurgists developed their idea that the reward of virtue was a further term of servitude in the bodily prison from which the soul had finally escaped? I have two observations to offer. The first is that there was a general precedent for the theurgists to follow in the Platonic philosophy that they revered so deeply, although, notably, it was not an eschatological precedent per se. One of the central tenets of Socrates' teachings was that the individual must help his fellow citizens. This benefited not only those whom the individual helped, but also the individual himself because it led to a more perfect city-state in which any sensible individual wished to live. The third and fourth books of Plato's *Republic* articulate this premise as follows.[34] The ideal guardian of the perfect city-state, says Socrates, is a man who has learned not to be distracted by pleasure. He declines ownership of private property, and his meals provide only such nourishment as he needs to survive. Because he possesses in his soul "the gold and silver of divinity," he rejects all payment for his services to the state. "By living so," Socrates concludes, "the guardians will save themselves and their city alike." Another participant in the dialogue objects: "But Socrates, what will be your defense when someone objects that you are not making these men very happy?" Socrates replies that, although it would not surprise him if these guardians *did* turn out to be the happiest of all men, this is beside the point. He desires to ensure not the exceptional happiness of the guardians themselves, however much they deserve it, but the greatest happiness for the greatest number of the city-state's inhabitants. Thus will the city-state become almost perfect.[35]

The theurgists understood their "city-state" to be the cosmos itself; as guardians, they had to help the gods and angels administer it. Having

---

[34] Plato, *Resp.* 3.416d3–417b9 and 4.419a1–421c6.

[35] Given the Platonic background of many doctrines we find in the *Hermetica*, it is probable that the idea of the soul spending its last incarnation as a king, before passing into permanent disincarnate bliss where it will gain godlike powers (see previous discussion), was also influenced by the passage of the *Republic* that I have just mentioned, although it also should be remembered that the idea of particularly pure and just souls being incarnated as kings goes as far back as Pindar, fr. 133. The concept that pure souls should reign in the material world, then, is not surprising; what is surprising, in our theurgic belief, is that they do so not as a punishment or (so far as our sources tell us) as a final stage in their preparation for some permanent escape from the material world, but rather as a reward in itself.

inherited the concept of the Platonic Ideas or Forms, they also believed that the cosmos had been created not only once, *illo tempore*, but rather that it was in need of continuous re-creation and reordering, *hoc tempore*.[36] This continuous renewal depended on the continuous emission of Light and Forms by the supreme, transcendent God – the theurgists called him the Father – and also on the demiurgic participation of lower cosmic orders, each of whom received the Father's Light and/or Forms, processed them, and passed them along to the next order below, right down to and including the material world and the humans who inhabited it.[37] One of the theurgists' obligations was to discover the proper ways in which material objects such as plants and stones could be manipulated so as to help sustain, promote, and enhance cosmic re-creation.[38] One of his other obligations, and that of every human soul, was simply to exist as an embodied human; every item and entity in the cosmos had a cosmogonic function to perform what was closely tied to its intrinsic nature.[39] The properly maintained and continuously re-created cosmos, in turn, provided soteriological benefits to those who inhabited it and knew how to use its properties correctly.[40] Thus, the Socratic guardian of the political city-state may have served as a model for the theurgist not only insofar as, like the angelicized theurgist, the guardian had to reject the rewards he deserved for the greater good of the whole, but also insofar as he had to reject them precisely because he did not stand alone. He was one

---

[36] On administration of the cosmos, Iamblichus, *De anima* 1.379.6–7 and 1.458.16–19. On continuous recreation of the cosmos, see Iamblichus, *Myst.* 1.21, 65.4 and cf. Shaw, *Theurgy*, who mentions the idea throughout, e.g., 23–5, 56–7, 124–5, 129–32.

[37] See Majercik, *Chaldean Oracles*, 6–7, for an overview; also S. I. Johnston, "Fiat Lux, Fiat Ritus: Divinity as Light and the Late Antique Defense of Ritual," in *The Presence of Light: Divine Radiance and Transformative Vision*, ed. M. Kapstein (Chicago, forthcoming).

[38] Shaw, *Theurgy*, 47–50, 130–69, esp. 144–52, 158–9, and 163–9, which quote several of the crucial passages from Iamblichus' *Myst.* in translation; also B. Nasemann, *Theurgie und Philosophie in Jamblichs De mysteriis* (Beiträge zur Altertumskunde 11; Stuttgart, 1991), 231–82, esp. 247–82.

[39] Shaw, *Theurgy*, 81–126, with particular attention to the following passages from Iamblichus' *de Anima*, which Shaw quotes in translation on pp. 85 and 115: 1.378.25–379.6; 1.458.17–21. These focus on Iamblichus' view that the soul's embodiment in a human body was (as Shaw expresses it) "...simply the pivot through which the eros of Demiurge returned to itself.... For a theurgist, his experience in a corporeal form was the linchpin of the cosmos; embodiment was a creative and sacramental act." See also J. Dillon, *Alcinous: The Handbook of Platonism* (Oxford, 1993), 155–8, and R. Edmonds' discussion of "positive descent" in this volume.

[40] Shaw, *Theurgy*, as cited in n. 39, but with particular attention to 110–11 and 116.

cog in a larger cosmic machine and served himself best when he served the machine best.

My second observation starts from the obvious point that, in developing their eschatology, the theurgists applied Socrates' theories of how to live a good *life* to the *after*life – that is, what Socrates expected from his living guardians the theurgists expected from their souls. This contrast is characteristic of the relationship between the Platonic dialogues – which show little interest in eschatology per se and use eschatological myths mainly to drive home lessons about how to live correctly here and now – and the work of the theurgists, who were deeply concerned with eschatology and believed that eschatological lessons were cryptically embedded in the Platonic dialogues.

Which ends up making theurgy a very interesting beast for the student of ancient Mediterranean religions for, implicit in the theurgists' eschatology, is a challenge to one of our favorite dichotomies – the one between, as J. Z. Smith has famously expressed it, locative and utopian worldviews.[41] The Platonic worldview, like that of the classical Greek religious system under whose influence it developed, was strongly locative: that is, it was highly concerned with identifying the proper nature and functions of every item in the cosmos and then keeping each in its proper place so that its function could best be fulfilled. In Greek religion, generally, this meant, among other things, deep concern with pollution *à la* Mary Douglas' famous analysis.[42] In the Platonic dialogues, it is exemplified not only by locatively oriented treatments of pollution – in the ideal city-state, the corpses of executed parricides are to be thrown outside the city boundaries at the place where three roads meet, for instance – but also, for example, by a drive to determine which individuals in the ideal state properly belonged to each of three mutually exclusive classes of citizens with mutually exclusive duties and dwelling places: guardians, warriors, demiurgoi.[43] For the Platonic world to work, everyone had to be in the right place, doing the right thing. Theurgy, and Neoplatonism more generally, took locative concerns in new directions, including up. From the earth to the heavens, the Neoplatonic cosmos was highly stratified. Gatekeeping entities were poised between strata, both to prevent entities from

---

[41] J. Z. Smith, *Map Is Not Territory: Studies in the History of Religion* (Leiden, 1978), *passim*, esp. 101–3, 132–43, 160–70, 185–9, 291–4, 308–9.

[42] M. Douglas, *Purity and Danger: An Analysis of the Concepts of Pollution and Taboo* (London, 1996). Its manifestations in the Greek world are explored most thoroughly by R. Parker, *Miasma: Pollution and Purification in Early Greek Religion* (Oxford, 1983).

[43] Corpses of parricides: Plato, *Leg.* 873b–c; three classes: see esp. Plato, *Resp.* 3.415b–c.

passing into strata where they did not belong and to help alter the nature of entities or materials that needed to pass so that they might do so.[44] Each individual and object within the theurgic cosmos, moreover, fell under the care of one particular deity who ruled it; the individual had to learn to which deity's train he belonged before he could really live properly, in accordance with his particular nature. He also had to know which physical objects – animals, stones, plants – to sacrifice to each god as he interacted with him or her.[45] The locativity of the theurgic worldview is also demonstrated by the fact that both personal salvation and salvation of the cosmos as a whole depended on continuous cosmic re-creation and reordering.

And, yet, theurgy emerged in a Mediterranean world in which utopian religions, notably Judaism and Christianity, were arguing that the material part of the cosmos was insignificant and that blessedness was possible only when it was rejected. This had its effect. The central goal of the theurgic mysteries was to enable the soul of the theurgist, while he was still alive, to ascend above the material realm and look on beautiful sights that would improve it.[46] The theurgist's postmortem goal, to cause his soul to rise into the higher realm of the angels, speaks to this as well. The theurgists clung to the older, "locative" worldview insofar as they believed that it was essential to keep the *entire* cosmos – including its material portions – properly organized, but they were utopian insofar as they considered the nonmaterial realms of the cosmos to be more perfect and desirable and strove to lead their souls upwards into them.[47]

Which brings us back, at last, to theurgy's puzzling eschatology. In ascending and then redescending, in doffing materiality and then once again donning it, the theurgic soul simultaneously reaps the reward of its virtue by rising into a heavenly realm and then confirms its virtue by agreeing to participate in it properly so as to maintain it in as close to a perfect form

---

[44] Most importantly Hekate; see S. I. Johnston, *Hekate Soteira: A Study of Hekate's Roles in the Chaldean Oracles and Related Literature* (ACS 21; Atlanta, 1990), Chap. 4. See also Majercik, *Chaldean Oracles*, 9–12.

[45] Shaw, *Theurgy*, 144–51, 166–8.

[46] This point has often been discussed. For overviews with references to earlier works, see Majercik, *Chaldean Oracles*, 30–45, and Johnston, "Rising."

[47] In contrast to my suggestions here, Shaw, *Theurgy*, 9–17, has argued (1) that Plotinus and Porphyry (like many others of their time) turned away from the traditional Greek locative worldview toward a strictly utopian one; and (2) that, in contrast, Iamblichus and other theurgists embraced a traditional locative worldview, albeit in a "highly sophisticated way" (p. 14).

as possible. Or, to put it in other words, the theurgist's reward for virtue and knowledge of the cosmos was an enhanced opportunity to put them to work. Considering that the theurgic gods and angels themselves spend their time ordering the cosmos, this was a great reward indeed. In an environment within which utopian worldviews and ascents to heaven were all the rage, it is not surprising that theurgy developed utopian aspects; but, in the end, it clung to the locative system of traditional Greek religion.

So the analogy that I offered earlier in this paper, in which I compared the theurgic soul to an associate professor unhappily laden with new administrative work, was not quite right. Now that we have taken a closer look at theurgic eschatology, can the analogy be refocused? Is it only the adverb "unhappily" that needs to be changed – should we compare the theurgist to that *rara avis*, the professor who thrives on administrative work? Or should we, rather, shift the analogy out of the real academic world and into an imaginary one? Let us imagine a professor of philosophy being told to run his university according to the tenets of his favorite theorist. The admirer of Seneca would apply a Stoic approach, the admirer of Maimonides would refer to *A Guide for the Perplexed*, and the admirer of Epicurus would advocate a little more fun and a little less worrying about the future. The opportunity to put into effect the theoretical knowledge one had acquired as a student would surely provide occasion to rejoice. Similarly, for the theurgist, the opportunity to spend one life putting into effect what he had spent all of the last one learning constituted Paradise indeed.

PART TWO

INSTITUTIONALIZING HEAVEN

6

Earthly Sacrifice and Heavenly Incense: The Law of the Priesthood in *Aramaic Levi* and *Jubilees*

Martha Himmelfarb

I t is difficult to overstate the centrality of the Temple for Judaism in the Second Temple period. Yet, as far back as the *Book of the Watchers* in the third century B.C.E., many Jews were deeply critical of the priestly establishment that ran the Temple. Some critics, including the community at Qumran, came to view the Temple as defiled and were unwilling to participate in its cult. Even as they criticized the current state of affairs, however, they nonetheless continued to hold fast to the ideal of the Temple. One type of response to the distressing reality of the present appears in texts such as the *Temple Scroll* and 4QMMT, which offer detailed legal prescriptions for the proper governance of the Temple and its cult. Another type of response is attention to the heavenly Temple on which biblical tradition understands the Jerusalem Temple to be modeled. Thus, for example, the *Book of the Watchers* describes Enoch's ascent to heaven as if he were entering a Temple and treats the angels he encounters as priests, while the *Songs of the Sabbath Sacrifice* describes the liturgy of the heavenly Temple.

This paper begins on earth, with the "law of the priesthood" (13) in *Aramaic Levi* (13–61).[1] Here Levi, the ancestor of all priests, receives instruction from his grandfather Isaac on a range of topics concerning proper cultic procedure. These rules have sometimes been understood as an example of the kind of criticism of the Jerusalem Temple through the legal prescription I have already noted. But, after a thorough examination of these rules in comparison to the laws of the Torah and other texts concerned with the Temple cult, I argue that this is not the case. *Aramaic Levi* may have offered implicit criticism of the Jerusalem Temple through a description of the heavenly

---

[1] For text and translation of this work, preserved in Aramaic manuscripts from Qumran and the Cairo Geniza and in a Greek manuscript from Mt. Athos, I use R. A. Kugler, *From Patriarch to Priest: The Levi-Priestly Tradition from* Aramaic Levi *to* Testament of Levi (SBLEJL 9; Atlanta, 1996).

Temple, although unfortunately the content of Levi's vision of heaven is lost (supp. 21). In the law of the priesthood, however, the only area in which *Aramaic Levi* is critical of the priestly establishment is its marriage practices. In other areas, I suggest, the law of the priesthood supplements the laws of the Torah to provide priests with the information necessary for them to do their jobs.

From *Aramaic Levi*, I turn to the *Book of Jubilees* and its adaptation of the law of the priesthood (*Jubilees* 21). One notable feature of *Jubilees* is its emphasis on aroma in sacrifice. According to other sources of this period, aroma is the essence of the cult in the heavenly Temple. If the biblical tradition understands the earthly Temple as modeled on the heavenly, it is a scholarly commonplace, of course, that the biblical tradition has it backwards. For scholars, depictions of the heavenly Temple inevitably reflect the realities of the earthly Temple. But this view of the matter does not do justice to the significance of the heavenly Temple in the imagination of ancient Jews. Here, I argue that *Jubilees'* concern for aroma in the earthly cult is an instance in which descriptions of the heavenly Temple have influenced prescriptions for the earthly Temple.

The Law of the Priesthood

Because Levi lived before the revelation at Sinai, it is clear that he could not learn to be a priest by consulting the Torah. Thus, *Aramaic Levi* has Isaac teach him about a variety of subjects of importance to a priest: proper marriage partners (16–18); washing before and during sacrifice (19–21, 26, 53–55); the types of wood to be used for sacrifice (22–24); the order of sprinkling blood and laying the parts of the sacrificial animal on the altar and the requirement to salt the parts (25–29); the sacrifice of flour, oil, wine, and incense that accompanies the animal sacrifice (30); the amount of wood necessary for different types of offerings (31–36); the weights of the salt, fine flour, oil, and frankincense that accompany different kinds of offerings (37–46); the relationships among the different weights (46–47); keeping the priest's garments free of blood (53); and covering and avoiding the consumption of blood of animals slaughtered for food (56).[2]

---

[2] The last part of the instructions, 51–60, repeats and summarizes some of the material that comes before it. This has led some scholars to suggest that this portion is not original to the text. See Kugler, *From Patriarch*, 108, for references. *Jubilees'* version of the instructions includes keeping the garments free of blood and covering blood (21:17), subjects that

Yet, even if Levi had had the Torah in front of him, much of how a priest fulfills his duties would have been left to his imagination; for, despite the profusion of detail it offers, the priestly source of the Torah is certainly not a handbook for priests. Anyone attempting to perform a sacrifice on the basis of the laws in Leviticus and Numbers alone would be left wondering how to proceed at many points. There are so many questions P neglects to answer. How, for example, is the slaughter of sacrificial animals to be carried out? What sort of wood is to be used on the altar? How much salt is required for salting the sacrifices? Surely, P did not intend to leave decisions about the many points of procedure it neglects to clarify to the individual priest – it would be too dangerous, as the story of Nadav and Avihu's ritual innovation and its fatal consequences (Lev 10:1–3) demonstrates. Clearly, P presupposes a more elaborate and detailed body of tradition to be taught to young priests as they came of age to officiate in the Temple.

The body of priestly tradition that was not committed to writing is, of course, lost to us, and it would be naive to read Isaac's instructions as a straightforward report of what a priestly father was expected to pass on to his son. It is clear that, by the later Second Temple period, the Jerusalem Temple involved a physical plant, a bureaucracy, and a workload far beyond what P's picture of Aaron and his sons officiating in the wilderness tabernacle prepares us for. The *Letter of Aristeas*, probably from sometime in the second century B.C.E., describes priests functioning on an assembly line that would make an efficiency expert proud (92–95). The *Temple Scroll*, which probably also dates to the second century B.C.E., mandates a Temple with many architectural elements and equipment unknown from the Bible (cols. 30–45). More than a century after the Temple's destruction, the Mishnah recalls an even more elaborate Temple complex and provides information about how its bureaucracy was organized.[3] Although none of these texts can be taken as a simple representation of reality, they point to a far busier and more bureaucratic institution than P envisions.

Even if the Temple in pre-Maccabean times was a simpler operation than is reflected in these somewhat later sources, the lone priest sacrificing apart from an institutional setting is a requirement of the pseudepigraphic setting of *Aramaic Levi*, not a reflection of contemporary reality. Indeed, it may well

---

Aramaic Levi treats only in this concluding portion (53, 56). Thus, if the conclusion of the instructions is a later addition to *Aramaic Levi*, it had already been added by the time *Jubilees* was written.

[3] M. *Tamid* and m. *Middot* are particularly relevant.

be that by the time *Aramaic Levi* was written, which I take to be some time in the late third or early second century B.C.E.,[4] the indoctrination of young priests was no longer a task for fathers and grandfathers, but had become institutionalized. Still, it seems to me that Isaac's instructions to Levi contain precisely the sort of information a young priest would need to know before undertaking service in the Temple.

Robert A. Kugler has recently argued that *Aramaic Levi* is intended as a critique of the Jerusalem priesthood, offering the figure of Levi as a model of a pure and pious priest in contrast to the priestly establishment.[5] Kugler sees the differences between Isaac's instructions and the commands of the Torah as *Aramaic Levi*'s criticism of the practice of the priestly establishment. Yet, the only place in Isaac's speech where there is any hint of polemic is in his advice about marriage: "Take for yourself a wife from my family so that you will not defile your seed with harlots" (17). We know from other sources of the Second Temple period that marriage between priests and women from nonpriestly families was not uncommon. Isaac's position, that priests must marry only women from priestly families, appears also in the *Book of the Watchers* and 4QMMT, both texts critical of the priestly establishment.[6] The *Book of the Watchers*' condemnation of the Watchers' marriages to human women, in my view, reflects criticism not of priests' marriages to foreign women – marriages that would have been widely viewed as unacceptable – but rather of priests' marriages to Jewish women from nonpriestly families. 4QMMT's condemnation of the "harlotry" taking place among the people that it compares to a violation of the laws of mixed kinds also seems to reflect the position found in *Aramaic Levi*. On the question of marriage, then, *Aramaic Levi* rejects the dominant priestly practice in favor of a rigorist position shared by other antiestablishment works.

If Kugler's view of the instructions as critique is correct, however, it is remarkable how well the intent of the passage has been concealed on every topic except marriage. I now propose to look at the rest of the instructions contained in *Aramaic Levi*'s law of the priesthood and their relationship to the laws of the Torah. On some subjects, Isaac's directions complement the Torah's relatively terse instructions; there is no question of contradiction or

---

[4] M. E. Stone, "Enoch, Aramaic Levi and Sectarian Origins," *JSJ* 19 (1988): 159–60, n. 2.

[5] Kugler, *From Patriarch*, 108–11.

[6] See M. Himmelfarb, "Levi, Phinehas, and the Problem of Intermarriage at the Time of the Maccabean Revolt," *JSQ* 6 (1999): 1–24.

critique. On other points, Isaac's directions stand in a certain tension with the Torah, but nowhere, I hope to show, do they straightforwardly contradict the Torah.

Washing

Isaac's instructions about washing are one example of the way *Aramaic Levi* supplements the laws of the Torah. Isaac echoes the command of Exod 30:19–21 that priests wash before entering the sanctuary and before approaching the altar (19, 21), but adds a command to wash after donning the priestly garments (20) and after sprinkling the sacrificial blood on the side of the altar (26). *Aramaic Levi* also demonstrates a concern absent in P for washing up at the end of the process of sacrifice. In his concluding remarks, Isaac tells Levi to wash his hands and feet "from all the flesh" (presumably of the sacrifice) on leaving the sanctuary and to be sure that there is no blood on him (53–55). These ablutions reflect a greater anxiety about sacrificial blood than the priestly document of the Torah shows, but going beyond the demands of the Torah in washing appears to have been standard operating procedure in the Second Temple period in many areas of life. Indeed, a wide range of sources from Philo to the Dead Sea Scrolls demonstrates that washing had become a popular pious practice.[7] It would not be surprising if ablutions beyond those required by the Torah were standard priestly practice in the Second Temple.

Blood on Garments

Sacrifice must have been an extremely messy ritual. Although P does not appear to be worried about blood on priests' garments, the Mishnah contains some indications that it expected priests to change their garments frequently. A list of Temple officials includes a certain Phineas who was in charge of the garments (*m. Sheqalim* 5:1); he had a chamber designated for his use (*m. Middot* 1:4). We also learn that there were niches in which priests kept their garments when not participating in the service (*m. Tamid* 5:3). But in the

---

[7] For a recent discussion, see E. Regev, "Pure Individualism: The Idea of Non-Priestly Purity in Ancient Judaism," *JSJ* 31 (2000): 176–202. I think Regev's term for this purity is confusing, and I do not accept many aspects of his argument.

fictive world of *Aramaic Levi*, there is no room for Temple personnel whose task it is to keep the officiating priests in fresh garments. Thus, the best thing a priest can do is to take care not to get blood all over himself in the first place, and so Isaac urges Levi to avoid blood stains on his garment (53) and on himself (54–55).

Wood for the Altar

The Torah decrees arranging wood on the altar (Lev 1:7), but it is silent on the kind of the wood to be used and its qualities. Isaac's instructions (23–25) remedy that lack with a list of twelve trees suitable for use in the sacrifice because of their pleasant aroma. Isaac also cautions that the wood must be inspected for worms (22). As we shall see, a list of trees similar but not identical to that in *Aramaic Levi* appears also in *Jubilees* (21:12); the differences could reflect the vicissitudes of translation and transmission or changes in priestly practice over time. The passage in *Jubilees* places particular emphasis on the aroma of the trees. The passages in rabbinic literature that discuss the subject show some overlap with these lists, although they are much shorter; this is not surprising in texts written centuries after the Temple had ceased to function.[8]

Order of Sacrifice

One set of rules in *Aramaic Levi* that might be read as contradicting the laws of the Torah is Isaac's instructions to Levi about the order of the sacrifice (25–27).[9] Leviticus first commands the priests to dash the blood on the sides of the altar (1:5) and then to stoke the fire[10] and lay wood on the altar (1:7). According to Isaac, Levi is to dash blood on the altar as the fire begins to burn the wood he has laid there (25). From a practical point of view, there is much to recommend the order of *Aramaic Levi*, in which the wood was already laid on the altar and the fire burning adequately before the priest sprinkled the blood and arranged the parts of the animal on the altar. Although *Aramaic Levi* is explicit about the timing of these acts in relation

---

[8] For references to these texts and to secondary literature, see Kugler, *From Patriarch*, 104, n. 152.

[9] Kugler, *From Patriarch*, 105, sees "considerable differences" between the laws of the Torah and Isaac's instructions on the order of sacrifice.

[10] J. Milgrom, *Leviticus 1–16* (AB 3; New York, 1991), 157.

to each other, however, the Torah does not call for a particular order. It is possible that the order in which the commands appear is intended to be the order in which they are performed, but this is by no means evident.[11] So it is certainly not necessary to read Isaac's instructions as intended to contradict the order of the Torah. Indeed, the more practical order of *Aramaic Levi* might well reflect actual Temple practice.

Isaac goes on to decree the order for laying the parts of the offering on the altar:

> Let the head be offered up first, and cover it with fat, but do not let be seen upon it the blood of the slaughtered bull. After it its neck, and after its neck its forequarters, and after its forequarters the breast with the base of the rib, and after this the haunches with the spine of the loins, and after the haunches the hindquarters washed with the inner parts. (27–28)

Isaac's words designate the victim, a bull, but do not make explicit the type of sacrifice. The content of the instructions suggests that it is the *'olah*, the burnt offering. This is the first sacrifice to be discussed in the laws of Leviticus; it comes in three forms, "from the herd" (Lev 1:3–9), "from the flock" (Lev 1:10–13), and birds (Lev 1:14–17). For both cattle (herd) and sheep or goats (flock), Leviticus decrees cutting the sacrificial animal into sections (Lev 1:6, 12). As for cattle, the type of victim in the instructions in *Aramaic Levi*, Leviticus decrees the following arrangement:

> Aaron's sons, the priests, shall lay out the sections, the head and the suet,[12] on the wood that is on the fire upon the altar. Its entrails and legs shall be washed with water, and the priest shall turn the whole into smoke on the altar as a burnt offering. (Lev 1:8–9)[13]

Aramaic Levi offers more detail than Leviticus about the parts of the sacrificial animal. Leviticus refers to the "sections," but *Aramaic Levi* lists the remaining pieces of the bull, leaving nothing to chance.

When we turn to the order of laying out the parts of the sacrifice, we see once again that Leviticus offers an order only by implication, but *Aramaic Levi* makes one quite explicit. One piece of evidence against viewing the laws of Leviticus as dictating order when order is not explicit is the requirement

---

[11] Thus, Kugler is overstating the case when he writes, "Lev 1:5 requires sprinkling of blood *before* laying the fire in v. 7" (*From Patriarch*, 105).

[12] I adjust the translation of NJPS, "*with* the head and the suet," to make it more literal. The Hebrew is a list: the sections, the head, *and* the suet. RSV translates in the same spirit I do.

[13] All translations of biblical texts come from NJPS unless otherwise indicated.

that all sacrifices be salted. Not until it has commanded the salting of meal offerings does Leviticus add, "With all your offerings you must offer salt" (Lev 2:13). Thus, salting turns out to apply to the burnt offerings of Leviticus 1, but there is no retrospective indication of when in the process of sacrifice the salting is to take place. *Aramaic Levi* does not command salting at a particular moment, but it does refer to the pieces of the sacrifice to be placed on the altar as "salted" (26); an explicit command to salt the pieces comes only at the end of the list of parts of the sacrificial animal to be arranged on the altar: "And all of them salted with salt as is fitting for them, as much as they require" (29). Is this an echo of Leviticus' delayed command? The absence of language about order in Leviticus again means that it is possible that *Aramaic Levi*'s order represents actual priestly practice.

It is worth noting that *m. Tamid* also indicates the order in which the parts of the daily burnt offering, the *tamid*, were to be offered. This order differs considerably from that implied by Leviticus and stated by *Aramaic Levi*, although all three texts begin with the head. Like *Aramaic Levi*, the Mishnah provides a more detailed accounting of the parts of the sacrificial animal than Leviticus, but in keeping with its picture of the Temple as the bustling stage for highly complicated rituals requiring the carefully synchronized services of an elaborate priestly bureaucracy, it depicts a whole corps of priests participating in the offering of the *tamid* (*m. Tamid* 4:3, 7:3).

The *Minḥah* Accompanying Animal Sacrifices

To accompany the animal sacrifice he describes, Isaac decrees that Levi offer "the fine flour[14] mixed with oil, and after everything pour wine and burn over them frankincense" (30).[15] Until the mention of frankincense, Isaac's directions echo the Torah's rules for the meal offering, the *minḥah*, that is to accompany certain animal sacrifices (Numbers 15).[16] The priestly source requires frankincense as part of an uncooked *minḥah* that stands by itself

---

[14] Kugler, *From Patriarch*, translates "fine meal"; I prefer "flour" to be consistent with my previous translations. The term *nyšpˀ* is not the usual Aramaic equivalent for the biblical *solet*, fine flour, but it appears (in slightly different form) also in the phrase *swlt nyšpˀ* in the passage from the *Genesis Apocryphon* (10:16), as will be discussed (M. Morgenstern, E. Qimron, and D. Sivan, "The Hitherto Unpublished Columns of the Genesis Apocryphon," *Abr-Nahrain* 33 [1995]: 30–54; for discussion of this term, 35).

[15] Kugler translates *lbnh* (30) as "incense," but he translates *libanōtos* (45) and *libanos* (46) as "frankincense." It seems to me that *lbnh* should also be translated as "frankincense."

[16] Kugler, *From Patriarch*, 106, does not note this possible contradiction.

(Lev 2:1, 15), although not as part of a cooked *minḥah* (Lev 2:4, 5, 7).[17] But it does not mention frankincense when it describes the *minḥah* that accompanies animal sacrifices (Num 15:3–11). Does the omission in Numbers suggest that the priestly writers deemed the meat that formed the main part of the sacrifices described there adequate for providing the sweet smell, whereas the purely vegetal offering of Leviticus 2 required spice for achieving the requisite aroma? Or does the rule in Numbers assume the frankincense Leviticus has set out and thus feel no need to mention it?

For P, smell serves to play down the anthropomorphic understanding of God implicit in offering sacrifices: God does not eat or even taste the sacrifices, but partakes of the sacrifice only by means of an aspect of the sacrifice that is almost without physical reality. The recurrent references in Numbers 15 (vv. 7, 10, 14) to the *reiaḥ-niḥoaḥ* [pleasing odor] of the sacrifices could provide support for the view that the *minḥah* accompanying animal sacrifices should include frankincense despite the silence of Numbers 15.

Aramaic Levi appears to offer a harmonizing reading of the Torah that brings Numbers 15 in line with Leviticus 2. But it is possible that adding frankincense to the *minḥah* that accompanies the animal sacrifices was actually the practice, both before the codification of the Torah and after. Menahem Haran suggests that the use of the verb *qṭr* in the *hifʿil* for offering sacrifices, which he calls "especially characteristic" of P, as well as the term *reiaḥ-niḥoaḥ* itself, points to the possibility that priests added spices to animal and bird sacrifices despite the absence of a command to do so in the Torah.[18]

It is, of course, impossible to be certain that *Aramaic Levi* reflects Temple practice on this point because we do not know what Temple practice was. There is no indication in Isaac's rhetoric, however, that *Aramaic Levi* understands the practice it decrees as controversial. Furthermore, the practice is reflected in other texts of the Second Temple period. The *Temple Scroll* does not make any mention of such a practice,[19] but at this point, it may simply be following its biblical model. *Jubilees* offers several examples of such a practice, which I shall discuss in some detail. Here let me note that, according to

[17] Milgrom, *Leviticus*, 198–9, explains the difference as a concession to the poor who could not afford frankincense.

[18] M. Haran, *Temples and Temple Service in Ancient Israel*, repr. ed. (Winona Lake, Ind., 1985), 230–31.

[19] It is difficult to be certain because there are significant lacunae in the relevant passages in the *Temple Scroll* (cols. 13–14). Still, reconstruction of the text according to the Torah seems adequate.

the *Genesis Apocryphon*, which – unlike *Jubilees*, gives no indication of sectarian provenance – the *minḥah* that accompanies the sacrifice Noah offers on
emerging from the ark includes frankincense (10:16).[20]

Weights and Measures

A considerable portion of Isaac's speech concerns the amounts of wood,
salt, fine flour, oil, wine, and frankincense to accompany different sacrificial
animals (32–46). After the middle of the first verse, the passage is preserved
only in Greek and thus the units of measure are in Greek. The measures
of wood are given by weight in talents and minas (32–36). The measures of
frankincense are also given by weight, but in a smaller unit, the sheqel (45–
46). The unit in which the measures of salt, flour, oil, and wine are given is the
saton, Greek for Hebrew *se'ah*, a measure of volume that appears once in the
Torah, although not in the priestly document, and several times elsewhere
in the Bible (37–44).[21]

The Torah is just as silent about the proper amount of wood to lay upon the
altar as it is about the types of wood suitable for use, and it does not provide
measures for salt or frankincense. Thus, no direct comparison of *Aramaic Levi*
to the Torah on these points is possible. According to Isaac's instructions,
larger animals require larger amounts of wood, salt, and frankincense. A
correlation between the amount of the auxiliary materials and the size of
the animal being sacrificed is also evident in the Torah's instructions for the
minḥah that accompanies animal sacrifices (Num 15:3–11). It seems unlikely
that a decision about the proper amount of wood, salt, and frankincense for
various sacrifices was left to the judgment of individual priests, and, as far
as I can see, there is no reason why Isaac's instructions in *Aramaic Levi* could
not reflect standard Temple practice.

The Torah does provide measures for the fine flour and oil to be used in
the *minḥah* and the wine for the libation that accompany animal sacrifices.
In Numbers 15, the measure used for oil and wine is the *hin*, a measure of
volume for liquids. For the fine flour, the amount is given in tenths, although
the MT does not specify a unit of measure. But the instructions for the
minḥah (Num 28:5) in the opening passage in the list of festival offerings in

---

[20] For the text, Morgenstern, Qimron, and Sivan, "Genesis Apocryphon," 44. It appears that
the offering is explicitly designated *mnḥ'*, although the reading is not certain.

[21] Gen 18:6; 1 Sam 25:18; 1 Kgs 18:32; 2 Kgs 7:1, 16, 18.

Numbers 28–29 make it clear that it is the *ephah*, a measure of volume for solids, as the Septuagint indicates at Num 15:4.[22]

The measures for the meal offering and libation to accompany animal sacrifice according to the Torah (Numbers 15) are as follows:

Sacrificial Animal	Fine Flour	Oil	Wine
Sheep (vv. 4–5)	1/10 [*ephah*] (v. 4)	1/4 *hin* (v. 4)	1/4 *hin* (v. 5)
Ram (v. 6)	2/10 [*ephah*] (v. 6)	1/3 *hin* (v. 6)	1/3 *hin* (v. 7)
From the herd (vv. 8–9)	3/10 [*ephah*] (v. 9)	1/2 *hin* (v. 9)	1/2 *hin* (v. 10)

Aramaic Levi offers a somewhat different list of animals to be accompanied by a *minḥah*, but it is not difficult to see the correspondence between the categories in *Aramaic Levi* and those in the Torah. Both texts distinguish three size groupings, although *Aramaic Levi* lists the animals in descending order of size, in contrast to the Torah, which lists them in ascending order. Here in chart form are the measures from *Aramaic Levi*:

Sacrificial Animal	Fine Flour	Oil	Wine	Frankincense
Large bull, second bull, heifer (41)	1 *saton* (41)	1/4 *saton* (43)	=oil (44)	6 sheqels (45)
Ram, he-goat (42)	2 portions of a *saton* (42)	1/6 *saton* (44)	=oil (44)	3 sheqels [1/2 of 6 sheqels] (45)
Lamb, goat kid (42)	1/3 *saton* (42)	1/8 *saton* (44)	=oil (44)	2 sheqels [1/3 of 6 sheqels] (45)

The amount of fine flour for midsize animals, "two portions" of a *saton*, is meaningless. The text is preserved in a single manuscript, so there is no other reading to turn to; however, on the basis of its position in the list and the relations among other measures, I would guess that the correct measure is 1/2 *saton*.

---

[22] The book of Ezekiel orders different amounts in its sacrificial instructions: an *ephah* of flour and a *hin* of oil as accompaniments to animal sacrifices for Passover and Sukkot (45:23–25; cf. 46:11, in which the same measures are given for the prince's offering of bulls and rams, but in which there are no fixed amounts for his offering of sheep). For the daily offering, it decrees a sixth of an *ephah* of flour and a third of a *hin* of oil (46:13–14). As far as I can tell, these proportions have no influence on *Aramaic Levi*.

The most striking difference between the measures in *Aramaic Levi* and the Torah is that *Aramaic Levi* replaces the *ephah* and the *hin* with a single unit of measure, the *saton*, which it uses for both solids and liquids. As I already noted, the *se'ah*, the Hebrew translated by *saton*, appears several times in the Bible, although not in P. The relationship between the *saton* and the *ephah* is crucial for determining whether *Aramaic Levi* intends to expand on the rules of the Torah or to correct them. The Septuagint is not very helpful on this question. It usually translates *se'ah* with the generic *metron*, which it sometimes uses for *ephah* as well.[23]

At the conclusion of the passage of instructions about measures, *Aramaic Levi* offers several equivalences for the measures it uses, among them, "... a third of a *saton* is a third of an *ephah* ... " (46). If, in fact, it wishes to claim that the *ephah* and the *saton* are equivalent, *Aramaic Levi* differs from the Torah quite significantly. Its measures of fine flour would be about three times as large as those of Numbers. Yet, if its measures represented a purposeful rejection of the Torah's directions, one would expect some hint of this in its rhetoric. There is none. Furthermore, the text of *Aramaic Levi* raises questions. If the *saton* and the *ephah* are equivalent, why not say so directly? Why equate *one-third* of a *saton* with *one-third* of an *ephah*? A text that originally read, "A *saton* is one-third of an *ephah*," would provide an equivalence that brings *Aramaic Levi* and the Torah quite close, and it is not hard to imagine a scribal error that could introduce the extra "one-third" into such a text. Furthermore, scholars have sometimes suggested identifying the *se'ah* with the *shalish*, or "third" of Isa 40:12, which they take to be a third of an *ephah*.[24] Isaac's instructions to Levi perhaps provide further evidence for this identification.

On the assumption that *Aramaic Levi* understands a *saton* as one-third of an *ephah*, a comparison of the amounts of fine flour in *Aramaic Levi* and the Torah look like this:

Sacrificial Animal Size	Torah (Numbers 15) Fine Flour in *ephah* Measure	*Aramaic Levi* Fine Flour in *ephah* Measure (*saton* = 1/3 *ephah*)
Small	1/10 (0.1)	1/9 (0.11)
Medium	2/10 (0.2)	1/6 (0.167)
Large	3/10 (0.3)	1/3 (0.33)

[23] Deut 25:14; Ezek 45:10, 11, 13; 46:14; Zech 5:6–10.
[24] O. R. Sellers, "Weights and Measures," *IDB* (1962): 4.834–35.

If my suggestion for correcting the text of *Aramaic Levi* is accepted, the amounts it proposes are quite close to those of the Torah, especially for large and small animals.

Like the Torah, *Aramaic Levi* calls for equal amounts of oil and wine; indeed, it does not bother to provide measurements for the wine, but simply indicates that the wine should be equal to the oil. As we have seen, the Torah, unlike *Aramaic Levi*, uses different measures for its solid ingredient, fine flour, and its liquids, oil and wine. But if an *ephah* was roughly equivalent to 22 liters and a *hin* to 3.6 liters,[25] we can see that the ratios of fine flour to liquid in the Torah and *Aramaic Levi* are fairly similar:

Animal Size	Torah (Numbers 15) Flour/Liquid	*Aramaic Levi* Flour/Liquid
Large	3.67 : 1	4 : 1
Mid-size	3.67 : 1	3 : 1
Small	2.44 : 1	2.67 : 1

Again, the similarity points toward understanding *Aramaic Levi*'s measures not as an effort to correct the Torah, but rather as a different way of expressing the same measures. I have no explanation for why *Aramaic Levi* translates the measurements of the Torah into different terms. Further, I recognize that my effort to reduce disagreement on measures between *Aramaic Levi* and Numbers 15 is quite speculative. Still, although I would not want to place too much emphasis on the emendation I suggest, I do want to remind the reader that *Aramaic Levi* is attested at this point in only a single manuscript and that scholars have sometimes suggested on other grounds that a *se'ah* is one-third of an *ephah*. But I believe that the most important piece of evidence for *Aramaic Levi*'s basic agreement with the Torah is the absence of any indication that it understands its instructions as in conflict with anyone else's position.

The Law of the Priesthood and Sectarianism

It seems to me that this point holds true for the *Aramaic Levi*'s law of the priesthood as a whole. There are hints elsewhere in *Aramaic Levi* of at least one position that will come to be sectarian: adherence to a solar calendar

[25] Baruch Levine, *Numbers 1–20* (AB 4A; New York, 1993), 391.

(63–65).[26] Further, the protosectarian author of *Jubilees* and the sectarian author of the *Damascus Document* valued *Aramaic Levi* enough to use it, and it was preserved in several copies at Qumran. Despite these sectarian associations, however, as I have already argued at perhaps tedious length, there is no reason to understand *Aramaic Levi*'s rules for priests as sectarian. It is true that certainty on this point is beyond our grasp, not only because of the fragmentary state of *Aramaic Levi*, but also because we are so ill informed about Temple practice that it is impossible to say whether *Aramaic Levi*'s law of the priesthood deviates from it. And it is, of course, possible for a position to *become* sectarian, as adherence to the solar calendar did. Still, although it is not impossible that the practices Isaac passes on to Levi were later viewed as sectarian, as far as I can see there is no evidence from the later Second Temple period to suggest this. At the very least, the rhetoric of the law of the priesthood suggests that the author of *Aramaic Levi* did not understand the instructions as opposing the practices of others, with the significant exception of his prohibition of certain kinds of marriages.

Jubilees' Adaptation of the Law of the Priesthood

One central concern of the *Book of Jubilees* is to demonstrate that many of the laws of the Torah were in practice before the giving of the Torah. Thus, it describes the establishment of various festivals and sacrifices in the period of the patriarchs. Festivals and sacrifices require priests, and for *Jubilees*, Adam, the first man, was also the first priest (3:27). Priesthood then passes to Enoch, Noah, Abraham, Isaac, and Jacob, before Levi's ordination (32:3).

Jubilees places its adaptation of *Aramaic Levi*'s law of the priesthood in Abraham's mouth as part of his exhortation to Isaac before his death (*Jubilees* 21).[27] It is noteworthy that *Jubilees* makes Abraham the authority for priestly behavior, as in *Jubilees'* account he stands at the beginning of the hereditary

---

[26] Kugler, *From Patriarch*, 116; J. Greenfield and M. E. Stone, "Some Remarks on the Aramaic Testament of Levi from the Geniza," *RB* 86 (1979) 224–25; Stone, "Enoch, Aramaic Levi," 159–60, n. 2, 168–70.

[27] I understand *Jubilees* as drawing on and reworking *Aramaic Levi*. See my comment in n. 2. For a more extended discussion, see C. Werman, "Levi and Levites in the Second Temple Period," *DSD* 4 (1997): 220–1; the law of the priesthood figures prominently in Werman's discussion, but she considers other points as well. Stone also argues for direct dependence of *Jubilees* on *Aramaic Levi* ("Enoch, Aramaic Levi," 159–60, n. 2; 170). See Kugler, *From Patriarch*, 146–7, for a brief discussion of the views of scholars who argue against direct dependence in favor

priestly line that leads to Levi. For *Jubilees* what is significant about Levi is not that he is the founder of the priesthood, which he is not, but rather that he is the first priest to hold the office of priest in a generation in which there are other possible claimants.[28] *Aramaic Levi*, of course, glorifies Levi as the founder of the priestly line, yet even there Isaac's role as Levi's instructor implies that Levi is by no means the first priest for it requires that Isaac himself be a priest. This strongly suggests that in the background of *Aramaic Levi*'s exaltation of Levi stood a view of the history of the priesthood not unlike *Jubilees*'.

Both the opening of Abraham's speech (*Jub.* 21:2–5) and the conclusion (*Jub.* 21:21–25) preach righteousness of a kind relevant to those descendants of Abraham in future generations who will not serve as priests. It is the instructions for sacrifice in the central portion of the speech (*Jub.* 21:7–17) that draw on *Aramaic Levi*'s law of the priesthood. The speech has been composed quite carefully. Rules involving blood, the cultic substance *par excellence*, in contexts relevant to nonpriests (*Jub.* 21:6, 18–20) serve as transitions between the exhortations to righteousness at the beginning and the end of the speech and the cultic material in the middle. It is worth noting that the prohibition on eating blood (*Jub.* 21:6, 18) echoes a similar prohibition at the end of the law of the priesthood in *Aramaic Levi* (56).

All the topics of the section of Abraham's speech concerned with the cult appear in *Aramaic Levi*: procedure for sacrifice (*Jub.* 21:7–11, parallel to *Ar. Levi* 27–30), wood for the offering (*Jub.* 21:12–15, parallel to *Ar. Levi* 22–25), and washing and avoidance of blood on one's garments (*Jub.* 21:16–17, parallel to *Ar. Levi* 19–21, 26, 53–54). *Jubilees*' version of the instructions is smoother than *Aramaic Levi*'s, and it has eliminated the somewhat confusing repetition at the end of *Aramaic Levi*'s instructions. *Jubilees* also stays closer to the text of the Torah than does *Aramaic Levi*. For example, unlike *Aramaic Levi*, *Jubilees* specifies the type of sacrifice with which its instructions are concerned, the peace offering (Leviticus 3; 7), and it uses language that recalls the Torah's description of this sacrifice (Lev 3:11): "the food of the offering to the Lord" (*Jub.* 21:9).[29]

of a common source, and 147–55 for a defense of this position based on the relationship of *Jub.* 30:1–32:9 to *Aramaic Levi*.

[28] In my view, *Jubilees* plays down Levi's role as priest (M. Himmelfarb, "'A Kingdom of Priests': The Democratization of the Priesthood in the Literature of Second Temple Judaism," *Journal of Jewish Thought and Philosophy* 6 [1997]: 91–2).

[29] All translations of *Jubilees* are taken from J. C. VanderKam, *The Book of Jubilees* (CSCO 511; Louvain, 1989). See also his note to *Jub.* 21:9.

Frankincense and the *Minḥah*

The Torah distinguishes two kinds of peace offerings, one of thanksgiving, the other votive or freewill, with somewhat different rules for each (Lev 7:11–18). The passage in question describes the *minḥah* of the thanksgiving peace offering, four different varieties of cakes or wafers, in some detail, but it does not specify the nature of the *minḥah* to accompany the votive and freewill peace offerings. It also provides different limits for the time during which the sacrificial meat may be consumed: the day of the sacrifice only for the thanksgiving offering, that day and the next day for the votive and freewill offerings (Lev 7:15–17). The peace offering *Jubilees* has in mind must be the votive or freewill version because Abraham tells Isaac that it can be eaten until the third day (*Jub.* 21:10). This identification explains the *minḥah* that *Jubilees* requires: fine flour mixed with oil (21:7). This is the *minḥah* that accompanies animal sacrifices according to Numbers 15, which does not specify that the sacrifices in question include peace offerings, but does identify them as votive or freewill offerings.

Abraham's speech places great emphasis on aroma, including the aroma of the wood to be used on the altar (*Jub.* 21:13–14), a characteristic *Aramaic Levi* mentions but does not emphasize (23). Yet, in keeping with the Torah, Abraham does not mention frankincense as part of the *minḥah* to accompany the votive peace offering:

> If you slaughter a victim for a peace offering that is acceptable, slaughter it and pour their blood onto the altar. All the fat of the sacrifice you will offer on the altar with the finest flour; and the offering kneaded with oil, with its libation – you will offer it all together on the altar as a sacrifice. [It is] an aroma that is pleasing before the Lord. As you place the fat of the peace offering on the fire which is on the altar, so also *remove* the fat.... All of this you will offer as a pleasant fragrance which is acceptable before the Lord, with its sacrifice and its libation as a pleasant fragrance – the food of the offering to the Lord. (*Jub.* 21:7–9)

Despite the absence of frankincense in the *minḥah* in Abraham's instructions to Isaac, frankincense forms part of all but one of the sacrifices *Jubilees* details.[30] Noah adds frankincense to the sacrifices he offers on emerging

---

[30] The sacrifice in which frankincense is missing is *Jubilees'* version of the covenant between the pieces (Genesis 15; *Jub.* 14:1–20). *Jubilees* transforms the covenant ceremony of passing between the severed pieces of the animals, which it must have found exceedingly strange, into

from the ark (*Jub.* 6:3), as in the *Genesis Apocryphon*, and in celebration of the new wine (*Jub.* 7:4–5). In the first sacrifice, Noah puts frankincense not on the *minḥah* but on everything; in the second, the frankincense seems to be almost a separate sacrifice:

> Then [Noah] took a bull, a ram, a sheep, goats, salt, a turtledove, and a dove and offered (them as) a burnt offering on the altar. He poured on them an offering mixed with oil, sprinkled wine, and put frankincense on everything. He sent up a pleasant fragrance that was pleasing before the Lord. (*Jub.* 6:3)

> [Noah] offered all their meat on the altar. On it he placed their entire sacrifice mixed with oil. Afterwards he sprinkled wine in the fire that had been on the altar beforehand. He put frankincense on the altar and offered a pleasant fragrance that was pleasing before the Lord his God. (*Jub.* 7:4–5)

Abraham adds frankincense to his sacrifice for the feast of the first fruits of the wheat harvest. As in Noah's sacrifice on emerging from the ark, the frankincense is added to the sacrifice as a whole, not to the *minḥah* in particular.

> [Abraham] offered as a new sacrifice on the altar the first fruits of the food for the Lord – a bull, a ram and a sheep; (he offered them) on the altar as a sacrifice to the Lord together with their (cereal) offerings and their libations. He offered everything on the altar with frankincense. (*Jub.* 15:2)

Jacob adds frankincense to the sacrifices he offers for the feast of booths. In this sacrifice, the existence of the *minḥah* is questionable, and as in Noah's sacrifice on the festival of new wine, the incense appears to be a separate sacrifice:

> On the fifteenth of this month [Jacob] brought to the altar 14 young bulls from the cattle, 28 rams, 49 sheep, 7 kids, and 21 goats – as a burnt offering on the altar and as a pleasing offering for a pleasant aroma before God. This was his gift because of the vow which he had made that he would give a tithe along with their sacrifices and their libations. When the fire had consumed it, he would burn frankincense[31] on the fire above it; and as a peace offering two young bulls, four rams, four sheep, four he-goats, two year-old sheep, and two goats. (*Jub.* 32:4–6)

a sacrifice, even adding a *minḥah* and a libation of wine (*Jub.* 14:9), but it does not mention frankincense.

[31] VanderKam, *Jubilees*: "incense." The Ethiopic word here is *sᵉhna*, the same word VanderKam translates as "frankincense" in the passages just discussed. I would like to thank Annette Reed for checking the Ethiopic of these passages for me.

The Incense Offering

To make sense of the status of frankincense in the descriptions of sacrifices just quoted, it is helpful to consider *Jubilees'* interest in the incense offering. The Torah decrees that Aaron was to offer *qetoret sammim* ("aromatic incense") twice daily, morning and evening, on a special altar for the purpose (Exod 30:7–8). *Jubilees* clearly views this twice-daily ritual as of great importance. It claims that morning incense was the first sacrifice ever offered – by Adam as he left the Garden of Eden (3:27).[32] The evening incense offering, according to *Jubilees*, goes back to Enoch (4:25). Not only does *Jubilees* note the establishment of the incense offerings, but it also mentions Abraham's incense offerings during his observance of the feast of booths (16:24).[33]

Jubilees further stresses the importance of incense in its Sabbath laws at the end of the book:

> For great is the honor which the Lord has given Israel to eat, drink, and be filled on this festal day; and to rest on it from any work that belongs to the work of mankind except to burn incense and to bring before the Lord offerings and sacrifices for the days and the Sabbaths. (*Jub.* 50:10)

It is striking that burning incense is not simply included in the larger category of sacrifice, but rather is treated as a category in its own right. Indeed, it receives special emphasis as the first category of activity that must be specially authorized for the Sabbath. It is also worth noting that God's commands about Sabbath observance at the conclusion of creation are said "to rise as a fine fragrance which is acceptable in his presence for all times" (2:22).

We have seen that the Torah does not mention frankincense as part of the *minhah* accompanying animal sacrifices. But we have also seen some evidence to suggest that priests in the Temple did add frankincense to the *minhah*. The rather loose relationship between the *minhah* and frankincense in *Jubilees'* descriptions of sacrifice appears to reflect both the practice of adding frankincense to the *minhah* attached to the animal sacrifice under the influence

---

[32] It reports the four components of Adam's incense as "frankincense, galbanum, stacte, and aromatic spices." This list presumably echoes the Torah's list of spices for incense, stacte, onycha, galbanum, and frankincense (Exod 30:34); the difference may well be the result of the vicissitudes of translation.

[33] The seven "fragrant substances: frankincense, galbanum, stacte, nard, myrrh, aromatic spices, and costum," include the four Adam offered; perhaps the theory is that more is better. *Jubilees'* description of the spices as "beaten, equally mixed, pure" (*Jub.* 16:24) appears to echo Exodus, "expertly blended, refined, pure, sacred" (Exod 30:35).

of the freestanding *minḥah* and *Jubilees'* taste for incense offerings, so that the frankincense is sometimes described as if it were a separate offering.

Incense and the Heavenly Temple

Why are the incense offering and the aroma of sacrifices so important to *Jubilees*? Perhaps it is because aroma plays so prominent a role in descriptions of the liturgy of the heavenly Temple from the centuries around the turn of the era. The heavenly cult presents certain obvious difficulties. Even for people who saw sacrifice as an essential mode of connection between God and humanity, it must have been hard to imagine the blood and fat of animals on a heavenly altar. Although a few texts refer explicitly to sacrifice in heaven, I do not know of any that mentions animals, blood, or fat. The least problematic aspect of sacrifice from this point of view, the most ethereal and suitable to heaven, was its aroma, the pleasing smell to which the priestly source of the Torah refers so often. For the same reason, the offering of incense seems more appropriate to heaven than does animal sacrifice. Thus, the opening of the last of the *Songs of the Sabbath Sacrifice* mentions "the sacrifices of the holy ones," "the odor of their offerings," and "the odor of their drink offerings" (11QShirShabb 8–7, lines 2–3). In the Book of Revelation, at the opening of the seventh seal, an angel offers up incense together with the prayers of the saints (Rev 8:3–4). The *Testament of Levi* imagines angels in the sixth heaven offering "a pleasant odor, a reasonable and bloodless offering" (*T. Levi* 3:6).[34]

Jubilees never mentions a heavenly Temple explicitly, but its claim that the Sabbath (2:18) and the Feast of Weeks (6:18) are celebrated in heaven may imply a heavenly Temple because on earth both Sabbath and feast require sacrifices. Indeed, after noting that the Feast of Weeks was observed in heaven before it was observed on earth, *Jubilees* goes on to ordain sacrifices for the Israelites' observance of the feast (6:22). Finally, Isaac's blessing of Levi depicts priests on earth as counterparts of the angelic priests in heaven: "May he make you and your descendants (alone) out of all humanity approach him / to serve in his Temple like the angels of the presence and like the holy ones" (31:14).

Ancient Jews understood the Jerusalem Temple as modeled on the heavenly Temple. Modern scholars are inclined to reverse the relationship and to view the heavenly Temple and its rituals as reflecting the earthly Temple

[34] M. Himmelfarb, *Ascent to Heaven in Jewish and Christian Apocalypses* (New York, 1993), 33–6.

and its practices. Yet, *Jubilees* provides an example of an effort to make the cult on earth more like the cult in heaven through its stress on aroma and incense. *Jubilees*, then, is an instance in which both ancient Jews and modern scholars are correct. The picture of the heavenly Temple is indeed formed by the rituals of the earthly Temple, but once sacrifice has been adapted to its new location, the adaptation exerts its influence on the depiction of sacrificial practice on earth.

7

Who's on the Throne? Revelation in the Long Year

John W. Marshall

When Vespasian had "pacified" Galilee and the Judaean environs of Jerusalem – razing villages, enslaving inhabitants and survivors, and killing combatants and the unserviceable elderly[1] – and surrounded the holy city of Jerusalem, word came that Nero had died and that Servius Galba had been raised to the imperial purple. Vespasian sent his son Titus westward to greet the new ruler. But while Titus crossed the isthmus at Corinth on his way to the capitol, news came that Galba had fallen, Otho was now hailed by Senate and people as emperor, and Vitellius was leading the German legions in arms against Otho. Tacitus put Titus's dilemma pithily:

> If he should go on to Rome, he would enjoy no gratitude for an act of courtesy intended for another emperor, and he would be a hostage in the hands of either Vitellius or Otho; on the other hand, if he returned to his father, the victor would undoubtedly feel offence; yet, if his father joined the victor's party, while victory was still uncertain, the son would be excused; but, if Vespasian should assume the imperial office, his rivals would be concerned with war and have to forget offences. (*Hist.* 2.1)

"If ... on the other hand ... yet ... but ... ": Titus's need for knowledge outstripped the information available to him through the usual channels of rumor and rumination and, according to Tacitus, Titus sought divine guidance in the sanctuary of Paphian Venus on Cyprus. The question on Titus's mind, a question that would determine his course of action and indeed the course of his life, concerned the imperial succession: Who would rule the Empire? With supportive omens and favorable entrails left behind him, he

---

[1] In *J.W.* 3.540, Josephus describes the execution of 1,200 noncombatants and 36,000 consigned to slavery. By 6.420, he tabulates a total of 97,000 captives and claims that 1.1 million perished in the siege of Jerusalem. No matter what compensations are made in the hope of correcting any exaggeration on Josephus's part, the Judaean War stands as unambiguously brutal – a crisis in the course of any ethnicity or religion.

struck out to Syria to support his father's bid for the imperial office (see Tacitus, *Hist.* 2.2–4).

While Titus coasted along Achaia and Asia at sea, a Jew named John worried on land – probably in Ephesus – over the same question: Who would rule? Perhaps more accurately, it should be said that he worried about how the truth of which he was convinced would actually come about. How would the God of Israel and his appointed and anointed Lamb exert God's power as Lord of the universe, vindicate God's people, and bring the nations into his kingdom? John looked out at the same circumstances as did Titus: Vespasian's army surrounding the holy city on one hand, chaos and civil war in Italy on the other. John's Revelation addresses the same question that Titus posed to the priests of the Paphian Venus.

Although the understanding that events and structures on earth stand as reflections of more basic and more real events in heaven is particularly vivid in Jewish and Christian apocalyptic literature, it is also characteristic of Graeco-Roman understandings of rulership. In the political events of the "long year," 69 C.E., we see both Roman historians and Jewish visionaries working from the principle "on earth as it is in heaven" as they strive to explain their world and to justify their judgments of the past and their hopes for the future.

The book of Revelation is commonly studied within an interpretive framework that focuses primarily or even exclusively on an exigency arising in a Christian context, such as persecution, perceived persecution, self-definition in relation to and in distinction from Judaism, and rivalry among Christian prophets. Revelation is also studied, nearly ubiquitously, under the assumption that it may be unproblematically understood as a *Christian* document, with all the attendant preunderstandings that the term "Christianity" gathers. I have argued against these conditions of interpretation and suggested that Revelation is properly interpreted as a Jewish document responding to the questions that pressed on Diaspora Jews during the Judaean War of 66–70 C.E.,[2] in one mode, and that in another mode pressed on any inhabitant of the Empire with an interest in the imperial succession.

---

[2] Concerning the dating that this provenance for Revelation implies, see my more extensive argument in *Parables of War: Reading John's Jewish Apocalypse* (Waterloo, Ont., 2001), esp. 88–97. For a date of around the year 70 C.E., see also J. C. Wilson, "The Problem of the Domitianic Date of Revelation," *NTS* 39 (1993): 587–605; C. Rowland, *The Open Heaven: A Study of Apocalyptic in Judaism and Early Christianity* (London, 1982), 403–12. A later Domitianic date commands somewhat wider support; see A. Y. Collins, *Crisis and Catharsis: The Power of the Apocalypse*

Naming Revelation as a Jewish text does not serve to insulate it from the Graeco-Roman world, but names the location from which John engages that world (even by calling for disengagement from it). To be sure, there is much in John's apocalypse that is essentially an "inner-Jewish" conversation, especially its extensive intertextuality with materials from the Hebrew Bible. This does not prevent it from participating, albeit in a mode substantially based in John's Jewish heritage, in a speculative conversation concerning the nature and future of world rulership that shares several of its motifs and structures with the wider Graeco-Roman world.

My argument for a shared discourse among John and certain Graeco-Roman historians is undertaken through juxtaposition, allowing fragments of these historians to stand puzzling beside John as both scrutinize the heavens, hoping for a sign that will clarify the chaos according to their convictions. Their texts stand as intertexts and interpretants[3] for John's. While Jewish apocalyptic literature may be one of the most elaborately developed threads of this shared discourse, John's activities in the realm of Jewish apocalyptic literature share with Greek and Roman historians important understandings of the relation between heavenly phenomena and earthly rule. This sharing does not involve a claim that specific portents or signs related by later historians were specifically known in Asia Minor, but only that dispositions to regard the heavens as a source of knowledge about the dynamics of rule on earth were common across the lines that we are accustomed to drawing between religions. Although working at cross purposes during the Judaean War and the events of the long year, John and his pagan counterparts share in a discourse that examines the heavens to answer a question that traditional avenues of inquiry seemed, at least in the crucible of those tumultuous times, increasingly unable to address: Who is really on the throne?

(Philadelphia, 1984), 54–83; G. K. Beale, *The Book of Revelation: A Commentary on the Greek Text* (Grand Rapids, 1999). D. Aune creates a complex source-critical hypothesis that results in multiple dates of composition and redaction, ranging from Nero to Trajan (*Revelation*, 2 vols. [Dallas, Tex., 1997–8]).

3 J. Deely, *Basics of Semiotics* (Bloomington, Ind., 1990), 26, describes an interpretant thus: "whether a given interpretant be an idea or not, what is essential to it as interpretant is that it be the ground upon which the sign is seen as related to something else as signified." Thus, I am proposing that the Graeco-Roman historians stand as a context for interpreting John's own text and enabling readers to see them both pointing to a shared discourse in antiquity. As I use it here, the "interpretant" functions in a manner similar to the more widespread notion of "intertextuality." See J. Kristeva, *Revolution in Poetic Language*, trans. M. Waller (New York, 1984), 59–61.

SIGNS OF POWER

And a great portent appeared in heaven, a woman clothed with the sun, with the moon under her feet, and on her head a crown of twelve stars ... she brought forth a male child, one who is to rule all the nations with a rod of iron, but her child was caught up to God and to his throne. (Rev 12:1, 5)	The astrologers also – a tribe of men untrustworthy for the powerful, deceitful for the ambitious, a tribe which in our state will always be both forbidden and retained – they also urged him [Otho] on, declaring from their observations of the stars that the year would be a glorious one for Otho. (Tacitus, *Hist.* 1.22)

At the end of the long year, neither Otho nor Jesus exercised rule over the nations. Otho had committed suicide at Brixellum (Tacitus, *Hist.* 2.33, 39, 46–49), and Jesus had not returned on the earth or on the clouds. John bided his time in Asia, confident that what he saw in the heavens would prove a guide to events on the earth. The supporters of Vespasian, too, assured themselves that the omens of his reign were trustworthy, that he would hold the office that three men had been unable to hold for even a year, and that his son Titus would complete the work that he had begun in Judaea. Vespasian's supporters were correct, although, as Tacitus wryly notes, such oracles could be believed only after they had been accomplished.[4] With no such hindsight available at the time, the tumultuous long year is littered with portents, prodigies, visions, and omens. John's vision is the most well known, but Roman historians of the period also have a long list of enigmatic indicators of who would take, and hold, the office of emperor. Both John and his Roman counterparts testify to the intensity with which, in the chaos that flooded the Empire in that year, its residents scanned the heavens for signs of who would hold earthly power.

Preliminary Discussions of Kingdom

In John's apocalypse, the theme of rulership starts in the combination of literary forms that John deploys in Rev 1:4–6 with a threefold claim: that the source of John's revelation is the one on the eternal and heavenly throne ("he who is and who was and who is to come"), that the one whom John reveals is "the ruler over the kings of the earth" [ὁ ἄρχων τῶν βασιλέων τῆς γῆς], and that the community of those devoted to him are themselves a true

---

[4] Tacitus, *Hist.* 1.11: "The secrets of Fate and the signs and oracles which predestined Vespasian and his sons for power, we believed only after his success was secured."

kingdom (1:6, cf. 1:9), priests to the true God. The self-identification of God that follows – "'I am the Alpha and the Omega,' says the Lord God, who is and who was and who is to come, the Almighty" (1:8) – clinches the claim that this section is about power in all its particulars: the locus of authority and the duration of rule. The discussion of who is the ultimate ruler (God), who are the ruled (those who claim rulership on earth), and who constitutes citizens of the realm (John's coreligionists) stands at the front of John's discourse and remains in the center of the stage throughout.

The vision/audition that follows the narrative of Patmos offers an impressive description of the "one like a son of man" – robes, girdle, sword, shining face, and hair (Rev 1:12–16) – and provokes the action of obeisance that the ruler of the universe should expect, complete prostration: "I fell at his feet as though dead" (1:17). The allusion to Daniel, however, draws in an intertext that intensifies the rulership theme. Dan 7:13 describes the entrance of "one like a son of man" onto a scene of judgment in which the Ancient of Days subjugates a sequence of worldly kingdoms, symbolized by the beasts of Dan 7:1–8. The kingship won from the beasts is given to the "one like a son of man":

> And to him was given dominion and glory and kingdom, that all peoples, nations, and languages should serve him; his dominion is an everlasting dominion that shall not pass away, and his kingdom is one that shall not be destroyed (Dan 7:14).

Drawing on Daniel's discourse of divine empire, John's introduction lays out his question: Who will rule?

The messages to the seven assemblies are the words of the viceroy of the Almighty, the παντοκράτωρ, to the local assemblies of his people. In a time when edicts, oaths, and rumors concerning who was really in charge sprouted from Rome with disturbing frequency and consistently arose from murder, battle, or suicide, the messages to the seven assemblies were affirmations of the stability of an order led by one who has been in charge since "the beginning of God's creation" – and who, in fact, *is* that beginning (Rev 3:14).

The promise in the first message, to an angel of the assembly at Ephesus, is that they who conquer shall wear a crown (Rev 3:10). The set of messages is bracketed with royal promises, and the final message (to Laodicea) also makes a royal promise: "He who conquers, I will grant him to sit with me on my throne, just as I myself conquered and sat down with my Father on his throne" (3:21). Here, shared rule is not a strategy pursued among the height of the elite to avoid being deposed – compare Otho's repeated and seeming embarrassingly public overtures to Vitellius that they rule jointly[5] – but a substantial element of the promise that Revelation makes. Its readers will be a kingdom as well as kings. The middle message, as well, to Thyatira, holds up the royal promise in the midst of the heavenly messages: "He who conquers . . . I will give him power of the nations" (2:26). The opposite side of the rulership analysis is the ruler systems of pagan society. John's view is clear in the messages in 2:13: "I know where you dwell, where Satan's throne is." There is no need to link the messages to the particular cities. What ties all the messages together and specifically to elements of the political struggles of the long year is the repeated urge to "conquer," which in that year was the goal to which leaders of the various factions were also inspiring their true-believing followers: in Italy on either side of the Alps, in Judaea on either side of the walls of Jerusalem, and in Asia as John communicated on behalf of his would-be warrior–sovereign.

The Throne Vision

After the messages/proclamations to the assemblies, there is a slight slip out of the visionary narrative state established in Rev 1:10, or at least a reference to the consciousness of being ἐν πνεύματι, but the voice that pulled John into the spirit the first time calls him again, and he ascends to the heavenly throne room (4.1–2). Before any specific Temple imagery, the account emphasizes the royal aspect of the vision that occupies Revelation 4–5. It continues with a description of the heavenly throne room, the attendant council of elders (crowned and on thrones themselves), and the praise they

Thus Galba was declared emperor, just as Tiberius had foretold when he said to him that he should have a taste of the sovereignty. The event was likewise told by unmistakable omens. For it seemed to him in a vision that Fortune told him that she had now remained with him for a long time, yet no one would grant her admission to his house, and that, if she should be barred out much longer, she would take up her abode with somebody else. (Dio Cassius, *Hist.* 34.2)

offer the one on the throne. The imagery of worship enters the scene most closely with the description of the four beasts that modulate the throne/heaven/Temple vision of Ezekiel and their ascription of the praise of Isa 6:3 to the one seated on the throne.

[5] Suetonius, *Otho* 8; Dio Cassius, *Hist.* 64.10.

Two elements deserve note in an effort to situate Revelation in the context of the struggles for rulership that characterized the period of the civil wars after Nero: The motifs of victory, kingdom, and priesthood are continued from the prior sections of Revelation, and the qualities ascribed to the one on the throne in the songs of praise are precisely those qualities that combined in strong candidates for the imperial office

> Having in this way through the favor of three emperors been honored not only with political positions but distinguished priesthoods as well, he [Vitellius] afterwards governed Africa as proconsul. (Suetonius, *Vit.* 5)

as well. Rev 5:5 introduces the messianic center of Revelation as cosmic conqueror and the heir of Israel's political patriarch Judah and exemplary ruler David. The praise to the Lamb in 5:10 makes a twofold claim of what he has done: (1) gathering – buying, in fact – people from every tribe, tongue, people, and nation, and (2) making them into a kingdom of priests who shall exercise kingship over the earth. The first claim competes directly with the prerogatives of the world-ruling empire,[6] but the second constitutes an attack on Rome by suggesting that all the subjects shall be kings and shall be the rulers rather than the ruled.

The antiphonal songs of praise that span Revelation 4–5 ascribe to the one on the throne and his Lamb glory, honor, power, wealth, wisdom, vigor (ἰσχύς), praise, and might. These are the powers that accompany kingship as qualifications or benefits. P. Touilleux argues that the hymns in Revelation mirror the hymns composed in honor of Roman emperors.[7] John has not created his hymnic texts in a vacuum; the speculation concerning succession that preoccupied the subjects of the empire in 69 C.E. and the speculation concerning the results of the Judaean War that preoccupied Jews at the same time are the context that give his hymnic texts and his throne vision a direct relevance that praise in the abstract cannot.

Seals, Trumpets, Thunders

The drama of the opening of the seven seals that governs Rev 6:1–8:5 falls into two parts: the first four seals in which the four horsemen are released to work their malevolence on the earth indiscriminately, and the final three

---

6   The "tribes, tongue, peoples, and nations" phrase is a development of similar phrasing in the book of Daniel, in which it is the language of Babylonian imperial proclamations (3:7, 21; 4.1; 6:25) and is claimed for the God of Israel by Daniel (5:18–19) and for the "one like a son of man" (7:14).
7   P. Touilleux, *L'Apocalypse et les cultes de Domitien et de Cybèle* (Paris, 1935), 100–3.

seals that selectively preserve the people of God and punish the enemies of God. The primary attributes of the horsemen are their martial ambitions: The first wears a crown and conquers (6:2), the second provokes war among men and removes peace from the earth with a great sword (6:3), and the third comes forth with a balance in his hand while a "voice from the midst of the four creatures" announces the exorbitant prices that accompany war (6:5–6).[8] The fourth rider is given *potestas* (δύναμις, "power") over a fourth of the earth and kills wantonly (6:7–8).

It is common to interpret these horsemen in the most general sense. Aune's summary is representative: "The first cavalier primarily represents warfare, and each of the three following cavaliers represents one of the stereotypical evils of war: sword, famine, plague."[9] Although Aune describes all of Revelation 6 as John's "First Edition" of his apocalypse compiled about 70 C.E. and having "the events leading up to and following the first Jewish revolt (A.D. 66–73)" as its *Sitz im Leben*, his interpretation of 6:1–8 does not make any direct connection to that context. Here, I think that the customary practice of viewing Revelation as a Christian document creates an unwarranted and highly problematic reading of the text. Whether this problem results from dogmatic concerns, or merely from the conditions that this interpretive category forces on the document, reading Revelation as a Christian document distracts scholars from noting the connections between John's portrayal of conquering horsemen and the events and turmoil of the long year. Thus, an overly general reconstruction of the exigency of the document is not merely the product of sober historical–critical caution, but may actually serve the requirements of theological interpretations, often grounded in the conviction that "timeless truth" will necessarily be found in canonical documents.

On the contrary, in the year 69 C.E., the Judaean War seemed to await its climax, while shocking news of the civil war in Italy and of the bloody procession of emperors, pretenders, claimants, and successors coursed through the rumor mills of the Empire; this is crucial to the interpretation of the

---

[8] On the wheat, barley, oil, and wine oracle, see David Aune, *Revelation*, 1:316 and S. Krauss, "Die Schonung von Öl und Wein in der Apokalypse," *ZNW* 10 (1909): 81–9.

[9] Aune, *Revelation*, 2:395. The exception to this sort of generalizing interpretation is the readings of Rev 6.6b that attempt to make a strong connection with the edict attributed to Domitian first in Suetonius, *Domitian* 7.2, curtailing viticulture in favor of grain production. Aune treats the history of this interpretation and notes the manifold difficulties in (1) reliably attributing the decree and its implementation to Domitian, (2) reading it as relevant to writers in Asia Minor, and (3) resolving the several inconsistencies between the decree attributed to Domitian and the oracle of Rev 6:6b (*Revelation*, 2:398–400).

horsemen. There is no way to avoid consideration of the narrative of four crowned conquerors stealing peace from the earth and scattering devastation and war in their wake. The second rider spreads war among men, just as Otho brought assassination and civil war into the forefront of the succession procedure for the first time since Augustus had established the *Pax Romana*. The third rider holds the scales, an emblem of Libra, the sign under which the third emperor of 69 C.E., Aulus Vitellius, was perhaps born.[10] The fourth rider is more horrible for several reasons: the increasing intensity narratively demanded of a cycle such as that of the seven seals, the degeneration of a sequence of four kingdoms necessitated by the widespread trope of ancient world histories reworked here on a microscale for the aftermath of Nero, the particular animus that John would obviously have against Vespasian who prosecuted the brutal suppression of the Judaean Revolt and who remained in charge (either directly or through his son Titus) of the Roman army that surrounded the holy city of John's God. John weaves together narrative resources from the ancient world, from the history and scriptures of Judaism, and from the concrete situation that his readers face and his text addresses.

Interpreting the first four seals in relation to the succession of four emperors changes the signification of the latter three seals. The fifth seal looks specifically to the heavens to inquire into how the succession of violence on the earth will be broken, to ask, in the words of the souls of the martyrs dwelling beneath the altar of the heavenly Temple, "How long, O Sovereign holy and true, until you will judge and avenge our blood upon those who dwell on the earth?" (6:10). The answer is "Not long." The sixth seal begins the process of vengeance, and the heavens proclaim the catastrophe that will befall "the kings of the earth and the great men and the generals and the rich and the strong and every one, both slave and free" (6:15). The punishments in this case rain down from the heavens: "There was a great earthquake; and the sun became black as sackcloth, the full moon became like blood, and the stars of the sky fell to the earth as the fig tree sheds its winter fruit when shaken by a gale" (6:12–13). This is the vengeance that many Diaspora Jews would surely imagine while

> The great confusion which under these conditions prevailed in the camp of Vitellius was increased that night by an eclipse of the moon . . . it appeared both blood colored and black and gave out still other terrifying colors. (Dio Cassius, *Hist.* 44.11.1)

---

[10] Suetonius, *Vit.* 3.2, gives two possible birthdates for Vitellius (September 7 or 24), only the latter of which falls within the sign of Libra.

Roman troops lay siege to the holy city – the vengeance that they sought in reading the heavens and that they were convinced that their enemies would see in the heavens when the time came.

Following the seventh, sabbatical, seal, the seven trumpets recapitulate the structure and action of the seven seals. The first four trumpets are incidents and omens of destruction on a cosmic scale. Subsequent destruction is specific to those who do not have the seal of God on their foreheads. The fifth and sixth trumpets describe the catastrophes in direct military language. The locusts of the fifth trumpet are arrayed for battle, like warhorses, clad in scales like armor, and sounding like a battalion of chariots (9:7–9). The origin of these locusts is beyond the earth; it is a fallen angel who unlocks the abyss and releases them (9:1–3). What looks like battle and a struggle for kingship on earth by military means is nothing but a scourge released by evil powers as the world speeds toward its end.

The period of the sixth trumpet, like that of the sixth seal, contains action related directly to the seventh, as well as intercalated scenes that set up the climax of the seventh member of the sequence. In the immediate aftermath of the sixth trumpet, a massive army is released to destroy a third of humanity. Again, military language colors the description of the agents of destruction (9:16–17). Before the seventh trumpet, several scenes intervene: the seven thunders whose voice is sealed (10:1–7), the prophetic commissioning of the visionary (10:8–11), and the content of that prophecy in the holy city and the great city (11:1–14). The last provides the most direct means of comment on the Judaean War and on the simultaneous struggle for supremacy at Rome.

The Holy City and the Great City

Drawing on images from the prophet Zechariah (Zech 2:2–8), Rev 11:1–14 describes the current distress and subjection of the holy city Jerusalem – the outer courts of its Temple will be given over to the trampling of the nations for a period – and the prophetic indictment of the great city of Rome. The call for repentance made by the two prophets of 11:3 is ignored, and the prophets are killed, only to rise again for the judgment of the great city and its partial destruction.[11] This scene draws together three elements of a situation that John would have known well: the Roman siege of Jerusalem, the chaos of the city of

---

[11] See Marshall, *Parables of War*, 169–73.

Rome in the period of civil war,[12] and the presence of a community there dedicated to the worship of Jesus. After the earthquake devastates the city, the seventh trumpet sounds, and the angel's proclamation announces what has been at stake all along: "The kingdom of the world has become the kingdom of our Lord and of his Christ and he shall reign forever and ever" (11:15).

The seals, trumpets, and thunders are all about who reigns over the earth and over the heavens. After the angel's announcement, praise follows in the heavenly throne room:

> We give thanks to thee, Lord God Almighty, who is and who was, that you have taken your great power and begun to reign. The nations raged, but your wrath came, and the time for the dead to be judged, for rewarding your servants, the prophets and saints, and those who fear your name, both small and great, and for destroying the destroyers of the earth. (Rev 11:17–18)

Finally, according to John, God will seize his own power, putting to rest the conflicts of the nations and dealing justice and judgment to those who deserve them. The episode concludes with auditions and portents from the heavenly Temple of God:

Then God's Temple in heaven was opened, and the ark of his covenant was seen within his temple; and there were flashes of lightning, voices, peals of thunder, an earthquake, and heavy hail. (Rev 11:19)	In all parts of the country chariots were seen in the air and armed battalions hurtling through the clouds and encompassing the cities. . . . the priests on entering inner court of the temple . . . reported that they were conscious first of a commotion and a din and after that of a voice as of a host, "we are departing hence." (Josephus, *J.W.* 6.299–300)

John and Josephus both know that the Temple of God is where victory or defeat is determined and announced. Josephus has the advantage of hindsight and the burden of an imperial patron.

---

[12] John describes gratuitous feasting over the fate of the witnesses (Rev 11:10). Tacitus, *Hist.* 2.95, concentrated on the morally revelatory function of the gratuitous feasting of Vitellius.

War in Heaven

Revelation 6–11 depicted a war on earth that had been unleashed by heavenly agents and resolved by divine intervention. Revelation 12–16 retells that story with a more direct eye to the heavenly conflict that animates the earthly. In a time when prophecies of leadership were rampant, John's vision in Revelation 12–14 joins the fray. He suggests that the child who will "rule the nations with an iron rod" – far from being Galba's adopted Piso, Otho's prospective offspring, Vitellius's stammering boy, or Vespasian's militant sons Titus and Domitian – is the child of mother Israel, hidden from the current distress, waiting on God's own throne to claim earthly rule. Josephus' prophecy, supposedly widespread, that the ruler of the world would come from the East may be in view here[13]:

These portents [tame oxen, dog bearing hands, uprooted trees] needed interpretation, but not so the saying of a Jew named Josephus: he, having earlier been captured by Vespasian and imprisoned, laughed and said: "you may imprison me now, but a year from now, when you have become emperor, you will release me." (Dio Cassius, *Hist.* 65.1.4)	He [Galba] was encouraged too … because the priest of Jupiter at Clunia, directed by a dream, had found in the inner shrine of his temple the very same prediction, likewise spoken by an inspired girl two hundred years before. And the purport of the verses was that one day there would come forth from Spain the ruler and lord of the world. (Suetonius, *Galb.* 9.2)

What more than all else incited them [the Jews] to war was an ambiguous oracle, likewise found in their sacred scriptures, to the effect that at that time one from their country would become ruler of all the world. (Josephus, *J.W.* 6.312; cf. Tacitus, *Hist.* 5.13)

All parties have prophecies of their victory. Some, such as those recounted by Suetonius concerning Galba and by Josephus concerning Vespasian, are suspiciously similar.

Before matters are resolved on earth, they are resolved in heaven. The combat between the archangel Michael and the dragon resolves in Michael's

[13] Josephus' own account predicts unabashedly that Vespasian will be emperor, but he does not cast his initial account as a fulfillment of a prophecy already known to Vespasian (*J.W.* 3.401), although Josephus mentions the oracle in terms more reminiscent of Tacitus in *J.W.* 6.312. He does, however, cast himself a messenger of God. Cf. Tacitus, *Hist.* 5.13 and Suetonius, *Vesp.* 4.

favor, and the dragon is cast down to the earth for an epilogue of violence. It is at this point, when the program and justification for the resolution of the conflict on earth has been laid out in Revelation 12, that John depicts the Roman imperial struggles and power most starkly. The beast from the sea with seven heads and ten horns, the dragon that requires worship, and the beast from the land that works signs in the heavens and enforces the worship of the beast – these are the subject of numerous reconstructions and identifications juggling options like the provincial elites who supported the imperial cult for the beast from the land, the empire or the emperor for the beast from the sea, the heavenly adversary for the dragon.[14] All of this climaxes with the *gematria* of 13:18 that identifies Nero, perhaps Nero *redivivus*, with the final beast.[15]

Standing in opposition to this cohort of beasts is the company of the Lamb, arrayed as holy warriors standing on Zion. In consonance with the holy war tradition, standing faithfully seems to be sufficient, and the destruction of Babylon is announced proleptically in Rev 14:8. At this point, the son of man takes charge of reaping the earth (14:19–20). As elsewhere in the apocalypse, the "great city" is consistently Rome. The promise of the son of man's judgment is that wrath of God and the blood of its victims will be poured out upon Rome.

Revelation 15 forms the heavenly Temple scene in which the kingship of God is confirmed in the praise of the saints in heaven and the final phase of the conflict which brings down Rome is prepared: the seven bowls of plagues to be poured out on the earth. Among the plagues – consisting usually of boils, portents, scorching fire, and so on – two are most notable. The fifth plague is poured out "on the throne of the beast," darkening its kingdom. The sixth plague dries up the river Euphrates and prepares the way for the "demonic spirits, performing signs, who go abroad to the kings of the

> Apartment houses had their foundations undermined by the standing water and then collapsed when the flood withdrew. The moment people's minds were relieved of this danger, the very fact that when Otho was planning a military expedition, the Campus Martius and the Flammian Way, over which he was to advance, were blocked against him was interpreted as a prodigy and omen of impending disaster rather than as the result of chance or natural causes. (Tacitus, *Hist.* 1.86)

---

[14] On the relation of these images to Roman imperial apparatus, see Collins, *Crisis and Catharsis*.

[15] A. A. Bell has made an extensive case that the most intense speculation on a revived or returning Nero took place soon after his death ("The Date of the Apocalypse: The Evidence of Some Roman Historians Reconsidered," *NTS* 25 [1979]: 93–102). Cf. Tacitus, *Hist.* 2.8–9.

whole world, to assemble them for battle on the great day of God the Almighty" (16:14).[16] Like the climax of the cycle of seals, trumpets, and thunders, this cycle peaks with the destruction of the great city of Rome which – together with the cities of the gentiles (ἐθνῶν) – is afflicted by lightning, earthquakes, hail, and made to "drain the cup of the fury of [God's] wrath."

Judgment and Celebration

The final chapters of Revelation celebrate the defeat of the powers of Rome and the triumph of God and his Lamb. Here, John makes most starkly and most vulnerably his claim that what he has seen in the heavens will transpire on the earth solving the question of rule that has animated him and his opponents. Within this narrative, John's concerns are clearly to identify Rome as the primary referent of his metaphors, to identify the kings of the earth as complicit in the demonic power of Rome, to emphasize the effectiveness of the army of heaven against Rome, to recount the economic symptoms of the illegitimacy of Roman hegemony, and to proclaim a reconciliation under God that exceeds *Pax Romana*. Such identifications are not exhaustive and, in terms of John's theology, they may not be the most important. It is in terms of his immediate social circumstances and the practical effect his work might have on its audience that these references gain primacy. Revelation 17 takes on the task of identifying the woman on the beast, "with whom the kings of the earth have fornicated" (17:2), with Rome. The imagery of kings obviously refers to clientage, but the mounted-woman image calls forth more intentional explanation. An angel explains the mystery: The seven heads of the beast on which she sits are the seven hills:

> they are also seven kings, five of whom have fallen, one is, the other has not yet come, and when he comes he must remain only a little while. As for the beast that was and is not, it is an eighth but it belongs to the seven, and it goes to perdition. (Rev 7:10–11)

Counting these "kings," as emperors were styled in the East, is a controversial business. What is not controversial is the idea that one is counting Roman emperors. Rev 17:18 sums up the identification most clearly: "And the woman who you saw is the great city which has dominion over the kings of the earth."

---

[16] Cf. the astrologers retained by Otho (Tacitus, *Hist.* 1.22; Suetonius, *Otho* 4) and Vespasian (Suetonius, *Vesp.* 25; Tacitus, *Hist.* 2.78).

Revelation 18 concentrates the economic critique of Rome that has surfaced elsewhere in the vision. Songs and laments illustrate the changing allegiances during periods of civil war (cf. 17:16), and most of all they indict those who have profited by assimilation to the Roman economy: merchants, kings, sailors. Revelation 18 concludes its critique of Rome, which focused on economics, the consumption of costly spices, jewels, foods, and so on, by making the claim that "in her was found the blood of prophets and of saints, and of all who have been slain on earth" (18:24). Here, the author is striving to explain the well known – namely, violence by and for Rome – by means of his conviction about a substantial channel of Rome's influence: its effect on the trading and economic patterns of the Mediterranean world. Obviously, such judgments are situated and ideological, but John is confident, perhaps overconfident, that his perspective coincides with a truly universal perspective and that his narrative of the master is the master's narrative.

> His [Vitellius's] besetting sins were luxury and cruelty. He divided his feasts into three, sometimes into four a day, breakfast, lunch, dinner, and a drinking bout; and he was readily able to do justice to all of them through his habit of vomiting. Moreover, he had himself invited to each of these meals by different men on the same day, and the materials for any one of them never cost less than four hundred thousand sesterces. (Suetonius, *Vit.* 13.1)

The celebration of the marriage supper of the Lamb that begins in Revelation 19 commences with a celebration of the virtues of the groom's father: He has destroyed the Harlot and "has avenged on her the blood of his servants" (Rev 19:2). After the narrator (a master of ceremonies in at least a narratological sense) elaborates the praise of the father, comments briefly on the beauty of the bride's attire (19:8), and puts in a kind word concerning the guests (19:9), the encomium focuses on the groom. A military man of sorts, the groom surpasses any warrior or leader known in the current conflict that wracks the Roman world. The visionary's epideictic description is so dense that any paraphrase would vitiate its force:

> Then I saw heaven opened, and behold, a white horse! He who sat upon it is called Faithful and True, and in righteousness he judges and makes war. His eyes are like a flame of fire, and on his head are many diadems; and he has a name inscribed which no one knows but himself. He is clad in a robe dipped in blood, and the name by which he is called is the Word of God. And the armies of heaven, arrayed in fine linen, white and pure, followed him on white horses. From his mouth issues a sharp sword with which to smite the nations, and he

137

will rule them with a rod of iron; he will tread the wine press of the fury of the wrath of God the Almighty. On his robe and on his thigh he has a name inscribed, "King of kings and Lord of lords." (Rev 19:11–16)

Followed by an immense wedding party of holy warriors,[17] the groom's entry completes the conditions necessary for dinner to start. The angel announces the "great supper of God." On the menu are the rival suitors and their retinues: kings, captains, mighty men, horses and their riders, the enslaved and the free, the small and the great (19:18). Unconventionally, the groom is not the carver for this meal, but rather the butcher, slaughtering those listed on the menu by the "sword of his mouth" (19:19). With the exception of two delicacies deep-fried in the lake of burning sulfur – namely, the false prophet and the beast – the menu is served raw, although by this point only the birds have retained their appetite (19:19–20). Emphasizing the peculiarity of this wedding prompts the question of what drove John to the contortions such a scene contains. No mystical union of Christ and the assembly of his followers is in focus here. This is a celebration of victory in rivalry: the warrior of the God of Israel victorious over the beast and his legates in heaven and on earth. It is a celebration of the prowess of the groom and his witnesses, and the "church" is his trophy wife.

> The war was shown by numerous representations, in separate sections, affording a very vivid picture of its episodes. Here was to be seen a prosperous country devastated, there whole battalions of the enemy slaughtered.... The spoils were borne in promiscuous heaps; but conspicuous above all stood out those captured in the temple at Jerusalem. (Josephus, *J.W.* 7.142–144, 148, describing the triumphal procession)

In the spirit of *bonhomie* that a wedding supper can stimulate, the remaining text of Revelation has peacemaking as one of its major functions. Like the *Pax Romana*, this is a peace imposed by a victor, but a peace nonetheless. Although Satan is chained in the abyss for a millennium to come and although some types of people – "the cowardly, the faithless, the polluted, as for murderers,

> When his mother died, he [Vitellius] was suspected of having forbidden her being given food when she was ill, because a woman of the Chatti, in whom he believed as he would in an oracle, prophesied that he would rule securely and for a long time, but only if he would survive his parent. (Suetonius, *Vit.*, 14.5)

---

[17] Rev 19:14: "the armies of heaven, arrayed in fine linen." Cf. 14:1–4. For arguments concerning the status of the 144,000 of 14:1–4, to which the army of 19:14 clearly corresponds, see Collins, *Crisis and Catharsis*, 127–32; Marshall, *Parables of War*, 140–1, 151–2, 160–3.

fornicators, sorcerers, idolaters, and all liars" – are exiled to the lake of burning sulfur (21:8), John's depiction of the holy

[Under Vitellius] the astrologers were banished from Italy. (Tacitus *Hist.* 2.62)

city includes a prominent place for reconciliation. The conversion of at least some of the kings of the earth is one witness to this reconciliation motif, as is the declaration that the leaves of the trees that line the river of the central street of the holy city are "for the healing of the nations" (21:24–27). Who can be healed, of what, under what conditions is ambiguous; yet, John's conviction that innumerable Gentiles will be healed and brought into God's people is crystal clear.

Conclusion: The One on the Throne

For John, the God of Israel is the only acceptable answer to the question, "Who is really on the throne?" At first, the one on the throne is not named and, as is fitting for a sovereign, not met with a direct gaze. John claims to see "the scroll from the right hand of him who was seated on the throne" (Rev 5:7). At this point, the face of the one on the throne is not revealed but is instead surrounded with transparent objects, jewels, fire, glass, water, as if to indicate that, except in the right conditions, it cannot be seen. In fact, when the fourth seal is broken, the kings of earth beg to be hidden from "the face of him who is seated on the throne" (6:15). It cannot be seen without peril by those not bought by the Lamb; audience with a ruler is notoriously dangerous. At the climax of the first cycle of destruction in which the great city is brought down by earthquakes (11:13), the Ark of the Covenant is seen once again in God's heavenly Temple. Voices from the throne continue (17:17; 19:5; 21:3) and, finally, after the visionary has gazed on him who is on the throne (20:11), all the servants of God gain the privilege of seeing his face (22:4). The slow unveiling of the one on the throne is a mirror of the slow resolution of the civil wars, even though John is confident of a very different resolution than any of the contending parties sought.

The means by which John sought to know, however, are shared with the contenders for the imperial office, their supporters, detractors, and chroniclers. Galba's rise was portended in a personal vision of Fortune, a ghost ship full of arms, a foaling mule, a young temple attendant's hair turning quickly to white, the seeings of seers, the death of the Augustan chickens, heads rolling from statues, a prophesy by Emperor Tiberius, lightning striking and leaving in its wake "unmistakable tokens of supreme power [*imperii signum*]," oracles from the priest of Jupiter and the predictions of a noble girl, the discovery of a magical ring, rampant oxen drenching him in blood, earthquakes, and mooing sounds.[18] Conversely, soothsayers predicting assassination and god-sent storms indicated his fall.[19]

Otho too was supported by astrologers,[20] but, according to a dream in which Galba haunted him, warning of improperly performed rites, the wailings of the worshippers of Cybele, unfavorably positive indications in an offering to Dis, floods of the Tiber, animated statues, temple apparitions, a talking ox, and the brief appearance of an uncommon bird in a popular grove, Otho was destined for a bad ending.[21]

Vitellius plotted his ascension[22] on the basis of horoscopes of future power, the flight of eagles, the breaking of statues, and the behavior of birds, but his downfall was foreseen and foretold by astrologers lampooning him in public, comets, lunar eclipses, multiple suns indicating his ill prospects, giant footprints in the Capitol, the moon turned to blood and, when vultures interfered with his sacrifice, the end was surely near.[23] All was for naught, and Vitellius found himself huddling in a dog kennel, pretending to be a slave, begging for his life only shortly after rising to the imperial office.

Vespasian was destined for glory[24] by an ox that did obeisance, a dog that fetched a human hand, a tree surprisingly uprooted, a dream of Nero losing a tooth, the prophecy of a Jewish captive, the flooding of the Nile, his own healing of the blind and the lame, comets and stars that attended his endeavors, a cow giving birth to a lamb, heavenly voices, suddenly spouting oak trees, an oracle from the priest at Mount Carmel, an apparition of the priest of Serapis, the predictions of soothsayers, and his ever-trusted horoscopes. Tacitus's admission that only retrospect can make such signs trustworthy (*Hist.* 1.11) ought not to blind us to the myriad of portents that would surely have foretold Vespasian's downfall, if it had been as swift or as ignominious as those of his predecessors.

Jesus was, according to his devotee John, prophesied and destined by his prophets and his father. The dense intertextual relations between Revelation

---

[18] Dio Cassius, *Hist.* 53.30.3; Suetonius, *Galb.* 1; 4.1–3; 8.2; 9.2; 10.4; 18.1–2.
[19] Suetonius, *Galb.* 19.1; Tacitus, *Hist.* 1.38.
[20] Tacitus, *Hist.* 1.22; Suetonius, *Otho* 4.
[21] Suetonius, *Otho* 7.2; 8.3; Tacitus, *Hist.* 1.86, 89; 2.50.
[22] Suetonius, *Vit.* 3.2; 9; Tacitus, *Hist.* 1.52.
[23] Dio Cassius, *Hist.* 53.30.3; 54.8.1–2, 11.1, 16.1; Suetonius, *Vit.* 14.4–5; cf. Tacitus, *Hist.* 2.62.
[24] Josephus, *J.W.* 4.626; 6.289, 292, 301; Suetonius, *Vesp.* 5.1, 4–6; 7.1–3; 25; Dio Cassius, *Hist.* 55.1.2–4, 8.1; Tacitus, *Hist.* 2.78; 5.13.

and the Hebrew Bible make this clear. Jesus also, for John, dwelt truly in the heavens and commanded the angels that are the visible stars and so it made perfect sense to seek him there.[25] Without the benefit of the hindsight of a historian, John's text precedes any effort to reconcile the promise of victory with the disappointment of defeat that the destruction of the Temple in Jerusalem constituted.

This study has proceeded with primarily narrative literary data, but the understandings of heaven and earth that underpin the conversations I have tracked have their roots in a more widely distributed coordination of heavenly and earthly rule. In first-century Asia Minor, the cults of Roman rulers, which grew from the cults of Alexander before them, offer another angle on the phenomenon under investigation here.[26] Revelation is usually read as standing in incompatible contrast to this element of its historical context, and there is no doubt that John found such a cult abhorrent. Tracking the conversation in literary terms, rather than being guided by the distinction John draws so desperately, enables us to see him and his form of first-century Asian Judaism as standing in continuity with the environment that is also a source of such vehement tension.

During the long year, a conversation concerning the heavens and the throne grew loud in every corner of the empire; it echoed for generations after in the Graeco–Roman historians in one mode and shows up vividly in John's apocalypse in another. In their allegiances, John and Tacitus would disagree; but when Tacitus writes that, in the long year,

> there were prodigies in the sky and on the earth, warnings given by thunderbolts, and prophecies of the future, both joyful and gloomy, uncertain and clear. For never was it more fully proved by awful disasters of the Roman people or by indubitable signs that the gods care not for our safety but our punishment . . . (*Hist.* 1.3)

John of Patmos might have thought that Tacitus was, briefly, on the right track and perhaps that direct conversation was possible.

---

[25] On the astrological interpretation of Revelation, see B. J. Malina, *On the Genre and Message of Revelation: Star Visions and Sky Journeys* (Peabody, Mass., 1995); J. M. Chevalier, *A Postmodern Revelation: Signs of Astrology and the Apocalypse* (Toronto, 1997).

[26] See S. R. F. Price, *Rituals and Power: The Roman Imperial Cult in Asia Minor* (Cambridge, 1984); S. J. Friesen, *Imperial Cults and the Apocalypse of John: Reading Revelation in the Ruins* (New York, 2001).

8

The Earthly Monastery and the Transformation of the Heavenly City in Late Antique Egypt

Kirsti B. Copeland

As it is done in heaven, so also on earth.   (*Apoc. Paul* 29, Paris MS)

As it is on earth, so it is also in heaven.   (*Apoc. Paul* 29, Arnhem MS)

Few Christian apocryphal texts have been as widely preserved and as influential in Late Antiquity, the Middle Ages, and Byzantium as the *Apocalypse of Paul*. A product of late fourth-century Egypt,[1] this apocalypse is extant in more than a dozen languages, including Greek, Latin, Coptic, Syriac, and Arabic. The text was not only copied in monasteries but also was read aloud in churches throughout the Mediterranean by those who believed

I am grateful to Martha Himmelfarb, Peter Brown, Elaine Pagels, Ra'anan Boustan, and Annette Reed for their comments on this paper. The opening translations are my own. Subsequent translations of the *Apocalypse of Paul* are from J. K. Elliott, *Apocryphal New Testament* (Oxford, 1993), 616–44, and K. Copeland, "Mapping the Apocalypse of Paul: Geography, Genre and History" (Ph.D. diss., Princeton University, 2001), 188–248.

[1]   I date the *Apocalypse of Paul* after the consular date found in its preface, 388 C.E.; other scholars have placed it in the second or the third century (notably, C. Carozzi, *Eschatologie et Au-delà: Recherches sur l'Apocalypse de Paul* [Provence, 1994], and R. P. Casey, "The Apocalypse of Paul," *JTS* 34 [1933]: 1–33). Dates before the end of the fourth century have very little to support them, as our first secure witnesses to the *Apocalypse of Paul* are Augustine's 98th tractate on the Gospel of John (416 C.E.) and Sozomen's *Ecclesiastical History* (443 C.E.). Moreover, contrary to the assertions of those who favor an earlier date, Origen does not refer to the *Apocalypse of Paul* in the third century; Bar Hebraeus' *Nomocanon* 7.9 misquotes Origen in the thirteenth century. See further P. Piovanelli, "Les origines de l'*Apocalypse de Paul* reconsidérées," *Apocrypha* 4 (1993): 25–64, and Copeland, "Mapping," 21–35. Although the date of the *Apocalypse of Paul* is secure, some question may legitimately remain with regard to provenance. Plausible arguments can be made that the apocalypse was composed in Egypt, Palestine, or Asia Minor. In my opinion, Egyptian provenance remains the most convincing on the basis of the sheer number of parallels with Egyptian Christian apocryphal and monastic literature; for example, the *Apocalypse of Elijah*, the *Apocalypse of Peter*, the *Apocalypse of Zephaniah*, the *Testament of Abraham*, the second *Sibylline Oracle*, the Coptic *Life of Pachomius*, and Paul of Tamma's *Cell*.

it to be the authentic revelation of the apostle Paul. Its impact can be felt in Christian literature across the spectrum, from late Coptic apocrypha to Dante's *Inferno*. The *Apocalypse of Paul*'s importance as a reflection of the religious atmosphere of Late Antiquity is borne out by this volume, in which no fewer than three other articles refer to it.[2]

This critically important Christian composition contains within it the most spectacular description of the heavenly Jerusalem since the Book of Revelation. At the end of the fourth century, when the *Apocalypse of Paul* envisions its "City of Christ," the earthly Jerusalem has been an iconic center of Christendom for several decades. Yet, Constantine's Christian city does not inform this apocalypse's image of the heavenly Jerusalem despite its relative proximity to Egypt.[3] The description of the City of Christ in the *Apocalypse of Paul* contains no trace of the recently constructed Church of the Holy Sepulcher or any of Constantine's other building projects. The City of Christ is not, however, entirely ethereal and distant, with no connection to the physical world. Its this-worldly counterpart has merely shifted; it is to be found not in the earthly Jerusalem, but in a different Christian city much closer to home: the Egyptian monastery.

I must clarify that, although Paul's *angelus interpres* once refers to the City of Christ as the "heavenly Jerusalem" (29), this city is not actually located in the heavens; it is situated in the mystical and otherworldly lands beyond the river Ocean. The city is heavenly in state, but earthly in location. Thus, in a very discrete manner, it addresses the desire for a renewed earthly Jerusalem. Nonetheless, the City of Christ of the *Apocalypse of Paul* is divorced from eschatological hopes about the restoration of the political entity of Jerusalem in the geographical region of Judea.

To understand the significance of the *Apocalypse of Paul*'s vision of the City of Christ, it is necessary to situate this Christian apocalypse within the history of Jewish and Christian traditions about the heavenly Jerusalem, from the Babylonian Exile to late antique Egypt. In sharp contrast to earlier visions, the *Apocalypse of Paul* neither envisions the built environment of heaven in the image of the Temple nor hopes for a heavenly Jerusalem to descend to earth in lieu of the conquered terrestrial city. For the *Apocalypse of Paul*, the City of

---

[2]   See J. Bremmer, F. Graf, and S. I. Johnston in this volume.
[3]   B. Kühnel has demonstrated that the closer a Christian artist was to Christian Jerusalem, the more likely it would be for the heavenly Jerusalem to be depicted with attributes of the earthly; *From the Earthly to the Heavenly Jerusalem: Representations of the Holy City in Christian Art of the First Millennium* (Rome, 1987), esp. 166.

Christ is not intimately linked to the earthly city of Jerusalem. Instead, as I subsequently demonstrate, the *Apocalypse of Paul* reflects attitudes prevalent among late antique Egyptian Christians and pilgrims to Egypt, who regarded the monastery as a new model for the heavenly Jerusalem.

The Heavenly Jerusalem, One with the Earthly Jerusalem

For the *Apocalypse of Paul* to link the heavenly city to the monastery represents an unusual twist in the long history of this otherworldly metropolis. Earlier generations of Jews and Christians saw the heavenly and earthly Jerusalems as inextricably united – in one sense imagining them as a single city, in another sense envisioning the unassailable heavenly Jerusalem as divine compensation for an earthly city overrun too many times by the invading armies of foreign kings. Time and again, Jerusalem's turbulent political history shaped the development of her otherworldly counterpart, underscoring just how connected the two cities once were.

The idealized city that becomes the heavenly Jerusalem first appears not as a supernal city, but as another kind of imagined city, an earthly one. In the writings of Israelites exiled to Babylon in the sixth century B.C.E., such as Ezekiel and second Isaiah, the hopes for the restoration of the earthly Jerusalem are articulated through exalted images of the city.[4] Ezekiel's prophecy culminates with a vision in which he is taken to the land of Israel to view a high mountain and the city upon it (Ezekiel 40–48). Although he sees the whole land of Israel, his vision focuses on the restored Temple.[5] In verse after verse of painstaking detail, Ezekiel describes the courts of the Temple, their measurements, gates, and functions. His vision is a divine blueprint of the holy Jerusalem, but this city does not belong in heaven. Although it is built on a grand scale, its dimensions are of this world.[6] In contrast to the fire and precious stones of Ezekiel's celestial realms (e.g., 1, 10), the Temple

---

[4] See R. L. Wilken, *The Land Called Holy: Palestine in Christian History and Thought* (New Haven, Conn., 1992), 11–17; Kühnel, *From the Earthly*, 34–35.

[5] Elsewhere, Ezekiel speaks of Jerusalem as the center of the earth: "Thus says the Lord God: This is Jerusalem; I have set her in the center of the nations, with countries all around her" (Ezek 5:5, NRSV). As J. D. Levenson has noted, Ezekiel's geography does not derive from scientific fact; Jerusalem is here the center of the world, the cosmic mountain of ancient Israel (*Sinai and Zion* [Minneapolis, Minn., 1985], 115–16; idem, *Theology of the Program of Restoration of Ezekiel 40–8* [Missoula, Mont., 1976], 8, 17).

[6] For instance, the gateways of Ezekiel's city are comparable in size to Solomonic gateways found at Megiddo, Gezer, and Hazor.

and its altars are built from the simple materials of stone and wood (40:42; 41:22). For Ezekiel, this holy Temple will be built on earth after the exile has ended; his idealized Jerusalem will stand in exactly the same place as the city that he was forced to leave behind. There are not yet two cities, one heavenly and one earthly, but only a single Jerusalem, past and future.[7]

The restored Jerusalem described by second Isaiah (Isaiah 40–55) is no longer a city of wood and stone, but a city of precious jewels with "pinnacles of rubies" and "walls of precious stones" (54:11–12). Nevertheless, second Isaiah also imagines a city that is both eschatological and earthly. Although his utopian city lacks the detailed correspondence to the Jerusalem Temple that marks Ezekiel's vision, his idealized city and the political entity of Jerusalem are still one and the same.

The first vivid images of a celestial Jerusalem would appear long after the return from exile and the restoration of Jerusalem and her Temple by Persian monarchs. The ascent of Jerusalem to heaven may, in fact, have occurred because the rebuilt city did not live up to the idealized city of earlier hopes. Although earlier Jewish texts suggest that there is a heavenly "pattern" of the Jerusalem Temple, it is not until the *Book of the Watchers* (1 Enoch 1–36; third century B.C.E.) that this pattern becomes the veritable built environment of heaven.[8] The description of the heavenly cityscape is so evocative of the earthly Jerusalem and her Temple that it provides an apt contrast for the *Apocalypse of Paul*'s City of Christ. Both texts are written in periods when Jerusalem stands, but only the *Book of the Watchers* mirrors the earthly city in the heavenly one. The *Book of the Watchers*' heaven evokes the Jerusalem Temple: The "fiery Cherubim" that Enoch sees in heaven (14:11) recall the decorations found on the woven tapestry of the tabernacle and in the engravings of the Temple walls. The three houses through which Enoch must pass before he reaches the throne of God (14:9–17) correspond to the three chambers of the Temple: the vestibule, the sanctuary, and the holy of holies.[9]

---

[7] In Levenson's apt phrase, the restoration of Jerusalem will be "the fulfillment of Israelite history, a fulfillment which assumes the resolution of the tensions that produce history" (*Theology*, 18).

[8] See Exod 25:9, 25:40; 26:30; 27:8. M. Himmelfarb, "Apocalyptic Ascent and the Heavenly Temple," *SBLSP* 26 (1987): 211. Before the *Book of the Watchers*, the imagery of the royal court dominated the heavens (e.g., 1 Kgs 22:19; Isa 6:1; Ps 82; Zech 3:1–10; Job 1:6–12; 2:1–6); see idem, *Ascent to Heaven in Jewish and Christian Apocalypses* (New York, 1993), 14.

[9] The Ethiopic refers to a wall and two houses, but the Greek describes three houses. See further Himmelfarb, "Apocalyptic Ascent," 210; idem, *Ascent*, 14. M. Black argues that the

Visions of heaven as a Temple appear in nearly every ascent text of the apocalyptic tradition after the *Book of the Watchers*: 2 Enoch, the Enochic *Similitudes*, the *Apocalypse of Abraham*, the *Testament of Levi*, the *Ascension of Isaiah*, 3 Baruch, and the *Apocalypse of Zephaniah*.[10] The *Apocalypse of Paul* belongs to this same genre and was influenced by some of these texts.[11] Thus, it is all the more significant that the *Apocalypse of Paul* does not identify the heavenly city with the Jerusalem Temple.

The near identification between the earthly Jerusalem and the heavenly one continues after the second destruction of Jerusalem and her Temple by the Romans in 70 C.E. The authors of 4 Ezra and 2 Baruch both express sorrow at the loss of Jerusalem and deep desire for the return of the city, and both contain the promise by God that a heavenly Jerusalem will descend to earth.[12] Like Ezekiel and second Isaiah, the authors of 4 Ezra and 2 Baruch write while the earthly Jerusalem is not under Jewish control, and they seek the restoration of the terrestrial city. However, their visions are influenced by the idea of the heavenly Temple that appeared during the Second Temple period, and they imagine that Jerusalem is currently in heaven and that it will descend to earth.

The author of 4 Ezra bemoans the loss of Jerusalem, arguing with the angel of the Lord about how God could turn Israel over to her enemies (6:57–59). Like Ezekiel, Ezra is then given a promise of a restored Jerusalem. The angel comforts him, saying, "For indeed the time will come to pass, that the city that now is not seen shall appear, and the land that now is hidden shall be disclosed" (7:26).[13] Ezra sees this restored Jerusalem in a vision of a grieving mother who transforms herself into the holy city (10:27). This is the "city of

---

"building" of the first house in the Greek is actually an encircling city wall (*The Book of Enoch or I Enoch: A New English Edition* [Leiden, 1985], 146). Translations of 1 Enoch come from Black's edition.

[10] Himmelfarb, "Apocalyptic Ascent," 212. According to G. W. MacRae, "in the apocalyptic literature we find the notion of a temple in heaven full blown and even taken for granted" ("Heavenly Temple and Eschatology in the Letter to the Hebrews," *Semeia* 12 [1978]: 179–99; quotation on 183).

[11] At the very least, the *Apocalypse of Paul* draws on the *Apocalypse of Zephaniah*.

[12] Because of the broad scope of my survey, I emphasize the similarities in the expectations of 4 Ezra and 2 Baruch. For a detailed look at the differences, see G. Sayler, "2 Baruch: A Story of Grief and Consolation," *SBLSP* 21 (1982): 497–9; A. B. Kolenkow, "The Fall of the Temple and the Coming of the End: The Spectrum and Process of Apocalyptic Argument in 2 Baruch and Other Authors," *SBLSP* 21 (1982): 243–50.

[13] Ezra's Jerusalem is a "new creation" that can only be born from the destruction of the old; see Kolenkow, "Fall of the Temple," 249.

the Most High" (10:54), the heavenly Jerusalem that will descend to earth as the answer to Ezra's prayers.

Just as Ezra challenges God for allowing Jerusalem to be conquered, so does Baruch in 2 Baruch. The divine response is remarkably similar. Baruch is assured that the destruction is only temporary and that Jerusalem will be rebuilt, superior to the city that was destroyed (4:1–3). The author of 2 Baruch draws on the image of Jerusalem carved on God's palm in second Isaiah (Isa 49:16). Second Isaiah, however, refers only to a pattern of the holy Jerusalem to be restored on earth, and not to a celestial city. In 2 Baruch, God speaks of an actual building that is with him now, something more than a mere pattern. Nevertheless, the proper place for that building is on earth, after a certain period of time has passed. The celestial Jerusalem and the earthly, eschatological Jerusalem are identical. They remain, at this point, inextricably linked.

Like his fellow Jews, the first-century John of Patmos both envisions a celestial counterpart to the earthly Jerusalem and harbors the eschatological expectation that the heavenly city will eventually descend to earth (Rev 21:1–2).[14] Although John differs from the authors of 4 Ezra and 2 Baruch in that he believed Jesus to be the messiah, his political and eschatological hopes were, like theirs, Jewish.[15] Thus, we should not be surprised that his final Jerusalem comes from above but ultimately belongs on this earth. What is even more intriguing is that later generations of Gentile Christians would continue to believe that, at the end of history, Christ would reign on earth in this New Jerusalem.

The most renowned supporter of this early Christian chiliasm is the church father Irenaeus (second century C.E.). Irenaeus draws his image of the New Jerusalem primarily from second Isaiah and Revelation (*Adv. haer.* 5.34.4). He discerns that Isaiah's Jerusalem is not a celestial image, but ultimately an earthly one. He understands that these images exist in type in heaven only in order to be rebuilt on the earth. Like the author of 2 Baruch, Irenaeus appeals to second Isaiah's pattern of Jerusalem sketched onto the palm of

---

[14] It seems clear to me that the descent of Jerusalem in Revelation is a characteristic shared with both 4 Ezra and 2 Baruch and not something that sets it apart. Contrast "the idea that Christian Jerusalem descends from heaven while Jewish Jerusalem does not" (Kühnel, *From the Earthly*, 59).

[15] J. Marshall has argued that John of Patmos was a Jew reacting to the difficulties that the Judaean War caused Diaspora Jews in the years 66–70 C.E. See his article in this volume and *Parables of War: Reading John's Jewish Apocalypse* (Waterloo, Ont., 2001), 88–97.

God's hand (*Adv. haer.* 5.35.2). And, like John of Patmos, Irenaeus is waiting for this Jerusalem to come to rest on top of the ruins of the earthly Jerusalem, marking the beginning of Christ's reign on earth.

Although the connection between the earthly and heavenly Jerusalems remains as relevant for Irenaeus as it was for first-century Jews, some argue that other second-century Christians, known as the New Prophets or Montanists, divorced the heavenly Jerusalem from the earthly one. According to the fourth-century heresiologist Epiphanius, one of their prophetesses uttered an oracle that the New Jerusalem would descend not in Judaea, but rather in their hometown of Pepuza in Asia Minor (*Pan.* 49.1). Although we cannot be certain about the veracity of Epiphanius' claim in this instance,[16] there is corroborating evidence in that Montanus renamed the city of Pepuza "Jerusalem."[17] At the very least, this renaming suggests that some Phrygian Christians were disillusioned with the earthly Jerusalem and figuratively re-created the holy city in Asia Minor.

However, we cannot assume that this disenchantment with the earthly location of Jerusalem was widespread, even for the followers of the New Prophecy. In fact, there is evidence to the contrary: When Tertullian (second/third centuries C.E.), a believer in the New Prophecy, writes about the new Jerusalem, he does not associate it with Pepuza; instead, he remarks that the city has been seen hovering over Judaea, where it will descend and begin a thousand-year kingdom on earth.[18] Notably, Tertullian makes it explicit that he does not share the association held by his Jewish contemporaries between the political entity of Jerusalem and the heavenly city. Even as he associates the heavenly Jerusalem with the *geographical* region of Judaea, he testifies to the growing separation in Christian discourse between the heavenly Jerusalem and the *political* entity of Jerusalem.

Irenaeus and Tertullian write more than a century after the destruction of the Second Temple. Much has happened to the city in the interim. Two quashed Jewish uprisings have led Emperor Hadrian to change the name of the city from Jerusalem to Aelia Capitolina. Aelia Capitolina is a Roman city, with prominent statues of Hadrian and Zeus. Some Christians react

---

[16] On the questionable reliability of Epiphanius's testimony, see R. Heine, *The Montanist Oracles and Testimonia* (Macon, Ga., 1989), 5, and D. Groh, "Utterance and Exegesis: Biblical Interpretation in the Montanist Crisis," in *The Living Text*, eds. D. Groh and R. Jewett (New York, 1985), 80–1.

[17] Eusebius, *Hist. eccl.* 5.18.2, quoting Apollonius of Ephesus (ca. 180–210).

[18] Tertullian, *Marc.* 3.24.

to the effacement of Jerusalem by renaming their small village of Pepuza "Jerusalem" in order to maintain the connection between the heavenly and earthly Jerusalems. Others, like Irenaeus and Tertullian, continue to see the geographical region of the earthly Jerusalem, if not the political entity, enmeshed with the heavenly Jerusalem. Their writings underscore both the general necessity of an earthly complement to the heavenly city in Christian chiliasm and the fact that, for these early Christian authors, that earthly complement is located in Judaea.

Jerusalem, a City in Judaea No Longer

In the centuries following the destruction of the Temple and the establishment of Aelia Capitolina, rabbinic Jews persist in hoping for a renewed, earthly Jerusalem, even as they place more emphasis on its heavenly counterpart. The essential inseparability of the earthly and heavenly Jerusalems is encapsulated in a midrash attributed to Rabbi Yohanan (third century C.E.): "The Holy One blessed be he said, 'I will not enter the Jerusalem above until I can enter the Jerusalem below.' Is there a Jerusalem above? Yes, for it is written: 'Jerusalem, you are built as a city that is compact together.'"[19] Although this sentiment is shared in part by second-century Christians like Irenaeus and Tertullian, by the third and fourth centuries, the same is no longer true for many Egyptian Christians, who begin to make a sharp distinction between the earthly and heavenly Jerusalems. The former has fallen; the latter alone remains. There are no wistful musings about the return of the earthly city. All hope is placed on the supernal Jerusalem.

Origen is highly influential in dissolving the connection between the heavenly and earthly Jerusalems. Unlike earlier Christians, Origen is not waiting for the heavenly Jerusalem to descend to earth. On the contrary, he is adamantly opposed to such beliefs, which he condemns as worthless, absurd, and "Judaistic" (*Princ.* 2.11.2). Instead of reading biblical passages about Jerusalem as referring to the earthly, eschatological Jerusalem, Origen insists that these passages promise only a heavenly Jerusalem. In *Against Celsus*, for instance, he speaks against the Christian and Jewish beliefs that Judaea is the Promised Land, and he proposes that the Promised Land of Exodus 3 is the homeland of the righteous in heaven. For him, the description

---

[19] *B. Ta'an.* 5a, cited after Wilken, *Land Called Holy*, 41. Also idem, "Early Christian Chiliasm, Jewish Messianism, and the Idea of the Holy Land," *HTR* 79 (1986): 306.

of "a land flowing with milk and honey" simply cannot apply to a physical place on earth; he therefore attributes them to "that pure land, goodly and large, in the pure region of heaven, in which is the heavenly Jerusalem" (7.28–29). In *On First Principles*, he likewise contrasts the land of Judaea and the heavenly Jerusalem:

> For we believe that the prophets were speaking about this heavenly country by means of mystical narratives whenever they uttered prophecies concerning Judaea or Jerusalem.... All statements or prophecies, therefore, which are made concerning Jerusalem we must understand, if we listen to the words of Paul, as being those of Christ speaking in him, to refer in the thought of Paul himself to that country which he calls the heavenly Jerusalem, and to all those regions or cities which are said to belong to the holy land, the mother city of which is Jerusalem. (*Princ.* 4.3.8)[20]

For Origen, the heavenly Jerusalem has completely eclipsed the earthly one. In his view, the promise that is associated with Jerusalem in both the Hebrew Bible and the New Testament can refer to only the heavenly Jerusalem. His heavenly Jerusalem, unlike those of earlier interpreters, has nothing to do with the earthly city.

Despite their long-term impact, Origen's views did not immediately prevail throughout Egypt. Chiliastic movements expecting an earthly kingdom persisted in the Egyptian countryside, most notably in the controversy that surrounded Nepos, bishop of Arsinoë, and Coracion, a local prophet (ca. 260–270).[21] Our details about this event come from Eusebius' *Church History*, which preserves portions of Dionysius of Alexandria's first-person narrative of his trip to Arsinoë to refute the movement's literal interpretation of Revelation. Unfortunately, Dionysius does not specify where or how the movement imagined the earthly kingdom would come to rest; we can only guess that the circles around Nepos and Coracion followed Revelation literally enough that they imagined that the New Jerusalem would come to rest in Palestine.[22]

Even though the chiliastic hope of an earthly kingdom in Jerusalem continues in third-century Egypt, Origen's disassociation of the heavenly Jerusalem from the earthly city would be enormously influential in

---

[20] Butterworth, trans., *Origen on First Principles* (Gloucester, Mass., 1973), 301.

[21] Eusebius, *Hist. eccl.* 7.24.4.

[22] The same lack of specificity about the city is true for the *Apocalypse of Elijah*, which also attests continuing millennialism in third-century Egypt. D. Frankfurter, *Elijah in Upper Egypt* (Minneapolis, Minn., 1993), 270–8.

subsequent Christian theology, and his opposition to a "literal" reading of the promise of the earthly Jerusalem would ultimately become normative in Christianity. In Egypt, in particular, Origen's opinions are echoed by the early fourth-century Alexandrian bishop, Athanasius. Athanasius views the destruction of Jerusalem as a sign that the Word of God has come:

> For a sign and a great proof of the coming of God the Word is this: no longer does Jerusalem stand, nor does a prophet arise, nor is vision revealed to them – and rightly so. For when he who was signified has come, what need is there of those that signify? ... [S]ince the holy of holies is at hand, rightly have vision and prophecy been sealed, and the kingdom of Jerusalem has ceased. (*On the Incarnation* 40.4–13)[23]

Athanasius attempts to downplay the earthly Jerusalem. For him, Jerusalem is properly "a 'spiritual concept,' not a geographical one."[24] Christians are "children of the higher Jerusalem, of which the one that Solomon built was a pattern" (*Epist. fest.* 45).[25]

Athanasius writes his second *Letter to Virgins* to discourage the current trend of pilgrimage to the holy land.[26] Here, the Alexandrian bishop tries to convince the virgins, who have themselves recently returned from Palestine, that the "true Jerusalem ... was in heaven, and the virgin's journey there took place within her, in her 'mind,' by means of her 'way of life.'"[27] He tells them, "Let your bodies be on earth, but your mind in heaven. Your dwelling-place is your [earthly] father's house, but your way of life is with the heavenly Father" (*Epist. virg.* 2.6).[28] In so doing, Athanasius not only devalues the physical city of Jerusalem, currently the city of Aelia Capitolina, but he foreshadows what is to become the earthly counterpart of the heavenly Jerusalem for many late antique Egyptian Christians – namely, the monastery. Although Athanasius addresses virgins who have remained in their parents' homes, his arguments operate on the same principle as later associations between the monastery

---

[23] R. W. Thomson, trans., *Contra Gentes and De Incarnatione* (Oxford, 1971). See D. Brakke, *Athanasius and Asceticism* (Baltimore, 1995), 39.

[24] Brakke, *Athanasius*, 38.

[25] Cited after D. Brakke, "'Outside the Places, Within the Truth': Athanasius of Alexandria and the Localization of the Holy," in *Pilgrimage and Holy Space in Late Antique Egypt*, ed. D. Frankfurter (Leiden, 1998), 448.

[26] Brakke, *Athanasius*, 36–9. On pilgrimage, see E. D. Hunt, *Holy Land Pilgrimage and the Later Roman Empire A.D. 312–460* (Oxford, 1982); J. Wilkinson, *Egeria's Travels to the Holy Land* (London, 1971).

[27] Brakke, *Athanasius*, 38.

[28] Cited after Brakke, *Athanasius*, 38.

and the heavenly Jerusalem: It is the pious inhabitants, not the holy buildings or sacred geography, that constitute the city.

Monastery as Heavenly Jerusalem, Heavenly Jerusalem as Monastery

In the centuries following Origen and Athanasius, the separation between the earthly and heavenly Jerusalems becomes widespread in Egyptian Christianity. However, the heavenly Jerusalem does not remain long without an earthly counterpart. Different imagery is pressed into service that can once again connect heaven and earth. Some Egyptian Christians find that link in the institution of the church[29]; others find it in the institution of the monastery. Images of the church have encroached on the heavenly Jerusalem and the Temple from the beginnings of Christianity,[30] but the relationship between the monastery and the heavenly Jerusalem can only arise in this period after the monastery had a profound impact on the imaginations of late antique Christians. In a twist of symbols, then, a heavenly city based on a specific earthly location begins to define a different space, as the monastery is increasingly seen as the representation of the heavenly Jerusalem on earth, both by visitors to Egypt and by the monks and virgins themselves.

In contrast to the centrality of the Temple in earlier images of the heavenly Jerusalem, the monastery becomes the terrestrial complement of the heavenly city through the elevation of the living monk to a heavenly status. The prologue of the *History of Monks in Egypt*, for example, states that the monks "have citizenship in heaven" [*en ouranois politeuontai*].[31] The text even adds that, "some of them [the monks] do not even know that another world exists on earth."[32] Likewise, Jerome describes the monks of Egypt as "the heavenly family upon earth" (*Epist.* 3.1).[33] Some of the great figures of the Egyptian monasticism subsequently use this growing association between monks and angels to control the behavior of other monks. Shenoute, abbot of the White Monastery from the late fourth to the mid-fifth century,

[29] See, for example, the *Martyrdom of Paese and Thecla*, fols. 77v–78r in E. A. E. Reymond and J. W. B. Barns, eds., *Four Martyrdoms from the Pierpont Morgan Coptic Codices* (Oxford, 1973), 175.
[30] See Eph 2:19–21; Herm., *Sim.* 9.
[31] A.-J. Festugière, *Historia Monachorum in Aegypto* (Brussels, 1961), 7.
[32] Cited after J. E. Goehring, "The Encroaching Desert: Literary Production and Ascetic Space in Early Christian Egypt," *JECS* 1 (1993): 284.
[33] See G. Frank, "Miracles, Monks, and Monuments: The *Historia Monachorum in Aegypto* as Pilgrim's Tales," in *Pilgrimage and Holy Space*, 483.

fumes: "we do abominable, sinful deeds in the community of God, which is being called the 'heavenly Jerusalem' by those who come to it from many places, cities and regions."[34] His successor, Besa, similarly seeks to convince an errant nun that the community "is truly the heavenly Jerusalem, and it is the hill which God has blessed."[35] In all of these examples, the monastic institution is closely linked to the heavenly Jerusalem.

In his contribution to this volume, Adam H. Becker examines the language that scholars use to discuss the relationship between earthly and heavenly institutions. He contrasts the use of metaphor and simile with an understanding that an earthly institution is a microcosm of a macrocosmic heavenly institution. Although the relationship between the heavenly Jerusalem and monastery in many of the texts previously mentioned is more closely related to Becker's use of microcosm and macrocosm than it is to simile or metaphor, the language of "complement" and "counterpart" comes even closer to describing the actual relationship between the City of Christ of the *Apocalypse of Paul* and the Egyptian monastery. First, the reciprocity implied by the words "complement" and "counterpart" is inherent in the *Apocalypse of Paul*'s description of the City of Christ. It is in this context that we find the passage quoted at the opening of this paper: "As it is done in heaven, so also on earth" (*Apoc. Paul* 29, Paris MS; cf. Matt 6:10). Notably, a later copyist saw the connection between heaven and earth in the *Apocalypse of Paul* as so thoroughly reciprocal that he consciously or unconsciously altered it to read, "As it is on earth, so it is also in heaven" (*Apoc. Paul* 29, Arnhem MS). Second, "complement" and "counterpart" refer to two parts that complete one another. The *Apocalypse of Paul*'s heritage from early Christian chiliasm, in which the earthly and the heavenly cities are combined, insists that it describes an otherworldly city on the basis of an earthly counterpart, the mundane location that literally completes it by joining heaven and earth.

One of the most obvious and general connections between the City of Christ and the monastery is the emphasis placed on celibacy in the *Apocalypse of Paul*. The main criterion for entering the City of Christ is virginity or chastity. This is made explicit in the text both before and after Paul enters the City of Christ. Before Paul enters the city, he sees a beautiful and bountiful

---

[34] É. Amélineau, *Oeuvres de Schenoudi: Texte Copte et Traduction Française* (Paris, 1907–1909), 1:92. Cited after H. Behlmer, "Visitors to Shenoute's Monastery," in *Pilgrimage and Holy Space* in *Late Antique Egypt*, ed. D. Frankfurter (Leiden, 1998), 363.

[35] K. H. Kuhn, trans., *Letters and Sermons of Besa* (CSCO 157; Louvain, 1956), 106; Behlmer, "Visitors to Shenoute's Monastery," 363–4.

Land of Promise. The vision divides the good things of the Land of Promise and the City of Christ into rewards for two separate categories of people. Paul's angelic guide, referring to the extraordinary things that Paul has just seen in the Land of Promise, informs him that, "These particular promises belong to the secular ones who kept their marriage holy, but those who abstain from these things and the virgins will receive things seven times more excellent than these" (26; trans. Copeland). In this passage, righteous married individuals, *kosmikoi*, are explicitly contrasted with virgins, *parthenoi*. The former will inherit the Land of Promise, whereas the latter will receive a superior inheritance: the City of Christ.

Inside the city, Paul is shown a gathering of souls at the River of Milk who are greeted by the infants slain by Herod. They are described, according to the Latin version, as "all who keep their chastity and purity" (26; trans. Elliot).[36] A parallel text can be found among the writings of Horsiesios, a disciple of Pachomius, the founder of communal monasticism. Horsiesios links monastic purity with entering the city of God: "We have been taught: O wretched man, keep purity, and you will enter into the city of God. And the foolish man says, 'I wish to enter the city, but the pleasures of impurity I cannot renounce.'"[37] As in the *Apocalypse of Paul*, here it is the purity of the monastic life that brings a soul into the city of God.

These pure, virginal, monastic souls at the River of Milk are not, however, the first group of souls that Paul meets after he leaves the Land of Promise and sails across the waters of the Acherusian lake to the city. He first encounters the souls of men who are failed monks. The Coptic version of the *Apocalypse of Paul* is particularly revealing here because it uses a number of Greek words with specifically monastic connotations, possibly reflecting the original Greek[38]:

These are renouncers [*apotaktikoi*],[39] keeping a [monastic] regime [*politeuesthai*] and fasting [*nasteuein*], but they are more arrogant than all men, praising only

---

[36] The Coptic and Syriac versions of the *Apocalypse of Paul* independently refer to virginity, not to chastity.

[37] Hors. Frg., CSCO 159, 81–2; A. Veilleux, trans., *Pachomian Koinonia* (Kalamazoo, Mich., 1982), 3:169.

[38] This is one of the many places in which the later Greek version (G2) shows extreme, artless editing. G2 mentions the men and then launches into a discussion on pride. The description of the men as it appears in the Coptic, Latin, and Syriac has been cut out of G2.

[39] Lat. *abrenunciauerunt*. The Greek word used in the Coptic manuscript has a range of meanings from hermit to anchorite to coenobitic monk; all meanings are monastic.

themselves, despising, for their part, their neighbors. If it pleases them, they greet men. If it doesn't please them, they do not greet anyone. (24; trans. Copeland)

It is worth noting that these monks do not dwell within the walls of the City of Christ; they are only in its vicinity, directly outside its gates. They are penitent monks whose ascetic works qualify them for a place near the City of Christ, but whose lack of hospitality and great pride keeps them from entering its golden gates.

It is certainly not unusual for a monastery to have a number of monks living outside of its walls. True, in this period some hermits do so by choice, but there is also evidence that penitent monks may have been kept just outside of the monastery gates. The *Life of Theodora of Alexandria* describes the Oktokaidekaton[40] as an enclosed structure with a solid door, outside of which penitent monks lived in a hut.[41] The renouncers outside of the City of Christ in the *Apocalypse of Paul* must repent for the actions that they committed while they were still alive. Just as penitent monks are kept outside of monasteries, so these souls are punished by being kept just outside the City of Christ.

Within the gates of the City of Christ, there are two gatherings of souls that are the positive foils of the penitent monks who are unable to enter the city. Some enter the city because they gave proper hospitality to strangers, whereas others find a place in the city because they have no pride in themselves. As with the pure, chaste souls associated with the River of Milk, these souls are greeted at rivers flowing in and around the City of Christ.

At the River of Oil, the men who have "no pride in themselves" also "rejoice in the Lord God and sing psalms to the Lord with their whole heart" (*Apoc. Paul* 28; trans. Elliot). The very image of these humble men who greet visitors by singing psalms occurs repeatedly in monastic literature. For example, the party of the *History of Monks in Egypt* describes their approach to one monastery as follows: "they came running to meet us, singing psalms. For this is what they generally do with their visitors" (8.48).[42] This psalmodic

---

[40] The monastery was so-called because it was eighteen miles from Alexandria.

[41] K. Wessely, "Die Vita s. Theodorae" in *Fünfzehnter Jahresbericht des k. und k. Staatsgymnasiums in Hernals* (Vienna, 1889), 24–44. J. Gascou, "Oktokaidekaton," *Coptic Encyclopedia* (New York, 1991), 1827. The actual monastery may have looked quite different, consisting not of a single structure, but of multiple communities. Nonetheless, the literary construction remains.

[42] N. Russell and B. Ward, trans., *The Lives of the Desert Fathers: The Historia Monachorum in Aegypto* (Kalamazoo, Mich., 1980), 77.

greeting of newcomers to the City of Christ thus reflects a common monastic practice of welcoming visitors.

At another river in the city, the River of Honey, there are souls described as "every one who shall have afflicted his soul and not done his will because of God" (*Apoc. Paul* 25; trans. Elliot). Rejecting one's own desires both in favor of the will of God and in favor of the will of a spiritual father is a virtue often found among the desert monks. To give but one example among many, Poemen said "To throw himself before God, not to assess himself, and to cast his own will behind him: these are the tools of the soul."[43] Once again, a monastic virtue is embodied in the souls who inhabit the City of Christ.

Yet another group of souls demonstrates how the late antique monastic culture reinvented the heavenly city in the *Apocalypse of Paul*. Near the center of the city, there are a number of simple fools who sit upon thrones. When Paul asks for an explanation, the angel makes this reply:

> They are guileless [*akeraios*] and simple [*haplous*] men, making themselves fools for the sake of God, who do not know many [passages] in the scriptures, nor many psalms, but only the sayings that they heard from the scriptures by men of God, keeping to a strict [monastic] regime [*politeia*], their hearts upright towards God. And the righteous inside the City of Christ are amazed, saying "Look and see these uneducated ones who do not know the scriptures who have received this great honor from God because of their simplicity." (29; trans. Copeland)

These simple monks are well known in the monastic literature of the fourth and fifth centuries. The *Lausiac History*, written by Palladius around the year 420, lauds the blessed Innocent who was simple beyond measure. Palladius describes Innocent as "guileless [*akakos*] and simple [*haplous*]" (44. 3).[44] The influence of late antique Egyptian monasticism is again apparent.

Even when the *Apocalypse of Paul* uses imagery traditionally associated with the heavenly Jerusalem, it does so in a manner that reinforces its connection with the monastery, rather than with the earthly Jerusalem. For example, the City of Christ is, quite literally, the city of David:

> I saw in the midst of this city a great altar, very high, and there was someone standing near the altar whose countenance shone as the sun, and he held in his hands a psaltery and harp, and he sang saying, "Alleluia!" so that the foundations of the city were shaken; and I asked the angel and said, "Sir, who is this of

---

[43] Poemen 36, cited after G. Gould, *The Desert Fathers on Monastic Community* (Oxford, 1993), 34.
[44] R. T. Meyer, trans., *Palladius: The Lausiac History* (London, 1965), 121. A. Lucot, ed., *Palladius Histoire Lausiaque: Texte grec, introduction et tranduction française* (Paris, 1912), 298.

such great power?" And the angel said to me, "This is David. . . . [I]t is necessary that David should sing psalms in the hour of the oblation of the body and blood of Christ." (29; trans. Elliot)

It is, however, worth noting that the city of David is no longer necessarily the earthly Jerusalem. In late antique Egypt, David is found performing the Eucharist at the altar in the monastery. Shenoute reputedly said, "For behold, a chorus of angels surrounds him, making the responses and behold the prophet David stands beside him, giving him the words which are right for him to say."[45] For many late antique Egyptian Christians, David's city is the monastery, not the earthly Jerusalem.

The fact that the City of Christ is patterned after the monastery and not after the terrestrial city of Jerusalem is all the more striking because the *Apocalypse of Paul* explicitly mentions the earthly Jerusalem. The preface to the vision claims that the text was found in a marble box under the floorboards of the house once owned by Paul in Tarsus. The man who found the box sent it to Emperor Theodosius, who subsequently had the text copied. The emperor kept one of the copies for himself and had the other sent to Jerusalem. The discovery tale demonstrates that the author is familiar with Jerusalem as a Christian city. The fact that he nevertheless opts to represent his heavenly Jerusalem with the characteristics of a monastery, rather than with those of the earthly Jerusalem, emphasizes just how complete the transformation of the heavenly Jerusalem is for him.

The association of the heavenly Jerusalem with the monastery becomes even more pronounced in later centuries, as shown by the *Life of Matthaius the Poor*. In this Coptic hagiography, it is even more explicit that the entire heavenly city is intended solely for monks. In the *Life*, Matthaius recounts the following vision:

> I saw in ecstasy, two brother monks standing above me in great glory. They answered and said to me: "Rise, come quickly to meet the fathers of the schema Anthony and Pachomius and Theodore and our father Apa Moses and the holy elder and prophet Apa Shenute the Archimandrite." . . . They said to me: "It is good that thou shouldst come with us to the Heavenly Jerusalem." Then I saw a great tower and a very high wall, ... I then entered in fear and trembling. I saw a great walk, . . . , it would be two or three miles long. . . . From end to end of the

---

[45] I. Leipoldt, "Sinuthi Archimandritae Vitae et Opera Omnia. Sinuthi Vita Bohairice," CSCO, *Scriptores Coptici*. Series 2, 41 (1946): 46.2; V. MacDermot, trans., *The Cult of the Seer in the Ancient Middle East: A Contribution to Current Research on Hallucinations, Drawn from Coptic and Other Texts* (Berkeley, Calif., 1971), 443–4.

walk stretched a great multitude of thrones, with great multitudes of monks sitting upon them in great glory.[46]

In the tradition of the *Apocalypse of Paul*, the *Life of Matthaius* has further developed the theme of heavenly city as monastery.

Late antique Egyptian Christians do not see the heavenly Jerusalem as being united with the earthly Jerusalem. Unlike the authors of the *Book of the Watchers* and other early Jewish apocalypses, they do not see the image of Jerusalem's Temple dominating the heavens. David's altar is the place for the Eucharist, a central location in any monastery, not a Temple altar. In contrast to earlier Jews and Christians, who hoped for a restoration of the earthly city of Jerusalem through the descent of the heavenly city, late antique Egyptians live in an era of a Christian Jerusalem and do not wait for the heavenly Jerusalem. Surprisingly, however, this Christian Jerusalem does not influence their image of the heavenly city. Part of this, no doubt, arises from Origen's separation of the heavenly Jerusalem from both the Jewish city of Jerusalem and the Roman city of Aelia Capitolina, a rift that is not easily repaired when Jerusalem comes under Christian control. More important, however, when the heavenly Jerusalem is drawn back toward the earth in Egypt, it finds its counterpart in the local images of the monastery, not in the distant ones of Christian Jerusalem. This emphasis on local images is simultaneously a testimony to the prominence of the monastery in the late antique Egyptian geographical and cultural landscape and an indication that heaven is more easily built from materials at hand than from distant quarries.

---

[46] W. Till, "Matthaeus der Arme," in *Koptische Heiligen und Martyrer Legenden* (OrChrAn 102; Rome, 1935), 8–22 (20.3); MacDermot, *Cult of the Seer*, 505.

9

Contextualizing Heaven in Third-Century North Africa

Jan N. Bremmer

In the earliest stages of the movement of Jesus' followers, heaven was no issue. They looked out for his speedy return and were in no need of a detailed description of the "life everlasting."[1] It can, therefore, hardly be chance that the most important texts in the gospels about the afterlife, the story about Dives and Lazarus (Luke 16:19–31) and Jesus' words on the cross to the criminal ("Truly, I say to you, today you shall be with me in Paradise"; Luke 23:43), both occur only in Luke, the youngest gospel.[2] And, indeed, toward the end of the first century, the situation had changed. It had become clear that Jesus would not return within his followers' lifetimes; yet, the persecutions required an elaboration of the afterlife in order to sustain those Christians who were prepared to die for their faith. Given the absence of any authoritative description, it is surprising how early the main features of heaven became accepted in Christian tradition.[3] Nevertheless, the absence of an authoritative tradition also gave scope for individual appropriations of the standard views. We should never forget that precisely in this area there was always room for more idiosyncratic ideas, as the more interesting visions of heaven invariably contain a personal touch.

---

[1] My investigation builds upon and sometimes makes use of my earlier investigations into early Christian afterlife: *The Rise and Fall of the Afterlife* (London, 2002), 56–70; "Perpetua and Her Diary: Authenticity, Family and Visions," in *Märtyrer und Märtyrerakten*, ed. W. Ameling, (Stuttgart, 2002), 77–120; "The Vision of Saturus in the *Passio Perpetuae*," in *Jerusalem, Alexandria, Rome: Studies in Ancient Intercultural Exchanges in Honour of A. Hilhorst*, ed. F. García Martínez and G. P. Luttikhuizen (Leiden, 2003), 55–73.

[2] For the origin of the term "Paradise," see most recently A. Hultgård, "Das Paradies: vom Park des Perserkönigs zum Ort der Seligen" in *La cité de dieu = Die Stadt Gottes*, ed. M. Hengel et al. (Tübingen, 2000), 1–43; Bremmer, *Rise and Fall*, 109–19 (text), 178–84 (notes).

[3] For these ideas, see most recently A. Lumpe and H. Bietenhard, "Himmel," *RAC* 15 (1991): 173–212; J. B. Russell, *A History of Heaven: The Singing Silence* (Princeton, N.J., 1997); J. E. Wright, *The Early History of Heaven* (New York, 2000); B. Lang and C. McDannell, *Heaven: A History*, 2nd ed. (New Haven, Conn., 2001).

In my contribution, I present a commentary on one of these more personal
pictures of heaven: a vision of a North African martyr in the middle of
the third century C.E. Such visions illustrate the ways in which individual
Christians had accepted *and* modified more traditional ideas. At first sight,
a thematic discussion might perhaps better fulfill this volume's goals, but
a more comprehensive survey of North African ideas of heaven would be
possible only after a detailed analysis of all available evidence, and we have
not yet reached that stage. Christian North Africa, compared with other areas
of the Roman Empire, was unusually interested in visions, and, as a first step
towards a thematic discussion, I naturally adduce parallels from other visions
to show that the idea of heaven in this particular vision sometimes followed
traditional views.[4] Subsequently we look at our source, the *Passio Sanctorum
Mariani et Iacobi* (henceforth *Marian*; §1), the court scene in the vision (§2),
its landscape (§3), its fountain (§4), and its vision of heaven in general (§5).

The Passio Sanctorum Mariani et Iacobi

Our source derives from the description of the martyrdom of a group of
North African Christians who were arrested near Cirta in Numidia during
the Valerian persecution.[5] They were executed in the spring of 259, a few
weeks before Montanus, Lucius, and others at Carthage, but after the martyrdom of Cyprian in the autumn of 258 (§2).[6] The description itself dates
from the early fourth century, but it has used an earlier eyewitness report.[7]
The final editor had read the *Passion of Perpetua*, as a number of verbal echoes
demonstrate, and was fully in command of Roman stylistic devices such

[4] For an enumeration of the African visions, see G. W. Clarke, *The Letters of St. Cyprian of Carthage*
(New York, 1984), 1:150, 3:218. I have presented a detailed analysis of the visions in the *Passio
Perpetuae* (henceforth *Perpetua*) in my "Perpetua and Her Diary," 95–119, and "Vision of
Saturus."

[5] I use the text and translation (albeit adapted) of H. Musurillo, *The Acts of the Christian Martyrs*
(Oxford, 1972), 194–213, which is based on P. Franchi de' Cavalieri, *La Passio SS. Mariani
et Iacobi* (Rome, 1900), 42–63. For a French translation, introduction, and some notes, see
V. Saxer, *Saints anciens d'Afrique du Nord* (Vatican City, 1979), 88–103. For the date, see the
excellent discussion by A. R. Birley, "A Persecuting Praeses of Numidia under Valerian," *JTS*
42 (1991): 598–610 at 603. For the "genre" of the *Acta martyrum* and the problem of their
trustworthiness and authenticity, see Bremmer, "Perpetua and Her Diary," 78–80.

[6] For the *Passio Montani et Lucii* (hence *Montanus*), see the most recent edition by F. Dolbeau,
"La Passion des saints Lucius et Montanus," *REAug* 29 (1983): 39–82; see also R. Herzog and
P. L. Schmidt, eds., *Handbuch der lateinischen Literatur der Antike* (Munich, 1997), 4:429–30 (by
A. Wlosok, with the most recent bibliography).

[7] Herzog and Schmidt, *Handbuch*, 4:427–29 (by A. Wlosok).

as "chiastical parallelism, symmetry, alliteration and homoioteleuton."[8] In short, he clearly possessed some literary training. *Marian* contains several visions, of which we discuss here the one by the lector Marian, one of the protagonists of the martyrdom, as it is the most informative one about heaven.

After Marian had been subjected to a grueling torture, he had the following vision:

> I was shown, brothers, the towering front of a shining, high tribunal [*tribunalis excelsi et candidi*], on which, instead of the governor, a judge of a very handsome countenance presided. There was a scaffold [*catasta*] there, whose lofty platform was reached not merely by one but by many steps and was a great height to climb. And up to it were brought ranks of confessors, group by group, whom the judge ordered to be executed by the sword. It also came to my turn. Then I heard a loud, clear voice of somebody saying, "Bring up Marian!" And when I climbed up to that scaffold, look, all of a sudden Cyprian appeared, sitting at the right hand of that judge, and he stretched out his hand and lifted me up to a higher spot on the scaffold. And he smiled at me and said: "Come, sit with me."
>
> And so it happened that the other groups were interrogated, while I too was an assessor of the judge. And the judge rose, and we escorted him to his residence [*praetorium*]. Our road lay through a place with lovely meadows, clad with the joyous foliage of flourishing woods, shaded by tall cypresses and pine trees that beat against the heavens, so that you would think that the entire spot all round was crowned with fertile groves. A hollow in the center abounded in fertilizing watercourses and pure water from a clear spring.
>
> And lo! all of a sudden that judge vanished from our sight. Then Cyprian picked up a cup [*fiala*], that lay at the edge of the spring, and when he had filled it from the spring like a thirsty person, he drank. And filling it again he handed it to me, and I drank gladly. And when I said "Thank God," I woke [he said] by the sound of my own voice. (*Marian* 6.6–15)

The Court Scene

At first sight, it seems that the vision starts with a normal court scene. This should not be surprising. At the moment of his vision, Marian had already been tortured, and he was now waiting for his interrogation by the judge. In the Roman legal system, the proconsul held judicial assizes in the main provincial cities.[9] During the actual interrogation, the judge and his assessors

---

[8]   See Cavalieri, *Passio SS. Mariani*, 13, n. 1; J. Aronen, "Marianus' Vision in the Acts of Marianus and Iacobus," *Wiener Studien* 97 (1984): 169–86 at 172–3 (quote).

[9]   For the Roman system, see C. Habicht, "New Evidence on the Province of Asia," *JRS* 65 (1975): 64–91; G. P. Burton, "Proconsuls, Assizes, and the Administration of Justice under

were sitting on a semicircular tribunal, or βῆμα.[10] In front of him there was a platform (*catasta* or *ambon*, somewhat confusingly sometimes also translated with βῆμα), on which suspects were interrogated and tortured; apparently, this platform often had only one step, although it could also be higher.[11] Here, however, the future martyr does not see the typical court arrangement, such as it must have been familiar to him from experience or hearsay. On the contrary, Marian sees an extremely high, white tribunal; moreover, he does not see the normal Roman governor but an extremely handsome judge. Inasmuch as white was typical of angels and other beings in heaven in early Christianity,[12] the color evokes a heavenly tribunal, as is also suggested by its impressive height and the handsome judge.[13] In other words, we are already in heaven, even though we are not told how Marian ascended.

Marian was not the only martyr who dreamed of a court tribunal. In his *Life of Cyprian*, Pontius relates that on the day when Cyprian's exile started, the Carthaginian bishop had the following vision:

> There appeared to me [he said], when I was not yet enveloped in the quiet of sleep, a youth taller than man's measure. When this person led me, as it were, to the residence, I seemed to be conducted toward the tribunal of the proconsul who was sitting there. As he looked at me, the latter immediately began to note on his tablet a sentence which I did not know, for he asked me nothing in the usual manner of interrogation. Indeed, however, [another] young man who was standing behind him read the notation with great curiosity. And because he could not express it in words, he showed by an explanatory nod what were the contents of the writing on that tablet. With his open hand as flat as a blade he imitated the stroke of the customary punishment, thus expressing as clearly as by speech what he wanted understood.[14]

---

the Empire," *JRS* 65 (1975): 92–106; J. den Boeft and J. N. Bremmer, "Notiunculae Martyrologicae III," *VC* 39 (1985): 110–30 at 119.

[10] *Acta Pauli et Theclae* 16; H. Gabelmann, *Antike Audienz- und Tribunalszenen* (Darmstadt, 1984), 172–4; L. Robert, *Le martyre de Pionios, prêtre de Smyrne* (Washington D.C., 1994), 107–8.

[11] *Perpetua* 6.2; *Acta Phileae* (Latin) 1; *Martyrium Theodoti* 6; Eusebius, *Hist. eccl.* 8.9.5; P. Franchi de' Cavalieri, *Scritti agiografici* (Rome, 1962), 1:57, 94, 231.

[12] For many examples, see U. Körtner and M. Leutzsch, *Papiasfragmente: Hirt des Hermas* (Darmstadt, 1998), 386, n. 71, 480, n. 202.

[13] Christ is regularly pictured as a "handsome youth" in the apocryphal *Acts of the Apostles*; cf. E. Peterson, *Frühkirche, Judentum und Gnosis* (Rome, 1959), 191–2.

[14] Pontius, *Vita Cypriani* 12.3–5 Bastiaensen; the translation is slightly adapted from R. J. Deferrari, *Early Christian Biographies* (Washington, D.C., 1952), 17. For the dream, see esp. J. Amat, *Songes et visions: L'au-delà dans la littérature latine tardive* (Paris, 1985), 131–8.

For our purpose it is sufficient to note that Cyprian similarly dreamed of being led to a tribunal. We know that he was immensely influential among African Christians; this is suggested, for instance, by his presence in *Marian* and *Montanus*,[15] in which he is even consulted as the most important expert regarding the question of whether the final deathblow would be painful. Although both future martyrs would have been naturally preoccupied by their impending court cases, a certain influence of Cyprian's dream on *Marian* can hardly be excluded, given the great prestige of this bishop in North Africa.

In his dream, Marian conflates an earthly court scene with a heavenly one. The former is reflected in Marian's vision of many groups of *confessores* being brought up and condemned by the judge to the sword, as is the case with Cyprian. *Confessores* were those Christians who had confessed the name of Christ and thus were likely to become martyrs. Cyprian often mentions this confession in his contemporaneous letters.[16] To pronounce the verdict of capital punishment was the prerogative of the Roman governor,[17] and death by the sword was the most merciful death[18]; other methods of execution – for example, death through a bear – were dreaded by future martyrs.[19]

At this point, however, the scene abruptly shifts away from the normal proceedings during a court case on earth. Marian hears a voice commanding him to appear before the judge. When he starts to climb the steps of the scaffold, he suddenly sees Cyprian sitting at the right hand of the judge,[20] another testimony to the enormous respect accorded to the bishop. Cyprian lifts up Marian to the higher spot and smiles at him. We also find such smiles elsewhere in early Christian literature. When in the *Acts of Paul* (7) the apostle Paul is in prison, there appears a young man of great beauty (like the judge in Marian's vision) who smiles and loosens his bonds and, in the *Acts of Peter* (16), Jesus appears smiling to Peter in prison. The motif clearly derives from pagan epiphanies in which the appearing deity traditionally smiles to

---

[15] *Marian* 6.9, 14 and *Montanus* 11.2, 13.1, 21.3.

[16] Cyprian, *Epist.* 5.1.2, 6.1.1, 21.1.1, and *passim*.

[17] Cf. J. Ermann, *"Ius gladii* – Gedanken zu seiner rechtshistorischen Entwicklung," *ZRGG* (Rom. Abt.) 118 (2001): 365–77.

[18] B. de Gaiffier, *Recherches d'hagiographie latine* (Brussels, 1971), 70–6.

[19] *Perpetua* 19.4: Saturus dreads a bear and hopes to be killed by one bite of a leopard.

[20] This was the normal place of honor; see the many parallels in Körtner and Leutzsch, *Papias-fragmente: Hirt des Hermas*, 407–8 (by Leutzsch).

Jan N. Bremmer

reassure anxious mortals.[21] His words "Come, sit with me" meant that Marian would immediately ascend to heaven and sit on the judgment tribunal at Christ's right hand. It was indeed a widely shared idea among early Christians that after their execution, martyrs would ascend straight to heaven, where they would become assessors of Christ[22]; the idea of an immediate ascent would exert a long-lasting influence and was even taken over by the Jews during the time of the Crusades.[23] Although this small sentence might seem natural to us, it may betray a world of frustration, as on earth Cyprian would have normally sat only with presbyters: minor clergy, such as the lector Marian, had always to remain standing in deference in his presence.[24]

The Heavenly Landscape

After the completion of the trial, Cyprian and Marian escorted the judge to his residence [*praetorium*][25]:

> Our road lay through a place with lovely meadows [*locum pratis amoenum*], clad with the joyous foliage of flourishing woods, shaded by tall cypresses and pine trees that beat against the heavens, so that you would think that the entire spot all round was crowned with fertile groves. A hollow in the centre abounded in fertilizing watercourses and pure water from a clear spring. (*Marian* 6.12-13)

The journey confirms our impression that in this vision Marian is already in heaven and, therefore, no longer needs to cross a difficult terrain. Whereas Perpetua (*Perpetua* 10.3), Hermas (*Vis.* 1.1.3), and the girls in Methodius of Olympus' *Symposium* (5: §4) must pass through a rough countryside before they reach their proper goal, Marian's journey is smooth and easy. The

---

[21] Note also *Acts of John* 73. For many parallels, see O. Weinreich, *Antike Heilungswunder* (Giessen, 1909), 3, n. 2; M. Puelma, "Die Dichtersbegegnung in Theokrits Thalysien," *MH* 17 (1960): 144–64 at 149.

[22] Hermas, *Vis.* 3.1.9 (martyrs at God's right hand); Tertullian, *Mart.* 2.4; Hippolytus, *Comm. Dan.* 2.37.4; Cyprian, *Epist.* 6.2.1; 12.2.1, 15.3, 31.3; *Ad Fort.* 13; Eusebius, *Hist. eccl.* 6.42.5; K. Berger, *Die Auferstehung des Propheten und die Erhöhung des Menschensohnes* (Göttingen, 1976), 374, n. 489; Bremmer, "Perpetua and Her Diary," 101–2.

[23] S. Shepkaru, "To Die for God: Martyrs' Heaven in Hebrew and Latin Crusade Narratives," *Speculum* 77 (2002): 311–41.

[24] Cf. Cyprian, *Epist.* 1.1.1, 39.5.2, 40.1.2, 45.2, 59.19.1; *Gesta apud Zenophilum*, CSEL 26.186-187 (standing); Clarke, *Letters* 1:150.

[25] For the development in meaning of *praetorium*, see R. Egger, "Das Praetorium als Amtssitz römischer Spitzenfunktionäre," *SÖAW* 250 (1966): 3–47; A. Martin, "Praetoria as Provincial Governor's Palaces," in *Historia testis: Mélanges T. Zawadski* (Fribourg, Switzerland, 1989), 229–40.

landscape shows certain elements of a *locus amoenus* but, unlike Saturus in the *Passion of Perpetua*, Marian does not enter into much detail and mentions only a few characteristics.[26]

The element of height occurs in other pictures of lovely gardens, such as in that of Alcinoös in the *Odyssey* (7.114) and in that encountered by Socrates and Phaedrus in Plato's *Phaedrus* (230B). It even occurs in the much later, late fourth-century *Apocalypse of Paul* (24), in which Paul sees *arbores magnas et altas valde* before entering Paradise. In all these instances, height hints at the shade that is so desirable in the Mediterranean world. Pines can grow to 80 feet and were common shade trees in Greece and Italy. They are mentioned in idyllic landscapes, and Ovid fondly remembered (one is nearly tempted to say "pines for") the pines of his gardens during his exile in faraway Pontus.[27] The presence of cypresses is more problematic. It fits the context insofar as the cypress was considered one of the tallest trees,[28] but it also held a strong funerary connotation: "Its branches were placed at the door of the mourning house, on the funerary altar and the pyre itself."[29] Yet, the context does not evoke associations with death, and here the cypress must have been chosen rather for its shade-evoking qualities. The author may well have had in mind its place in contemporary parks and gardens of the local grandees, such as can still be seen on North African mosaics of the time.[30]

The cypress is also evoked in another North African vision. In the *Passion of Perpetua*, the spiritual guide of Perpetua, Saturus, relates how, after his death, he was carried by four angels beyond the present world to an intense light. Here,

> there appeared to us a great open space, which looked like a kind of park (*viridiarium*), with roses as tall as trees and all kinds of flowers. The trees were as tall as cypresses and their petals were constantly falling. (*Perpetua* 11.5–6)

[26] G. Schönbeck, "Der Locus Amoenus von Homer bis Horaz" (Ph.D. diss., University of Heidelberg, 1962); J. Ntedika, *L'évocation de l'au-delà dans la prière pour les morts* (Louvain, 1971); Amat, *Songes et visions*, 117–20; P. Hass, *Der locus amoenus in der antiken Literatur* (Bamberg, 1998).

[27] Theocritus 1.1–2; Ovid, *Ars am.* 3.692, *Pont.* 1.8.43–44; R. Nisbet and M. Hubbard, *A Commentary on Horace*, Odes, *Book II* (Oxford, 1978), 58–9.

[28] Servius on Virgil, *Ecl.* 1.25: *cupressus vero arbor est maxima*. Note the combination of the pine and the cypress in Horace, *Carm.* 4.6.10.

[29] Nisbet and Hubbard, *Commentary on Horace*, Odes, II, 236.

[30] M. Blanchard-Lemée et al., *Mosaics of Roman Africa*, trans. K. D. Whitehead (London, 1996), 167–77; M. Guggisberg, "Vom Paradeisos zum 'Paradies': Jagdmosaiken und Gartenperistyle in der römischen Herrschaftsarchitektur Nordafrikas und Siziliens," *Hefte Arch. Sem. Univ. Berns* 17 (2000): 21–39.

Apparently, Saturus also thinks of the local parks [*viridiaria*], and his reference to roses evokes spring, inasmuch as the rose was the spring flower par excellence in antiquity.[31] Indeed, in Roman times, eternal spring had become a recurrent feature of the Golden Age and the *locus amoenus*.[32] It is not surprising that it thus was incorporated into descriptions of heaven as well.[33] A gardenlike picture of the hereafter is also alluded to by the Carthaginian Tertullian,[34] and he and Saturus may well have been influenced by the *Apocalypse of Peter* (ca. 135 C.E.), in which God

> showed us a great open garden. [It was] full of fair trees and blessed fruits, full of fragrance of perfume. Its fragrance was beautiful and that fragrance reached to us. And of it.... I saw many fruits.[35]

Yet, the closest parallel to Marian's vision can be found in a sermon, formerly believed to have been by Cyprian, which probably dates to the first years of the 250s and may well have originated in Carthage itself. After a graphic picture of the torments that await the unrighteous, the author continues with the pleasures of Paradise,

> where in the verdant fields the luxuriant earth clothes itself with tender grass, and is pastured with the scent of flowers; where the groves are carried up to the lofty hilltop, and where the tree clothes with a thicker foliage whatever spot the canopy, expanded by its curving branches, may have shaded. There is no excess of cold or of heat, nor is it necessary that in autumn the fields should rest, or, again in the young spring, that the fruitful earth should bring forth her bounty. All things are of one season: fruits are borne of a continued summer, since there neither does the moon serve the purpose of her months, nor does the sun run his course along the moments of the hours, nor does the banishment of the light make way for night. A joyous repose possesses the people, a calm home shelters them, where a gushing fountain in the midst issues from the bosom

---

[31] Theophrastus, *Hist. plant.* 6.8.2; Cicero, *Verr.* 5.27; Columella 12.28.3. Note also the combination of spring and roses in a vision related by the late seventh-century Valerius of Bierzo, *Dicta ad beatum Donadeum*; cf. M. Diaz y Diaz, *Visiones del Más Allá en Galicia durante la Alta Edad Media* (Santiago de Compostela, 1985), 45–7.

[32] Virgil, *Georg.* 2.149–150; Ovid, *Met.* 1.107 with F. Bömer *ad loc.*, *Fast.* 5.207–208; Lucian, *Ver. hist.* 2.12; Claudian, *Epithal.* 55.

[33] Cyprian, *Carm.* 6.227.

[34] Tertullian, *Nat.* 1.19.6, *Apol.* 27.14, 47.13, *Or.* 3.3.

[35] For an introduction and the translation, see *New Testament Apocrypha* 2:620–38. Our quote derives from *c.* 16 of the Ethiopic translation, which is the most complete text we have.

of a broken hollow, and flows in sinuous mazes by a course deep sounding, at intervals to be divided among the sources of rivers springing from it.[36]

There are a number of verbal echoes of this sermon in Marian's description of the heavenly Paradise,[37] and it seems virtually certain that our author knew this sermon – not surprisingly, if it was in fact written in Carthage. The passage elaborates on the Arcadian aspect in comparison with Marian's vision, but it also points to another aspect that is not uncommon in descriptions of idyllic places: Instead of an eternal spring, the seasons have now disappeared altogether. We find the same abolishment of the seasons in the description of the fate of the just in the second of the *Sibylline Oracles* (327), which in this respect may eventually go back to the Greek utopian tradition. In a description of life in the reign of Kronos, Plato (*Pol.* 272A) already mentions that the seasons had been tempered so as to cause primeval man no grief, and in the utopian picture of Horace's *Epode* 16 (56), Jupiter is said to be "moderating each of the two (extremes of climate: *utrumque rege temperante caelitum*)."

In this heavenly Paradise, there is no more night or day, but light forever. The eternal light may well derive from Revelation (21:23; 22:5), in which it is said that there will be no more sun or moon because the splendor of the Lord will give light. In turn, Revelation may have been influenced by the prophecy in Zechariah (14:6–7) that "it shall come to pass in that day, that the light shall not be clear, nor dark, but it shall be one day which shall be known to the Lord, not day, nor night: but it shall come to pass that at evening time it shall be light." Before entering heaven, Saturus also saw an intense light (*Perpetua* 11.4), and many passages show that light was indeed *the* characteristic of heaven for the early Christians.[38]

The Fountain and the Cup

The final part of this description is a fountain, and this aspect brings us back to Marian's vision, in which he saw a crystal spring with fertilizing

---

[36] Pseudo-Cyprian, *De laude martyrii* 21; the translation is slightly adapted from R. E. Wallis, *The Writings of Cyprian*, 2 vols. (Edinburgh, 1868–9) = *Ante-Nicene Fathers* 13:245–46; cf. Amat, *Songes et visions*, 155–6. For date and place, see the concise discussion by J. Doignon in Herzog and Schmidt, *Handbuch*, 4:578.

[37] Aronen, "Marianus' Vision," 180–1.

[38] Bremmer, *Rise and Fall*, 60.

watercourses and pure water. The detail is not elaborated on and is hard to explain from his vision only. Fortunately, the picture in pseudo-Cyprian helps us on our way. Here, the spring is the source of rivers, and such a spring we also find elsewhere. In an imitation of Plato's *Symposium*, a Christian author of the later third century, perhaps Bishop Methodius of Lycian Olympus, has a number of virgins discuss themes of Christian theology in the Garden of Virtue. This passage features several themes that we have already discussed, such as light, fragrance, trees, and shade:

> The spot was extraordinarily beautiful and full of a profound peace. The atmosphere that enveloped us was diffused with shafts of pure light in a gentle and regular pattern; and in the very centre was a spring from which there bubbled up, as gently as though it were oil, the most delicious water; and the crystal-clear water formed into little rivulets. These, overflowing their banks, as rivers do, watered the ground all about with their abundant streams. And there were various kinds of trees there, laden with mellow, ripe fruit hanging gaily from their branches – a picture of beauty. The ever-blossoming meadows, too, were dotted with all kinds of sweet-scented flowers, and from them there was wafted a gentle breeze laden with perfume. Now a stately chaste-tree [*vitex agnus castus*] grew nearby; here under its far-spreading canopy we rested in the shade.[39]

The description clearly alludes to the beginning of Plato's *Phaedrus*, but instead of settling beneath a plane tree – an influential motif in ancient literature – the virgins settled under an *agnus castus*, a tree symbolic of chastity.[40] For our subject, it is important to note that here too we find a spring in the very middle of a landscape that is explicitly called a "new Eden." In other words, the spring in Marian's vision is clearly the spring in Paradise from which the four great rivers (Pishon, Gihon, Tigris, and Euphrates; Gen 2:10–14) originated.[41] The similarities between the Carthaginian and the Lycian descriptions of the spring suggest an earlier source, which must unfortunately remain obscure. The spring is not yet mentioned in Genesis, and the "source and the river flowing from it" in the Garden of Eden mentioned in

---

[39] Methodius, *Symp.*, Prelude 7–8, trans. H. Musurillo, *St. Methodius, The Symposium: A Treatise on Chastity* (Westminster, 1958), 40–1. For the Greek text and the author, see H. Musurillo and V.-H. Debidour, *Méthode d'Olympe, Le Banquet* (Paris, 1963).

[40] Plane tree: Plato, *Phdr.* 229A; Cicero, *De or.* 1.29; Apuleius, *Met.* 1.18; Achilles Tatius 1.2.3; Marcellinus, *Life of Thucydides* 25. Agnus castus: See the brilliant study by H. von Staden, "Spiderwoman and the Chaste Tree: The Semantics of Matter," *Configurations* 1 (1992): 23–56.

[41] For the rivers, see most recently E. Noort, "Gan-Eden in the Context of the Mythology of the Hebrew Bible," in *Paradise Interpreted*, ed. G. P. Luttikhuizen (Leiden, 1999), 27–34.

the early Jewish *Apocalypse of Abraham* (21.6) can hardly have been at the basis of the later descriptions. The same is true of the *Apocalypse of Paul*; the apostle sees "a tree planted from whose roots water flowed out, and from this was the beginning of the four rivers" (45).[42] It is not impossible, then, that the spring in Marian's vision is the product of a Christian development.[43]

After Cyprian and Marian had arrived at the spring, the judge suddenly vanishes from our sight:

> Then Cyprian picked up a cup [*fiala*], that lay at the edge of the spring, and when he had filled it from the spring like a thirsty person, he drank. And filling it again he handed it to me, and I drank gladly. And when I said "Thank God," I woke [he said] by the sound of my own voice.

Unlike Perpetua, who explains her visions several times in the *Passion of Perpetua* (4.10, 7.9, 8.4, 10.14), Marian does not interpret his own vision, but his editor continues with this: "Then James also recalled that a manifestation of the divine favor had hinted this crown would be his" (7.1). In other words, using an immensely popular metaphor from athletics, the editor suggests that Marian will become a martyr. But how did he arrive at this interpretation? We may find an answer if we look more closely at the two other visions in which a *fiala* occurs.

When in a vision Perpetua had seen her deceased brother Dinocrates in a sorry state, she prayed intensely for him, and after a few days she had another vision:

> I saw that place that I had seen before and Dinocrates with a clean body, well dressed and healthy. And where the wound was, I saw a scar; and the basin that I had seen before now had its rim lowered to the level of the boy's waist. And water incessantly flowed from it. And above the rim there was a golden cup [*fiala*] full of water. And Dinocrates drew close and drank from it, yet that dish did not run short. And when he was satisfied he began to play with the water, as children do, full of happiness. And I woke up. Then I realized that he was liberated from his penalty. (*Perpetua* 8)

Rather remarkably, the *fiala* also returns in *Montanus*, where a mother, Quartillosia, whose husband and son had just been martyred and who herself would also soon be a martyr, saw in a vision her martyred son coming to

---

[42] For a discussion of the passage, see A. Hilhorst, "A Visit to Paradise: Apocalypse of Paul 45 and its Background," in *Paradise Interpreted*, 128–39.

[43] For a representation of this source on a Tunisian vessel, see A. Grabar, *Christian Iconography* (Princeton N.J., 1968), Fig. 39.

prison. "He sat down at the rim of the water-trough and said: 'God has seen your pain and tribulation.' And after him there entered a young man of remarkable size who carried two cups [*fialas*] full with milk in his hands." The young man offered everyone drinks from these cups, but they were never emptied. Afterward, the window of the prison suddenly became bright and heaven became visible. Then the young man put down his two cups and said, "Look, you are satisfied and there is more: still a third cup will be left over for you." And then he left (8).

Although the two later visions have clearly been influenced by Perpetua's vision, they each appropriate her visions in their own way.[44] Yet, they can perhaps help us to find a meaning in this at first sight rather enigmatic symbol. In *Montanus*, the young man (an angel?) hands out cups with milk. Now, the newly initiated faithful received milk and honey after baptism,[45] which was then immediately followed by the Eucharist.[46] A connection between milk and the Eucharist is supported by the fact that on the day after the vision, the future martyrs received *alimentum indeficiens* instead of their daily ration of food from two fellow Christians *velut per duas fialas* (9.2), a clear reference to the two cups in Quartillosia's vision. The young man's promise that there is still a third cup left seems to point to the impending martyrdom of Quartillosia.

In the case of Marian's vision, the connection is much less clear. The text interprets the vision itself as a revelation by *divina dignatio* to confirm his hope of salvation (*ad fiduciam spei salutaris*; 6.5), and Marian's vision is immediately followed by a report of a vision of James, which is also interpreted as a manifestation of the *divina dignatio* that the martyr's crown would be his (7.1). In other words, the context suggests a link between the cup and martyrdom.[47] Now, in a discussion of the penitent, Cyprian rhetorically asks, "How can we make them fit for the cup of martyrdom [*ad martyrii poculum*], if we do not first allow them the right of communion and admit them to drink, in the

---

[44] See the subtle analysis by V. Lomanto, "Rapporto fra la 'Passio Perpetuae' e 'Passiones' africane," in *Forma futuri*, 566–86, who at 581–5 discusses the parallels between *Perpetua* and *Marian*.

[45] Tertullian, *Cor.* 3.3, *Marc.* 1.14.3, *Scorp.* 1.12; Hippolytus, *Trad. ap.* 21; still useful, H. Usener, *Kleine Schriften* IV (Leipzig, 1910), 398–417 ("Milch und Honig").

[46] Tertullian, *Idol.* 7: *manus admovere corpori Domini*; Cyprian, *Epist.* 58.9.2, *Laps.* 15; Cyril of Jerusalem, *Catecheses mystagogicae* 5.21; Chrysostomus, *Hom.* 47 (*PG* 63, 898); Franchi, *Scritti agiografici*, 1:236, n. 3.

[47] See also Mark 10:38–39.

church, the cup of the Lord?"[48] Our *fiala*, then, is clearly a representation of this "cup of martyrdom" and, by gladly drinking from it, Marian accepts his forthcoming martyrdom.

There is a striking difference, though, between the vision of Perpetua and that of Marian. In Perpetua's vision, her brother takes the cup himself, but in Marian's vision, Marian receives the cup from Cyprian. Perpetua seems to have been a highly self-confident young woman, who felt assured enough to ask for a vision from God (*Perpetua* 4.1–2); consequently, she imagined her brother as taking the cup by himself. Marian, however, occupied a lowly position in the Christian clergy, and he could imagine receiving the cup only from his revered bishop.

After he had drunk from the cup, Marian said *Deo gratias*. The words may seem normal to us, but they would have been more significant to contemporaneous African readers. When a group of martyrs from Scillium was condemned to death by Proconsul Saturninus,[49] they answered with *Deo gratias*; the same words were pronounced by Cyprian and the young recruit Maximilian.[50] Apparently, this was the standard African Christian reaction to the pronouncement of their death sentence. And it is by the sound of these so fateful words that Marian is awakened. Similarly, Perpetua woke up from her first vision after those present in heaven had said "Amen!" (4.9).

Marian's Heaven

Having come to the end of our discussion of Marian's vision of heaven, what can we conclude? First, it is clear that heaven is above us. Marian has to ascend a high tribunal, just as in the *Passion of Perpetua*. Perpetua has to climb a high ladder (4.3); similarly, her teacher Saturus relates that after his death, he was carried by angels as if they were climbing a gentle hill (11.3).[51] Although Marian's vision does not stress the vertical symbolism to the same

---

[48] Cyprian, *Epist.* 57.2.2; the expression *poculum martyrii* also occurs in 37.2.2. Elsewhere, he speaks of *poculum salutare* (28.1.2) and *calix salutis* (76.4.2); see also *Martyrium Polycarpi* 14.2; Tertullian, *Scorp.* 12; Origen, *Mart.* 28; Franchi, *Scritti agiografici*, 2:244, n. 1.

[49] For the proconsul, see J. Nollé, *Side im Altertum* I (Bonn, 1993), 239f.

[50] *Passio Sanctorum Scillitanorum* 15, 17; *Acta Cypriani* 3².6 Bastiaensen; *Acta Maximiliani* 3.2; Franchi, *Scritti agiografici*, 2:243–45.

[51] L. Beirnaert, "Le symbolisme ascensionnel dans la liturgie et la mystique chrétiennes," *Eranos-Jahrbuch* 19 (1950): 41–63; see now esp. F. Graf in this volume.

extent as Perpetua's vision, in which she had to climb a dangerous ladder,[52] it clearly situates heaven above us.

Second, there is a close connection between heaven and martyrdom in our texts. Perpetua, Saturus, and Marian all dream that they ascend straight to heaven after their martyrdom. This was indeed a widespread belief among the early Christians, which must have sustained them during their arrests and executions.[53]

Third, in his *Peregrinus* (13), the pagan satirist Lucian had already noted that Christians persuaded themselves that they were immortal and would live forever. It is, therefore, not surprising that they must have been curious as to what heaven looked like. We know about this curiosity from an intriguing passage in *Montanus* (7.3–5). Here, a presbyter, Victor, relates that in a vision he saw a youth [*puer*], "whose face shone with an indescribable brilliance," entering his prison. Victor realized that he was the *Dominum de paradise*, and, rather surprisingly, asked him where heaven was. When the youth answered, "It is outside this world," Victor said "Show it to me." But the youth refused to do so and replied, "And where would your faith be?" Thus, if a presbyter could already be curious, how much more so the average Christian?

Fourth, heaven in Marian's vision is depicted as a garden but not in great detail. Both aspects deserve some comments. From the description in the *Apocalypse of Peter* (§3), it is clear that the Christians had adopted the identification of heaven with Paradise already at an early stage. The garden is virtually absent in New Testament eschatology, but it is important in Jewish eschatology, as the projection in the *Endzeit* of the *Urzeit* Garden of Eden.[54] Descriptions of this garden are elaborated with details from the traditional *locus amoenus* and contemporary parks (§3). Yet, Marian presents fewer details than some of the other descriptions quoted. It is not impossible that in his case we find influence from Cyprian, who was rather reticent about the content of fate after death[55]: This reticence seems to be reflected in the scarcity of details about heaven in both *Marian* and *Montanus*.

Finally, I have called my contribution "contextualizing heaven" not without a reason. Whether we believe or not, we all carry with us certain

---

[52] For the ladder, see Bremmer, "Perpetua and Her Diary," 98–100.

[53] C. Hill, *Regnum caelorum: Patterns of Millennial Thought in Early Christianity*, 2nd ed. (Grand Rapids, Mich., 2001), 203–6; Bremmer, *Rise and Fall*, 58–9.

[54] See now the various studies in Luttikhuizen, *Paradise Interpreted*; J. P. Brown, *Israel und Hellas* (Berlin, 2001), 3:138–40.

[55] Amat, *Songes et visions*, 153–4.

stereotyped images of heaven. Yet, we should always remember that these images are the fruit of a two-millennia-long tradition. In the first centuries of the new faith, the Christian faithful could still contribute to that tradition. Marian's vision shows that his picture of heaven was already influenced by the intertestamentary tradition of Paradise in heaven, but also by his knowledge (experience?) of the legal procedure during the interrogations of Christians, his impending martyrdom, and his admiration of Cyprian. His idiosyncratic vision demonstrates that traditions must always be appropriated, and this process is conditioned by the context in which we find ourselves: be it on earth or, as in Marian's case, in heaven.[56]

---

[56] Unfortunately, B. Shaw, "Judicial Nightmares and Christian Memory," *JECS* 11 (2003): 533–63, which is highly relevant to my section on "The Court Scene," appeared too late to be taken into account.

10

Bringing the Heavenly Academy Down to Earth: Approaches to the Imagery of Divine Pedagogy in the East Syrian Tradition

Adam H. Becker

The School of Nisibis was a semimonastic East Syrian institution of exegetical learning that flourished in the sixth century C.E.[1] Several examples of an East Syrian genre of "Cause" literature are extant, some composed by members of this school.[2] The most interesting of these texts is the *Cause of the Foundation of the Schools*, a late sixth-century address to the incoming class at Nisibis that purports to give a history of education, beginning with God's instruction to the angels at the time of creation and concluding with the tenure of Henana of Adiabene, the head of the school at the time of the speech's composition.[3] The *Cause* employs rich pedagogical imagery in recasting cosmogonic, Israelite, pagan, and Christian history as a long series of different schools. The few scholars who have commented on this bizarre text have suggested that the *Cause* is heavily dependent on the ideas of Theodore of Mopsuestia, particularly his notion of divine *Paideia*. This supposition is no doubt true. The purpose of this paper, however,

I would like to thank the editors as well as an anonymous reader and Leyla B. Aker for their helpful criticisms.

[1] The most detailed treatment of the School of Nisibis remains A. Vööbus, *History of the School of Nisibis* (CSCO Subsidia 26; Louvain, 1965). "East Syrians" are also traditionally referred to as "Nestorians," "Dyophysites," and the "Church of the East." Each of these appellations has its limitations.

[2] On this genre, see E. Riad, *Studies in the Syriac Preface* (Studia Semitica Upsaliensis 11; Uppsala, 1988), 136–7.

[3] A. Scher, *Barhadbeshabba of Holwan, Cause de la fondation des écoles* (PO 4.4; Paris, 1907), 317–404 [1–90]. A better translation of the title would be *The Cause of the Establishment of the Session of the Schools*; however, this was probably not the original title of the work, if it even had one, as it seems to refer to only a section at the end of the text (i.e., 79–80). For discussion of the meaning of the title, see R. Macina, "L'homme à l'école de Dieu, D'Antioche à Nisibe: Profil herméneutique, théologique et kérugmatique du mouvement scoliaste nestorien," *Proche-Orient Chretien* 32 (1982): 116–17, n. 22.

is to propose that other factors also lie behind the pedagogical imagery of the *Cause*. After demonstrating the *Cause*'s dependence on Theodore, I propose three other approaches to understanding the origins of this striking imagery.

The Heavenly Classroom in the *Cause of the Foundation of the Schools*

Although my analysis has bearing on the *Cause* as a whole, I focus particularly on a passage that describes the heavenly classroom at the time of creation. This passage comes from an earlier part of the *Cause*, which includes a detailed discussion of the epistemological inaccessibility of God and of how rational creatures – that is, angels and humans – are nevertheless able to know God. The passage ends with a discussion of the angelic school in heaven at the time of Creation and the different roles of the angels in the celestial hierarchy. This discussion of angelic learning sets the stage for the next section, a narrative description of the various human schools, which makes up the majority of the *Cause*.

I begin by quoting the passage in full (34.4–35.13) and then briefly summarize the other relevant parts of the *Cause*:

> Because the spiritual powers are first in creation and more excellent in substance, God brought forth his teaching to them, lest they should fall in error and falsely suppose great things about themselves. He wrote a scroll of imperceptible light with his finger of creative power, and with his command upon it[4] he had them read with an audible voice: "Let there be light, and there was light" [Gen 1:3] and because there was an understanding mind in them, at that very moment they understood that everything that comes into being came into being from another and everyone who is in authority is commanded by someone who is in authority, and from this they knew exactly that the one who brought this excellent nature into being also created them. Therefore, all of them in a group with an audible voice repaid their creator with thanks, as it is said in Job, "When I was creating the stars of dawn, all my angels shouted with a loud voice and praised me" [Job 38:7].
>
> In a similar manner we have a practice: after we have a child read the simple letters and repeat them, we join them one to another and from them we put together names that he may read syllable by syllable and be trained. The eternal teacher did the same: after he had them repeat the alphabet, he then arranged it [i.e., the alphabet] with the great name which is the construction of the

---

4   The meaning of *'law(ḥy)* here is unclear.

firmament and he read it in front of them that they might understand that he is the creator of them all, and as he orders them, they complete his will, and because they are quick-witted, they receive teaching quickly; in six days he taught them a wholly accurate teaching; at one time in the gathering together of the waters and in the growth of the trees; at another in the coming into being of the creeping things; and then at another in the creation of the animals and in the division of the luminaries, with these then also in the birds of wing, up until he made them comprehend the number ten; and he taught them again something else in the creation of the human being; and thence did he hand over to them the visible creation, that like letters they might write them in their continuous variations and read syllable by syllable with them the name of the creator and organizer of all. And he let them go and allowed them to be in this place of the school, more spacious than the earth.[5]

According to the *Cause*, there are two types of angelic students: the lazy and the diligent. In what may be a subtle warning to the speech's freshman audience, we are told how the lazy angels began to complain when God commanded them to pay honor to human beings and how they were beaten by their master and cast out of the school of heaven, whereas the diligent angels were given various positions in the celestial hierarchy (36–38).[6]

After the angelic classroom of creation, the *Cause* describes the long history of human schools, which begins when God establishes a school for Adam in the Garden. Adam erases the law from the tablet he is given and is ejected from school (38–40). The schools of Cain and Abel, Noah, and Abraham then follow (40–42). When God makes Moses the headmaster [*rabbaytā*] of the "great school of perfect philosophy" (42.6), humans are no longer just pupils, but begin to be instructors in their own schools (42–45). Joshua receives this school from Moses; later, Solomon and the prophets have their own schools as well (45–48).

The *Cause* then describes the schools of the different Greek philosophers, of the Zoroastrians, and of others who failed in their attempt to imitate the schools previously established by God (48–53). After this period of decline, Jesus came and "renewed the first school of his father" (53). He "made John

---

[5]   The Syriac of the last line is awkward: *'aršel šbaq 'ennon da-bhā na bayta rwi(y)ha d-beyt yulpā na d-men 'ar'a* (35.12–13).

[6]   Angelic resentment of humans for the honor accorded to them is a common theme. Its immediate source here, however, seems to be Theodore's commentary and Narsai's metrical homilies, which depend on it. With regard to my subsequent discussion, it is worth noting that this theme is also found in rabbinic literature; see P. Schäfer, *Rivalität zwischen Engeln und Menschen: Untersuchungen zur rabbinischen Engelvorstellung* (SJ 8; Berlin, 1975).

the Baptist a reader and instructor [*maqryānā wbādoqā*] and the apostle Peter the headmaster [*rabbaytā*]" (53.13–54.1). The *Cause* goes on to describe the schools of Paul and the apostles (59–60); the school of Alexandria, where Scripture is first interpreted (61–62); the various post-Nicene schools, including that of Theodore of Mopsuestia (62–67); the School of Edessa and its closure (67–72); and then, finally, the different heads of the School of Nisibis (72–79).

The Influence of Theodore of Mopsuestia

Theodore of Mopsuestia's influence can be seen specifically in the preceding passage's exegesis of Genesis 1 and more generally in the way that the *Cause* depicts all of human history as a sequence of schools. A description of Theodore's exegesis of Genesis 1 and a discussion of his idea of divine *Paideia* illustrate both of these points of influence.

Insofar as it can be reconstructed, Theodore's commentary on Genesis clearly lies behind the *Cause*'s understanding of Genesis 1.[7] He divides the creation narrative into two parts. The heavens, the earth, and various other entities whose creation is not mentioned by Scripture (e.g., fire, darkness, and the angels) came into being by God's will alone. Gen 1:1 – "In the beginning God created the heavens and the earth" – is Moses' abridged description of this earlier creation. The second creation comes about through God's verbal fiats: "Let there be light!" "Let there be a firmament!" and so forth. Of course, God did not need his word to bring about this second creation, but he used it to teach the angels that it is he who is the creator of everything and that he wields authority over all. During the first creation, "there was no one for whom it was fitting to learn anything from his word"[8]; hence, God's silence.

Theodore's understanding of the transcendence and omnipotence of God directs his exegesis of Genesis 1. Although some early Christians would

---

[7] The most significant collection of fragments of Theodore's commentary on Genesis is E. Sachau, *Theodori Mopsuesteni Fragmenta Syriaca* (Leipzig, 1869). Fragments can also be found in R. M. Tonneau, "Théodore de Mopsueste: Interprétation (du Livre) de la Genèse," *Mus* 66 (1953): 45–64; and T. Jansma, "Théodore de Mopsueste, Interprétation du Livre de la Genèse: Fragments de la version syriaque (B.M. Add. 17,189, fol. 17–21)," *Mus* 75 (1962): 63–92. Quotations from the Greek text can be found in the *Catena* tradition as well as in John Philoponus' refutation of Theodore's ideas in C. Scholten, trans., *De Opificio Mundi* (Freiburg, 1997).

[8] Sachau, *Fragmenta Syriaca*, 4.18–19.

use God's ability to create with his word alone as evidence of his power, in Theodore's view, it seems to limit the divine omnipotence, which can cause things to be by will alone. Thus, Theodore requires another reason for the creation by fiat, and he finds it in the unknowability of God. The angels recognize the creator through the effect that his creative word exerts on the world. Furthermore, by comparing the objects of this world through a process of analogy, the angels use their reason to learn about God.[9] By using his word [Gr. *logos*, Syr. *melthā*], God allows himself to be recognized by the angels who are rational [Gr. *logikos*, Syr. *mlilā*].[10]

In the preceding quotation from the *Cause*, the creation of the angels before the six days of creation, God's desire to teach the angels about himself, the angels' rational inference of God's authority, and even the use of Job 38:7 derive from Theodore's commentary on Genesis. Theodoran influence can be seen more broadly in the pedagogical schematization of history that follows the passage. As Macina, Wallace-Hadrill, and Reinink have suggested,[11] the *Cause* is dependent on Theodore's idea of divine *Paideia*, in which divine providence directs the present age until the future age of immortality and endows us with rational minds to make decisions, laws to guide us, and bodily existence to develop and test our virtues.[12] Scholars have certainly been correct in emphasizing that the theological roots of the *Cause* lie in Theodore's writings. Often referred to by the East Syrians as "the Interpreter," Theodore was considered by them and later scholars as the exegetical and theological authority of the East Syrian tradition, and

---

[9] See use of *pehma* in Sachau, *Fragmenta Syriaca*, 1.15, 2.3, 2.8; contrast *Cause* 21.3.

[10] Sachau, *Fragmenta Syriaca*, 1–4.

[11] G. J. Reinink, "'Edessa Grew Dim and Nisibis Shone Forth': The School of Nisibis at the Transition of the Sixth-Seventh Century," in *Centres of Learning: Learning and Location in Pre-Modern Europe and the Near East*, ed. J. Drijvers and A. A. MacDonald (Studies in Intellectual History 61; Leiden, 1995), 83–5. See also D. S. Wallace-Hadrill, *Christian Antioch: A Study of Early Christian Thought in the East* (Cambridge, 1982), 63; R. Macina, "L'homme à l'école de Dieu."

[12] Theodore's comments on Gal 2:15–16 are a good starting point for this. See H. B. Swete, ed., *Theodori episcopi Mopsuesteni in epistolas B. Pauli Commentarii* (Cambridge, 1880–2), 1:24.14–32.5 (e.g., 26.9–15: "dedit autem nobis praesentem hanc vitam mortalem, ut dixi, ad exercitationem virtutum et doctrinam illorum quae nos convenient facere. Multas in ea patimur vertibilitates, quasi qui et in natura mortali; nunc quidem hoc, nunc eligentes illud et facientes; in quibus non modica de illis quae non convenient et lege sunt interdicta facimus. Omni autem ex parte rationabilitas in nos et eligendi potestas exercetur"). For divine *Paideia*, see U. Wickert, *Studien zu den Pauluskommentaren Theodors von Mopsuestia als Beitrag zum Verständnis der antiochenischen Theologie* (BZNW 27; Berlin, 1962), 89–101; R. Macina, "L'homme à l'école de Dieu."

his works have been seen as providing the foundation for much East Syrian thought.

However, the rich and detailed imagery that we find in the *Cause* has no parallel in Theodore's works. To be sure, the Greek *paideuein* can be found behind the extant Syriac of his commentary on Genesis, but the imagery goes no further than this. Moreover, just as the *Cause* takes Theodore's exegesis of Genesis to another level, so its presentation of human history as a succession of schools puts Theodore's idea of divine *Paideia* into far more concrete terms. Theodore may have understood God as instructing the angels at creation and humans throughout history, but he does not speak of classrooms and schools. His works fail to explain the genesis of the rich imagery of the *Cause*.

The Pedagogical Tendency in Syriac Literature

An alternative approach to understanding this imagery is offered by a more nuanced interpretation of the history of East Syrian thought. The East Syrian reliance on Theodore was not as complete as scholars, often following the statements of the East Syrians themselves, have suggested.[13] Although the East Syrians continued to pay lip service to Theodore's authority – perhaps because his name had become an emblem of their resistance to western Christological formulations – they relied on other sources and at times even engaged in exegetical activities of which Theodore would have disapproved, such as allegorical exegesis.[14]

Furthermore, recent scholarship has revealed the complex relationship between early Antiochene and Edessene exegesis. Whereas the earlier model held that Theodore's ideas were introduced into the Syriac milieu when his books were brought to Edessa and translated into Syriac, we now know that previous exegetical contact existed between Edessa and Antioch. For example, Eusebius of Emesa (d. ca. 359), whose work has only recently been

---

[13] Theodore's name was invoked in Synods from the late sixth century onward, perhaps in reaction to his posthumous condemnation at the fifth ecumenical council in 553. For example, see S. Brock, "The Christology of the Church of the East in the Synods of the Fifth to Early Seventh Centuries: Preliminary Considerations and Materials," in *Studies in Syriac Christianity* (Brookfield, Vt., 1992), 127, 130, 135.

[14] The use of allegory, or "spiritual exegesis," increased among the East Syrians, particularly in the seventh century. For an English translation of the seventh-century Dadisho's defense of this practice, see S. Brock, *A Brief History of Syriac Literature* (Kottayam, India, 1997), 226–9. For the full text and French translation, see R. Draguet, ed. and trans., *Commentaire du livre d'Abba Isaïe (logoi I–XV) par Dadišo Qatraya*, 2 vols. (CSCO 326–327; Louvain, 1972).

studied, came from Edessa, but is considered part of the Antiochene school of exegesis.[15] This dual identity in a writer who predates Theodore suggests closer ties between Antiochene and Edessene exegesis than previously assumed, ties prior to the influx of Theodore's works into Edessa. Thus, the East Syrian attraction to the writings of Theodore may be due to their sharing a similar intellectual background with him.[16]

Another church writer to have a major impact on East Syrian thought is Ephraem the Syrian (or, of Nisibis; d. 373). Like Theodore, Ephraem emphasizes the ontological divide between the creator and the created. For him, the immense gap between humans and God is overcome by three different yet related "modes of divine self-revelation"; that is, God allows himself to be known through the types and symbols found in both Nature and Scripture, through his "putting on" of the various names that he allows himself to be called, and through his incarnation.[17] Although Ephraem does not use the language of the classroom, it is clear that he is working with a model in which God acts as an instructor.[18]

Theodore was not the sole major influence on the East Syrians; rather, he shared a similar, broad tradition with them as well as certain ideas about divine self-disclosure. Furthermore, the idea that God instructs his creatures and the notion that religious history is a history of didacticism were not rare in early Christianity. Early Christians had for some time used pedagogical terminology borrowed from the institutional discourses of the Graeco-Roman world to talk about themselves and their movement. Christianity could be

[15] See R. B. ter Haar Romeny, "Eusebius of Emesa's Commentary on Genesis and the Origins of the Antiochene School," in *The Book of Genesis in Jewish and Oriental Christian Interpretation: A Collection of Essays*, ed. J. Frishman and L. Van Rompay (Louvain, 1997), 125–42.

[16] L. Van Rompay, "Quelques remarques sur la tradition syriaque de l'oeuvre exégétique de Théodore de Mopsueste," in *IV Symposium Syriacum 1984: Literary Genres in Syriac Literature*, ed. H. J. W. Drijvers, R. Lavenant, C. Molenberg, and G. J. Reinink (OrChrAn 229; Rome, 1987), 33–43. Note that the Synod of 486, which has been interpreted as evidence for the Nestorianization of the Church of the East, was merely reiterating the traditional Antiochene–Syrian anti-Theopaschite Christology; cf. S. Brock, "Christology of the Church," 126, 130. On links between Theodore's theology and the Syriac milieu, see H. J. W. Drijvers, "Early Forms of Antiochene Christology after Chalcedon," in *Studies in Theology and Church History Offered to Albert van Roey*, ed. C. Laga, J. A. Munitiz, and L. van Rompay (OLA 18; Louvain, 1985), 99–113.

[17] I take this formulation from S. Brock, *The Luminous Eye: The Spiritual World Vision of St. Ephraem* (Kalamazoo, Mich., 1992), 40–3.

[18] In one of Ephraem's metrical homilies, "learning" [*yulphānā*] is hypostasized into a being that stands below God and acts as an intermediary between teacher and student; cf. E. Beck, ed., *Ephraem the Syrian, Sermones de Fide*, 2 vols. (CSCO 212–13; Louvain, 1961), Memra V 1.

characterized variously as a new nation [*ethnos*] or "polity" [*politeia*], as a kind of family, as the "true" Israel, or as a school among the many philosophies of the day.[19] Even in the first century, Philo and Josephus describe Judaism as a "school of thought,"[20] and the gospels present Jesus and his followers as a teacher (rabbi) and students (disciples). This pedagogical model is present in the Christian appropriation of the term *hairesis* (originally meaning school of thought) from the ancient classroom to talk about those who were theologically aberrant.[21] This model is also apparent in the fact that many ecclesiastical documents were referred to as "Teachings."[22]

In the Syriac milieu, in particular, we can see this tendency to scholasticize discussions of Christianity. The Pethion–Adurhormizd–Anahid cycle from the *Persian Martyr Acts* repeatedly employs words associated with the realm of learning to describe the Christianization of the Zoroastrian upper class through several generations, up to the persecution under Yazdgard II (ca. 446–448).[23] An excellent early example of this pedagogical tendency can be seen in the Syriac version of Eusebius' *Ecclesiastical History*, translated perhaps in the late fourth century.[24] Indigenous Syrian terminology creeps into the text of Book II, in which Eusebius uses Philo's account of the Therapeutae (*De Vita Contemplativa*) as evidence for early Christian monasticism. Words associated with early Syriac asceticism, such as *iḥidāyā* [solitary] and

---

[19] For Christianity as family, see D. K. Buell, *Making Christians: Clement of Alexandria and the Rhetoric of Legitimacy* (Princeton, N. J., 1999). Bibliographies on the Christian appropriation of Jewish/Israelite history can be found in the large corpus of secondary literature on early Christian anti-Judaism; esp. M. Simon, *Verus Israel: A Study of the Relations Between Christians and Jews in the Roman Empire, 135–425*, trans. H. McKeating (New York, 1986).

[20] See Josephus' descriptions of the different "schools" of Judaism (*J.W.* 2.119–166; *Vita* 10–12; *Ant.* 13.171–173; 18.11–22). For Philo: D. Runia, "Philo of Alexandria and the Greek Hairesis-Model," *VC* 53 (1999): 117–47. For first-century Judaism and early Christianity: S. Mason, "*Philosophiai*: Graeco-Roman, Judean, and Christian," in *Voluntary Associations in the Graeco-Roman World*, ed. J. S. Kloppenborg and S. G. Wilson (New York, 1996), 31–58.

[21] Much has been written on the history of the word *hairesis*. Although somewhat out-of-date, see M. Desjardins, "Bauer and Beyond: On Recent Scholarly Discussions of *Hairesis* in the Early Christian Era," *SecCent* 8 (1991): 65–82.

[22] There are several works with this or a similar title, e.g., the *Didache* and the *Didascalia Apostolorum*.

[23] There is a full summary and a translation of the Anahid portions of the story in S. Brock and S. A. Harvey, eds., *Holy Women of the Syrian Orient* (Berkeley, Calif., 1987), 66–7, 82–9. For the Syriac text of the whole, see P. Bedjan, ed., *Acta Martyrum et Sanctorum* (Hildesheim, 1968), 2:559–631.

[24] The older of the two manuscripts of the *Ecclesiastical History* is dated to 462–463 C.E. (St. Petersburg Codex). The manuscript of Eusebius' *On the Theophania* dates to 411 (British Library Add. 12150). Neither are autographs.

qaddishutā [holy celibacy], replace more familiar Greek words. However, the translator also imports pedagogical terminology into the Syriac version; for example, "ones who have become pupils" [*mettalmdin*] for "acquaintances" [*gnōrimoi*], "instruction, discipleship" [*tulmādā*] for "the race" [*to genos*], and "learning, doctrine" [*yulphānā*] for "way of life" [*politeia*].[25] Thus, before the translation of Theodore's works into Syriac, there was both the idea of God as pedagogue and the understanding of Christianity as learning in the Syriac milieu.

Parallel "Earthly" Institutionalization

The pedagogical relationship between God and the human being may have been a common theme in early Christian, especially Syriac, literature; however, it does not sufficiently explain the origins of the concrete imagery of the classroom in heaven found in the *Cause*. We must employ another approach to understanding this imagery, one offered by setting it within its institutional context. The imagery of the *Cause* may be closely related to the ideas of Ephraem and Theodore, but the internal development of East Syrian thought does not explain why the *Cause* scholasticizes heaven and all of human history in such an extreme way. The socio-historical context, or "earthly reality," of the *Cause* was radically different from that of Theodore and Ephraem, and this too may explain its "imagined realm." Theodore came from a world of *paideia*, in which figures such as John Chrysostom (d. 407) and Rabbula of Edessa (d. 435), or even the later John of Tella (d. 538) – young Christian elites nourished on Homer and Demosthenes – shocked their parents by rejecting the appurtenances of their class and starving themselves in the wilderness; however, these same men often passed through this rejectionist phase – doubtlessly to the relief of their parents – and went on as bishops to distinguish themselves in a manner befitting ancient elites.[26] The real Ephraem, contrary to his exciting and almost completely fictitious

---

[25] W. Wright and N. McLean, eds., *The Ecclesiastical History of Eusebius in Syriac* (Cambridge, 1898), 87 (Chap. 17.6); 88 (Chap. 17.7); 89 (Chap. 17.15).

[26] See, for example, P. R. L. Brown, *Power and Persuasion in Late Antiquity: Towards a Christian Empire* (Madison, Wisc., 1992), 35–41. On the early portion of the *vita* of Rabbula of Edessa, see G. W. Bowersock, "The Syriac Life of Rabbula and Syrian Hellenism," in *Greek Biography and Panegyric in Late Antiquity*, ed. T. Hägg and P. Rousseau (Berkeley, Calif., 2000), 255–71. For a recent discussion of the education of John of Tella and literacy in the Syriac milieu in general, see S. Brock, "Greek and Syriac in Late Antique Syria," in *Literacy and Power in the Ancient World*, ed. A. K. Bowman and G. Woolf (Cambridge, 1994), 149-60.

vita tradition, seems to have led a simple life as a deacon who whiled away his time composing poetic masterpieces for the church.[27]

In contrast, the *Cause* was composed in the School of Nisibis more than 150 years after Theodore's death and more than 200 years after Ephraem's. From the late fifth century onward, a scholastic movement had been developing within the East Syrian church in Mesopotamia.[28] The School of Nisibis was founded by members of the School of Edessa who had fled the confines of the Roman Empire in the late fifth century when Cyrus, the bishop of Edessa, with the help of the emperor Zeno, closed the school because it was a bastion of Nestorianism.[29] The *Cause* comes from a world in which the roles of scholar and ascetic have become inextricably conflated. For example, in the *Life of Mar Aba*, Aba converts to Christianity after meeting a Christian scholar [*eskolāya*].[30] It is not the scholar's fancy speculation or theology that impresses Aba, but rather his outer appearance and way of life. Scholasticism was a lifestyle with its own distinct institutions and practices. The conflation of scholar and ascetic in the *Life of Mar Aba* is mirrored in the extant collections of school rules, as well as in the constant traffic between monastery and school that we find in the prosopography of contemporary East Syrians.[31] Behind the fabulous metaphors of divine pedagogy found in the *Cause* lie real institutions and the lives people led within them. As

---

[27] S. Griffith, "Ephraem, the Deacon of Edessa, and the Church of the Empire" in *DIAKONIA: Studies in Honor of Robert T. Meyer*, ed. T. Halton and J. P. Williamson (Washington, D.C., 1986), 22–52; J. P. Amar, "Byzantine Ascetic Monachism and Greek Bias in the *Vita* Tradition of Ephrem the Syrian," *OCP* 58 (1992): 123–56.

[28] For "scholasticism" as a broadly defined comparative religious category, see J. I. Cabazón, ed., *Scholasticism: Cross-Cultural and Comparative Perspectives* (Albany, N. Y., 1998); the East Syrians aptly fit Cabazón's eight suggested criteria as he outlined on pp. 4–6. The one work that addresses East Syrian scholasticism as such is Macina, "L'homme à l'école de Dieu."

[29] The exact date and number of expulsions from Edessa have been debated. For a discussion of possible dates and the sources, see Vööbus, *History*, 33–47. The only exact date presented by the sources is 489, but, relying on inconsistencies among some of the sources, scholars have suggested alternative dates or even more than one exodus from Edessa.

[30] P. Bedjan, ed., *Histoire de Mar-Jabalaha et trois autres Patriarches* (Paris, 1895), 206–87. For his conversion, see 211–15. There is a German translation in O. Braun, *Ausgewählte Akten persischer Märtyrer* (Bibliothek der Kirchenväter 22; Munich, 1915), 188–221. On Mar Aba, see J. Labourt, *Le christianisme dans l'empire Perse, sous la dynastie Sassanide (224–632)* (Paris, 1904), 163–91; Baumstark, *Geschichte*, 119–20; S. Brock, "From Antagonism to Assimilation: Syriac Attitudes to Greek Learning," in *East of Byzantium: Syrian and Armenia in the Formative Period*, ed. N. G. Garsoïan, T. F. Mathews, and R. W. Thomson (Washington, D.C., 1984), 22.

[31] A. Vööbus, ed., trans., and comm., *The Statutes of the School of Nisibis* (Stockholm, 1961). Prosopographical material can be found in A. Baumstark, *Geschichte der syrischen Literatur* (Bonn, 1922).

these earthly institutions developed, so did those that were projected into heaven.

The works of Narsai clearly demonstrate the ways in which the institutionalization of heaven evolved along with this concomitant institutionalization on earth.[32] Narsai was of the first generation of students in Edessa to study Theodore's works in Syriac translation. He was head of the School of Edessa until the exodus to Nisibis, where he oversaw the formalization of its official rules. Narsai's metrical homilies on creation reflect this process of institutionalization:

> And he taught them a new book which they did not know,
> As if [they were] children he wrote a sound [ba(r)t qālā] instead of letters,
> And he had them pronounce in the writings, "Let there be light."
> In the form of a verse he directed the sound [qālā] before their eyes,
> And they began to shout, "Blessed is the creator who created the light."
>   (2.250–254)

> As if with a finger he was showing them the power of his essence,
> "See, angels, that I am the power over every power,"
> As if with a pen he was writing for them a book in the mind,
> And he was making them read syllable by syllable [or meditate on] the
>   writings of the creator of all.
> In the likeness of a Master [Rabbā] his gesture was standing at the head of
>   their rows,
> And he was repeating [tāne] to them the power of the meaning of his hidden
>   things. (2.352–357)

This passage is thoroughly Theodoran. Yet, at the same time, its use of concrete scholastic metaphors represents a clear departure from Theodore's more abstract philosophical analogies. In fact, we witness in this excerpt precisely the same type of elaboration that we have seen Theodore's ideas receive at the hand of the author of the *Cause*.

However, although Narsai is the first to describe creation as a school lesson with books, pens, and other accoutrements, his language is often qualified by simile markers (i.e., it is *like* a classroom). Narsai has enriched the metaphorical meaning of Theodore's *paideuein*, but it nonetheless remains metaphor. Like Narsai's similes, the *Cause* makes an analogy between heaven and earth; yet, it goes a step beyond metaphor when it suggests that

[32] For full text and French translation of Narsai's metrical homilies on creation, see P. Gignoux, *Homélies sur la Création: Édition critique du texte syriaque, introduction et traduction française* (PO 34.3–4; Paris, 1968).

God teaches with a "scroll of imperceptible light" (34.6). This is not a simile, but rather the projection of a mundane practice into heaven. Similarly, when the *Cause* reports that God "had them read [*'aqri*] aloud," it is clear that he is being imagined in the role of the "reader" [*maqryā nā*], one of the offices in the School of Nisibis.[33] Such a correlation between earthly and heavenly institutions is, of course, not uncommon: For example, in her contribution in this volume, Kirsti Copeland demonstrates how the real world of the monastery caused some Christians to reimagine the heavenly city in monastic terms. Transformations above often conform to developments below.[34]

The Rabbinic Comparandum

Despite a clearly delineable internal history, the development of the idea of heaven as a classroom is not a phenomenon exclusive to the Church of the East. Another approach to this imagery is provided by comparing it with the very similar material found in rabbinic literature from contemporary Mesopotamia. A simple comparison between the *Cause* and the various instances in which the expression *metivta de-reqi'a* (study circle of the firmament) appears in the Babylonian Talmud produces some interesting results[35]: the two traditions employ similar imagery in rather different ways. This comparison is particularly apt because both traditions, rabbinic and East Syrian, use the very same word for the school "session": Jewish Aramaic *metivta* and Syriac *mawtbā*, both deriving from the root meaning "to sit" and clearly cognate with the Hebrew *yeshivah*.

The passages in the Babylonian Talmud in which *metivta de-reqi'a* is found betray a pronounced thematic consistency: an emphasis on the horizontal relationship between the earthly *metivta* below and the parallel *metivta* above. The uses to which the Babylonian Talmud puts the *metivta de-reqi'a* are schematized in the following chart:

---

[33] Vööbus, *Statutes*, 51, 83, 88, 92, 104.

[34] I would tentatively suggest that the changeover from the use of metaphor to the use of "spiritual" equivalents of earthy entities would have been facilitated by the influx of Neoplatonic literature into the School of Nisibis in the sixth century. See, for example, discussions in S. Brock, "From Antagonism to Assimilation" and Riad, *Studies*, 39–72.

[35] For a general introduction, see "Academy on High," in *Oxford Dictionary of the Jewish Religion*, ed. R. J. Zwi Werblowsky and G. Wigoder (New York, 1997), 13. An earlier example of a Christian heavenly school can be found in Origen, *Princ.* 2.11.6–7.

	b. Sotah 7b[36]	b. Gittin 68a	b. Berakhot 18b	b. Bava Metzi'a 85b	b. Bava Metzi'a 86a	b. Ta'anit 21b
Descent	X	X		X	X	
sleq (he ascended)	X	X	X	X		
Death	X		X	X	X	
Angel/Demon	X	X		X	X	
The Dead Speak			X	X		
la mə'ayyəlin (they obstruct ascent)	X	X	X			
Message from Heaven					X	X

Not counting doublets, six passages contain the expression *metivta de-reqi'a*. Of these, four feature a descent from heaven; four use the verb *sleq*, meaning "to ascend"; death occurs in four; four have angels or demons; the dead speak in two; two have angels that hinder ascent into heaven (Aramaic *la mə'ayyəlin*); and two have messages sent down from heaven.

To understand this material better, it is helpful to situate it within the broader history of early Jewish and Christian descriptions of the heavenly Temple. George MacRae has argued that Jews in the Second Temple period conceptualized the heavenly Temple in two distinct ways. On the one hand, it could be seen as a paradigm of the earthly Temple, in which case we have a parallelism between heaven and earth. On the other hand, it could be seen as the inner sanctuary of a Temple-centered universe. In the latter case, the Temple of the earth is a microcosm of the macrocosmic Temple in heaven.[37]

I believe that the difference between the rabbinic Jewish and Syriac Christian understanding of heavenly pedagogy parallels these two distinct streams of thought concerning the heavenly Temple. The rabbis seem to have thought that the pedagogical debate that took place in their classes and courtrooms could also be found in heaven. Thus, heaven may be seen as a paradigm for earth. For example, in *b. Gittin* 68a, Asmodeus, the prince of demons, "every day goes up to heaven and studies the heavenly lesson [*metivta de-reqi'a*] and then comes down to earth and studies the lesson of

---

[36] Parallels are found in several places, e.g., *b. B. Qam.* 92a and *b. Makkot* 11b.

[37] G. W. MacRae, "Heavenly Temple and Eschatology in the Letter to the Hebrews," *Semeia* 12 (1978): 179–99, esp. 184.

the earth."[38] *B. Berakhot* 18b reports that when Samuel asked the dead in the cemetery where his father was,

> They replied: "He has gone up to the Academy of the Sky." Meanwhile he saw Levi sitting outside. He said to him: "Why are you sitting outside? Why have you not gone up [to heaven]?" He replied: "Because they said to me: 'For as many years as you did not go up to the academy of Rabbi Efes and hurt his feelings, we will not let you go up to the Academy of the Sky.'"[39]

This passage illustrates well that the *metivta* of the earth and the *metivta* of heaven were imagined as separate, though parallel, spheres.[40] Furthermore, the centrality of the ascent/descent motif corresponds well with contemporaneous Jewish speculation concerning the human capacity to gain access to heaven.[41]

In contrast to the rabbinic material, in which the *metivta* of the firmament is a parallel and contemporary paradigm for the *metivta* of the earth, the material in the *Cause* attests a different way of conceptualizing the relationship between the earthly and heavenly schools. The classroom in heaven takes place at the time of creation and apparently ends when the angels proceed to their respective careers in the celestial hierarchy. This classroom serves as a *precursory* heavenly model for the schools of the earth. However, following the earlier Syriac idea that the revelation found in Scripture is similar to that found in Nature, the *Cause* broadens the analogy between the earthly, scriptural school and the school of the whole of the created world (and not the school at the time of creation). In this model, the individual wonders of creation are analogous to the letters of the alphabet by which we read Scripture. These wonders can be arranged in different ways to spell out God's authority, just as the letters of the alphabet offer us God's revelation in Scripture. This model does not require movement by ascent and descent between the school above and the school below because the earthly school is a microcosm of the macrocosmic school of the created world. The various earthly schools are an extension or outgrowth of a broader cosmic pedagogy.

---

[38] I. Epstein, trans., *The Babylonian Talmud, Seder Nashim*, Vol. 7, *Gittin* (London, 1936), 323.

[39] I. Epstein, trans., *The Babylonian Talmud, Seder Zera'im*, Vol. 1, *Berakhot* (London, 1948), 112.

[40] This vertical spatial relationship fits well within the cosmological tradition analyzed by P. Schäfer in this volume.

[41] See especially *b. B. Metzi'a* 85b in which connections to Hekhalot literature are readily apparent. I. Chernus suggests that this is the only passage showing any relationship to Merkabah mysticism (*Mysticism in Rabbinic Judaism* [Berlin, 1982], 93, n. 32).

The idea that there is an analogy between the interpretation of Nature and Scripture is common in Syriac literature. For example, Jacob of Serug, the West Syrian poet contemporary to Narsai, writes

> Behold, by you are the evenings and dawns brought forth to their ears,
> And day to day your homily [or: a homily of you] is poured forth to the
>   listeners,
> On the corners and edges [of the earth] the sun runs in its path,
> And it is made as a herald to the creation for you.[42]

In this paraphrase of the beginning of Psalm 19, Jacob depicts the changing of the days as a homily by and about God. The wonders of creation are the daily lesson in the classroom of the world, just as Scripture, another form of divine self-disclosure, is the object of study in the East Syrian exegetical schools.

The Problem of "Influence"

Clearly, then, there are significant differences in the way that rabbinic and East Syrian sources used the imagery of the heavenly classroom. Nevertheless, the many similarities in the content and language of these two traditions – such as their common use of technical terminology,[43] their similar projection of academic institutions into the biblical past concomitant with the projection into heaven, and their shared focus on the creator's employment of the letters of the alphabet at the time of creation – complicate the task of assessing their relationship. Indeed, if this imagery derives in large measure from earlier Syriac precedents, as I have previously detailed, how can we explain the fact that the practice of projecting earthly scholastic institutions into heaven developed in rabbinic culture at precisely the same time and place as it did among their Syriac-speaking neighbors?

Because the rabbis in Babylon and the East Syrians shared similar Scripture, spoke similar languages, and had similar educational institutions while living on the margins of Greek culture as minorities in the same empire, one could argue that the similarity of heavenly imagery is a case of homologous

---

[42] *Memra* 96 (P. Bedjan, ed., *On the Decapitation of John the Baptist, Homiliae Selectae Mar-Jacobi Sarugensis* [Paris, 1905–1910], 3:664).

[43] For example, compare the usage of *qibbel* and *qabbel* in *m. Avot* 1:1 and *Cause* 73.9, both referring to a diadochic succession; another example of shared technical terminology can be seen in the East Syrian use of *mawtba*, the Syriac equivalent of *metivta*, for the school session (e.g., *Cause* 79.5).

evolution – that is, that similar circumstantial factors have led to the development of similar imagery. However, evidence suggests that Jews and Christians did not belong to communities hermetically sealed off from one another. In fact, in some sectors an ambiguous social dynamic remained.

This is certainly not the place to delve into the complicated and largely unresolved question of the development of distinct Jewish and Christian identities in Late Antiquity; however, a few words are in order for the future study of how these imageries and the scholastic cultures from which they derive relate to one another. Although some scholars have recently argued that anti-Jewish polemic often attests only the existence of an autonomous Christian discourse rather than providing evidence of actual Jewish–Christian controversy,[44] most continue to believe that the large corpus of Christian anti-Jewish polemical literature reflects social proximity.[45] According to this latter view, certain sources suggest that the clear-cut distinctions between Jews and Christians were softer on the margins of orthodoxy, and that rabbis and bishops were the most prominent peaks arising from a wide and interconnected range of religious practices.[46]

Both East and West Syrian Christians maintained a vibrant anti-Jewish polemical tradition; this may suggest that social interaction, albeit frequently negative, occurred between Jews and Christians.[47] Although Sebastian Brock has argued that exegetical material tends to stop crossing the denominational divide into Syriac by the late fourth century,[48] well into the medieval

---

[44] M. S. Taylor, *Anti-Judaism and Early Christian Identity: A Critique of the Scholarly Consensus* (StPB 46; Leiden, 1996); see also D. Satran, "Anti-Jewish Polemic in the *Peri Pascha* of Melito of Sardis: The Problem of Social Context," in *Contra Iudaeos: Ancient and Medieval Polemics between Christians and Jews*, ed. O. Limor and G. G. Stroumsa (TSMJ 10; Tübingen, 1996), 49–58.

[45] For a discussion of the debate about extrapolating social realities from anti-Jewish literature, see especially G. G. Stroumsa, "From Anti-Judaism to Antisemitism in Early Christianity?" in *Contra Iudaeos*, 1–26; A. H. Becker, "Anti-Judaism and Care of the Poor in Aphrahat's *Demonstration* 20," *JECS* 10 (2002): 305–27; A. Jacobs, "The Lion and the Lamb: Reconsidering Jewish – Christian Relations in Antiquity," in *The Ways That Never Parted: Jews and Christians in Late Antiquity and the Early Middle Ages*, ed. A. H. Becker and A. Y. Reed (TSAJ 95; Tübingen, 2003), 95–118.

[46] For Judaizing Gentile Christians in fourth-century Antioch, see R. L. Wilken, *John Chrysostom and the Jews: Rhetoric and Reality in the Late Fourth Century* (Berkeley, Calif., 1984). For later material, see G. Dagron, "Judaïser," *Travaux et Mémoires* 11 (1991): 359–80.

[47] A. P. Hayman, "The Image of the Jew in the Syriac Anti-Jewish Polemical Literature," in *"To See Ourselves as Others See Us": Christians, Jews, "Others" in Late Antiquity*, ed. J. Neusner and E. S. Frerichs (Chico, Calif., 1985), 423–41; S. Kazan, "Isaac of Antioch's Homily Against the Jews," *OrChr* 45 (1961): 30–53; 46 (1962): 87–98; 47 (1963): 89–97; 49 (1965): 57–78.

[48] S. Brock, "Jewish Traditions in Syriac Sources," in *Studies in Syriac Christianity*, 231–2.

Adam H. Becker

period Syriac texts unmistakably show that social interaction between Jews and Christians continued. Aphrahat's *Demonstration* on the care of the poor provides evidence of Christians visiting synagogues for charity in the fourth century.[49] Similarly, the sixth-century *Life of Mar Aba* takes for granted that a Zoroastrian could confuse the identities of a Jew and a Christian.[50] This situation continued even into the Islamic period. In the eighth century, Sergius the Stylite quotes a hypothetical layman who attends both church and synagogue, refusing to put all his eggs in one religious basket.[51] In the ninth century, the Jewish philosopher Dāwūd ibn Marwān al-Muqammis converted to Christianity under the Christian intellectual and apologist Nonnus of Nisibis, before converting back to Judaism and polemicizing against Christianity.[52] Such intellectual contacts may also be evidenced by the fact that the Targum of Proverbs is based on the Peshitta version.[53]

Thus, although Christianity and Judaism had become separate traditions, the boundaries between them remained permeable. Furthermore, if it is true, as some scholars have suggested,[54] that the real break between Church and Synagogue did not occur until the peace of the church in the fourth century, how are we to assess the relationship between them in areas outside of the Roman Empire, such as Mesopotamia?[55] Besides the few examples of contact just described, it is difficult to establish a clearly verifiable and specific locus of interaction where "influence" may have occurred without positing vague notions such as a shared Mesopotamian cultural milieu.[56]

[49] Becker, "Anti-Judaism and Care of the Poor."

[50] For this passage, see Bedjan, *Histoire de Mar-Jabalaha*, 213–14; German translation: Braun, *Akten*, 189–90. For a treatment of this passage, see D. Boyarin, *Dying for God: Martyrdom and the Making of Christianity and Judaism* (Stanford, Calif., 1999), 22–3.

[51] A. P. Hayman, *The Disputation of Sergius the Stylite Against a Jew* (CSCO 338–39; Louvain, 1973), 2:77 (XXII 15): "This man in his madness is undecided with regard to them both, and in his folly he thinks thus: If Christianity is good, behold, I am baptized as a Christian. But if Judaism is also useful, behold, I will associate partly with Judaism that I might hold on to the Sabbath" (also cited in Hayman, "Image of the Jew," 440).

[52] For his attack on Christianity, see S. Stroumsa, *Dawud ibn Marwan al-Muqammis's Twenty Chapters* (Etudes sur le judaïsme médiéval 13; Leiden, 1989).

[53] M. P. Weitzman, *The Syriac Version of the Old Testament: An Introduction* (Cambridge, 1999), 109–110.

[54] Boyarin, *Dying for God*, 18.

[55] On this issue, see A. H. Becker, "Beyond the Spatial and Temporal *Limes*: Questioning the 'Parting of the Ways' Outside the Roman Empire," in *Ways That Never Parted*, 375–94.

[56] On "influence," see P. Schäfer, *Mirror of His Beauty: Feminine Images of God from the Bible to the Early Kabbalah* (Princeton, N. J., 2002), 229–35.

Conclusion

In this paper, I have proposed several different approaches to explaining the pedagogical imagery of the *Cause*, notably its description of the heavenly classroom at the time of creation. My examination has moved from an analysis of the influence of Theodore of Mopsuestia to (1) a more nuanced understanding of the history of Antiochene–Syriac thought and the early Christian tendency to use pedagogical terminology, (2) an awareness of the development of East Syrian scholastic institutions, and, finally, (3) a comparison with similar imagery in the Babylonian Talmud. The different explanations these approaches offer are obviously not exclusive of one another: "Since things are called causes in many ways, it happens that there are many causes of the same thing" (Aristotle, *Physics* 195a4–5). Whatever the proper balance between them, it is clear that the gradual institutionalization of learning among Syriac Christians (and perhaps their Jewish neighbors) played a crucial role in the development of a scholastic ideology. In turn, the pedagogical understanding of Christianity fostered in these new scholastic institutions made it all the more likely that pedagogical practice would be projected into heaven. Of course, once this "scholasticization of heaven" had begun to crystallize in this emerging discourse of divine pedagogy, the heavenly classroom could function as an idealized image on which earthly institutions themselves were modeled, thereby making the earthly school seem both natural and inevitable. By implicitly raising the mundane academy to a heavenly level, the heavenly classroom – as well as the series of mythical schools leading up to the School of Nisibis – rooted everyday life at the school of Nisibis firmly within the great pedagogue's cosmic plan.

PART THREE

TRADITION AND INNOVATION

11

Angels in the Architecture: Temple Art and the Poetics of Praise in the *Songs of the Sabbath Sacrifice*

Ra'anan S. Boustan

Since the first partial publication of the *Songs of the Sabbath Sacrifice* (henceforth, the *Songs*) forty years ago,[1] scholars have explained the cycle's repetitive and sonorous language as a device intended to induce intensified states of "religious" feeling or consciousness. This approach views the syntactic and grammatical anomalies of the *Songs* – broken syntax, odd vacillations between singular and plural forms, and in particular dense participial and nominal clusters – primarily as *epiphenomena* of their ritual-liturgical function. Even those who have been wary of using transhistorical categories, such as "mysticism" or "mystical experience," to account for the formal features of *Songs* have nonetheless resorted to functionalist explanations when confronted with the idiosyncratic poetics of the cycle, often relying on supposed phenomenological affinities between the *Songs* and the hymnic material found in the Hekhalot literature.[2]

---

[1] All text designations and translations for the *Songs* unless otherwise indicated follow C. A. Newsom, "Shirot 'Olat Hashabbat," in *Qumran Cave 4*, Vol. 6, *Poetical and Liturgical Texts, Part 1*, ed. E. Eshel, H. Eshel, C. Newsom, B. Nitzan, E. Schuller, and A. Jardeni (DJD 11; Oxford, 1998), 173–401; I have also consulted Newsom's original critical edition of the cycle, *Songs of the Sabbath Sacrifice: A Critical Edition* (HSS 27; Atlanta, Ga., 1985). The material from Cave 11 is cited according to F. García Martínez, E. J. C. Tigchelaar, and A. S. van der Woude, "11QShirot 'Olat ha-Shabbat," in *Qumran Cave 11*, Vol. 2, *11Q2–18, 11Q20–31* (DJD 23; Oxford, 1998), 259–304.

[2] On the formal and verbal affinities between the *Songs* and later Jewish "mystical" poetry, see esp. L. H. Schiffman, "Merkavah Speculation at Qumran: The 4Q Serekh Shirot Olat ha-Shabbat," in *Mystics, Philosophers, and Politicians: Essays in Jewish Intellectual History in Honor of A. Altmann*, ed. J. Reinharz and D. Swetschinski (Durham, N.C., 1982), 15–47; Schiffman revises his position slightly in idem, "Sifrut Ha-Hekhalot ve-Kitve Qumran," *Jerusalem Studies in Jewish Thought* 6 (1987): 121–38 [Hebrew]; J. M. Baumgarten, "The Qumran *Sabbath Shirot* and Rabbinic Merkabah Traditions," *RevQ* 13 (1988): 199–213. Recently, several review articles have addressed the difficulties and implications of situating the *Songs* within the history of early Jewish mysticism: E. Hamacher, "Die Sabbatopferlieder im Streit um Ursprung und Anfänge der Jüdischen Mystik," *JSJ* 27 (1996): 119–54; J. R. Davila, "The Dead Sea Scrolls and Merkavah Mysticism," in *The Dead Sea Scrolls in Their Historical Context*, ed. T. H. Lim

For instance, despite taking Carol Newsom to task for applying the term "mysticism" to the *Songs*,[3] Johann Maier has written that "the style of the *Songs* is in all their parts formalistic and stereotypical and altogether results in a very solemn and overloaded diction, ceremonious and even static, less expressing thoughts or describing events than giving a numinous impression."[4] Maier's characterization, thus, largely recapitulates Gershom Scholem's assessment of the later Hekhalot hymns as "the *non plus ultra* of vacuousness,"[5] which was itself indebted to the assertion made by the nineteenth-century scholar Philip Bloch that the hymns "do not in the least assist in the process of thought but merely reflect emotional struggle."[6] The dominant paradigm used to interpret the *Songs* – especially those portions of the work that have been characterized as "numinous" – is, thus, deeply committed to the notion that their style represents a purposeful and cultivated meaninglessness.[7]

In this chapter, I take issue with this interpretative framework, which I believe has unnecessarily foreclosed consideration of the central role of the cycle's poetics in generating discursive content. In fact, I show that the cycle achieves its primary conceptual objective: namely, the systematic collapse of the boundary between angelic beings and architectural elements in what might best be termed the "angelification" of the celestial Temple, by means

---

(Edinburgh, 1999), 249–64, esp. 250–3; M. S. Swartz, "The Dead Sea Scrolls and Later Jewish Magic and Mysticism," *DSD* 8 (2001): 182–93, esp. 184–8.

[3] J. Maier, "Shire 'Olat hash-Shabbat: Some Observations on Their Calendrical Implications and on Their Style," in *The Madrid Qumran Congress: Proceedings of the International Congress on the Dead Sea Scrolls, Madrid 18–21 March, 1991*, ed. J. Trebolle Barrera and L. Vegas Montaner (STDJ 11; Leiden, 1992), 2:553; cf. idem, "Zu Kult und Liturgie in der Qumrangemeinde," *RevQ* 14 (1990): 543–85, esp. 572–4. See also E. R. Wolfson, "Mysticism and the Poetic-Liturgical Compositions from Qumran: A Response to Bilhah Nitzan," *JQR* 85 (1994): 185–202, which similarly critiques the use of the term "mysticism" in B. Nitzan, "Harmonic and Mystical Characteristics in Poetic and Liturgical Writings from Qumran," *JQR* 85 (1994): 163–83.

[4] Maier, "Shire 'Olat hash-Shabbat," 557. On the poetics of the *Songs* in general, see also Newsom, *Songs*, 5–21; B. Nitzan, *Qumran Prayer and Religious Poetry* (Leiden, 1994), 173–200; J. R. Davila, *Liturgical Works* (Grand Rapids, Mich., 2000), 86–8; S. Segert, "Observations on Poetic Structures in the *Songs of the Sabbath Sacrifice*," *RevQ* 13 (1988): 215–23.

[5] G. Scholem, *Major Trends in Jewish Mysticism* (New York, 1941), 57–8.

[6] P. Bloch, "Die *Yorde Merkavah*, die Mystiker der Gaonenzeit, und ihr Einfluss auf die Liturgie," *MGWJ* 37 (1893): 18–25, 69–74, 257–66, 305–11, here 259.

[7] Scholem first applied the category of the "numinous" to the study of Jewish mystical poetry in his seminal comments on the Hekhalot hymns in *Major Trends*, 57–63; cf. idem, *Jewish Gnosticism, Merkabah Mysticism, and Talmudic Tradition* (New York, 1965), 20–30. For formal analysis of "numinous" poetics in Hebrew mystical poetry, see especially J. Maier, "Serienbildung und 'numinoser' Eindruckseffekt in den poetischen Stücken der Hekhalot-Literatur," *Semitics* 3 (1973): 36–66.

of its distinctive poetic style. This studied juxtaposition and subsequent collapse of the animate and inanimate spheres reveals the generative relationship that existed between Second Temple angelology and the plastic arts of the Jerusalem cult.[8]

After situating the *Songs* within their specific historical context and generic framework, I argue that the cycle possesses a coherent narrative arc as it moves from conventional angelological material to descriptions of animate Temple art and architecture singing the praises of God. Moreover, this broader thematic movement is prefigured in the internal narrative structure of the cycle's seventh and middle song, which betrays a parallel shift in emphasis from angelic actors to angelified Temple structures. I then show that it is through transfer of the verbs of praise so central to the liturgical framework from angelic host to celestial architecture that this narrative trajectory is realized. More interesting still, not only does the cycle describe the cultic art and architecture as participating in the quintessentially angelic activity of singing hymns of praise to God, but it also methodically portrays the angelic creatures in material terms as images inscribed, carved, or woven into the Temple's walls, furnishings, and tapestries. In this way, a single, common semantic field – the vocabulary of praise – is applied both to the plastic arts of the Jerusalem cult and to the angelic creatures who serve God in his supernal Temple. These descriptions of angels and Temple are not drawn from a single base text, such as Ezekiel, but instead incorporate the verbal and conceptual fluidity that is already present in a wide variety of biblical ekphrastic passages describing the Jerusalem Temple.

Songs of the Sabbath Sacrifice: Textual History and Performative Setting

The cycle of thirteen songs was discovered in nine separate manuscripts at Qumran, eight from Cave 4 and a ninth from Cave 11.[9] Yigael Yadin

---

[8] Note that I do not use the word "angelology" to refer to a coherent body of speculative knowledge regarding the angelic realm because, as P. Schäfer has forcefully argued, there existed no single system of angelology among Jews in Antiquity (*Rivalität zwischen Engeln und Menschen* [SJ 8; Berlin, 1975], 8–9). It is here intended in the looser, more variegated sense suggested by the German word *Engellehre*.

[9] Paleographic analysis dates the earliest manuscript copy of the cycle (4Q400) to the late Hasmonaean period (ca. 75–50 B.C.E.), whereas the latest copies from Qumran date from the middle of the first century C.E. The Cave 11 fragments date to ca. 20–50 C.E. and those from Masada to ca. 50 C.E. A concise description of the various manuscripts appears in Davila, *Liturgical Works*, 85–6.

identified a tenth among the textual remains of the Masada excavations.[10] Because of the large number of manuscripts of the *Songs* found at Qumran, as well as a number of thematic and formal features they share with sectarian material, the work is best viewed within the larger literary and historical context of the Qumran community.[11] At the same time, the copy of the cycle found at Masada and the absence of explicit sectarian terminology in the cycle warrant caution concerning the work's origins. In her most thorough and nuanced treatment of this question, Newsom argues that the *Songs* were produced outside the sect, but came to play an important and influential role within the community.[12] Thus, although we cannot assume absolute conformity between the cycle and other liturgical and hymnic material found at Qumran, the sect undoubtedly served as one of the text's primary sites of performance and transmission.

The cycle was apparently recited during the thirteen Sabbaths of the first quarterly period of the 364-day calendar used in the Qumran community.[13] Consequently, the *Songs* have often been understood as representing the text of a liturgical act of worship.[14] Yet, it is clear that they do not represent a

[10] The Masada fragments were first published in C. Newsom and Y. Yadin, "The Masada Fragment of the Qumran Songs of the Sabbath Sacrifice," *IEJ* 34 (1984): 77–88.

[11] I base this observation on the following criteria: (1) The liturgical form of the document points to a highly organized, coherent community as the functional setting for the cycle; (2) despite the absence of other, more explicit signs of sectarian self-consciousness, the use of eschatological and predestinarian language in song 5 indicates ideological and speculative concerns in line with those of the sect; (3) the absence of self-consciously sectarian language might best be explained by the function of the text as an internal document, not per se intended to demarcate the boundaries of the community; (4) the many verbal parallels between the *Songs* and two clearly sectarian works, *Songs of the Maskil* (4Q510 and 4Q511, ed. Baillet) and the Berakhot texts from Cave 4 (4Q286–290, ed. Nitzan) indicate the cycle's influence on the sect's written tradition and perhaps its own sectarian origins; and (5) most significant, the title *maskil* found in the opening formula of each of the songs serves as a name for a sectarian office (1QS iii 13, 1QS ix 26–x 5, and 1QSb).

[12] C. Newsom, "'Sectually Explicit' Literature from Qumran," in *The Hebrew Bible and Its Interpreters*, ed. W. Propp, B. Halpern, and D. Freedman (Biblical and Judaic Studies 1; Winona Lake, Ind., 1990), 167–87.

[13] Maier argues that the numerical month designations in the *exordium* indicate that the cycle was limited to the Nisan season ("Shire 'Olat hash-Shabbat," 546–52). Newsom entertains the possibility that the cycle could have been recited throughout the four parallel periods of the year (*Songs*, 19–20). C. R. A. Morray-Jones, "The Temple Within: The Embodied Divine Image and Its Worship in the Dead Sea Scrolls and Other Early Jewish and Christian Sources," *SBLSP* 37 (1998): 410, argues that the cycle climaxes in the twelfth song, which would have been recited immediately following the covenant-renewal ceremony held on the Feast of Weeks according to the community's calendar.

[14] Maier, "Shire 'Olat hash-Shabbat," 552–3.

conventional liturgy in which the actual words of praise or petition are given. On a strictly formal level, the genre of "liturgical praise" assumes two basic patterns. The first reports the actual words of praise, as in the Christian *Trishagion* and the Jewish *Qedushah*, as well as in narrative apocalypses such as the *Apocalypse of Abraham* (17:1–3). The second basic form is the "liturgical invitation." Although probably intended for recitation, this form emphasizes the order and manner of praise, often leaving the actual words of the liturgy unrecorded.[15] Bilhah Nitzan has rightly assigned the *Songs* to the second category.[16] The cycle is primarily descriptive, classifying and ordering the hymnic praise to be recited. Each of the songs begins with a call to praise followed by descriptive material ranging from the activities performed by the angels to the architectural features of the heavenly Temple structures and the clothing of the angelic high priest. The content of angelic speech is entirely absent; the praise of God himself is never repeated. Instead, the *Songs* describe and detail the order and conduct of the liturgical activities performed in the supernal realms. It is the angelic host itself – its hierarchies, its speech, and its activities – that forms the focus of the cycle of songs. The cycle is structured both as a summons to a list of worshippers and as an invitation to praise.

The Narrative Trajectory of the Cycle: From Angels to Architecture

Despite the cycle's emphasis on description, it fails to offer a coherent and ordered depiction of a heavenly Temple or even of a series of celestial sanctuaries. Even Newsom comments that "just how the heavenly realm is conceived of in the *Songs* remains elusive."[17] Martha Himmelfarb likewise offers only a partial explanation for the anomalous descriptions of celestial structures in the *Songs*: "the loose correspondence of heavenly temple to earthly seems to reflect the belief that the heavenly temple so transcends the earthly that the correspondence cannot be exact."[18] This puzzlement stems in part from the natural desire to assimilate the *Songs* into a set of conventions for describing

---

[15] Compare passages such as Pss 148, 150:1–2, and the *Song of the Three Youths* (LXX Dan 3:28–68) in which the various categories of heavenly and earthly creatures are called on in a hierarchical order to praise God.

[16] Nitzan, *Qumran Prayer*, 183–9, 195–200.

[17] Newsom, *Songs*, 377.

[18] M. Himmelfarb, *Ascent to Heaven in Jewish and Christian Apocalypses* (New York, 1993), 16.

the heavenly Temple, which certainly underlies the cycle.[19] However, at the same time that the cycle draws on this long-standing tradition, its multiplication and animation of celestial structures challenges the conventions for describing an ordered and stable celestial sphere.

Scholars have universally recognized that the *Songs* shift their focus as the cycle progresses, turning from an interest in angelology to a description of the art and architecture of the Temple. However, the question of how exactly to understand this shift remains controversial.[20] This question has had direct bearing on how scholars have divided the thirteen songs of the cycle. For Newsom, the seventh song constitutes the dramatic peak of the cycle; she has thus discerned a tripartite division in the work, grouping together songs 1–5, 6–8, and 9–13 in order to highlight the centrality of the middle section.[21] By contrast, Devorah Dimant has suggested that the cycle reaches its climax at the end (i.e., in song 13) and, hence, has supported a bipartite division of the composition.[22] In opposition to these atomizing approaches, Christopher Morray-Jones perceives a sense of dramatic movement in the cycle as a whole. In his reading, song 7 functions as a preliminary crescendo, whereas song 12 serves as the climax of the cycle and song 13 as its dénouement.[23]

Morray-Jones' insight into the dramatic arc of the cycle suggests the possibility of a concomitant narrative trajectory, which would account for the thematic shift from the protocols and hierarchies of the angelic priesthoods to the detailed description of the heavenly Temple. Seen from this perspective, the seventh and middle song represents a microcosm of the work as a whole. The seventh song is less formally rigid in composition than the sixth

---

[19] On the diverse exegetical sources and strategies employed in the *Songs* to generate its image of the "macrocosmic temple," see especially J. R. Davila, "The Macrocosmic Temple, Scriptural Exegesis, and the Songs of the Sabbath Sacrifice," *DSD* 9 (2002): 1–19. That the Tabernacle and then the Solomonic Temple were built according to a heavenly model or blueprint [תבנית] is attested to at Exod 25:9, 40; 1 Chron 28:11–12.

[20] See, most recently, C. H. T. Fletcher-Louis, *All The Glory of Adam: Liturgical Anthropology in the Dead Sea Scrolls* (STDJ 42; Leiden, 2002), 252–394, esp. 325–35, which unconvincingly tries to account for this thematic movement as a shift from the angelic host described in the song's first half to the transformed and deified human community that he believes is described in the cycle.

[21] Newsom, *Songs*, 13–17; idem, "Merkabah Exegesis in the Qumran *Shabbat Shirot*," *JJS* 38 (1987): 11–30, esp. 13.

[22] D. Dimant, "The Apocalyptic Interpretation of Ezekiel at Qumran," in *Messiah and Christos: Studies in the Jewish Origins of Christianity Presented to David Flusser on the Occasion of His Seventy-Fifth Birthday*, ed. I. Gruenwald, S. Shaked, and G. Stroumsa (TSAJ 32; Tübingen, 1992), 31–51, esp. 41, n. 40.

[23] C. Morray-Jones, "Temple Within," 417–20.

and the eighth, which frame it. Song 7 is divided into two sections. The first consists of an expansion of the call to praise with which each of the Sabbath songs opens, whereas the second begins with the words: "With these (angels) let the f[oundations of the hol]y of holies praise, the uplifting pillars of the supremely lofty abode, and all the corners of its structure" (4Q403 1 i: 41). In the second section, the beams, the walls, and the "crafted furnishings of the *devir*" – in particular, multiple chariot thrones (4Q403 1 ii: 15)[24] – engage in song and praise alongside the "godlike spirits" who have been the subject of songs 1–6.

The thematic progression within song 7 – from angels who offer praise to architectural structures that offer praise – mirrors the narrative arc of the entire cycle, which similarly moves from detailed angelologies to rich and animated descriptions of the architecture of the heavenly sanctuary. The "architectural" participation in singing praise to God reflects the progressively intensified identification between the animate angelic beings described in the first half of the cycle and the animated Temple structures of the second half. Rather than functioning as the climax of the cycle, this song points forward to the realization of the cycle's ultimate emphasis on the animation and praise performed by the celestial structures.

Song 7, thus, functions as the cycle's narrative hinge. In contrast to the angelologies of the first half of the cycle, songs 9–12 focus almost exclusively on the praise offered by the supernal sanctuaries. These descriptions appear to move from the outer structures inward, beginning with the vestibules and ending with the holy of holies itself. Newsom has suggested that this trajectory is modeled on the "Temple tour" contained in Ezekiel 40–48, in which the sanctuary is likewise described "from the outside in," although she readily admits that this order might merely follow the logical sequence of the worshiper's experience of moving into the progressively sacred precincts of the Temple.[25] Her attempt to rationalize these descriptive passages, however, is complicated by the absence of simple unidirectional movement within the cycle's narrative trajectory. Although song 9 does mention the "vestibules of their entryways" (4Q405 14–15 i: 5), it quickly skips to describe the "structure of the [m]ost holy [sanctuary] in the inner-sancta (*devirim*) of the King"

---

[24] Besides this passage, multiple *merkavot* appear three times in song 11 (4Q405 20 ii–21–22: 3–5), twice in song 12 (4Q405 20 ii–21–22: 11 and 11Q17 vii: 14), and once in song 13 (11Q17 x: 7). Note, however, that these multiple *merkavot* are not simply synonymous with the single *merkavah* that they occur alongside of in song 12.

[25] Newsom, *Songs*, 54–7.

(4Q405 14–15 i: 6–7). Song 10 then returns to describe the vestibule, brick-work, pavement, and chariot thrones before resuming its discussion of the tapestry (or tapestries) that hangs outside of the *devirim* (4Q405 15 ii–16: 2–16 and 4Q405 17: 1–9). Song 12, in turn, describes the procession of the angels through the vestibules and gates of the celestial Temple. The pro-gression of this sequence, which is circular rather than linear, resists facile comparison with the methodical movement of Ezekiel's description of the future Temple (Ezekiel 40–48).

Not only does the cycle deviate from Ezekiel's ordered plan, but it also draws on a broad range of biblical precedents, belying simple intertextual dependence on Ezekiel.[26] Several key words from songs 9–12 do not occur in Ezekiel's description of the Temple. The terms פרוכת,[27] זבול,[28] and דביר[29] appear nowhere in Ezekiel; תבנית[30] occurs only at Ezek 10:8 and without the architectural associations ascribed to the term in the *Songs*.[31] Even where the *Songs* and Ezekiel do share terminology, this vocabulary is often not distinctive to the text of Ezekiel.[32]

In fact, no Jewish source from Qumran or related Jewish and Christian literature matches the *Songs'* cryptic and puzzling deployment of Temple imagery. These temples are at times intricate, like the concentric palaces pictured in Hekhalot literature; at times, they are even paradoxical, like the twofold heavenly palace in the *Book of the Watchers*, whose interior structure is said to occupy more space than the exterior one (1 Enoch 14:14–15). Despite a common interest in multiplicity and concentricity in some of these texts, Newsom herself concedes that "it is extremely difficult to supply parallels

---

[26] On the limited use of Ezekiel 1 and 40–48 in the *Songs* and the cycle's dependence on a broad range of other Scriptural sources, see Dimant, "Apocalyptic Interpretation," esp. 42, n. 44.

[27] The term *parokhet* is drawn instead from descriptions of the tabernacle (e.g., Exod 26:31; Lev 4:17; Num 18:7).

[28] The term *zevul*, meaning sanctuary, is rather rare in the Hebrew Bible. It is drawn from descriptions of the Solomonic Temple (e.g., 1 Kgs 8:13 and 1 Chron 6:2) and from Isa 63:15.

[29] The term *devir* appears in a wide variety of texts from 1 Kgs 6:19–20 and 2 Chron 2:16 to Ps 28:2. It does not once appear in Ezekiel, nor does Ezekiel devote significant space to descriptions of the inner sanctum of the Temple.

[30] The term *tavnit* seems to have specifically signified a model or blueprint, most likely of divine origin. It is used with regards to the Tabernacle at Exod 25:9, 40 and with regards to the Solomonic Temple at 1 Chron 28:18.

[31] "The cherubs appeared to have the form [תבנית] of a man's hand under their wings" (Ezek 10:18, JPS).

[32] Words such as אולם [vestibule], בדן [form], and צורה [shape] are equally prevalent in descrip-tions of the tabernacle and Temple of Solomon.

for the notion of seven heavenly sanctuaries."[33] More important, none of these descriptive passages offers a comparable account of the dynamic and active role played by the Temple structures in the liturgical act of praise. In fact, rather than betraying an interest in developing a coherent depiction of the heavenly Temple or in offering a systematic narrative reenactment of cultic ritual, the cycle's narrative structure highlights the essential affinities between the activities of the angelic priesthoods and those of the animated Temple.

Architectural Language and Temple Art in the *Songs*

If Ezekiel 40–48 and its tradition of describing the idealized, future temple do not constitute a privileged source for the *Songs*, what conception informed the text's deployment of architectural and figural language? In my view, the rich architectural and graphic detail found in the *Songs* grows out of an ekphrastic tradition in which angelological speculation was articulated through the language of the material cult. Scholars who have tried to account for the relationship among art, language, and visionary experience have tended to view the process in diachronic terms, as the progressive spiritualization of the cultic site.[34] Yet, it is clear that the Jerusalem Temple had long served as a privileged locus of prophetic and visionary experience in ancient Israel.[35] Saul Olyan has commented suggestively on the "tendency to divinize or accord special figurative treatment to divine attributes and aspects of temple and ritual . . . witnessed throughout the ancient Near East, and paralleled in later Jewish angelic exegesis of divine attributes and cultic terms."[36] As Isaiah's vision in the Temple plainly demonstrates (Isa 6:1–6), the media of the plastic arts, such as architecture and carvings, should not

---

[33] Newsom, *Songs*, 50.

[34] For particularly glaring examples of this tendency, see R. Elior, "Between the Earthly Sanctuary and Heavenly Sanctuaries: Prayer and Hymn in Hekhalot Literature and Their Relationship to Temple Traditions," *Tarbiz* 64 (1995): 341–80 [Hebrew]; idem, "From Earthly Temple to Heavenly Shrines," *JSQ* 4 (1997): 217–67.

[35] As J. D. Levenson, "The Jerusalem Temple in Devotional and Visionary Experience," in *Jewish Spirituality I: From the Bible Through the Middle Ages*, ed. A. Green (New York, 1985), 58, rightly states, "It was not that the Temple was spiritualized after its destruction. Instead, the spiritual role of the Temple after its destruction was a continuation of the role the Temple had long played in the devotional and visionary experience of Israel in the biblical period."

[36] S. M. Olyan, *A Thousand Thousands Served Him* (TSAJ 36; Tübingen, 1993), 119–20.

be seen to have priority over verbal description or visionary experience.[37] Instead, although the relationship between literary and artistic traditions is never seamless, the domains of art, language, and vision can best be understood as a triad of compatible media that clustered around the cultic center in Jerusalem, constituting a fluid and synchronic matrix in which each component shaped and was shaped by the others.

The history of the class of angels called the *ophannim* [lit. the wheels] perhaps best exemplifies the process by which the mythological can become frozen in statuary and then reused in textual form. Of the thirty times this word appears in the Hebrew Bible, twenty-eight citations come either from Ezekiel[38] or from the description of the wheels of the laver stand in 1 Kgs 7:32–37. Both sources employ the same distinctive technical prose when describing the *ophannim*. Language that seems so distinctively Ezekelian surfaces precisely in those sections of biblical historical prose passages that describe the Jerusalem Temple. For example, 1 Kgs 7:33 reports that "The structure of the wheels [ומעשה האופנים] was like the structure of chariot wheels [כמעשה אופן המרכבה]." In addition, these passages from Ezekiel and 1 Kings also echo the abstract language of the brief account of the Sinai theophany in Exodus: "And they saw the God of Israel: under his feet there was the *likeness* [כמעשה] of a pavement of sapphire, like the very sky for purity" (Exod 24:10). These verbal echoes suggest that the seemingly sober ekphrastic descriptions of the Temple and its art in historical sources are related to prophetic-visionary accounts of Temple theophanies in surprisingly intimate ways. Whatever the precise relationship between these various texts, they undoubtedly represent the threads of literary material out of which the *Songs* are woven. Rather than offering a unified and stable depiction of the heavenly sanctuary or sanctuaries, the *Songs* represent a highly developed elaboration of the enduring ekphrastic impulse already present in a wide range of biblical texts.

The graphic depiction of angels carved or woven into the physical structures of the heavenly sanctuary are particularly central to both the thematic unity and narrative trajectory of the cycle. It is this fluidity between angelic and architectural language that underlies the distinctive combination of architectural description and angelology pervading the latter half of the *Songs*.

---

[37] Indeed, as the massive laver referred to as "yam" or sea (1 Kgs 7:23) and perhaps also the enigmatic columns Yachin and Boaz (1 Kgs 7:21) show, the art of the Temple of Solomon reflects contemporary mythological figures and narratives.

[38] Ezek 1:15–22 is perhaps the most famous passage.

Songs 9–12 are often read as no more than a bewildering, kaleidoscopic accumulation of cultic vocabulary, intended to express the awesomeness of the ritual climate of the Jerusalem Temple. Yet, these intricate compositions do more than just create an evocative sense of place. They imbue the cultic art and architecture with the living force of the angelic beings depicted on them. This effect is apparent in a fragmentary passage assigned by Newsom to song 9[39]:

> (5) [And the liken]ess of living divine beings is engraved in the vestibules where the King enters, figures of luminous spirits, [. . . K]ing, figures [בדני] of glorious li[ght, wondrous] spirits; (6) [in] the midst of the spirits of splendor (is) a work of wondrous colors, figures of the living divine beings. [. . . in the] glorious *devirim*, the structure [מבנית] of the (7) [mo]st holy [sanctuary] in the *devirim* of the King, fig[ures of the di]vi[ne beings and from] the likeness of [. . .] of holiest holiness. (4Q405 14–15 i: 5–7)

Song 10 similarly describes the veil(s) of the inner sancta [*devirim*] as having angelic figures woven into it (them): "(3) Beauty upon the veil of the *devir* of the King . . . (4) in the *devir* of His presence, the mingled colors of . . . everything which is engraved upon the . . . , figures of hea[venly beings . . .] (5) the glory from both of their sides [. . .] the veils [פורכות] of the wondrous *devirim*" (4Q405 15 ii–16: 3–5). More striking still is song 11's description of the "wondrous mosaic" [דבקי פלא] composed of multihued "shapes of god-like beings" (4Q405 19ABDC: 3–7). Here, the animated figures engraved into the "floor" of the celestial shrine [מדרס דבירי פלא] and the brickwork under the divine chariot throne [ללבני כבודם] are explicitly equated with the "holy angels" who offer blessings and praise to God.

By contrast, in a passage from song 13, the fluidity of descriptive language progresses in the opposite direction; it is not the carvings or tapestries that are said to be animated like angels, but rather the angels who are compared to carved or woven figures:

> (7) . . . In their wondrous stations are spirits [clothed with] many colors, like woven work, engraved with figures of splendor. (8) In the midst of the glorious appearance of scarlet, the colors of most holy spiritual light, they stand firm in their holy station before the (9) [K]ing, spirits in garments of [purest] color in the midst of the appearance of whiteness. And this glorious spiritual substance

---

[39] Newsom, *Songs*, 280.

is like fine gold work, shedding (10) [lig]ht. And all their crafted [garments] are purely blended, an artistry of woven work. (4Q405 23 ii: 7–10)[40]

The crafted garments of the angels are continuous with the description of the woven tapestries described in songs 10 and 11. It is as if the angels themselves are formed from the raw materials used to construct the Temple.

Moreover, a number of passages play with variations on phrases built around the term בדן [figure] and its plural בדני as well as the similar word צורה [form]. Such passages link the discursive account of the hierarchies and activities of the various classes of angels in the first part of the cycle with these carved and woven figures.[41] In addition, the roots חקק [engrave],[42] מלח [blend],[43] חרת [inscribe],[44] פתח [engrave],[45] and חקה [engrave][46] appear multiple times in the cycle, all within the context of representations of angelic figures on the structures and implements of the supernal sanctuaries. The juxtaposition of this material vocabulary with the descriptions of the celestial host forges a powerful link between angelic speculation and the iconographic traditions of the Jerusalem Temple, thereby making the cycle's angelologies and its ekphrastic descriptions both thematically and verbally interdependent.

The *Berakhot* texts from Qumran Cave 4 (4Q286–290) further illuminate these patterns of thought and usage.[47] This liturgical work apparently served as an annual covenantal renewal liturgy performed within the sect.[48] Like the *Songs*, 4QBerakhot draws on ekphrastic description of the material cult to articulate its speculative knowledge concerning the angelic realm:

---

[40] Compare the many other similar passages in which terms from the plastic arts (e.g., בדן, חקה, חקק, חרת, מלח, פתח, צורה, רקם) are used to describe the angels, especially: 4Q405 14–15 i: 5–7; 4Q405 19: 5; 4Q405 23 ii: 7.

[41] For use of בדן in the context of the strictly angelological portion of song 7 before the shift to angelified architecture, see 4Q403 1 ii: 9.

[42] For example, 11Q17 vi: 6 and esp. 4Q405 19: 5–6: כ]בודם [ב]דני צורות אלוהים מחוקקי סביב ללבני.

[43] For example, 4Q405 19: 3–4 and 4Q405 20 ii–21–22: 11.

[44] For example, 4Q405 23 ii: 1–3.

[45] For example, 4Q405 14–15 i: 5.

[46] For example, 4Q405 15ii–16: 4.

[47] For critical edition and translation, I have used B. Nitzan, "Berakhot," in *Qumran Cave 4*, Vol. 6, *Poetical and Liturgical Texts, Part 1*, 1–74.

[48] According to Nitzan, the Berakhot texts seem to represent an expanded version of the ritual alluded to in the *Community Rule* (1QS i–ii), with which it shares many verbal affinities ("4QBerakhot[a–e] [4Q286–290]: A Covenantal Ceremony in the Light of Related Texts," *RevQ* 16 [1995]: 487–506).

(2) their [. . .] splendid [st]ructures (תב] ניות הדרמה]) [. . . (3) [walls of] their glorious [hal]ls, their wondrous doors [. . . (4) . . .] their [. . .] angels of fire and spirits of cloud [. . . (5) bri]ghtness of the brocaded spirits (רוקמת רוחי) of the holiest holi[ness (6) . . . [. . .]m and firmaments of holy [. . . (7) [spirits of the holiest] holiness [will sing in joy] in all the due time[s (8) and they will bless] the name of your glorious divinity. (4Q287 2ab: 2–8)

The language is reminiscent of the *Songs*, particularly in its use of technical terms such as תבנית (here in the plural translated as structures) and רוקמה (here translated as brocaded). And, as in the *Songs*, the boundary between the angels and their pictographic forms is fluid. By drawing on this rich verbal iconography, both of these liturgical collections achieve what I have termed the "angelification" of temple architecture.

Moreover, both works seem to abandon a systematic depiction of the supernal sanctuary. They emphasize instead the actual participation of the Temple in the liturgical act. The participation of the inanimate elements of the physical cult grows out of the traditional fluidity between the categories of angelic creatures, on the one hand, and of representational and architectural forms, on the other. Yet the existence of a reservoir of iconographic art and language does not in itself account for the cycle's success in merging the domains of angelology and architecture. In what follows, I explore how the cycle's rigorous and precise poetic composition produces this effect.

The Poetics of the *Songs of the Sabbath Sacrifice*, or the Strange Problem of Singular and Plural Forms

Beyond their semantic affinities, both 4QBerakhot and the *Songs* employ plural forms of architectural vocabulary in anomalous and surprising ways. The following passage from the *Berakhot* is typical of this grammatical phenomenon:

(1) the seat [מושב] of Your honor and the footstools [והדומי רגלי] of Your glory in the [h]eights of Your standing-place and the trea[d ([מדר]ך) (2) of Your holiness; and the chariots [ומרכבות] of Your glory, their *keruvim* [כרוביהמה] and their wheels [ואופניהמה] with all [their] councils; (3) foundations [מוסדי] of fire and flames of brightness, and flashes of splendor, li[ght]s of flames and wondrous lights. (4) Majes]ty and splendor, and height of glory, foundation of holiness and foun[tain of b]rightness, and height of beauty; wo[nder (5) of thanks]giving and a well of powers, splendor of praises and great in awesome deeds and healing[s (6) and miraculous works; a foundation of wisdom and a structure of

knowledge and a fountain of insight, a fountain of prudence (7) and a counsel of holiness, and a foundation of truth, a treasury of understanding; structures[49] [מבני] of justice and residences [מכוני] of hone[sty. (4Q286 1 ii: 1–7)

The plural forms scattered throughout this passage do not merely compli-cate the task of reconstructing the heavenly realm encoded in this text; they fundamentally call into question whether the poetic form represented by this work even assumes a stable representation of heaven. Like the *Songs*, this text multiplies and animates these architectural structures so that, like the figures carved on them, they can be depicted in the act of praising God. To un-derstand the function of the cycle's enigmatic descriptions of multiple heav-enly sanctuaries, its unique language – its repetitions, alternations between singular and plural forms, broken syntax, and sonorous language – must be understood as a mechanism to communicate the distinctive ideational content of the text.

As I have argued, the *Songs* alternate between two primary and contrasting poetic modes. On the one hand, the praise and blessings of the angelic orders are characterized by structured repetition and methodical uniformity, reflecting their interest in hierarchy and protocol. By contrast, the songs that describe the activities of the celestial Temple are marked by fractured irregularity. In this way, changes in poetic form mark significant shifts in thematic content and narrative development.

Song 6, for example, includes two separate hymnic cycles: a cycle of praises of the seven chief princes of the angels and a cycle of their blessings. The cycle of praise (4Q403 1 i: 1–7 and Mas1k ii: 1–19) contains seven twofold liturgical proclamations concerning the praises to God recited in order by the tongue of the seven chief princes. Each proclamation contains two parallel declarations: a noun phrase describing the type of praise to be recited and a verbal clause declaring its actual recitation.[50] Similarly, the blessings of the seven angelic chief princes (4Q403 1 i: 23–26) contains seven threefold blessings in which the chief princes are said to bless either angels or righteous

---

[49] It is telling that F. García Martínez and E. J. C. Tigchelaar, eds., *Dead Sea Scrolls Study Edition* (Leiden, 1999), 544–5, erroneously translate מבני צדק as "from the sons of justice."

[50] For detailed parsing of this unit's poetic structure, see Newsom, *Songs*, 178–80; Nitzan, *Qumran Prayer*, 297–301; R. S. Abusch, "Seven-fold Hymns in the *Songs of the Sabbath Sacrifice* and the Hekhalot Literature: Formalism, Hierarchy and the Limits of Human Participation," in *The Dead Sea Scrolls as Background to Post-Biblical Judaism and Early Christianity*, ed. J. R. Davila (STDJ 46; Leiden, 2002), 228–32.

people in the name of God.[51] These units constitute, in Nitzan's terms, "liturgical-ritual act(s) of sequential recitations by the heavenly entourage."[52] Song 8 likewise contains seven calls, depicting the praise to be recited by seven different figures, one after the other in a kind of liturgical chain. The praise is increased sevenfold each time permission is passed from one angelic prince to the next. In this case, it is quite simple to follow the poetic constraints the author has chosen:

> (27) And the tongue of the first [angelic prince] will grow strong sevenfold (joining) with the tongue of the one who is second to him. And the tongue of the one who is second with respect to him will grow strong] (28) sevenfold from [the sound of] the one who is third with respect to [him. And the ton]gue of the thi[rd will] grow strong sevenfo[ld from (the sound of) the one who is fourth with respect to him. And the tongue of the fourth will grow strong sevenfold (joining) with the tongue of the one who is fifth with respect to him. And the tongue of the fifth will grow strong sevenfold (joining) with the tongue of] (29) the one who is sixth with respect to him. And the tongue of the sixth will grow strong sevenfold (joining with) the] to[ngue of the one who is seventh with respect to him. And with the tongue of the seventh it will grow strong ... holiness of the sanctuary. (4Q403 1 ii: 27–29)[53]

This passage is typical of the phenomenon I have been discussing. The angelic priesthoods, founded by God in earlier songs, are here described as fulfilling their allotted functions. The formal parallelism and regularity of such passages thus enhance the impact of their depiction of a sphere dominated by prescribed rules of organization and activity.

By contrast, the descriptions of the praises of the Temple architecture are primarily litanies, which systematically intermingle angelic and architectural language. Songs 9–13, which contain these passages, are characterized by the following formal features:

1. lack of finite verbs,
2. elaborate construct chains,
3. nominal and participial sentences,
4. clustering and repetition of related vocabulary and imagery.

---

[51] Lacunae in this unit are supplied from 4Q404 2: 5–8 and 4Q405 3a ii: 15–19. For detailed parsing of this unit's poetic structure, see Newsom, *Songs*, 207–8; Nitzan, *Qumran Prayer*, 301–7; Abusch, "Seven-fold Hymns," 232–35.

[52] Nitzan, *Qumran Prayer*, 305.

[53] On the poetic structure of this unit, see Newsom, *Songs*, 242.

No hierarchy differentiates between animated creatures and animated structures. Temple structures do not function as a locus of activity, but as participants in praise. The litany form – its repetitions, its transferal of verbs from one type of being to another, and its absorption of disparate elements within a single scene or activity – invests this collapsing of categories with a sharply rhetorical note. The very performance of the litany or song enacts the dynamic relationship between angelic beings and temple structures that is so central to the thematic content of the cycle.

The lack of hierarchy and structure in passages of the *Songs* that contain a multiplicity of sanctuaries and Temple structures is enhanced by the interchangeable use of singular and plural forms. Their alternation makes it virtually impossible to extract a coherent and stable image of the heavenly sphere or the heavenly Temple structures that are said to inhabit it, thereby undermining the reader's capacity to systematize the use of architecture within the cycle. A single term alternates from singular to plural, seemingly at random within the same passage. For example, the twelfth song places one central chariot throne alongside a series of multiple *merkavot* (4Q405 23 i: 1–13). The latter half of song 7, which I have argued foreshadows the cycle's subsequent animation of the Temple, employs this same verbal technique:

(11)...And there is a voice of blessing from the chiefs of His *devir* [...] (12) And the voice of blessing is glorious in the hearing of the godlike beings and the councils of [...(13) voice of] blessing. And all the crafted furnishings of the *devir* hasten [to join] with the wondrous psalms of the *devi*[r...] (14) of wonder, *devir* to *devir* with the sound of the holy multitudes. And all their crafted furnishings [...] (15) And the chariots of His *devir* give praise together, and their *keruvim* and thei[r] *ophannim* bless wondrously [...] (16) the chiefs of the divine structure. And they praise Him in His holy *devir*. (4Q403 1 ii: 11–16)

In this passage, the antiphonal singing of the multiple inner sancta [*devirim*] is systematically juxtaposed to the singular *devir* of God. Similarly, at 4Q405 14–15 i: 7 and 8, the phrases "the inner-sancta of the king" [דבירי מלך] and "the inner-sanctum of the king" [דביר מלך] are found alongside each other without any thematic or narrative explanation for the shift. Elsewhere, the word מושב [seat or stool] appears in rapid succession in both singular and plural forms (4Q405 20 ii–21–22: 2 and 4). Even the word זבול [sanctuary] appears in the plural at the end of the cycle (11Q17 x: 8). All of these cases are equally difficult to rationalize.

Newsom herself seems to have been frustrated by the problem posed by these verbal and poetic techniques. She tries to explain several of the cases, such as the vacillation between the singular and the plural forms of the word *parokhet* [veil] at 4Q405 15 ii–16: 3 and 5 (בפרוכת and פרכות), by suggesting that "one sanctuary is hierarchically superior to the others of lesser sanctity."[54] Yet, the weight of the evidence forces her to articulate the inadequate position that "in translating the Sabbath songs, not all of the plural forms need be rendered as plurals, even though it is clear that in some contexts genuine plurality of sanctuaries is envisioned."[55] This solution does not yield convincing insights into the cycle's depiction of temple structures, nor does it elucidate the cycle's relationship to the Jerusalem Temple.

Certainly, there are precedents for the simultaneous depiction of single and plural forms of the same object. Revelation describes the twenty-four thrones of the elders with the same nomenclature as the one throne of God (καὶ κυκλόθεν τοῦ θρόνου θρόνους εἴκοσι τέσσαρας; Rev 4:4). The Hekhalot corpus, likewise contains this plural usage of the term *merkavah* and, in many cases, depicts these plural structures as participating in liturgical song.[56] In these cases, however, plurality is invariably maintained throughout a given passage and does not alternate at random with singular forms. In both Revelation and the Hekhalot corpus, the plural forms are uniformly linked to a consistent plural conception of heavenly structures, such as the twenty-four thrones of the elders or the multiple chariots in the multiple heavenly throne rooms. In neither case are the alternations as pervasive or as *ad hoc* as in the *Songs*. In my view, this vacillation is systematic and serves to emphasize the similarity between the multiplicity of angelic hosts and temple structures.

The process of "animation" inaugurated in Song 7 is brought to its completion at the end of the entire cycle in a fragment presumed to be from the thirteenth and final song, which typifies the cycle's nonliteral, nonrepresentational depiction of the supernal sanctuary/sanctuaries:

(6) for the angels of knowledge [למלאכי הדעת], in all … […] … holy upliftings
(7) for the thrones of His glory [לכסאי כבודו] and [His foot]stool (ולהדום ר]גליו)
[and for all] the [ch]ariots His majesty (מר]כבות הדרו) and for the *devirim* of his
[His] ho[liness] ([ולדבירי קו]דשו) […] and for the portals of the entrance [ולפתחי
מבוא]י of (8) [the Kin]g together with all the exits [מוצא]י of [… the cor]ners of its

54 Newsom, *Songs*, 49.
55 Newsom, *Songs*, 49.
56 See especially §§554–555. Paragraph designations follow P. Schäfer's *Synopse zur Hekhalot–Literatur* (TSAJ 2; Tübingen, 1981).

> str[uc]ture ([. . . פנ]ות מבניתו) and for all the dw[ellings . . .] ([ז]בולי) for the temples of His glory ([ו]להיכלי כבודו) and for the firmaments of [ולרקיעי]. (11Q17 x: 6–8)

The extremely fragmentary state of this passage makes it difficult to interpret. It seems to follow immediately after a detailed description of the clothing of the angelic high priest and the sacrificial offerings he makes in the heavenly Temple.[57] Although most scholars have naturally focused on the significance of this cultic scene, little attention has been paid to what the *Songs* have to say about its setting.[58] The use of *lamed* before this list of architectural features (e.g., "for the thrones of His glory" [לכסאי כבודו]) is peculiar. The grammatical function of the preposition in this series certainly parallels its use in the fragment's first phrase, "to the angels of knowledge." But what function does this particle serve when applied to the inanimate objects that follow this unambiguous angelic designation? Here, at the dénouement of the cycle, we might have expected the text to employ a *locative* designation to specify the celestial Temple as the site of the sacrificial action described earlier in the song. We find instead a passage that traces out the cycle's shifting architectural topography, beginning with God's throne and ending outside in the firmament.

As in the rest of the work, this blueprint cannot be reduced to its spatial coordinates; the heavenly Temple is not so much a locus of angelic life as its semantic and conceptual foundation. Indeed, seen from this view, the intimate relationship between Jewish angelology and the vibrant ekphrastic tradition in the Hebrew Bible may challenge long-cherished notions concerning the aniconism of early Judaism.

57 11Q17 ix: 3–9; 4Q405 23 ii: 1–13. See especially the cultic vocabulary in 11Q17 ix: 3–5: "suitable [offering]s" ([מנחו]ת רצון), "the sacrifices of the holy ones" [לזבחי קדושים], "the aroma of their offerings" [ריח מנחותם], and "and the ar[o]ma of their libations" (ר[י]ח נסכיהם). On the reasons for the primarily "aromatic" nature of heavenly sacrifice, see M. Himmelfarb in this volume.

58 For example, Fletcher-Louis, *Glory of Adam*, 356–91.

The Collapse of Celestial and Chthonic Realms in a Late Antique "Apollonian Invocation" (*PGM* I 262–347)

Christopher A. Faraone

One of the many remarkable changes in pagan religious outlook in the late Roman period is the growing tendency to focus on the heavens as the abode of a frequently transcendent god and to develop techniques of ascension to gain access to this (usually male) divinity or his divine knowledge. The presence of a powerful male god in the celestial, realm is not new, of course; the Greeks in archaic and classical times tend to divide up the supernatural into two fairly distinct categories, each with their own forms of ritual and address: (1) the Olympian or celestial, and (2) the chthonian. In the earlier periods, a person could search for supernatural knowledge or prophecy in either direction, upward: for example, by consulting an oracle of Apollo or Zeus, or downward by performing a necromantic ritual or (in mythic narratives) by making a journey to interrogate a ghost. In later antiquity, however, as pagan worshippers turned their eyes increasingly to heavenly deities for divine knowledge, necromancy and other forms of chthonian prophecy seem to diminish in importance.[1] This is not to say that the

An oral version of this paper was given at the conference in January 2001 from which this volume springs. I would like to thank my hosts at Princeton, Ra'anan Boustan, Annette Reed, and Peter Schäfer, as well as all of the other participants, for their helpful comments and questions. I also presented this paper one year later to a seminar on the Greek Magical Papyri that I cotaught with Hans-Dieter Betz, and I am thankful for the many comments of my colleagues and students in that venue as well. All of the mistakes, however, remain my own.

[1] By "necromancy" I mean – as the Greek etymology makes clear – a ritual designed to elicit prophecy [*manteia*] from a corpse [*nekros*]. For the rising unpopularity of necromancy in the Roman period, see F. Graf, "Magic and Divination," in *The World of Ancient Magic: Papers from the First International Samson Eitrem Seminar at the Norwegian Institute at Athens, 4–8 May 1997*, ed. D. R. Jordan, H. Montgomery, and E. Thomassen (Papers from the Norwegian Institute at Athens 4; Bergen, 1999), 295–6; R. Gordon, "Imagining Greek and Roman Magic," in *Witchcraft and Magic in Europe: Ancient Greece and Rome*, ed. B. Ankarloo and S. Clark (Philadelphia, 1999), 206–8.

chthonian forces were abandoned: Indeed, the hundreds of *defixiones* from around the Mediterranean attest the continued popularity and power of Persephone, Hermes, Hecate, and various underworld demons and ghosts during the late imperial periods. But, divination rites do seem to change with the times and increasingly to orient themselves in a celestial direction, suggesting that heaven alone was the source for divine wisdom and prophecy.

In this essay, I hope to show that necromancy was not simply forgotten, but rather that it was reused and redirected in spells that collapse the traditional Greek distinction between the celestial and chthonian realms. In particular, I offer a close reading of an intriguing late antique divinatory spell labeled an "Apollonian Invocation" (*PGM* I 262–347) in the hopes of revealing the process by which rituals and hymns ostensibly dedicated to Apollonian prophecy of the typically Olympian sort begin to expropriate, or attract to themselves, forms of necromancy or other kinds of chthonic prophecy. This development occurred primarily, but not exclusively, by means of the popular equation of Apollo and the sun god who, in Egyptian and Mesopotamian traditions, travels each night through the underworld. As we shall see, this metamorphosis of necromancy occurs on the level of imagery – the practitioner is directed to hold both the laurel bough of Apollo and the ebony wand of Hermes – and is also manifested by the confusion or disguise of explicit references to corpses and other markers of graveside necromantic ceremonies.

The Syncretistic Tendencies of Late Imperial Pagan Religion

Before we examine the material from the Greek Magical Papyri, we need to understand how the god Apollo evolved during Hellenistic and Roman times and gradually attracted many of the attributes of other powerful solar and celestial gods and how these deities are in turn connected to necromancy. A classic instance of the late Roman melding of Apollo and other, mainly solar, deities is a prose hymn composed by the third-century C.E. rhetorician Menander as an example of an epideictic speech in honor of a god:

> Now, O Sminthian and Pythian god, from you my speech began and to you it will end. With what titles shall I address you? Some people name you "Lycian," some "Delian," some "Akraion," and others "Actian." The Lacedaemonians call you "Amyclean," the Athenians "Patroan," the Melesians "Branchiate"

[="Didymian"]. Every city, land, and nation do you control; and just as you dance around the heaven having the choruses of stars around you, so you also control the entire inhabited realm of humankind. As "Mithras" the Persians address you, as "Horus" the Egyptians (for you lead the seasons [*horai*] in their cycle), and as "Dionysus" the Thebans address you.... From you the moon receives her ray. The Chaldeans address you as "Ruler of the Stars." (2.445.26–446.8)

Here, we see a maneuver typical of later pagan hymns; the speaker begins with a list of the god's various epithets, a common-enough feature of traditional Greek prayers and hymns, but then he proceeds to equate Apollo with various non-Greek solar or celestial divinities, who are often pancratic in nature. This late antique Apollo, therefore, is more powerful than his traditional Greek ancestor – for he has control over the entire world – and he is imagined as a heavenly being at the center of the dancing choruses of stars.

We find a somewhat different kind of mélange in a papyrus fragment of the lost *Kestoi* of Julius Africanus, a near contemporary of Menander Rhetor, who preserves a startling variant of the famous scene in the *Odyssey* in which Odysseus performs a necromantic ritual to summon up the spirit of Teiresias.[2] The text starts with two passages from the beginning of the traditional Homeric narrative (*Od.* 11.34–43, 48–50), in which Odysseus describes how he sacrificed sheep and drained their blood into a pit, how the spirits of the dead came up out of the underworld, and how he in fear drew his sword and did not let any of them drink the blood. In the standard Homeric text that has come down to us in the manuscript tradition, the shades of various heroes begin to appear at this point. However, in Africanus' variant text, the hero appeals to a series of supernatural entities – both celestial and chthonic – to fulfill his charm [*epaoide*] so that he can get the necessary information to find his way home. It is, in short, a full-fledged necromantic ritual that combines a typically chthonic form of sacrifice – slitting the throats of animals into a pit without burning them – and a long invocation in dactylic hexameters that begins as follows (lines 16–22):

2 *P. Oxy* 412. 14. *PGM* XXIII supplies only later non-Homeric material, whereas the translation of *PGM* XXIII in H. D. Betz, ed., *The Greek Magical Papyri in Translation*, 2nd ed. (Chicago, 1992), 262–4, returns the missing material. For text and general discussion, see R. Wünsch, "Der Zaubersang in der Nekuia Homers," *ARW* 12 (1909): 2–19; J.-R. Vieillefond, *Les "Cestes" de Julius Africanus: Étude sur l'ensemble des fragments avec édition, traduction et commentaire* (Florence, 1970), 277–91.

> O rivers, earth, and you below, who [?] punish
> men done with life, whoever has falsely sworn;
> Be a witness, fulfill for us this charm [*epaoide*].
> I have come to ask how I might reach the land
> of that Telemachus, my own son whom I left in a nurse's arms.

Odysseus goes on to invoke a series of Egyptian and Greek chthonic gods –
Anubis, Hermes, Infernal Zeus (=Hades), and Earth – and then some celestial
ones who are generally solar in nature (the Greek Helios, the Jewish Yahweh,
and the Egyptian sun god Re) and the so-called gods of magic whose names
are formulas themselves.

The last of these is the famous Abrasax, who is invoked cosmically as
an all-powerful deity, who rules the earth's rotation, the dance of the constellations, and the light of the bear constellation, much like Sminthian
Apollo in the prose hymn previously quoted from Menander Rhetor. Moreover, this invocation closes by again collapsing the celestial and the chthonic
worlds: Odysseus invokes "the infernal and heavenly one" and the dog star
Sirius, and then the traditional Homeric narrative resumes. All of the gods
in Africanus' inserted invocation – both celestial and chthonic – are asked
to come hither and "fulfill" or "bring to perfection" (the Greek verb is *telein*)
the charm that Odysseus sings, a fairly common topos in the preambles
to Greek incantations.[3] Africanus' spell is nonetheless quite puzzling: It is
all preamble, and there is no invocation to Teiresias himself asking him
to come forward and speak – for this should be the ultimate goal of the
spell.

From a text-critical perspective, we can see that these thirty-five lines of
invocation are a later composition. The polyglot content and style of these
additions obviously point to a late Roman date,[4] but it is crucial to note that
the forger is imagining a contemporary audience that would find no fault in
a necromantic scene that invokes celestial and solar gods in addition to the
traditionally chthonic ones. What we see here, I think, is a later Roman mind
trying to connect a very famous archaic narrative about the dead as a source
of prophecy with the growing influence of solar cults and the increasing
hegemony of the celestial realms in the area of necromancy. Apollo himself
does not, as it turns out, appear in this late antique version of Odysseus'

---

[3] C. A. Faraone "Aristophanes *Amphiaraus* Frag. 29 (Kassel-Austin): Oracular Response or
Erotic Incantation?" *CQ* 42 (1992): 320–7.
[4] Wünsch, "Der Zaubersang."

invocation, but many of the other solar and celestial gods associated with him in Menander's prose hymn are invoked, a practice that reappears in many of the divinatory spells discussed herein.

Now that we have some sense of Apollo's solar connections and the ease with which solar and celestial deities can show up in Hades, I turn to the divinatory recipes in the magical handbooks. But before I begin my analysis of the long and complicated "Apollonian Invocation," I offer a brief survey of a few other spells in *PGM* III and II that also invoke Apollo as the source of oracular knowledge, but in a simpler and more traditional manner. My hope is that these texts will provide a baseline against which we can examine and compare the necromantic additions to the "Apollonian Invocation."

Apollo as a Source of Oracular Inspiration in *PGM* III

The first of these Apollonian spells is a somewhat fragmentary recipe from *PGM* III (282–409) that calls itself a "Divinatory Procedure."[5] One section of great interest is titled "preparation for the operation" (292–320): It instructs us to create a miniature oracular shrine for Apollo, which includes a tripod, an image of Apollo carved from laurel wood, and a beaker or shell filled with pure water. Before performing the rite, we must keep pure for three days, wear clean white garments and a laurel wreath, and sacrifice to Apollo while singing special hymns [*paians*] to him at sunrise. Then we are to sing a formula (321–332); the text of this formula is, unfortunately, quite fragmentary, but we can make out that it requests foreknowledge and a kind of mind reading: "Make me know in advance each of the . . . from . . . and . . . toward the sunrise early [to know] each of the men [and] to know in advance [what things] each has in his mind [and] all their essence."

This "preparation for the operation" is quite simple and – unlike most *PGM* recipes – seems to be entirely Greek in content: We are directed to create (presumably in our home) a small mantic shrine, similar to Apollo's at Delphi with its tripod, statue, and laurel-wreathed prophet,[6] in the hope that Apollo will inspire us with divine knowledge. Other details, however, seem to point to procedures from two other famous Apollonian oracles, Didyma and Claros, which from the Hadrianic period onward had, in fact, eclipsed the Delphic

---

5 I follow W. C. Grese's interpretation in Betz, ed., *Greek Magical Papyri*, of the lacunose lines 305–20.

6 J. Fontenrose, *The Delphic Oracle* (Berkeley, Calif., 1978), 224–6.

sanctuary in importance.[7] At all three of these sanctuaries, the prophets (male at Claros, female at Delphi and Didyma) before the mantic session either drink or anoint themselves with water from a special spring, a practice that is perhaps alluded to by the beaker of pure water placed next to Apollo's tripod in this *PGM* III recipe. The recipe, moreover, seems to mimic two aspects of Apollonian mantic cult that are, to my knowledge, attested only at Didyma, where the priestess fasts for three days, as is required by the recipe, and a chorus sings hymns to Apollo to encourage his arrival at the mantic session (in the magic recipe, the practitioner makes a sacrifice and sings *paians* to Apollo).[8] That this recipe seems to conflate the mantic procedures from two or three different Greek shrines should not, however, surprise us, as these sanctuaries were all quite famous from the second century C.E. onward: The author or redactor of the spell either confuses the different oracles or (perhaps more likely) wants to increase the perceived efficacy of the invocation by alluding to as many famous procedures as possible. We shall see, however, that other Apollonian spells reveal a greater influence of the two oracles in Asia Minor, which in Late Antiquity did not decline as precipitously as the one at Delphi, but rather flourished well into the fourth century.

These instructions in *PGM* III for creating a personal and rather elaborate oracle in the home provide a good illustration of the common late antique practice of appropriating, shrinking, and domesticating, if you will, a public cult by a private individual.[9] Although this "preparation" section of the recipe seems to be mainly Greek in content - with the exception of the magical

---

[7] S. Eitrem, *Orakel und Mysterien am Ausgang der Antike* (Zürich, 1947), 47–52; H. W. Parke, *The Oracles of Apollo in Asia Minor* (London, 1985), 69–92, 125–70. On the decline of Delphi, see F. Ahl, "Apollo: Cult and Prophesy in Ovid, Lucan, and Statius," in *Apollo: Origins and Influences*, ed. J. Soloman (Tuscon, Ariz., 1994), 114–16.

[8] It is, of course, true that Apollo is closely connected at Delphi with music, where he is traditionally invoked as the "Leader of the Muses" and the focus of famous musical and choral competitions in the small theater that overlooks his temple. But only at Didyma is there a specific and very close connection between a hymn sung to the god and his oracular response. In a late imperial oracle from Didyma, Apollo addresses the Melesians and orders them "to sing a hymn in my sanctuaries, as before, just when the *axon* was about [to reveal] a word from the innermost shrine. I rejoice over every song . . . but chiefly if it is old." We do not know precisely what the *axon* is, but it is clearly an apparatus (like the Delphic tripod), which was set up in the inner sanctum at Didyma. Here, as Parke notes, the hymn seems to replace or be valued above the usual sacrificial rituals at other oracles - in other words, without the hymn, there will be no inspired oracle (*Oracles of Apollo*, 101–3).

[9] J. Z. Smith, "Trading Places," in *Ancient Magic and Ritual Power*, ed. M. Meyer and P. Mirecki (RGRW 129; Leiden, 1995), 13–28; Graf, "Magic and Divination," 291–2.

symbols that are inscribed on some of the apparatus – other parts betray the usual combination of Greek, Jewish, and Egyptian names and practices.[10] In the fragmentary lines that precede the "preparation," for example, some god, presumably Apollo or Apollo-Helios, is addressed as follows: "Continue without deception, lord, the [vis]ion [?] of every deed, according to the command of the holy spirit [hagion pneuma], the a[ng]el Phoibos, you yourself being pliable because of these songs [molpai] and psalms [psalmoi]" (287–288). This close causal connection between the hymns and the prophetic response of Apollo is, as I have said, reminiscent of the oracular procedure at Didyma, but the mention of a "holy spirit," an "angel," and "psalms" all point to the kind of syncretism of Jewish and Greek ideas that we saw in Africanus' text. And, in the lacunose text that follows the "preparation" (321ff), we find other invocations, which clearly reflect knowledge of Egyptian divine names and religious ideas.

A second and equally fragmentary spell from the same handbook (PGM III 187–262) directs us to offer Apollo some small, round honey-cakes while once again singing paeans [special hymns] to the god, who "will come...shaking the whole house and the tripod, and he will bring about an inquiry into the future." The text of two of these paeans – both hexametrical – follows. The first is to be recited "before Helios," which probably means at sunrise or sunset, and it seems to invoke the god by a series of different names, all which can loosely be called solar: "King Semea,"[11] the sacred scarab beetle of the Egyptians, the fiery angel of Zeus, Iao, Abrasax, Sabaoth, and Adonai (lines 198–229). The second hymn, however, contains only Greek material: It begins by invoking Apollo himself as healer, giver of oracles, and mentions Delos, Delphi, and Dodona (234–240).[12] After a

---

[10] The relative ethnic content of the PGM recipes – mostly inscribed in Greek but found in Upper Egypt far from the centers of Greek influence – is too complicated a question to discuss here. Suffice it to say that I believe that rituals and prayers from the Greek, Egyptian, and Jewish traditions are freely interspersed throughout the collection, but there are places where one tradition clearly dominates (as in the case of Greek dominance in this Apollonian spell). For a fuller and more detailed expression of my general views and my resistance to the recent arguments of Ritner and Brashear for the nearly complete domination of the Egyptian tradition, see my two essays: "The Mystodokos and the Dark-Eyed Maidens: Multicultural Influences on a Late-Hellenistic Incantation," in Ancient Magic and Ritual Power, 297–333; and "The Ethnic Origins of a Roman-Era Philtrokatadesmos (PGM IV 296–434)," in Magic and Ritual in the Ancient World, ed. P. Mirecki and M. Meyer (RGRW 129; Leiden, 2002), 319–43.

[11] See A. Mastrocinque, Studi sul mitraismo: Il mitraismo e la magia (Rome, 1998), 5-6, on Semea's solar connections.

[12] Dodona is a puzzle here, as that was the seat of a famous oracle of Zeus, not his son Apollo. Perhaps Apollo is seen to have appropriated the site by this poet. Because a similar "error"

lacuna in the papyrus, the text resumes with the request: "Come hither, seer (*mantis*), you who bring joy, O Smintheus. Give your response and hearken, Pythian Paian" (249–250).

The text then concludes confusedly with what appears to be an envoi to Daphne, who is imagined in this hymn as both a laurel tree (addressed as an "undying shoot") and a "Delphic maiden" for whom Apollo first sang songs. It seems she is asked to shake a (presumably laurel) bough and urge on Apollo, who is again addressed directly: "Well disposed and listening come to (your) prophet [*prophêtês*], hastening, you who run through the air, Pythian Paian" (256–570). This is a very traditional-sounding pagan hymn, which not only invokes Apollo, who is to come personally to the prophet (i.e., the practitioner), but also calls on Daphne, who seems to provide a charter myth for this ritual: for, like the practitioner, she is imagined to shake a laurel bough [*klados*] and to urge Apollo's arrival with her own song (for which the Delphians later praised her as "melodious").[13] There is, in addition, an erotic element here: The singer of this hymn, who is probably holding a laurel bough (like most of the *PGM* spells that invoke Apollo) and who is singing this hymn, seems to be playing the role of Daphne, of whom Apollo was famously enamored – a point to which I return in the next section.

Apollo as a Source of Oracular Inspiration in *PGM* II

Despite the generally fragmentary state of both of these recipes from *PGM* III, we can see that they share the same general goal: to create in one's home a miniature Apollonian oracle and to turn oneself into an inspired prophet, who – like the one at Didyma – wears the appropriate robe and laurel wreath,

appears in Prudentius (*Apoth.* 441), it is tempting to see "Dodona" as a scribal mistake for "Didyma." But the words have different metrical shapes and it would have been hard for a poet to confuse.

[13] The text is not entirely clear here. It seems to say that Daphne herself, because of her mythical success in attracting Apollo to Delphi with her song and laurel bough, was later made the object of songs at Delphi that praised her for being "melodious" [*eukelados*]. In fact, the extant literary versions of her story (all of Hellenistic or later date) stress her great reluctance to welcome Apollo and they make no mention of her own ability to sing. See T. Gantz, *Early Greek Myth* (Baltimore, 1993), 90–1; and Ahl, "Apollo," 122–5. It seems to me that we have a variant version of the myth of Daphne here in which she, like Branchus at Didyma and Cassandra at Troy, does not get transformed, but rather becomes a prophetess as the result of her contact with Apollo. It is interesting to note that Delphi, the original site of her transformation, was also the home of the Delphic Sibyl, whose name was Daphne; this Sibyl lived near Apollo's oracle and gave her own prophecies (see Fontenrose, *Delphic Oracle*, 160).

shakes a laurel bough, and sings a hymn to attract the god. A much fuller and better preserved spell in another handbook (*PGM* II 64–184) also treats Apollo as a completely heavenly source for divinatory knowledge in its traditional Greek form: hexametrical poetry.[14] In the ritual instructions for this recipe (64–75), we are asked to inscribe magical names onto the leaves of two laurel boughs (they are called both *klôn* and *klados* in the Greek) and to weave into each of them strands of white and red wool; the first is worn as a wreath on the head, and the second is probably carried in the right hand. In this regalia, we are to sacrifice a white rooster and a pinecone, both of which are to be burnt up completely in a fire and extinguished with wine (64–77).

Most of these items and actions – with the exception of the holocaust form of sacrifice – are typical of Olympian ritual, especially the white color of the rooster and the laurel wreath, which was, as we saw earlier, worn by the prophets at several of Apollo's sanctuaries.[15] The rooster, on the other hand, which greets each day with his crowing, is certainly an appropriate offering for a solar god who is hymned at sunrise.[16] It is not quite clear, however, precisely when the sacrifice is to be made because the rite starts the night before. But we are told quite explicitly that the next morning, at the break of day, we should recite an elaborate and lengthy hexametrical hymn that conflates Apollo, Helios, and the Egyptian sun god Re. Here, as in the case of the prose hymn of Menander Rhetor and the hexametrical hymns from *PGM* III, there is no hint of any chthonic associations. The first section of the hymn invokes Apollo in specific ways that evoke his famous shrine at Claros (*PGM* II 81–87):

> O Daphne (= Laurel), sacred plant of Apollo's oracular power, the leaves of which the scepter-holding lord once tasted and issued forth songs (*aoidai* = oracles). Iê iê famous Paean (= Apollo), dwelling in Colophon (= Claros), heed

---

[14] *PGM* II seems to contain one very long and multifaceted divinatory spell, whose precise nature is obscured because of its lacunose state. For discussion, see Graf, "Magic and Divination," 289–90, n. 14.

[15] Parke, *Oracles of Apollo*, 210–24.

[16] But it was also used in necromantic rites. Graf ("Magic and Divination," 291, n. 16) quotes Aineias of Gaza: "Among the Chaldeans, Egyptians and Greeks those who perform *teletai* tell that they sacrifice a rooster when they wake up and announce that they would call (*goêteuein*) the souls of the long dead, and thus they would call them up and make them visible." He wonders why magic and divination collapse together in the Augustan period onward and thinks that theurgy is the link – I would argue that *goêteia* already provided the link, as one calls up ghosts for many things: to curse an enemy, to leave a friend alone, and to prophesy. See S. I. Johnston, *Restless Dead: Encounters Between the Living and the Dead in Ancient Greece* (Berkeley, Calif., 1999), 82–126.

my sacred song [*aoidê*] and come quickly to earth from heaven and join me. Stand near me and from your ambrosial mouth breath songs into me [*aoidas empneuson*]. You yourself, lord of song [*molpês*], come, famous ruler of song. Hear me, blessed one, heavy in your wrath, stern. Now Titan, hear our voice, immortal one and don't ignore it. Stand near and from your ambrosial mouth speak [*ennepe*] quickly your oracular power [*mantosyne*] to me, who am your suppliant, all pure Apollo.

This hymn starts off oddly with an apostrophe to the laurel as the plant that allegedly inspired Apollo to prophesy after he ate it, a myth that is – as far as I have been able to ascertain – unattested elsewhere. It is true, however, that Lucian and one or two later sources claim that the Pythia and prophets at other sanctuaries were inspired by chewing the leaves, so perhaps this is an *aition* for the same mantic procedure.[17] The hymn then rather abruptly addresses Apollo (who dwells in Colophon) to come quickly to earth from heaven [*ouranothen*], and imagines him explicitly as a god, who – like the Muses – inspires song, in this case, presumably the singing of oracular hexameters. Thus, as in the preceding recipe from *PGM* II, the hexametrical songs of humans cause the arrival of the god, who will in turn inspire the practitioner to sing in another hexametrical genre: an inspired prophetic song.

The focus of this hymn on Apollo's eastern oracles is most obvious from the explicit reference to Colophon, which is the city nearest to the sanctuary of Apollo at Claros and whose name is often used by poets as an alternative to Claros. But here, too, many of the details seem to point as well to Didyma, where, as was noted previously, cletic hymns were (uniquely) sung to the god immediately before the mantic session. The hymn may also allude vaguely to one of the foundation myths of the sanctuary there, according to which Apollo became enamored of a local shepherd named Branchus and gave him three gifts: a kiss, a bough of laurel [*klados*], and the gift of prophecy.[18] The laurel, moreover, seems to have been extremely important for the shrine at Didyma. It shows up, for instance, in another story about Branchus in which he purifies "the Ionians" by sprinkling them with a laurel branch

[17] Fontenrose, *Delphic Oracle*, 225.
[18] For Branchus, see Parke, *Oracles of Apollo*, 5–6; Joseph Fontenrose, *Didyma: Apollo's Oracle, Cult, and Companions* (Berkeley, Calif., 1988), 53. The first line of prophets at Didyma were male descendents of Branchus, but after the oracle was destroyed by the Persians and then revived in Hellenistic times, a female prophet was chosen, perhaps in imitation of the (at the time) more famous Delphic practice.

dipped in water and singing a hexametrical hymn or incantation to Apollo. Furthermore, the first laurel bough that Apollo gave Branchus was planted in the sanctuary at Didyma and ultimately became the source of a sacred grove there, from which the prophetess (herself imitating Branchus) presumably took the two boughs that she used in her mantic sessions, placing one on her head as a wreath and holding the other in her hand. The hymn may perhaps also refer more subtly to the other two gifts of Apollo, in its references to the "ambrosial mouth of Apollo" (twice repeated) and in its request that the god "stand near me and ... breathe songs into me [*aoidas empneuson*]." The focus here on this intimate contact – which also occurs in Ovid's treatment of the Daphne story – suggests to me, at least, that the lover's kiss may have been the vehicle for the gift of Apollonian prophecy.[19]

The next section of this hymn in *PGM* II equates Apollo with Helios, all golden in his fiery chariot, who at the end of the day leads his horses down into the Ocean (87–96).[20] After the intonation of the seven vowels, the hymn returns again to Apollo, now as "leader of the Muses," and it reiterates the request to "come to me now quickly to earth" and "with ambrosian mouth give voice to my song" (97–102). The hexametrical verses end here, but the invocation continues in prose to call on the Egyptian sun god Horus, who rises in the East as a child sitting on the lotus and enlightens the world. In the end, however, this prose prayer returns yet again to Apollo (129–40) with strings of vowels, which seem to play on the traditional Apollonian refrain "iê iê Paian" and which are interspersed with Apollo's names in the vocative, both in his Delphian guises ("Pythian," "Parnassian," and "Castalian") and in his Clarian ones ("Colophonian" and "Clarian").

To sum up, then: This particular recipe from *PGM* II begins and ends as a rather traditional Greek ritual and hymn designed to summon Apollo away from his famous shrines and to the practitioner to inspire the latter with oracular hexameters. Like the previously discussed spells, with their miniature tripod and statue of Apollo, this recipe provides yet another example of the appropriation and domestication of the most famous cults of Apollo at Delphi, Didyma, and Claros. In this case, the practitioner dresses like Apollo's prophets at Didyma and Delphi (with a wreath and a handheld bough, both

---

[19] Daphne kissed: Ovid, *Metam.* 555–56 (in which the word *oscula* appears twice); see Ahl, "Apollo," 123, n. 6, for discussion. The idea that a god can "breathe" poetic and oracular inspiration "into" a poet is found (together with the gift of a laurel staff) at Hesiod, *Theog.* 22–23. Parke, *Oracles of Apollo*, 211, discusses the parallels.

[20] Trans. E. N. O'Neil in Betz, ed., *Greek Magical Papyri*.

of laurel) and turns his courtyard or rooftop into an oracular shrine in which he will presumably produce hexametrical poems as prophecies. In two of the three examples discussed, moreover, the hymn equates Apollo with a series of sun gods: Helios (imagined in Greek fashion as a charioteer who drives his steeds into the sea), the Jewish God, and various versions of the Egyptian sun god. We should not, however, hastily assume that this syncretism was solely the work of the author or redactor of this recipe, for these kinds of equations were commonplace in Late Antiquity (as we saw earlier in the prose hymn of Menander Rhetor) and even show up in anecdotes and oracles concerned with, and, perhaps, emanating from, Claros and Didyma. There was, for example, even in Hellenistic times a myth that the legendary first prophet at Didyma, Branchus, was the son of Helios,[21] and oracular responses of the late Roman period said to be from Clarus or Didyma address Apollo as "Helios, the bringer of light."[22] Other oracle texts from this period equate Apollo with the Jewish god Yahweh (Iao) or more vaguely as "one of God's angels."[23] I should stress again, however, that in all of these Apollonian oracles, rituals, and hymns, there is no mention of chthonic gods or necromantic ritual.

The Recipe for an "Apollonian Invocation" in *PGM* I

Let us turn at last to *PGM* I 262–347. More than a half-century ago, Eitrem pointed out that parts of this invocation – like the Apollonian spells discussed in the two previous sections – draw heavily on some of the traditional cults of the oracular Apollo.[24] Thus, this recipe directs us to equip ourselves in "prophetic gear" [*prophêtikon schêma*] and hold a seven-leaved branch [*klôn*] of laurel in our right hand. As in the previous Apollonian spell, these seven laurel leaves are inscribed with magical symbols. Further along in the spell we are asked to set up a lamp on the (presumably severed) head of a wolf

---

[21] This was believed because his mother had a dream that the sun entered her mouth, traveled down her body, and exited from her vagina, a bizarre concept discussed briefly by W. Burkert, "Olbia and Apollo of Didyma: A New Oracle Text," in *Apollo: Origins and Influences*, 51.

[22] A late third-century inscription from the sanctuary itself has one of the prophets (a man named Damianus) address the god as "you Didymaean Lord, Helios Apollo," and another oracle quoted by Eusebius seems to equate Apollo with "Helios the bringer of light." For discussion, see Parke, *Oracles of Apollo*, 98–100; Fontenrose, *Didyma*, 113–14, 219–20.

[23] Macrobius, *Sat.* 1.18.19, quoting Cornelius Labeo, perhaps a student of Porphyry, and the so-called "Tübingen Theosophy." For a discussion of both texts and their alleged connection with Claros and/or Didyma, see Parke, *Oracles of Apollo*, 163–8.

[24] Eitrem, *Orakel und Mysterien*, 47–52.

and a small altar for burning incense (compounded from spices and the eye of a wolf) and for offering cakes to the god in batches of seven (267–295). Although the head and the eye of a wolf may seem worthy of Shakespeare's weird sisters in *Macbeth*, the wolf is, in fact, an animal closely connected with Apollo in the East, as is the number seven.[25] The practitioner, moreover, by dressing in prophetic gear and holding a sprig of laurel in his right hand, seems once again to mimic the mythic figure of Branchus, the founder of Apollo's oracle at Didyma, who – as was mentioned earlier – began to utter oracles after Apollo kissed him and gave him a wreath and staff of laurel, similar to those still being used by inspired Didymean prophets in Roman times.[26] There may also be a reference in this recipe to the Didymian rites of abstention and purification: We are told to perform the rituals after refraining from "any unclean things, any eating of fish, and any sexual intercourse in order that you may bring the god into the greatest desire [*tên megistên epithumian*] towards yourself" (290–291). The mention of the erotic desire of Apollo here recalls, again, the myths of the god's desire for Daphne and Branchus, which are connected with the foundation of his Delphian and Didymian oracles.

Up to this point, then, it would seem that we are confronted with a purely Apollonian scene. There are, however, two small but not insignificant details in these arrangements that suggest this spell will be quite different from those discussed earlier. In the first line of the recipe, we are told that the goal of this spell is to summon "the Ouranian gods and the chthonic *daimones*" and, in addition to the laurel branch grasped in our right hand, we are also instructed to take up an ebony rod (*rhabdos*) in our left. Because ebony is a very dark wood associated in the Greek Magical Papyri and in Apuleius's *Apology* with Hermes, it is most likely that this rod is some version of the staff Hermes uses to conduct souls to the underworld.[27] Thus, the practitioner, grasping a laurel bough in his right hand and an ebony rod in his left, provides at the very beginning of this recipe a rather vivid illustration of the collapse of the Olympian and underworld realms.

---

[25] W. Burkert, *Greek Religion: Archaic and Classical*, trans. J. Raffan (Cambridge, Mass., 1985), 143–9, and idem, "Olbia and Apollo," *passim*.

[26] Fontenrose, *Delphic Oracle*, 78–9.

[27] For the connection between Hermes and ebony, see, e.g., the magician's boast of knowledge in *PGM* VII 12 ("I know your wood is ebony. I know you, Hermes, who you are, etc.") and the ebony statuette of Mercury described by Apuleius (*Apol.* 63) and discussed by A. Abt, *Die Apologie des Apuleius von Madaura und die antike Zauberai* (Geissen, 1908), 226–8.

Christopher A. Faraone

So much for the ritual setting. As was true for the other Apollonian spells, most of this recipe is then taken up with the invocation of the god in a hexametrical hymn, which begins as follows: "Give answer to my questions, lord. O master leave Mt. Parnassos and Delphic Pytho, whenever my priestly lips voice secret words." (298–300). This opening scene, then, is quite similar to that imagined in the recipes discussed earlier: The person who performs this spell imitates a prophet of Apollo and with a hexametrical hymn calls the god away from another of his oracular shrines – in this case, from Delphi – to answer in his own person questions about the future. The second section of the hymn, however, moves us away from the traditional form of a Greek cletic hymn and reveals once again the influence of Jewish traditions both in its content and in its form (300–306)[28]:

> First angel of [the god], great Zeus, Iao
> And you Michael, who rule heaven's realm,
> I call, and you archangel Gabriel.
> Down from Olympus, Abrasax, delighting
> in dawns, come gracious who view sunset from
> the dawn, Adonai, father of the world
> All nature quakes in fear of you, Pakerbêth.

Here, the hymn equates Apollo with Zeus' first angel Iao (usually = Yahweh) and then calls Michael and Gabriel to come down from Mount Olympus, along with Adonai, all of which recalls the similarly Jewish names that show up in Odysseus' invocation in Africanus' version of the Homeric *Nekuia* scene and in some of the other magical and oracular texts discussed earlier.

The hymn then takes the form of an exorcistic incantation (i.e., a series of short statements beginning with the Greek verb *exorkizo*, "I adjure you"), a genre that probably originated in a Jewish context in Palestine or Asia Minor at the end of the Hellenistic period.[29] The exorcistic formulae close at line 313 by requesting that these divinities send a "divine spirit" or "divine breath" [*theion pneuma*] to fulfill what is in the practitioner's heart and mind.

[28] Trans. O'Neil in Betz, ed., *Greek Magical Papyri*.

[29] See Roy D. Kotansky, "Greek Exorcistic Amulets," in *Ancient Magic and Ritual Power*, 243–77, who points out the obvious parallels between two heavily Jewish recipes for exorcism in *PGM* IV (1227–1264, 3007–3086), a series of first-century C.E. Greek *defixiones* from North Africa with obvious Semitic influence (e.g., *DT* 241.23ff: "I adjure you by the god above the sky, the one sitting over the Cherubim"), and an early papyrus love spell from Egypt dated to the first century C.E. that has affinities to the *philtrokatadesmos* under discussion (*PGM* XVI 9–10: "I adjure you, *nekydaimon*, by Adônaios Sabaôth ... cause Serapion ... to pine and melt away out of passion").

This last request represents, of course, a subtle but important change, for it recasts the classical Greek trope of divine inspiration into a new, but related form. In the previously discussed spells, Apollo was sometimes asked to come to the practitioner and breath directly into [*empneuson*] him – much like the Muses "inspire" Hesiod – so that he can sing inspired hexametrical oracles. In the first part of the hymn in this spell Apollo is also asked to come and answer questions himself. But here, in the second section of the hymn, Apollo is equated or connected with Jewish *angeloi* and asked to send instead a divine "breath" [*pneuma*], a word that is wonderfully ambiguous. It can, of course, refer to the Greek pneumatic theory of poetic inspiration, but in the demonological theories of the day and in many late-Roman-era exorcistic texts, the word *pneuma* comes to mean a separate supernatural entity apart from the god – for example, a demon.[30] In short, the syncretistic deity in this passage, at least, seems to be more distant from the practitioner, as he avoids the direct contact of lips upon lips and sends instead a *pneuma* as an intermediary.

The third section of this hexametrical invocation (which begins at line 315) quotes part of a hymn to Helios that was apparently quite popular among late antique sorcerers – it appears in the *PGM* corpus in four different recipes. The version in our spell, however, does not name Helios, and we are probably to assume that it is still addressed to Apollo, since the two gods were – as we have seen illustrated earlier – often conflated in postclassical Greece[31]:

> Hear blessed one, I call on you who rule heaven and earth and Chaos and Hades, where dwell ["ghosts (*daimones*) of men who once gazed on the light"]. At my sacred chants [*epaoidai*] send to me this ghost [*daimôn*], who moves by night to orders beneath your force, from whose own *skênos* this thing [*tode*] comes, and let him tell me in total truth all that my mind designs, and send him gentle, gracious, and pondering no thoughts against me.

Here, finally, we understand why this recipe at its beginning boasted the power to summon "heavenly gods and chthonic *daimones*," for Apollo–Helios himself is here addressed as the "ruler of heaven, earth, Chaos, and Hades" and asked to send up a ghost from the underworld to reveal true things.

---

[30] It is curious to note, however, that many of the Roman-era texts that discuss Delphic procedure explain that the Pythia gets inspired by coming into contact with a *pneuma* or a *spiritus*; see Fontenrose, *Delphic Oracle*, 198–201, who translates both words as "breeze" or "wind."

[31] The words quoted in the first set of square brackets have been supplied from the other versions of the hymn.

This long hexametrical hymn, then, makes three different but related requests to this very syncretistic god, all of which aim at prophecy:

Lines	God	Request
297–299	Delphic Apollo	Come from Delphi and answer my questions
300–314	the Jewish God or angels	Send down a *pneuma theion* to fulfill what is in my heart and soul
314–326	Helios	Send up from Hades a ghost to tell in total truth all my mind designs

One can see right away how this "Apollonian Invocation" differs from the previously discussed Apollonian recipes, in which the god is asked only to come in person either from another earthly spot (e.g., another sanctuary) or down to earth from heaven. Here, however, a third possibility arises: that Apollo in his Helian guise will send the ghost of a dead person up from Hades.

There remains, however, one very curious problem with this last part of the hymn: Why is the request for the ghost so specific? Why is the god asked to send "*this* ghost . . . from whose *skênos this* thing [*tode*] has come"? To which ghost precisely does the pronoun "this" refer? And what does the word *skênos* designate? The word is related to the more common Greek word *skênê* and similarly means a "tent" or a "hut." But it is also a poetic and philosophic word for "corpse," showing up in a dozen or so sepulchral epigrams, mostly of Roman date, usually as the first word in a hexameter, just as it does in this "Apollonian Invocation."[32] The word also shows up much earlier in Greek philosophic writers such as Democritus, Timaeus, and Plato, who use it most often – as do the epitaphs – to draw a contrast between the body that dies and the soul that does not. Thus, it apparently designates the body as the "tent" that covers or contains the soul. The word *skênos* is not very popular in magical spells, appearing only six times in all of the *PGM*: four times in the different versions of this same hexametrical hymn to Helios and twice in prose recipes for the interrogation of corpses. There is, in fact,

---

[32] The earliest extant use of it in poetry, as far as I can tell, is in a late Classical or early Hellenistic poem inscribed on a tombstone found near Boeotian Thebes; nearly all of the later poetic examples are of Roman date. The Hellenistic stone from Thebes is G. Kaibel, *Epigramata Graeca ex lapidibus conlecta* (Hildesheim, 1965), no. 502. All the other stones in his corpus that use the word *skênos* are of Roman date or later: nos. 97, 226, 250, 422, 502, and 711.

some confusion about precisely how to render the word when it appears in the *PGM*. In the "Apollonian Invocation" in *PGM* III, O'Neil, for instance, follows the German rendition of Preisendanz, and translates the word *skênos* as "tent," but elsewhere (e.g., *PGM* IV 449) both scholars translate in the word as "corpse."

This ambiguity in interpretation can be easily explained and defended by an examination of the fullest version of the hexametrical hymn to Helios from which lines 315–326 of our "Apollonian Invocation" have been adapted. We find this version of the hymn at the end of the well-known recipe for a *Philtrokatadesmos* [love-binding spell], an elaborate and much discussed recipe that includes the manufacture of an effigy of Ares stabbing a nude and kneeling figurine of a bound woman.[33] The recipe enjoins us to inscribe on a lead tablet a long incantation addressed to a corpse and to place it at sunset "beside the grave of one who has died untimely or violently." We are also instructed to sing a hexametrical hymn to the setting sun, "while holding magical material [*ousia*] from the tomb [*mnemion*]." In Greek magical texts, the word *ousia* usually refers to hairs or threads from the victim of the curse that are used as targeting devices to direct a supernatural attack narrowly at a single victim.[34] Here, the word must refer to parts of the corpse taken from a grave – items that are presumably used to compel the arrival of the ghost, whose corpse was buried there.

The hymn to be sung at the graveside for this erotic spell is a much fuller and more coherent version of the same hexametrical hymn to Helios (*PGM* IV 443–56):

> Hear blessed one, I call on you who rule heaven and earth and Chaos and Hades, where dwell the ghosts [*daimones*] of men who once gazed on the light. And even now I beg you, blessed one, unfailing one, the master of the world, if you go to the depths of the earth and search the regions of the dead, send *this* ghost [*daimôn*], from whose corpse [*skênos*] I hold *this* remnant [*leipsanon*].
>
> And send him [i.e., the ghost] gentle, gracious, and pondering no thoughts against me. And may you [i.e., Helios] not be angry with my potent chants

---

[33] *PGM* IV 335–406. A number of lead tablets and figurines apparently prepared according to this recipe have survived; see P. du Bourguet, "Ensemble magique de la période romaine en Égypt," *Revue du Louvre* (1975): 255–7; idem, "Une ancêtre des figurines d'envoutement percées d'aiguilles, avec ses compléments magiques, au Musée du Louvre," *MIFAO* 104 (1980): 225–38; W. M. Brashear, "The Greek Magical Papyri: An Introduction and Survey; Annotated Bibliography (1928–1994)," *ANRW* II 18.5 (1995): 3380–684, esp. 3416–17.

[34] D. R. Jordan, "Defixiones from a Well Near the Southwest Corner of the Athenian Agora," *Hesperia* 54 (1985): 251.

[*epaoidai*], but guard that my whole body come to light intact, for you yourself arranged these things among mankind for them to learn about the threads of the Moirai, and this is your advice.

In this hymn, which the practitioner sings at sunset at a graveside while holding part of a skeleton or a corpse, the deictic pronouns – *this* ghost, *this* remnant – make perfect sense and it is quite easy to translate the word *skênos* in its second meaning as "corpse." The practitioner is directed to hold in his hand a bone or part of the corpse of a person to ensure that the sun god can find the unhappy ghost of this particular person and then send it out of the underworld to the practitioner. This fuller version of the hymn in *PGM* IV is, of course, used in a complex erotic spell, and it is tempting to assume that the Helios hymn was originally designed for such a goal. But the mention of the Moirai [Fates] at the end of the passage previously quoted seems to me to suggest that this hymn was, in fact, originally designed solely for necromantic purposes: "for you yourself [i.e., Helios] arranged these things among mankind for them to learn about the threads of the Moirai." Here I imagine that "learning about the threads of the Moirai" must refer to a necromantic inquiry aimed at gaining knowledge of the precise hour and day of someone's death, a very popular question for diviners throughout Late Antiquity.

If we compare the two different versions of these verses and analyze them in a text-critical manner, we would probably say that the version in the "Apollonian Invocation" (in *PGM* I) is the more corrupt because it is missing a whole hexametrical line and the deictic pronouns ("... this ... this ...") make little sense. But this terminology is inappropriate here, because it implies that the text of this hexametrical invocation devolved from a pristine exemplar because of an accumulation of scribal errors and misunderstandings over a long stretch of time. In the case of Greek magical spells, however, there is often a very different process of experimentation and purposeful adaptation in play, and I would suggest that the somewhat incoherent version of the hymn in *PGM* I is probably not the result of incompetence, but rather of self-conscious editing on the part of the redactor who was trying (albeit with somewhat limited success) to resituate a graveside necromantic ritual to some other place, presumably – like most of the other Apollonian spells – to a courtyard or rooftop of a private house. Thus, their translations of the verses as they appear in the "Apollonian Invocation," both O'Neil and Preisendanz have in a sense captured this scribal adaptation and relocation by rendering the word *skênos* in the *PGM* I version in a more neutral or ambiguous fashion as "tent" and not "dead body" or "corpse."[35]

Conclusion

We have seen how the "Apollonian Invocation" in *PGM* I seems to combine and thereby collapse two realms – the celestial and the chthonic – that were originally kept apart, at least in traditional Greek cult and mythology. Indeed, it is instructive to recall that at *Odyssey* 12.382–383, Helios considers sinking into the underworld in shame if he does not avenge the eating of his cattle by Odysseus' men – an act that is clearly impossible for him or any Greek to imagine. It would be equally impossible, I should think, for a Greek in the archaic or classical period to contemplate donning a white robe and laurel wreath and invoking Apollo in a ceremony that also includes the summoning of ghost from the underworld. Although both rituals were performed separately in the Greek world in the earlier periods, their combination in this single spell is a clear sign of the times, when an increasingly all-powerful celestial god, who is invoked as Apollo among other names, can claim to himself the power of necromancy as well.

How did this come about? Clearly, the identification of Apollo–Helios with the Egyptian sun god Re and the Mesopotamian sun god Shamash was a crucial step in this development for, in both of those non-Greek religious traditions, the solar deity is closely involved with the underworld, because he is believed to descend into it each night and pass through its entire length until he reappears in the East again at dawn. This is, of course, precisely what we are required to say in the middle of the hexametrical hymn to Helios (see *PGM* I 314–326, previously quoted).

It is interesting to note, however, that in the three other extant versions of this hymn in the Greek Magical Papyri, this request is prefaced with a condition: "*If* you go into the hollow of the earth to the land of the dead, send this ghost." This is quite puzzling, of course, and suggests that this section of the poem or at least its contents did not, in fact, originate with Mesopotamian

---

[35] There is a slim possibility that the redactor of our *PGM* I spell, thinking of the Jewish elements in the preceding hymn, might have had a passage or two of the Septuagint in his mind when he stripped the Helios hymn from its necromantic context, for there are a handful of passages (e.g., Exod 31:3) in which the tabernacle is called the "tent (*skênê*: feminine noun) of the presence" of God. Could it be that he thought that the laurel bough held in the hand of the practitioner (always a good candidate for the referent of a deictic pronoun) was "this thing" [*tode*] that came from the "tabernacle" of Apollo–Yahweh?

or Egyptian sources, because in those cultures the visits of the sun god to the underworld are famously unconditional. Indeed, it is part of a necessary and irrevocable cycle that the sun should enter the underworld every day at sunset. I suspect, therefore, that the scribe or practitioner who put together this Apollonian spell adapted this hymn by removing the condition ("If you go into...") because he was, in fact, thinking of Apollo-Helios in broadly syncretistic terms as the equivalent of Re, who appears at the end of the hymn in his own right. The appearance of the condition, however, in the three other versions suggests that this request to send up a ghost from Hades was originally addressed to another god who makes uncyclical or random visits to the underworld: Hermes, the conductor of the dead. I would argue, in fact, that just as the grasping of Apollo's laurel bough in one hand and Hermes' ebony rod in the other reflects on an emblematic level the combination of the celestial and chthonian insignia of divination, this curiously hybrid hymn melds a cletic hymn to Apollo, originally designed to summon the god from heaven to inspire the practitioner with prophetic verses, with another Greek tradition of necromantic hexameters asking Hermes to send up a ghost from the underworld to speak to him.

13

In Heaven as It Is in Hell: The Cosmology of *Seder Rabbah di-Bereshit*

Peter Schäfer

"For [God] is on the earth below exactly as in the heavens above."
(Shneur Zalman of Lyadi)[1]

I

The most comprehensive Jewish cosmological tractate handed down to us from Late Antiquity, probably from the post-talmudic/early geonic period, is commonly known as *Seder Rabbah di-Bereshit* ["The Greater Order of Creation"].[2] It has never been edited in a critical edition,[3] nor has it been adequately translated into a modern language.[4] The manuscript tradition varies greatly as far as its structure, its contents, and even its title are concerned. The most common title, attested in the majority of manuscripts, is not *Seder Rabbah di-Bereshit* (in fact, this title is suggested in only one manuscript),[5] but rather *Maʿaseh Bereshit* ["The Work of Creation"].[6] This, of course, is an allusion to the famous mishnah in *m. Ḥagigah* 2:1:

---

[1] Shneur Zalman of Lyadi, *Tanya* (Vilna, 1937), 164.

[2] More precisely transliterated as *Seder Rabbah di-Vereshit*, henceforth, *SRdB*.

[3] The earliest scholarly, but by no means comprehensive, edition can be found in S. A. Wertheimer, ed., *Batei Midrashot*, 2nd ed. by A. J. Wertheimer (Jerusalem, 1950-3), 1:19–48; another version (from the Oxford manuscript), or rather a certain microform as part of the larger unit "*SRdB*," in *Batei Midrashot*, 1:365–69. The versions contained in MSS Oxford 1531, Munich 22, and Munich 40 are published in P. Schäfer, ed., with M. Schlüter and H. G. von Mutius, *Synopse zur Hekhalot-Literatur* (TSAJ 2; Tübingen, 1981), to which all paragraph numbers for *SRdB* and the Hekhalot literature refer.

[4] The only translation available so far is the French translation in N. Sed, *La mystique cosmologique juive* (Paris, 1981), 80ff.; see also idem, "Une cosmologie juive du haut moyen age: La Běraita di Maʿaseh Běrešit," *REJ* 123 (1964): 259–305; 124 (1965): 23–123. Sed did not, however, have all the relevant manuscript evidence at his disposal.

[5] MS Oxford 1531 (§832).

[6] MS Munich 22 (§429), and in most of the *Massekhet Hekhalot* manuscripts: see K. Herrmann, *Massekhet Hekhalot: Traktat von den himmlischen Palästen; Edition, Übersetzung und Kommentar*

Peter Schäfer

The laws of prohibited sexual relationships ['arayot] may not be expounded by [or: to][7] three persons, nor the "Work of Creation" [ma'aseh bereshit] by [or: to] two, nor the chariot [merkavah] by [or: to] an individual, unless he is a sage and understands on his own.

Anyone, who looks into [mistakkel be-] four things, it would be merciful for him if he had not come into the world: what is above, and what below, what is before, and what after.

Anyone, who has no concern for the glory of his creator, it would be merciful for him if he had not come into the world.

In prohibiting, or rather restricting, the "exposition" ['ein dorshin] of "prohibited sexual relationships," "creation," and "the chariot," the Mishnah clearly refers to exegetical exercises and distinguishes between the exegesis of the biblical texts dealing with these three topics: Lev 18:6–23, Genesis 1, and Ezekiel 1; 10. Hence, it is certainly not by accident that the text of SRdB is preserved in the manuscripts together with either Hekhalot material (Merkavah mysticism) or with the late tractate Massekhet Hekhalot ["Tractate of the [Heavenly] Palaces"], which focuses on God and his throne in the seventh heaven. SRdB (ma'aseh bereshit) and the literature of Merkavah mysticism (ma'aseh merkavah) represent, according to the medieval scribes, the two major disciplines of the three mentioned in the Mishnah: creation and the divine chariot.[8]

The mishnaic prohibition is most restrictive in the case of the chariot and slightly less so in the case of creation. Thus, it is not surprising that we have very little evidence of Merkavah mystical activity in the vast corpus of rabbinic literature.[9] The most salient example is the story in the Babylonian Talmud about R. Eleazar b. Arakh who, despite the prohibition of the Mishnah, expounds the "Work of the Chariot" in the presence of his master, Yohanan b. Zakkai, and who does it so successfully that fire comes down from heaven and an angel approves of his exposition: "This is the very 'Work of the Chariot'!" (b. Ḥag. 14b). However, as much as we learn about the extraordinary circumstances of this mystical event – we are even told precisely

(TSAJ 39; Tübingen, 1994), 229, n. 110, in which he also lists the other titles found in the manuscripts.

[7] Depending on the reading bisheloshah, etc. (which is attested to in most manuscripts) or lisheloshah, etc. (which is attested to in one manuscript only); see D. J. Halperin, The Merkabah in Rabbinic Literature (New Haven, Conn., 1980), 11, with n. 3.

[8] I here leave out the discussion of prohibited sexual relations, which obviously never became a discipline of their own.

[9] See Halperin, who emphasizes the fact that there is no evidence at all for the existence of a mystical praxis in the Palestinian rabbinic sources; it is only the Bavli that "offers positive evidence that the rabbis believed in some sort of ecstatic mysticism" (Merkabah, 179).

234

which song the trees were singing when they listened to Eleazar – we are not deemed worthy of any detail of his exposition! He was a student who "understood of his own" and, therefore, must have been taught the secrets of the chariot by his master Yohanan b. Zakkai. But the secret is kept as a secret and not transmitted to the unworthy.

Such oblique allusions to the actual content of the discipline of *ma'aseh merkavah* contrast sharply with the abundant evidence we have for exegetical activity related to the first chapter of Genesis. Much of it is preserved in the Midrash *Genesis Rabbah*. Two smaller units in *Genesis Rabbah* are particularly instructive because they betray a clear awareness of the mishnaic restrictions on *ma'aseh bereshit*. The first one is the *petiha GenR* 1:5, which interprets Gen 1:1 through the lens of Ps 31:19 ("Let the lying lips be dumb that speak arrogantly against the righteous with pride and contempt"). The "lying lips" that should be silenced are the lips of those who speak "arrogantly" ['*ataq*] against the will of the Righteous One on matters that he has withheld [*he'etiq*] from his creatures – that is, matters of creation. "With pride" [*be-ga'avah*] means, according to this interpretation, that they boast [*lehitga'ot*] and say, "I expound the 'Work of Creation,'" and "contempt" [*buz*] means that they have contempt for [*mevazzeh*] God's glory. This, of course, refers to the last part of the Mishnah, which is concerned with the glory of the creator. A parable is finally added to explain how exactly these people offend the glory of God and how this relates to Gen 1:1:

> In human practice, when an earthly king builds a palace on a site of sewers, dunghills, and garbage, if one says: "This palace is built on a site of sewers, dunghills, and garbage," does he not insult [the king]?! Thus, whoever comes to say: "This world was created out of *tohu* and *bohu* and darkness," does he not insult [God]?!
>
> R. Huna said in the name of Bar Kappara: "If the matter were not written, it would be impossible to say it: 'God created heaven and earth' (Gen 1:1) – out of what? Out of: 'And the earth was *tohu* and *bohu* [and darkness was over the surface of the abyss]' (Gen 1:2)."

The parable makes it abundantly clear, against the grain of the psalm, that the "lying lips" are to be silenced not because they are lying, but precisely because they speak the truth – a truth, however, that they are not permitted to utter. The palace of the earthly king *was* built on the site of rubbish and, accordingly, the world of the heavenly king *was* created out of *tohu, bohu,* and darkness – that is, unformed matter. This is true and stated in the Bible, but this truth is not meant to be communicated, at least not to everyone. There can be no doubt that this interpretation is based on the reading of the first three verses of Genesis that was later adopted also by Rashi in his biblical commentary[10]: namely, "When God began to create[11] heaven and earth – the earth being *tohu* and *bohu*, with darkness over the surface of the abyss, and a wind from God/the Spirit of God sweeping over the water – God said: 'Let there be light!'" This reading presupposes that *tohu*, *bohu*, darkness, and abyss were already present as some kind of raw material when God began his creation and that the first thing that God made was the light. It goes without saying that such a reading does not conform to the idea of *creatio ex nihilo*.

Hence, what we find in *GenR* 1:5 is the somewhat paradoxical assertion that proper exegesis of the biblical text can lead to troubling conclusions, which, although true, diminish the glory of the creator. The Mishnah's prohibition, the author of this unit argues, does not oppose such expositions of the "Work of Creation," but rather is, literally, against communicating them to others. But at the same time, he does precisely this: He communicates the horrible secret of the creator to his audience (whoever this is).

A very different conclusion is reached in another unit in the very same *parashah* of Genesis Rabbah (1:9):

> A philosopher asked Rabban Gamaliel, saying to him: "Your God was indeed a great artist, but he [nevertheless] had good materials[12] that helped him." He [Gamaliel] said to him [the philosopher]: "What are they?" He [the philosopher] answered: "*tohu, bohu*, darkness, water, wind, and the abyss." He [Gamaliel] said to him [the philosopher]: "May your spirit (lit. may the spirit of that man) burst! All of them are [explicitly] explained as having been created [by God]:

> *Tohu* and *bohu*: 'I make peace and create evil' (Isa 45:7).[13]
> Darkness: 'I form light and create darkness' (Isa 45:7).
> Water: 'Praise him, you highest heavens, and you waters [that are above the heavens]' (Ps 148:4). Why? 'For he commanded and they were created' (Ps 148:5).
> Wind: 'For it was he who formed the mountains and created the wind' (Amos 4:13).
> Abyss: 'When there was still no abyss, I was brought forth' (Prov 8:24).

Here we find the same interpretation of Gen 1:1–3 as in the previous passage, namely, that God used certain preexistent raw material for his creation of the world, but in this case, the idea is put in the mouth of a pagan philosopher.

---

[10] Rashi ad Gen 1:1.
[11] Reading *bereshit bero' Elohim* . . . instead of *bereshit bara' Elohim*.
[12] Reading *samemanim* instead of *semanim*.
[13] *Tohu* referring to peace, and *bohu* referring to evil.

Moreover, the rabbinic representative, Rabban Gamaliel, fiercely opposes this exegesis by offering scriptural support (however, not from Genesis itself) for the assertion that God was, in fact, responsible for creating all of the primordial materials. What is presented in *GenR* 1:5 as perfectly correct exegesis (albeit not to be communicated) is here disqualified as unacceptable exegesis, which must be neutralized by other verses from the same Hebrew Bible. Exegesis stands against exegesis, and everything depends on who is doing the interpreting. The exposition of Genesis 1 turns out to be a tricky task, and the fact that the redactor of *Genesis Rabbah* has included both of these conflicting exegeses within the same *parashah* (although prudently not placing one immediately after the other) does not make *our* task of exegesis any easier.

II

Genesis Rabbah is characteristic of the rabbinic approach to the discipline of the "Work of Creation." The rabbinic inquiry into "what is above, and what below, what is before, and what after" is primarily an activity of biblical exegesis, not of some other kind of experience. This activity may result in certain experiences, but – if there is any experience involved – it follows from exegesis. Not so *SRdB*. *SRdB* is by no means a uniform tractate; it has been transmitted in the various manuscripts in very different versions,[14] and some contain exegetical material. Nevertheless, the bulk of this relatively late work is nonexegetical, in stark contrast with earlier rabbinic treatments of the "Work of Creation."[15] This accords with what has been observed for some time already about Hekhalot literature, its counterdiscipline, which is also almost completely independent of biblical exegesis.

SRdB contains the microforms given in the following subsections.[16]

[14] See the unpublished M.A. thesis by my former student Christian Weinhag, "*Seder Rabbah di-Bereshit ('Die große Schöpfungsordnung')*" (M.A. thesis, Freie Universität Berlin, 1984). Weinhag was kind enough to put at my disposal some of the material collected for his not yet finished dissertation on *SRdB*; see also Herrmann, *Massekhet Hekhalot*, 230ff.

[15] The contrast between *GenR* and *SRdB* is between "exegetical" and "nonexegetical": The former exegetes and expands on the Bible, whereas the latter is to a large degree independent of the biblical text. The fact that biblical proof texts are still used or that the first unit subsequently discussed begins with a biblical exegesis of Gen 1:1 is not a counterargument. Biblical proof texts connect the new structure with the Bible, but they are not building blocks of the new structure; and if Gen 1:1 is still the "hook" on which the rest of the traditions are hung, the authors/tradents/redactors of *SRdB* choose to veer off into other directions. Moreover, if *SRdB* expands on a given text, it is the Bavli rather than the Bible (see subsequent discussion). I owe this clarification to a discussion with Annette Reed.

[16] I here follow Weinhag and Herrmann.

Midrash on Gen 1:1 (§§429–436 and §§832–854)

This microform is preserved as part of a larger macroform "*SRdB*"[17] as well as an independent unit.[18] Although it follows the classical midrashic style, it introduces material that is foreign to the traditional Midrash. Part of it is structured as a Midrash on *bereshit bara' Elohim*, and part of it is structured according to the work of creation on the six days (i.e., outlining precisely what God created on each of the seven days). We know from the Bible, the Midrash explains,[19] that God created the heavens (lit. plural!) and the earth on the first day, and this is taken as a starting point to mention briefly the seven heavens and the seven earths (strangely enough, the heavens are here called *ma'yanot* – fountains[20] – and the earths *tehomot* – depths; §431 [§842]). Only the names of the seven heavens and the seven earths are given, but the text explicitly emphasizes that each heaven corresponds to a certain earth[21]:

Seven Earths	Seven Heavens
1. [*Eretz*]	1. [*Shamayim*][22]
2. *Adamah*	2. *Raqia'*
3. *Haravah*	3. *Shehaqim*
4. *Yabashah*	4. [*Zevul*]
5. *Arqa*	5. [*Ma'on*]
6. *Tevel*	6. [*Makhon*][23]
7. *Heled*	7. *'Aravot*

[17] Only in MS Munich 22 (§§429–436) and in Wertheimer, *Batei Midrashot*, 1:19–26.

[18] In MSS Oxford 1531 (§§832–854), and in MSS Jerusalem 381 and New York 1746.

[19] §842, MS Oxford; §431, MS Munich.

[20] A scribe in MS Oxford 1531 corrected *ma'yanot* to *me'onot* [residences], which is certainly a hypercorrection.

[21] I follow the list in MS Oxford but have changed the sequence as indicated in brackets. The sequences in both MS Oxford 1531 and MS Munich 22 are corrupt, but it makes perfect sense if we adopt the sequence outlined in the major part of *SRdB* (see subsequent discussion). The only difference is that here the sequence of the seven earths is turned upside down: *Eretz* is the first earth – perfectly corresponding with *Shamayim* – and not the seventh earth (*Eretz ha-tahtonah*).

[22] *Eretz* and *Shamayim* are completely missing in MS Oxford 1531 but are mentioned as the first heaven and the first earth in MS Munich 22.

[23] The actual sequence in MS Oxford 1531 is in reverse order: *Makhon, Ma'on, Zevul*.

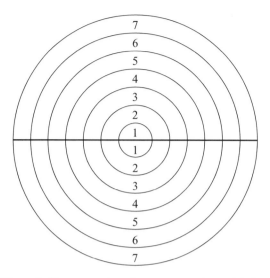

Figure 1. Heavens and earths as concentric semicircles.

Because the heavens and the earths all mirror one another, the most likely graphical representation is seven concentric semicircles representing the seven heavens completed by seven semicircles representing the seven earths, which meet each other at a central horizontal axis (or, imagined as spheres: seven concentric hemispheres completed by the corresponding hemispheres, which meet at an imagined central plane; see Figure 1). In a salient comment with which the microform concludes, an additional detail is added to this mirror-image cosmology: "He [i.e., God] spread out his throne above, and from his glory [*mi-kevodo*] he gave downwards." This statement indicates that God's throne was located in the seventh heaven *'Aravot* (quite common), whereas his glory (or something from his glory) was located in the seventh earth *Ḥeled* (very uncommon). The strange expression *mi-kevodo* seems to be an allusion to Ezek 48:2 ("and the earth was brightened by his glory [*mi-kevodo*]"). Whereas it is common biblical theology to assume that God's glory is not only in heaven but also on earth,[24] it is certainly much less common to propose that (part of) his glory is in the seventh earth/netherworld, of all places. Within the cosmological scheme of *SRdB*, however, this assertion makes perfect sense: Because the seventh heaven and the seventh earth

---

[24] See, e.g., Isa 6:3; Ezek 43:2; Pss 57:6, 12; 72:19; 102:16; 108:6; 148:13.

Peter Schäfer

literally meet one another, it is only logical to conclude that God's glory physically extends down into the seventh earth.

The Dimensions of the "World" (§§437–439)

In MS Munich 22, this brief microform directly follows the unit on Gen 1:1; in MS Vatican 288 and in MS Darmstadt 25, it is the very first microform of *SRdB* (titled in MS Vatican *Sidduro shel ʿolam* and in MS Darmstadt *Maʿaseh Bereshit*). The cosmos is again imagined as a circle [*ʿiggul*], surrounded above and below by waters (it seems as if these waters are kept outside the "world," i.e., beyond the semicircles or the hemispheres constituting the seven heavens and the seven earths, but they nevertheless "filter" through them to reach our earth, *Eretz*). They are called here "weeping waters" [*mayim bokhim*] because when God separated the upper and the lower waters, the latter wept and wanted to come closer to their creator (§438). God comforted them by allowing them to start his praise and letting the upper waters join in only later (a cosmologically oriented variation on the well-known motif that Israel begins God's praise on earth, whereas the angels in heaven are allowed to join in only after Israel has taken the lead).[25]

What follows (§439) is a brief description (or merely a list) of the seven earths and the seven heavens, beginning with *Eretz ha-taḥtonah* ["the lower earth"]. Between *Eretz ha-taḥtonah* and the next earth (i.e., the sixth, *Adamah*) are located a number of elements – water, pillars of *ḥashmal*, mountains of hail, storehouses of snow, waters of fire, abyss, *tohu, bohu*, wind, storm, the vault of the earth – that serve as a kind of buffer zone. The following earths and subsequent heavens are merely listed in a stereotyped language (in each case, for instance, they are said to be "hung on storm and tied to the vault" of the next earth/heaven). MSS Munich 22, Vatican 288, and Darmstadt 25 list the sequence of earths and heavens as follows[26]:

[25] See texts such as D. Hoffman, ed., *Midrash Tannaim ʿal sefer Devarim* (Berlin, 1909), 71; *b. Ḥag* 12b; *GenR* 65:21; *Midrash Psalms* 104:1 in the rabbinic literature and the unit §§174–179 in *Hekhalot Rabbati* (see P. Schäfer, *Rivalität zwischen Engeln und Menschen: Untersuchungen zur Rabbinischen Engelvorstellung* [SJ 8, Berlin, 1975], 164ff.).

[26] MSS Vatican 288 and Darmstadt 25 are not in Schäfer, *Synopse*; I follow the preliminary translation (in manuscript) by Christian Weinhag.

	Munich 22	Vatican 288	Darmstadt 25
Heavens			
	7. 'Aravot	7. 'Aravot	7. 'Aravot
	6.	6. Makhon	6. Makhon
	5. Zevul	5. Ma'on	5. Ma'on
	4. Makhon	4. Zevul	
	3. Shehaqim	3. Shehaqim	
	2. Raqia'	2. Raqia'	
	1. Shamayim	1. Shamayim	
Earths			
		Welon	Welon
	1. Heled	1. Heled	1. Heled
	2. Tevel		
	3. Arqa	3. Arqa	3. Arqa
	4. Yabashah	4. Yabashah	4. Yabashah
	5. Haravah	5. Haravah	5. Haravah
	6. Adamah		6. Adamah
	7. Eretz	7. Eretz ha-tahtonah	7. Eretz ha-tahtonah

Welon, between the first heaven (*Shamayim*) and the first earth (*Heled*), is actually the "curtain" separating heaven and earth and does not count as an additional heaven or earth. *'Aravot*, the seventh heaven, is "hung on the right arm" of God himself, which alludes to Deut 33:27, literally understood as "and below the arms: world" [*u-mittahat zero'ot 'olam*].[27]

Detailed Description of the Seven Earths and Seven Heavens (§§440–462 and 743–776)

This is the most important part of the composite tractate *SRdB*. Here, the various manuscripts vary greatly (subsequently discussed in more detail), and I follow now the most extensive microform as preserved in MSS Oxford 1531,

[27] Only in MSS Vatican and Darmstadt, but not in MS Munich 22 (§439 end).

Vatican 288, and Munich 22.[28] In a manner typical of the Hekhalot literature, the microform opens with the introductory formula "Rabbi Ishmael said." The text then immediately proceeds to discuss the *two* arms of God[29] from which the seven heavens and earths (called here the "seven dwellings [*me'onot*] that are in heaven/on earth") are said to be suspended. This discussion of the cosmological function of God's arms seems to pick up directly on the subject matter with which the "preceding" microform ended – although it is worth pointing out that the two microforms do not actually follow each other in any of the manuscripts. There is no attempt whatsoever to present this discussion as an exercise in biblical exegesis. Indeed, the verse Deut 33:27, which is quoted at the end of the paragraph, serves only as a supporting proof text and not as the starting point for the subsequent discussion.

The description of the heavens and earths begins with the seventh earth (*Eretz ha-tahtonah*, lit. the lowest earth), which is surrounded by a number of "shells," apparently arranged in the form of concentric semicircles. They contain elements such as water and fire, lightning and thunder, but also the "appearance of the *Hayyot*" and the sound of the heavenly praise (§744).

The following paragraphs (§§745–748) explain in more detail what §744 has just briefly outlined: On the "lowest earth" are located (1) the *Hayyot,* the four holy creatures known from Ezekiel 1 who carry God's throne, (2) the *Ofannim* (lit. the "wheels" of the throne, moved forward and backward by the *Hayyot*,[30] which later become a class of highest angels), (3) the Throne of Glory itself, and (4) above the heads of the *Hayyot,* the "feet of the Shekhinah." This remarkable inventory is essentially identical to the inventory of the highest heaven, 'Aravot (§§775–776: *Ofannim, Keruvim, Hayyot,* etc.; Throne of Glory; God). Hence, the lowest earth and the highest heaven contain precisely the same inventory: God himself and his immediate entourage! The only difference between 'Aravot and *Eretz ha-tahtonah* is that the lowest earth explicitly mentions the "feet" of the Shekhinah, whereas the highest heaven has the Shekhinah itself – probably indicating that only the feet of the Shekhinah are grounded on earth and, hence, envisioning an image of God as some kind of *macroanthropos,* extending from the lowest earth to the

---

[28] MS Oxford, §§743–776; MS Munich 22, §§440–462. MS Vatican 288 according to the translation by Weinhag.

[29] The reference to Deut 33:27 makes better sense here because it takes full advantage of the plural *zero'ot:* The seven heavens hang from the *right* arm of God, and the seven earths hang from his *left* arm.

[30] Ezek 1:15–21.

highest heaven. But this possible image is neutralized by the next sentence, which flatly states, with no distinction among various parts of God's body, "Just as his Shekhinah is above, so too is his Shekhinah below" (§745).

This is clearly one of the core statements of *SRdB*, if not its main message. To begin with, there can be no doubt that *SRdB* is not speaking about two manifestations of the Shekhinah or a double Shekhinah, but rather about the same Shekhinah who is present simultaneously above (in the seventh heaven) and below (on the seventh earth).[31] The biblical proof texts provided in MS Oxford[32] are Hab 3:3 ("His majesty [*hodo*] covers the heavens, and his splendor [*tehillato*][33] fills the earth") and Isa 66:1 ("The heavens are my throne, and the earth is my footstool") – two verses that are already used in classical rabbinic literature to describe the puzzling problem of God's simultaneous presence in heaven and on earth.[34]

What we encounter here is the very first case in the Jewish tradition in which a *cosmological* structure is outlined that maintains a perfect balance between heaven and earth. At their most extreme points – the highest heaven and the lowest earth – the differences between heaven and earth are abolished. God sits enthroned in the highest heaven just as he sits enthroned on the lowest earth. Heaven and earth form an exact pair (although, as we subsequently see, this is true only at their extreme extensions): The seventh earth is identical to the seventh heaven. It is obvious that such a daring cosmology works only if the seven heavens and the seven earths are depicted in seven concentric semicircles (or hemispheres) as illustrated in Figure 1. Moreover, it is precisely the seventh heaven and the seventh earth that physically meet in such a cosmological worldview, thereby enabling God to be simultaneously present in heaven and on earth.

The surroundings of the seventh earth as described here differ from §744 and are much more detailed. Thousands of angels encircle the feet of the Shekhinah, most likely still within the realm of the seventh earth. However, the text continues (§746) with 18,000 worlds that border the place of the feet of the Shekhinah, alluding to many more "worlds" laid in concentric

---

[31] See also the discussion by G. Scholem, *On the Mystical Shape of the Godhead: Basic Concepts in the Kabbalah* (New York, 1991), 173.

[32] MS Munich 22 does not give proof texts, and MS Vatican 288 has Hab 3:3 and Ezek 48:35 (the very last sentence of Ezekiel, describing the city of God and its Temple): "And the name of the city from that day on shall be: 'The Lord is there.'"

[33] Usually translated as "his praise," but here it refers to an aspect of God himself.

[34] See *Song of Songs Rabbah* 8:11, §2 and parallels (Schäfer, *Rivalität*, 159ff.).

circles like shells around the *Eretz ha-taḥtonah*. The number 18,000 is taken from Ezek 48:35, the last verse of the book of Ezekiel, which refers to the eschatological city of God in which he dwells forever ("Its circumference [*saviv*] [shall be] 18,000 [cubits], and the name of the city from that day on shall be 'The Lord is There' "). Here, *saviv* is understood as that which surrounds the seventh earth (the city of God!): namely, "surrounding it [*Eretz ha-taḥtonah*] are 18,000 [worlds]." These 18,000 worlds are divided in 4 × 4,500 worlds that extend to the north, south, east, and west of the seventh earth and are all full of God's praise. But this is not yet the end of the netherworld's cosmos. The 18,000 worlds are surrounded[35] by a long list of elements and (in MS Oxford) angels. There are walls of fire, fire and water, mountains of hail, hills of snow, walls of whirlwinds, and wings of storm (§747); the angels, according to MS Oxford, are flying cherubim, wings of wind, thousands of camps, thousands of troops, thousands of *Shin'an* (following Ps 68:18), myriads of chariots (again following Ps 68:18), those who sing songs, those who chant chants, those who blast the *shofar* horns, those who blow the trumpet, those who sweeten the melody, those who extol the songs of praise, those who say "holy" (following Isa 6:3), and those who say "blessed" (following Ezek 3:12).

There follows another, final layer of "shells" that surrounds the seventh earth (§748, in both MS Oxford 1531 and MS Vatican 288): thick mud [*tit ha-yaven*], abyss [*tehom*], *tohu* and *bohu*, and finally darkness [*ḥoshekh*], which is "unfathomable ['*ad 'ein ḥeqer*], innumerable ['*ein mispar*], immeasurable ['*ein shi'ur*], and infinite ['*ein takhlit*]."[36] "Up to this point," the text concludes, "you do have the permission to speak, but from this point and onwards consider yourself as someone who puts his finger on [his] eye!" The proof text is Sir 3:21–22: "Do not investigate things that are too wonderful for you and do not explore what is hidden from you! Consider what you have been permitted [to consider], but the concealed things are not your concern!"[37] In other words, there are innumerable worlds beyond those mentioned here, but they are inaccessible to human beings. It is the prerogative of God alone to roam through all of them, mounted on a cherub and gliding on the wings of wind

---

[35] Using the technical term *lehaqqif* – "to surround, encircle."

[36] The proof text is 2 Sam 22:12.

[37] In connection with the seventh heaven '*Aravot*, b. *Ḥagigah* 13a has "Up to this point you do have permission to speak, but from this point and onwards you have not permission to speak," followed by the same quotation from the Wisdom of ben Sira (see subsequent discussion).

(Ps 18:11). At this point, after such an exuberant expansion and exploration of the nether regions, the comment seems almost ironic. Indeed, *SRdB* has already gone very far in its exposition of "what is below" – certainly much further than the Mishnah would permit or could probably even imagine – such that the final "so far and no further" sounds like merely a formal reflex of the earlier rabbinic reticence about exploring such issues.

Paragraphs 750–776 describe in more detail the sequence and the inventory of the remaining six earths and seven heavens, progressing from the lowest earth to the highest heaven. The sequence of the earths, from the lowest to the uppermost, is as follows (according to §439): the seventh earth *Eretz ha-tahtonah,* the sixth *Adamah,* the fifth *Haravah,* the fourth *Yabashah,* the third *Arqa,* the second *Tevel,* and the first *Heled* Above *Heled,* the "curtain" [*Welon*] separates the upper earth and the lowest heaven, *Shamayim,* which is followed by the second heaven *Raqia',* the third *Shehaqim,* the fourth *Zevul,* the fifth *Ma'on,* the sixth *Makhon,* and the seventh and highest heaven *'Aravot.* Between each heaven a ladder is installed that connects one with another.

Insofar as the seventh earth (*Eretz ha-tahtonah*) and the seventh heaven (*'Aravot*) had practically identical inventories, we might expect the contents of the other earths to match those of their corresponding heavens. But, apart from one notable exception, there is almost no correspondence in their contents:

Seven Earths (Highest to Lowest)		Seven Heavens (Lowest to Highest)	
1. *Heled*	World of human beings, Torah	1. *Shamayim*	?
2. *Tevel*	Mountains, hills, fantastic creatures	2. *Raqia'*	Sun, moon, stars, constellations
3. *Arqa*	Seven departments of *Gehinnom*: punishment	3. *Shehaqim*	Manna for the righteous, the heavenly Jerusalem, and the heavenly Temple
4. *Yabashah*	Sea and rivers, dry land	4. *Zevul*	Michael, the heavenly high priest, offers sacrifices
5. *Haravah*	Channels and lakes	5. *Ma'on*	Ministering angels who sing during the day

(continued)

6. *Adamah*	Greatness and strength of *Qadosh Barukh Hu'*, power and beauty of *Yotzer Bereshit*	6. *Makhon*	Snow, hail, rain, wind, lightening, thunder etc.; rivers of fire, storm, vapor
7. *Eretz ha-tahtonah*	*Hayyot, Ofannim,* Throne of Glory, feet of the Shekhinah	7. *'Aravot*	Justice, life, blessing, etc., *Ofannim, Keruvim, Hayyot*, etc., Throne of Glory, God

The sixth earth, *Adamah,* contains the "greatness, strength, power, and beauty" of God, distinguishing between his roles as *Qadosh Barukh Hu'* [The Holy One blessed be he] and *Yotzer Bereshit* [Creator of the World]. We do not know what this distinction implies, but it may well point to an intentional differentiation between God in his quality as creator and God as seated on his throne on the seventh earth. Although there may be a certain degree of correspondence between *Adamah* and the sixth heaven *Makhon* (insofar as God has created all of the forces of nature in its inventory), it is hardly imperative for us to assume that the inventories of the sixth earth and the sixth heaven were purposefully paired with each other. There is even less connection between the inventories of *Haravah/Ma'on* and *Yabashah/Zevul*: Nothing at all links the channels and lakes in *Haravah* with the ministering angels in *Ma'on,* or the sea, rivers, and dry land in *Yabashah* with Michael and the heavenly sacrifice in *Zevul.*

The situation is different, however, with regard to the third earth, *Arqa,* and its corresponding heaven *Shehaqim.* To begin with, the description of *Arqa* and its inventory is by far the most detailed of all the heavens and earths. The text in all manuscripts starts abruptly with a list of what is called the "seven departments of *Gehinnom*" (§§754), presupposing that *Arqa* is subdivided in seven compartments with different names, all of which are taken from the Hebrew Bible. This seems to be an originally independent tradition that has been integrated into *SRdB*'s scheme of the seven earths/netherworlds. It also appears in the Bavli (*b. Eruvin* 19a), in which it is attributed to R. Yehoshua b. Levi, the first-generation Palestinian Amora, and consists merely of a list of the various (biblical) names of *Gehinnom* ("R. Yehoshua b. Levi stated: *Gehinnom* has seven names, and they are"). Because only the names are given, together with the appropriate biblical proof texts, the Bavli obviously does not refer to any elaborate cosmological fabric, and certainly not to a scheme in which *Gehinnom* is part of a well-defined substructure of the netherworld. The following chart shows the sequence of the names according to *b. Eruvin*, the three major manuscripts of *SRdB*, and *Midrash Konen* (a work that is closely related to, and presumably dependent on, *SRdB*)[38]:

b. Eruv. 19a	She'ol (Jon 2:3)	Avaddon (Ps 88:12)	Be'er shahat (Ps 16:10)	Bor sha'on (Ps 40:3)	Tit ha-yawen (Ps 40:3)	Tzalmawet (Ps 107:10)	Eretz ha-tahtit
SRdB, Vatican 288	Gehinnom	Sha'are mawet	Sha'are tzalmawet	Be'er shahat	Tit ha-yawen	She'ol/ Avaddon	Avaddon/ Sheol[39]
SRdB, Oxford 1531	She'ol tahtit	Avaddon	Be'er shahat	Tit ha-yawen	Sha'are mawet	Sha'are tzalmawet	Gehinnom
SRdB, Munich 22	She'ol tahtit	Avaddon	Mashhit	Tit ha-yawen	Sha'are mawet	Tzalmawet	Gehinnom
***Midrash Konen*[40]**	She'ol	Avaddon	Be'er shahat	Tit ha-yawen	Dumah		Be'er shahat = Eretz tahtit
***Midrash Konen*[41]**	She'ol (tahtit)	Avaddon	Be'er shahat	Tit ha-yawen	Sha'are mawet	Sha'are tzalmawet	(Gehinnom)

It would be futile to attempt reconstructing any "original" sequence of the seven departments of *Gehinnom*. Nevertheless, it seems likely that *b. Eruvin* served as the source for *SRdB*.[42] The disparities between the two texts can easily be accounted for: *Eretz ha-tahtit,* which is omitted in *SRdB*, is already

---

[38] See also the chart in Sed, *Mystique cosmologique juive*, 276.

[39] The sequence of *She'ol* and *Avaddon* varies at different places in MS Vatican 288.

[40] For text, see A. Jellinek, ed., *Beit ha-Midrash*, 3rd ed. (Jerusalem, 1967), 1:30.

[41] Jellinek, *Beit ha-Midrash*, 1:35.

[42] It may well be that *SRdB* reverses the order and regards *She'ol tahtit* as what the name says: the "lower *She'ol*," namely, the lowest of the seven departments, and *Gehinnom* the uppermost one. The various manuscripts seem to be confused about the order. Interestingly enough, in *Pirqe de-Rabbi Eliezer*'s version of Jonah's "sightseeing tour" through the waters of the depth, Jonah sees the *She'ol tahtit* and *Gehinnom* before he reaches the "Foundation Stone" [*even shetiyah*] beneath the Temple (*Pirqei de-Rabbi Eli'ezer ha-gadol* [Warsaw: Bi-defus T. Y. Bamberg, 1851/1852], Chap. 10, fol. 26a; English translation: G. Friedlander, trans., *Pirkê de Rabbi Eliezer* [New York, 1971], 71).

out of place in *b. Eruvin* – the talmudic editor was unable to provide a proof text from the Bible and thus refers to it as just "a tradition" [*gemara hu'*]. Of course, this compartment is identical to *Eretz ha-tahtonah*, the name of the seventh earth in the *SRdB* tradition. Also, *Bor sha'on* in *b. Eruvin* is similarly suspect: It is taken from the same proof text as *Tit ha-yawen* (Ps 40:3). On the other hand, *Dumah* in *Midrash Konen* is out of place in the *SRdB* tradition of the seven departments of *Gehinnom* because it belongs to, a different version of the seven netherworlds. And, finally, *Mashhit* in MS Munich 22 of *SRdB* is completely unique and not attested to in any of the traditions about *Gehinnom* or netherworlds/earths.

The text continues by describing the dimensions of the respective departments and the strength of the fire burning in them (§755). It is the perverse quality of *She'ol* (*tahtit*) that it consists both of fire and of hail so that the wicked are constantly forced from fire to hail and from hail to fire in order to fully appreciate both extremes. But who are these wicked who deserve this horrible (and eternal) punishment? The following paragraph (§756) explains that they are those "who had stretched out their hands against the Temple" – that is, the foreign nations that destroyed the Temple in Jerusalem. They are forced by the angel of death from fire to hail and back again (§757) and driven through each of the seven compartments of *Gehinnom* until they finally arrive at *Arqa*, from where they will never be released. Even though Israel and all the righteous petition God for mercy, he refuses to pardon those "who destroyed my house, burnt my Temple, and exiled my children among the nations" (§758).

What follows (§§759–764) is a collection of various traditions about *Gehinnom* and its seven compartments that differ from the preceding one and are inspired by classical rabbinic literature. The text now becomes even more specific, asserting that at the beginning of the process of creation, God created the seven compartments of *Gehinnom* "for the perfect wicked who transgress the Torah and the commandments, who annoy the Holy One blessed be he every day, deny the Holy One blessed be he, and accept idolatry" (§759), evidently referring to apostate Jews. This point is emphasized again, after a graphic description of the horrible punishment visited on those wicked in §764. There, the famous passage from the Tosefta, *t. Sanhedrin* 13:4–5, is quoted, according to which the "ordinary" sinners of both Israel and the nations are punished in *Gehinnom* for twelve months, after which their bodies will be burned and their souls will cease to exist. Concerning the various groups of Jewish apostates (the *minim, meshummadim,* and *apiqorsin,* those who deny the Torah, those who deny the resurrection of the dead, and those who sinned and tempted many others to sin, like Jeroboam and Ahab), the text asserts that "they will be judged in *Gehinnom* forever" – together with the Assyrians, the destroyers of the First Temple, and the Romans, the destroyers of the Second Temple – "and about them Scripture says: 'They will go out and gaze on the corpses of the men who rebelled against me: Their worms shall not die, nor their fire be quenched; they shall be a horror to all flesh' (Isa 66:24)." From this it becomes clear that *SRdB*, following *t. Sanhedrin*, pairs the apostate Jews with the pagan oppressors of Israel in the category of those destined for eternal damnation. It is for these gravest and most detested wicked that the seven compartments of *Gehinnom* are prepared, and not for ordinary sinners.

If we now compare the inventories of the third earth (*Arqa*) and the third heaven (*Sheḥaqim*), we discover again a conspicuous symmetry between the earthly and the heavenly realms. *Arqa,* the place for the appropriate punishment of the wicked, is balanced by *Sheḥaqim* as the place where the mills are located that grind the manna for the righteous in the world to come. Thus, the punishment for the wicked and the reward for the righteous are neatly distributed between the netherworld and the corresponding place in heaven. In placing the manna for the righteous in this heaven, *SRdB* follows *b. Ḥagigah* 12b. However, in contrast to the Bavli, *SRdB*'s *Sheḥaqim* is also host to the heavenly Jerusalem and the heavenly Temple, which *b. Ḥagigah* puts in the fourth heaven *Zevul,* together with the offering of the sacrifice by the heavenly high priest Michael. Notably, *SRdB* similarly locates Michael's sacrifice in *Zevul*. The result is an odd bifurcation of the heavenly Temple and the heavenly sacrifice, which *SRdB* must explain by resorting to the strange image of Jerusalem and the Temple "hanging on chains of fire" from *Zevul* into *Sheḥaqim* (§771).[43]

What is the reason for this strange separation between Michael's offering in *Zevul* and the location of the heavenly Jerusalem/Temple in *Sheḥaqim*? Comparison with its treatment of the seventh heaven and seventh earth (see preceding discussion) suggests that *SRdB* has moved the heavenly Jerusalem and the heavenly Temple from *Zevul* to *Sheḥaqim* to create a perfect

---

[43] Literally "from *Sheḥaqim* to *Zevul*" because the text is discussing first *Sheḥaqim* (the third heaven) and then *Zevul* (the fourth heaven), but because the fourth heaven is above the third heaven, the original place of Jerusalem and the Temple (with Michael's sacrifice) is in the fourth heaven.

balance between *Shehaqim* and its earthly counterpart *Arqa*.[44] Heaven and earth correspond again. The destroyers of both Temples are eternally punished on *Arqa* – together with their companions, the Jewish apostates – but God will mend this catastrophe of cosmic dimensions: He has prepared the new Jerusalem and the new Temple in *Arqa's* counterpart *Shehaqim*, where it is ready to return to our earth at the time of redemption.

Of the two remaining earths and heavens, the second earth (*Tevel*) contains the mountains and hills, but also a number of fantastic creatures, such as hybrids that are half-human and half-animal, creatures with two heads or four hands, and so on. Although they constantly quarrel with each other about their food, they are nevertheless perfectly righteous (§765). In the corresponding heaven (*Raqia'*) are the sun, moon, stars, and constellations, whose light radiates down to the lowest earth (§770). And, finally, *Heled*, the first earth, is our world, the world described in Genesis 1 – with all its creatures, including human beings and the most precious gift God gave to them: the Torah (§766). Its corresponding heaven (*Shamayim*) does not have an inventory at all according to the available manuscripts (§768).

The Area Beyond the Seventh Heaven (§§777–784 and 518–524)

The final major building block of the *SRdB* traditions is preserved in its most extensive version in MSS Oxford 1531 and Munich 22.[45] It adds a completely new cosmic dimension by extending the area of the heavens beyond the seventh heaven. The origins of this tradition clearly lie in the exegesis of Ezek 1:22: "And a form [*demut*] was above the heads of the *Hayyot*, an expanse [*raqia'*] in the likeness of the terrible ice [*ha-qerah ha-nora'*], spread out over their heads from above." This *Raqia'* above the heads of the *Hayyot* is understood as an additional heavenly realm already in *b. Hagigah* 13a, where the following dictum is attributed to R. Aha b. Jacob, the Babylonian *amora* of the fourth generation: "There is still another heaven above the heads of the *Hayyot*, for it is written [Ezek 1:22]." It may well be that this short Babylonian tradition served as the source for *SRdB*. If so, however, our author/editor expanded it considerably. Like *b. Hagigah*, he was obviously untroubled by the fact that this addendum to the seven heavens plainly

---

[44] Which is absent in *b. Hagigah* 12b because it does not include the seven earths. But Jerusalem and the Temple are located in *Shehaqim* also in *Re'uyyot Yehezqel*; see subsequent discussion.

[45] MS Vatican 288 has only §§780 and 783.

contradicts the earlier assertion that it is the seventh heaven 'Aravot that contains the throne of God and the Ḥayyot who (along with other angelic groups) carry it.

All in all, the contents of these additional heavens are as follows:

1. the feet, knees, necks, and heads of the Ḥayyot (§777); the realm above their heads is arranged in six more compartments,[46] most likely aiming at altogether seven additional "heavens" above the seventh heaven 'Aravot;
2. the arch of the rainbow (§779), reminiscent of the "bow" [qeshet], "which shines in the clouds on a day of rain" in Ezek 1:28;
3. the horns/rays of majesty/the Ḥayyot;[47]
4. the Raqia' of the "terrible ice" from Ezek 1:22 (§780);
5. the "appearance of the brightness" [mar'eh ha-nogah] from Ezek 1:28 (§781);
6. the Throne of Sapphire [kisse even sappir] from Ezek 1:26 (§782);[48]
7. the Throne of Glory [kisse ha-kavod].

As for the throne of God, there is a garment spread over it, on which the sun, the moon, and all the planets are "engraved." These images reflect, in a perfect astronomical correspondence of human fate in heaven and on earth, all the past and future deeds of human beings (§783).[49] Above this complex system of heavenly structures

> sits the Holy One blessed be he[50] on a high and lofty throne, surrounded by thickets of brightness, emerald, and sapphire, and the whole world is hung on his mighty arm like an amulet [hanging] with no effort from the hand of a hero – similarly there is no effort on his mighty arm, carrying the upper and the lower [worlds], as it is written: "and below the arms: world (u-mittaḥat zero'ot 'olam; Deut 33:27)." (§784)

This image of all the heavens and the earths hanging from God's mighty arm clearly refers back to §743, which opened the preceding microform (§§440–462 and 743–776). It may well be that it was intended to mark the

---

[46] After describing the measure of the Ḥayyot (§778).

[47] The manuscripts waiver between qarne hod and qarne ha-ḥayyot.

[48] In MS Munich 22 and in MS Oxford, §727 and §802; in §782 "a residence [ma'on] in the semblance of the terrible things [nora'im]."

[49] See also §§64–65 (3 Enoch): the curtain [pargod] that is spread in front of God and into which all the past and future deeds of human beings are woven.

[50] It is unclear whether God is located in the seventh compartment of the heavens above the seventh heaven, 'Aravot, or literally "above" this seventh compartment. It is also possible that what is counted here as the third compartment might be a later addition that confuses the sequence of the seven compartments (neither the "horns/rays of majesty" nor the "horns/rays of the Ḥayyot" fit very well here). If we delete point 3 from the list completely, there are seven compartments altogether with God in the seventh one.

end of this final microform and thus the end of the macroform *SRdB*, even though the text preserved in MSS Oxford and Munich 22 continues with two more microforms: the rivers of fire that stream forth from the sweat of the *Hayyot* carrying the Throne of Glory (§785)[51] and a long section about the heavenly praise and Israel's role in it (§§787–798), which is taken from the corresponding section in *Hekhalot Rabbati* (§§178–187). Whatever the formal end of *SRdB* (and the variations of the different manuscript traditions are significant), it is remarkable that the last microform that deals with the structure of the cosmos concludes with an image of God completely surrounded by light. This is quite in contrast to the preceding microform, which emphasizes the "darkness" [*hoshekh*], "clouds" [*'anan*], and "mist" [*'arafel*] surrounding God on his throne in the highest heaven, *'Aravot* (§776).[52] Hence, whereas the seventh heaven seems to vanish in impenetrable darkness – very much like its counterpart, the seventh earth – the farthest realm above the seventh heaven is completely immersed in light. The message that the editor of our microform wants to convey is clear: Not only can we look into the realm above the seventh heaven, but we can also know that the God present there is wholly light. With this he contradicts his presumable source, *b. Hagigah* 13a, which explicitly cuts off any discussion of the heaven above the head of the *Hayyot* by quoting the prohibition of ben Sira (Sir 3:21–22).[53]

III

To determine more precisely the profile of *SRdB*'s well-developed cosmological schema, we need to look at the prehistory of the concept of the seven heavens and seven earths/netherworlds/hells within the Jewish tradition. Even a cursory glance at the available material[54] immediately reveals that the earlier tradition is much more concerned with heaven and its subsequent multiplication than with the earth and its multiplication. Furthermore, the

---

[51] Another well-known motif that is derived from Dan 7:10.

[52] The same is true for the presumable source of this microform, *b. Hagigah* 12b/end, which has a problem with this "dark" note.

[53] Which the preceding microform has reserved for the realm beyond the surroundings of the seventh earth.

[54] Very helpful for this task are M. Himmelfarb's twin books on "what is below" and "what is above": *Tours of Hell: An Apocalyptic Form in Jewish and Christian Literature* (Philadelphia, 1983), and *Ascent to Heaven in Jewish and Christian Apocalypses* (New York, 1993); and see now J. E. Wright, *The Early History of Heaven* (New York, 2000), and A. E. Bernstein, *The Formation of Hell: Death and Retribution in the Ancient and Early Christian Worlds* (London, 1993).

expansion of the heavenly and earthly realms is closely linked to speculation about the places where the righteous are rewarded and the wicked punished.

The oldest biblical tradition does not distinguish between the "wicked" and the "righteous" but allocates the dead, irrespective of their deeds, to a dark and gloomy netherworld called *She'ol* (lit. "grave"),[55] which is somewhere below the surface of the inhabited earth (following the ancient Near Eastern tradition of a three-tiered universe consisting of "heaven" [*shamayim*] above, "earth" [*eretz*] in the middle, and "netherworld" [*she'ol*] below). God, of course, governs all three areas of the universe; there exists no "safe" place to hide from him, not in "heaven" and not even in *She'ol* (Amos 9:1–3; Ps 139:8). It is only when the old concept of after-death egalitarianism was questioned and felt to be unjust – when the idea of a divine judgment was introduced and when the categories of "wicked" and "righteous" were consequently extended into the time after death – that the expectation of an afterlife and of a resurrection from death finally arose – thereby necessitating the "separation of the dead"[56] and their assignment to different areas within the heavenly and earthly realms. It goes without saying that this separation and the subsequent diversification of the heavens and netherworlds did not occur at a certain point in history; rather, it was a process that unfolded over a long period of time (a process, moreover, that did not develop chronologically from "archaic" to ever-higher forms of "evolution" but moved dynamically in multiple – and sometimes conflicting – directions). In the following subsections, I briefly summarize some of its important "stages" within the prerabbinic traditions.

Heaven(s) and Hell(s) in Prerabbinic Literature

A major vehicle for the transportation of old and new ideas about the heavenly and earthly realms with their different contents and functions are the ascent apocalypses, which focus on the heavenly journey of a "biblical" hero. The first such account is preserved in the *Book of the Watchers*, which belongs to the oldest parts of the collection called 1 Enoch and presumably dates from the third century or the first quarter of the second century B.C.E.[57]

---

[55] See Bernstein, *Formation of Hell*, 140ff.

[56] This expression alludes to Bernstein's sixth chapter, titled "Dividing the Dead" (*Formation of Hell*, 154ff.).

[57] Himmelfarb, *Ascent*, 5. The oldest part of 1 Enoch seems to be the *Astronomical Book* (Chaps. 72–82), which belongs to the early third century B.C.E. It deals with the movements of the

Here, Enoch is first elevated into heaven before the divine throne (Chap. 14) and then taken by the angels on a kind of sightseeing tour, flying with them above the surface of the earth and exploring its four directions. During his first tour, he travels west and reaches the foundations of the earth (Chap. 18). At a "place, beyond the great earth, where the heavens come together" – we have yet to hear about "heavens" in the plural,[58] so obviously the place where "heaven" and "earth" come together is meant, the utmost end of the earth – Enoch sees a "deep pit[59] with heavenly fire on its pillars...a desolate and terrible place" (18:11–12). The *angelus interpres* accompanying him explains that this is indeed "the [ultimate] end of heaven and earth" and serves as the "prison house" for the stars that "did not arrive punctually" (18:14–15) and simultaneously for the rebellious angels of Genesis 6 (Chap. 19).

Enoch's second journey starts as a repetition of the first one: He sees the "empty place" of the stars that deviated from their appointed course and the "prison house" of the fallen angels (Chap. 21). Then he comes to "another place," also in the West, where the spirits/souls of the dead are located to await the day of judgment (Chap. 22). This seems to be the biblical *She'ol*, which is now, however, divided into three or four compartments, according to the deeds of the deceased during life.[60] Notably, Enoch hears the voice of Abel suing Cain and demanding the extermination of his seed from the earth (22:7). After this, he sees the perpetually burning fire at "the [extreme] ends of the earth" that feeds the luminaries of heaven (Chap. 23)[61] as well as seven mountains made of precious stone and surrounded by fragrant trees (Chap. 24). One of these mountains is the throne upon which God will sit when he descends to earth for the final judgment, and the most beautiful and fragrant tree is preserved for the righteous and pious who survive the judgment (Chap. 25). Turning to the center of the earth, Enoch sees the place of Jerusalem (Chap. 26) and an "accursed valley," which is "for those accursed forever" (Chap. 27) – probably the place for those who are sentenced (at the day of judgment) to eternal damnation. The journey continues to the East, where the Garden of Eden is located (Chap. 32) and where, at the "extreme

---

sun, the moon, and the winds in the (one) heaven and includes the "garden of righteousness" (77:4).

[58] One Ethiopic manuscript reads "waters" instead of "heavens"; see E. Isaac, "1 (Ethiopic Apocalypse of) Enoch," in *OTP* 1:23, n. "n."

[59] The same Ethiopic manuscript has "in the earth."

[60] See Bernstein, *Formation of Hell*, 185–6.

[61] Probably an adaptation of the Pythagorean belief in the "hearth of the earth" (see Wright, *Early History*, 121).

ends" of the eastern part of the earth, huge beasts and birds can be observed (Chap. 33). The East (more precisely, the place where heaven and earth meet) also accommodates the gates through which the stars enter the visible sky, whereas the West harbors the gates through which the stars make their exit (Chap. 35). Finally, the North contains the gates through which "cold, hail, frost, snow, dew, and rain" enter the world (Chap. 34), and the South is the entrance gate for the corresponding beneficent winds and rains (Chap. 36).

From this description, it becomes clear that the author of the *Book of the Watchers* follows the ancient Near Eastern (and early Greek) model of the earth as a flat disk,[62] which is covered, as it were, like a cheese dome with the vault of heaven.[63] At its extreme ends, heaven and earth meet, separated only by the "four winds which bear the earth as well as the firmament of heaven" (18:2) and that serve as a "buffer zone" between heaven and earth (18:3). The places for the punishment of the wicked and the reward of the righteous are separated in the West and the East, respectively, but they are clearly part of the earthly realm. Only the place for the deviating stars and the rebellious angels falls outside the physical geography of the earth: It is neither heaven nor earth but seems to hover somewhere in nowhere, a most desolate, chaotic, and terrible place (18:12; 21:2). The heaven (in the singular; there is no indication of several heavens), where Enoch is allowed to visit God before he undertakes his tour of the earth, is reserved for God alone (Chap. 14). However, God keeps a *pied à terre,* the throne on earth upon which he will take his seat on the day of the great judgment (and which is, therefore, located in the West).

The first unequivocal evidence for the belief in a resurrection of the dead and, hence, a life after death can be found in Daniel 12, written in the Hellenistic period around 165 B.C.E. Here it is said that "at a time of trouble," such as has never been seen before, "your people will be rescued [*yimmalet*], everyone who will be found written in the book" (12:1). This passage refers to the Hellenistic persecution and the Maccabean uprising: the people of Israel will be rescued, although apparently only those whose names are "written in the book." This interpretation is confirmed by the next verse, which emphasizes

---

[62] Wright, *Early History*, 123.

[63] The same cosmological structure is presupposed in 1 Enoch 106, the story about Noah's birth now affixed to the end of the *Epistle of Enoch*: When Methuselah wants to ask his father Enoch – who dwells with the angels – why Lamech's son Noah has such an unusual (i.e., angelic) appearance, he must go to the "ends of the earth," presumably because that is where heaven and earth are closest together and thus where Enoch will best hear him. (I owe this reference to Annette Reed.)

that "*many* of those who sleep in the dust of the earth will awake" (12:2). We do not know why only "many" will be resurrected, nor what the criteria will be for inclusion, but we do learn that these "many" will be transformed from sleeping in the dust of the earth (*She'ol?*) to another existence. Furthermore, this new life seems to depend on whether they have been righteous or wicked during their earthly existence: "some [of the many will awake] to eternal life [*le-hayye 'olam*], others to reproaches [*harafot*] and to eternal abhorrence [*dir'on 'olam*]" (12:2). Hence, although the resurrected are separated into two groups, obviously in accordance with their behavior on earth before death, they will share a common fate in that their new existence will be eternal.

Finally, and most important for our subject, what happens to the two groups of resurrected? Where do they go? The author gives the answer for the "righteous" only; the fate of the "wicked," who are destined for eternal reproach, remains unspecified: "The knowledgeable [*ha-maskilim*] will shine like the splendor of the firmament [*ke-zohar ha-raqia'*], and those who led the many to righteousness will be like the stars [*ka-kokhavim*] forever and ever" (Dan 12:3). The *maskilim* and "those who led the many to righteousness" are, of course, those who lived a righteous life before death. Whatever it means that they become *like* the stars (and not just stars), they obviously assume, as a reward for their earthly life, an astral existence among the stars of heaven[64]; in other words, they are no longer on earth but are elevated into heaven. Daniel 12, therefore, introduces for the first time in Jewish history the idea that the "righteous" – after a certain period in the "dust of the earth" – are resurrected for a new life within the realm of heaven. Although the nature of this heavenly existence is not further specified, there can be no doubt that the text has in mind the same single heaven in which it is said that God himself dwells. The wicked, despite their resurrection, disappear (or, rather, are no longer of any particular interest to our author).[65]

A greater differentiation between the postmortem fate of the righteous and the wicked and, accordingly, a differentiation between their respective dwelling places became the predominant theme of the apocalyptic texts

[64] Himmelfarb, *Ascent*, 50, points to the equivalence of angels and stars in biblical and post-biblical literature and suggests that "the widespread use of star terminology and associated language for describing transformation in these apocalypses may be due to the prominence of the idea of astral immortality in the contemporary Greco–Roman world."
[65] The "wicked" and the "knowledgeable" mentioned again in 12:10 are not the dead in their postmortem existence but human beings on earth before death (*pace* Bernstein, *Formation of Hell*, 174): The knowledgeable will and the wicked will not understand what is going on (and has been revealed to Daniel).

following the remarkable innovation of Daniel. The *Similitudes of Enoch* (1 Enoch 37–71), dating possibly from the first century B.C.E., continues the Danielic tradition: The righteous are located, close to God, in the heavenly realm (Chaps. 39; 71), and the wicked disappear (Chap. 51 says explicitly that on the day of judgment, God chooses and saves only the righteous, although *She'ol* "will return all the deposits that she had received"). Whether or not the retelling in Chaps. 70–71 (the "appendix" to the *Similitudes*) of Enoch's ascent in Chaps. 39 and onward indicates a two-tiered heaven and, therefore, a rudimentary multiple-heaven cosmology,[66] the first unequivocal evidence of multiple heavens appears in Paul's second letter to the Corinthians (second half of the first century C.E.).[67] Here, Paul reports an earlier ecstatic experience of his own, during which he was "carried off [*harpagenta*] into the third heaven" (2 Cor 12:2). Because this third heaven is identified with "Paradise" (*paradeisos*; 12:4), it is clear that Paul not only locates the dwelling place of the righteous in heaven, but that he also knows of several (at least three, probably more) heavens.

Paul is not interested in the taxonomy of the heavenly realm as such but only in his own ecstatic experience. It is striking, however, that one of the first apocalypses to propose an elaborate system of heavens similarly locates "Paradise" in the third heaven.[68] In the Slavonic *Apocalypse of Enoch* (2 Enoch) – which in its original "core" may belong to the late first century C.E.[69] – Enoch, when he reaches the third heaven, sees "Paradise," a place that is "inconceivably pleasant." In the midst of it is the "tree of life," the

---

[66] See Himmelfarb, *Ascent*, 60; Wright, *Early History*, 140ff. (Wright's distinction between these two units of text on pp. 124–5 and 140ff. seems rather artificial).

[67] Notably, Revelation, at the end of the first century C.E., still follows the one-heaven scheme (Chap. 4), closely resembling 1 Enoch 14. The same is true for the *Apocalypse of Zephaniah* (probably before the end of the first century C.E.; see Himmelfarb, *Ascent*, 514–55) with its different places for the sinners and the righteous.

[68] The other one (apart from the *Apocalypse of Paul*, which is clearly dependent on 2 Cor 12:1–4) is the *Apocalypse of Moses*, in which God hands over the dead Adam to the archangel Michael with the words: "Take him up into Paradise, to the third heaven, and leave [him] there until that great and fearful day which I am about to establish for the world" (37:5 and *Life of Adam and Eve* 25:3; see M. D. Johnson, "Life of Adam and Eve," in *OTP* 2:266, n. "a" in Chap. 25, and p. 291); Johnson dates the *Life of Adam and Eve* to the end of the first century C.E.

[69] A. Vaillant, *Le livre des secrets d'Hénoch, texte slave et traduction française* (Paris, 1952), viiiff., considers 2 Enoch to be an early Christian work; F. I. Andersen, "2 (Slavonic Apocalypse of) Enoch," in *OTP* 1:97, vaguely suggests that it is "early rather than late" (the title on p. 91 simply states "Late First Century A.D."); and Himmelfarb, *Ascent*, 38, favors the "standard view" of the book's provenance from first-century Egyptian Judaism (on pp. 85–6, she defines the "standard opinion" as "written in Egypt before the destruction of the Second Temple" and suggests Alexandria as the place of origin).

place where God takes a rest when he visits Paradise (Chap. 8).[70] The angels explain to him that this beautiful place has been prepared for the righteous as an "eternal inheritance" (Chap. 9). Yet, this idyll is balanced here by a counterimage: In the "northern region" of the third heaven, Enoch is shown that "frightful place" that has been prepared as an "eternal reward" for the wicked. It is a place of "all kinds of torture and torment," of "cruel darkness and lightless gloom" (Chap. 10). The righteous and the wicked are separated in afterlife according to their behavior on earth, but both are located on the same celestial plane, the third heaven; only the fallen angels and the "Watchers" are punished in different heavens: namely, the second (Chap. 7) and the fifth heaven (Chap. 18), respectively. The greater differentiation of heavenly realms allows for an increasing diversification of their inventories.

In 2 Enoch, there are altogether seven heavens (in the shorter version) or ten heavens (in the longer version). Whatever the "original" number of heavens, the seventh heaven is the highest heaven that Enoch can enter. Here, he is shown, "from a distance," the Lord, "sitting on his exceedingly high throne" (Chap. 20) in the seventh or in the tenth heaven.[71] The heaven is firmly established as a storehouse of a variety of items – angels, celestial bodies, meteorological elements, places of reward and punishment, and so forth – and God takes his place, as part of the heavenly "inventory," in the highest heaven.

The Greek *Apocalypse of Baruch* (3 Baruch) from the late first century C.E.[72] contents itself with five heavens. Here, the righteous and the wicked are separated in different heavens: The first heaven accommodates those who built the Tower of Babel (2:7) and the second heaven those who planned it (3:5); in the third heaven resides the stonelike serpent whose belly is Hades (5:3) and "which eats the bodies of those who pass through their lives badly" – that is, the third heaven is the place of the wicked (4:5), whereas in the fourth heaven, the souls of the righteous gather after death (10:5). Baruch does not get beyond the fourth heaven. We learn only that the fifth heaven is the one from which Michael appears to collect the prayers of Israel – and

---

[70] If not mentioned otherwise, I follow the longer version ("J") of 2 Enoch.

[71] The longer version calls the tenth heaven *Aravot* and is remarkably explicit about the appearance of God (Chap. 22).

[72] Himmelfarb, *Ascent*, 87; A. Y. Collins, following H. E. Gaylord, "3 (Greek Apocalypse of) Baruch," in *OTP* 1:655–56, prefers the second century C.E.; see her "The Seven Heavens in Jewish and Christian Apocalypses," in *Cosmology and Eschatology in Jewish and Christian Apocalypticism* (SJSJ 50; Leiden, 1996), 43.

disappears to bring them to God.[73] Whether God resides in the fifth heaven or somewhere above remains unspecified.

The relevant Jewish and Christian texts fluctuate among one-, three-, five-, seven-, and ten-heaven schemes, with a clear predominance of the one-heaven and seven-heaven structures.[74] Although the one-story heaven reflects the oldest pattern of the heavenly realm, it would be misguided to presume an evolutionary process from one heaven through three, five, and seven to finally ten heavens. The different patterns coexist with each other, and some texts even show conflicting tendencies within their own literary tradition (e.g., 2 Enoch or the Greek *T. Levi* 2:1–5:3,[75] which wavers between a three- and a seven-heaven scheme).[76] However, regardless of the number of heavens above the earth imagined in each text, this brief survey reveals a fundamental fact about this material that seems to have escaped the attention of most scholars: The authors of the ascent apocalypses and other relevant postbiblical Jewish and Christian texts are mainly preoccupied with the heaven(s)[77] and almost totally ignore or forget the netherworld, the third component of the ancient Near Eastern and biblical three-tiered heaven–earth–netherworld scheme. The earth expands upward into heaven but not downward into the netherworld.

Moreover, and more important, how should we envisage the multiple heavens in their relationship to the earth? J. Edward Wright sees here the Hellenistic astronomical model at work, which became known as the Ptolemaic geocentric model with the earth in the center surrounded by the seven

[73] It cannot be ruled out, however, that 3 Baruch "originally" contained seven heavens and that its present form is a later abridgment; see R. Bauckham, "Early Jewish Visions of Hell," *JTS* 41 (1990): 373–4; Himmelfarb, *Ascent*, 90; Collins, "Seven Heavens," 46.

[74] Himmelfarb, *Ascent*, 32, concludes that the ascent apocalypses from the first century C.E. or later "contain seven heavens, although the picture of a single heaven continues to appear in a wide variety of texts.... A number of the apocalypses with seven heavens are reworkings of earlier apocalypses with a single heaven." See also Wright, *Early History*, 199.

[75] *Aramaic Levi*, the major source of the Greek *Testament of Levi*, is dated to the middle of the second century B.C.E.; the Greek *Testament of Levi* in its present form is much later, probably from the first or more likely the second century C.E. (see Himmelfarb, *Ascent*, 127, n. 14).

[76] Himmelfarb, *Ascent*, 32, concludes "that the Testament of Levi recasts the contents of the ascent in the Book of the Watchers and the Aramaic Levi document to fill seven heavens." Collins, "Seven Heavens," 26, ponders the possibility that *Aramaic Levi* involved only three heavens and that the seven heavens were added at a later stage in the Greek *Testament of Levi*. In any case, she suggests that both the three-heaven and the seven-heaven schemes were influenced by Babylonian tradition and that the seven heavens in particular were inspired by Babylonian magic (pp. 28–9, 46).

[77] Apart from later Christian apocalypses that have tours of hell alongside tours of heaven; see Himmelfarb, *Tours of Hell*.

planets and the fixed stars. "While the biblical texts that were religiously authoritative for both Jews and Christians viewed the cosmos as a simple tripartite structure – heaven, earth, netherworld – these texts," he suggests, "adopted an entirely different image of the heavenly realm with multiple heavens above or encircling the earth."[78] Unfortunately, however, these Jewish and Christian authors misunderstood the Graeco–Roman models:

> Instead of having each heaven or sphere contain a separate planet, these texts...tend to put the planets, sun, moon, and stars in one or two different heavens...Thus, although adopting a multiple-heaven schema, these texts misunderstand the model and transform it into a schema whose true organizing principle centers around theological interests. The heavenly realms have become little more than places where people receive postmortem punishment or reward.[79]

The extent to which the Ptolemaic model was adopted by our Jewish and Christian authors is an intriguing question. I am not convinced, however, that the very fact of a multiple-heaven scheme in our texts necessarily points to the adoption of the Ptolemaic model. The problem is not so much that the planets are put in one or two heavens, or that the heavens are not planets. Much more disturbing is the fact that in none of these texts[80] do the heavens actually encircle the earth (as Wright optimistically assumes).[81] There are three, five, seven, or ten heavens, but these multiple heavens are piled up above the earth as in a sandwich; they do not *surround* the earth. Therefore, quite in contrast to Wright's thesis of a, however distorted, penetration of the Ptolemaic model into the backward worldview of Jews and Christians, our texts remain much closer to the ancient Near Eastern/biblical model than to the new discoveries of the Graeco–Roman world.[82] There is no real

---

[78] Wright, *Early History*, 183.

[79] Wright, *Early History*, 183, also 200.

[80] With the possible exception of 2 Enoch 30. Wright, *Early History*, 180, proposes that the cosmography of 2 Enoch 30 is "idiosyncratic" and that "this part of 2 Enoch is the only text discussed here that truly understands, albeit somewhat imperfectly, the Greco–Roman models of the cosmos." This fits well with Himmelfarb's conclusion that 2 Enoch might have originated from first-century Alexandria. The first to recognize in 2 Enoch 30 the early intrusion of the Ptolemaic model into Jewish cosmography was Gad Ben-Ammi Sarfatti in his article "Ha-qosmographiah ha-talmudit," *Tarbiz* 35 (1965): 145–6 [Hebrew]; he, however, considered this passage to be a later addition.

[81] His formulation "adopted an entirely different image of the heavenly realm with multiple heavens above *or* encircling the earth" is revealing: there is no "or"; the multiple heavens are "above," but do not "encircle the earth"!

[82] Collins, "Seven Heavens," 22, 54, comes to the same conclusion, although she is more concerned with rejecting the idea that the scheme of seven *planetary* heavens derives from

evidence in the texts surveyed so far that the Jews and Christians of the first few centuries C.E. adopted the Ptolemaic model of the cosmos.

The Heavens in Classical Rabbinic Literature

Turning now to the classical rabbinic literature, we discover a remarkable agreement with the apocalyptic tradition: Although the rabbis do not completely ignore the netherworld, they clearly put the emphasis on the multiplicity of the heavenly realm and are much less interested in the worlds below the surface of the earth. I begin with the heavens and summarize the most important traditions in the following chart (including the *SRdB* tradition)[83]:

RY1[84]	*Shamayim*	*Sheme shamayim*	*Zevul*	*'Arafel*	*Shehaqim*		*'Aravot*	*Kisse kavod*
RY2[85]	*Raqia'*/[86] *Shamayim*	*Sheme ha-shamayim*	*Zevul*	*'Arafel*	*Shehaqim*	*Makhon*	*'Aravot*	*Kisse kavod*
PRK 23 (Mandelbaum)[87]	*Shamayim*	*Sheme ha-shamayim*	*Raqia'*	*Shehaqim*	*Zevul*		*Ma'on*	*'Aravot: Ps 68:5*
PRK 23 (Buber)[88]	*Shamayim*	*Sheme shamayim*	*Raqia'*	*Shehaqim*	*Zevul*		*Ma'on*	*'Aravot: Ps 68:5*
LevR 29:11	*Shamayim*	*Sheme ha-shamayim*	*Raqia'*	*Shehaqim*	*Zevul*		*Ma'on*	*'Aravot*
DeutR 2:23 (32)	*Shamayim*	*Sheme shamayim*	*Raqia'*	*Shehaqim*	*Ma'on*		*Zevul*	*'Arafel*

Babylonian sources and served as the model for the seven heavens in Jewish and Christian apocalyptic writings, rather than with the Ptolemaic model.

83 I include 3 Enoch here (because of its obvious proximity to *b. Ḥagigah* and *SRdB*), although strictly speaking it belongs to the Hekhalot literature. However, this is yet another piece of evidence that 3 Enoch is more closely related to the classical rabbinic literature than the rest of the corpus; see Schäfer, *Hidden and Manifest God*, 136–8, 147–9.

84 I. Gruenwald, ed., "*Re'uyot Yeḥezqel*," *Temirin* 1 (1977): 115–16 [Hebrew]; A. Goldberg, "*Pereq Re'uyot Yeḥezqe'el*: Eine formanalytische Untersuchung," in *Gesammelte Studien*, Vol. 1, *Mystik und Theologie des rabbinischen Judentums*, ed. M. Schlüter and P. Schäfer (TSAJ 61; Tübingen, 1997), 6.1, 117–18.

85 Gruenwald, *Temirin*, 121ff; Goldberg, "*Re'uyot Yeḥezqe'el*," 8.1–15.1 (pp. 121–36).

86 It may well be that the second unit in *Re'uyot Yeḥezqe'el* begins counting the heavens with *Shamayim* and not with *Raqia'*, provided that *yam* in 9.1 has to be corrected to *shamayim* (see Goldberg, "*Re'uyot Yeḥezqe'el*," 124, n. 119).

87 B. Mandelbaum, ed., *Pesikta de Rav Kahana* (New York, 1962), 2:343.

88 S. Buber, ed., *Pesiqta ve-hi agadat erets Yisra'el meyuḥeset le-Rav Kahana* (New York, 1949), 154b.

b. Ḥag. 12b		Welon	Raqia'	Sheḥaqim	Zevul	Ma'on	Makhon	'Aravot
AdRN^A 37[89]		Welon	Raqia'	Sheḥaqim	Zevul	Ma'on	Makhon	'Aravot
Tg. Tosefta Ezekiel 1[90]		Welon	Raqia'	Sheḥaqim	Zevul	Ma'on	Makhon	'Aravot
3 Enoch 50		Shamayim	Raqia'	Sheḥaqim	Zevul	Ma'on		'Aravot
3 Enoch 21		Shamayim	Raqia'	Sheḥaqim	Zevul	Ma'on	Makhon	'Aravot
SRdB Vatican 288	Welon	Shamayim	Raqia'	Sheḥaqim	Zevul	Ma'on	Makhon	'Aravot
SRdB Oxford (§§767–777)	Welon	Shamayim	Raqia'	Sheḥaqim	Zevul	Ma'on	Makhon	'Aravot
Midrash Konen[91]			Raqia'	Sheḥaqim	Zevul	Ma'on	Makhon	'Aravot

Despite the obvious diversity of the traditions about the multiple heavens, the chart reveals some conspicuous clusters. First, except for a few deviations, the number of heavens is remarkably stable. The rabbis seem to have agreed on the seven-story image of heaven.[92] If we look now at the various traditions, the following textual groupings emerge:

1. *Re'uyot Yeḥezqel*
2. *Pesiqta de-Rav Kahana*, *Leviticus Rabbah*, and *Deuteronomy Rabbah*
3. Bavli *Ḥagiga*, *Avot de-Rabbi Nathan* (version A), Targumic Tosefta to Ezekiel 1, 3 Enoch, *SRdB*, and *Midrash Konen*.

The enigmatic *Re'uyot Yeḥezqel*, which according to Arnold Goldberg's penetrating form of critical analysis comes closest to a Midrash and has nothing to do with the "mystical" corpus of Hekhalot literature,[93] presents a unique

---

[89] S. Schechter, ed., *Avot de Rabbi Nathan* (New York, 1967), 110.

[90] Wertheimer, *Batei Midrashot*, 2:138.

[91] Jellinek, *Beit ha-Midrash*, 1:33.

[92] It is, therefore, all the more remarkable that a late Midrash like *Pirqe de-Rabbi Eliezer* resorts to the ancient model that the (one) heaven is spread like a tent over the waters of the ocean that surround the earth (*Pirqe de-Rabbi Eli'ezer* [Warsaw edition], Chap. 3, fols. 8a–b; Friedlander, *Pirkê de Rabbi Eliezer*, 16–17).

[93] Goldberg, "*Re'uyot Yeḥezqe'el*," 147.

collection of seven or eight heavens. Its mention of 'Arafel and Kisse ha-kavod [Throne of Glory] is particularly glaring, and it may well be that Kisse ha-kavod was, indeed, designed to be an eighth heaven above 'Aravot, usually the last and highest heaven. Presumably, the scribe of the first series (RY1) omitted Makhon in order to keep the traditional number of seven heavens, whereas the scribe of the second series (RY2) did not mind adding Kisse ha-kavod as the eighth heaven after 'Aravot.[94] If this supposition is correct, the author of Re'uyot Yeḥezqel may have followed a tradition similar to the one in Hekhalot Rabbati (§§100–101), in which God resides above 'Aravot and only at certain (liturgical) occasions descends to his throne in the seventh heaven 'Aravot.

The second group, which is relatively stable, is primarily interested in enumerating the correct number and names of the seven heavens. Deuteronomy Rabbah distinguishes between two separate traditions: One, communicated in the name of Rav[95] and derived from Deut 10:14 ("To the Lord, your God, belong the heaven [shamayim] and the heaven of heavens [sheme ha-shamayim]"), has only two heavens: namely, Shamayim and Sheme ha-shamayim; the other, communicated in the name of R. Eleazar, has the full number of seven heavens. The sequence and names of these seven heavens are identical with the other witnesses of this group, with the slight difference that Zevul and Ma'on are exchanged and that 'Arafel – otherwise found only in Re'uyot Yeḥezqel – replaces 'Aravot.[96] The other two texts in this group, Pesiqta de-Rav Kahana and Leviticus Rabbah, do not content themselves with merely enumerating the heavens. Instead, they take the form of an encomium to the number seven, according to which the seventh in a series is always the favorite [ḥaviv]: The seventh heaven, 'Aravot, is the favorite among the heavens because it is the residence of God ("Extol him who rides upon 'Aravot, the Lord is his name"; Ps 68:5).

The third group is extremely stable, with the sequence of (1) Shamayim, (2) Raqia', (3) Sheḥaqim, (4) Zevul, (5) Ma'on, (6) Makhon, and (7) 'Aravot. No doubt, this represents the classical sequence of the seven heavens in rabbinic

---

[94] Gruenwald, Temirin, 137; but see Goldberg, "Re'uyot Yeḥezqe'el," 118, n. 97.

[95] In b. Ḥagigah 12b in the name of R. Judah.

[96] The strange magical-mystical text Sefer ha-Razim comes closest to this group. It has seven heavens, but gives only the names of the first two or three: (1) Shamayim, (2) Shamayim (in the Geniza or in oriental manuscripts) or Sheme ha-shamayim (in European manuscripts), and (3) Ma'on (only in later European manuscripts). I owe this clarification regarding the manuscript groups to Bill Rebiger, Berlin.

literature.[97] Only the beginning deviates slightly in *b. Ḥagigah* (followed by *Avot de-Rabbi Nathan* and the Targumic Tosefta to Ezek 1:1) on the one hand and in *SRdB* on the other: whereas *b. Ḥagigah* counts *Welon* as the first heaven, *SRdB* appends it as a heavenly buffer zone, which belongs neither to the heavens nor to the earths (the description in both traditions nevertheless remains the same: *Welon* serves no purpose apart from dividing morning and evening). Accordingly, *SRdB* does not attribute to *Shamayim* any specific function or inventory and *b. Ḥagigah* leaves it out entirely. Other than this very minor discrepancy in the nomenclature of the first heaven, however, the inventories of *b. Ḥagigah* and *SRdB* are almost identical:

	b. Ḥagigah	*SRdB*	
		No purpose: morning/evening?	*Welon*
1. *Welon*	No purpose: morning/evening	?	1. *Shamayim*
2. *Raqia'*	Sun, moon, stars, constellations: Gen 1:17	Sun, moon, stars, constellations: Gen 1:17	2. *Raqia'*
3. *Sheḥaqim*	Manna for the righteous: Ps 78:23	Manna for the righteous: Ps 78:23 the heavenly Jerusalem, the heavenly Temple	3. *Sheḥaqim*
4. *Zevul*	Jerusalem, Temple, altar, Michael: 1 Kgs 8:13	Michael, the heavenly high priest, offers sacrifices	4. *Zevul*
5. *Ma'on*	Ministering angels who sing at night: Ps 42:9	Ministering angels who sing during the day: Ps 42:9	5. *Ma'on*
6. *Makhon*	Snow, hail, harmful dews, raindrops, storm, vapor: Deut 28:12	Snow, hail, rain, wind, lightning, thunder, etc., rivers of fire, storm,vapor	6. *Makhon*
7. *'Aravot*	Righteousness, life, peace, blessing, souls, dew, *Ofannim*, *Serafim*, *Ḥayyot*, ministering angels, Throne of God, the king, the living God: Ps 68:5	Treasure houses of justice, life, blessing, dew, souls, etc., *Ofannim*, *Keruvim*, *Ḥayyot*, wheels of the Merkavah, etc., Throne of Glory, God sitting on his throne above: Ps 68:5	7. *'Aravot*

---

[97] As has already been observed by Sed, *Mystique cosmologique juive*, 270ff., it is striking that the first two groups represent texts that can be classified as "Palestinian," whereas the third

The differences between the two inventories are restricted to *Welon/Shamayim* and *Shehaqim/Zevul*. In both cases, it makes sense to assume that *SRdB* depends on *b. Hagigah* or a very similar source. The reason why *SRdB* has moved the heavenly Jerusalem and its Temple from the fourth to the third heaven has already been discussed. And, in counting *Shamayim* as the first heaven, *SRdB* simply follows the overwhelming majority of texts that just enumerate the seven heavens; but because *b. Hagigah*, its presumed *Vorlage*, did not contain *Shamayim* – and, accordingly, no inventory of *Shamayim* – it was forced to leave *Shamayim* empty.

The only other text that presents a full inventory of the heavens is *Re'uyot Yehezqel*.[98] For the sake of clarity, I again provide a chart summarizing the inventories of the heavens in this work:

1. *Raqiaʻ*   Sun, moon, stars, and constellations; Merkavah Shelrekhesh
2. *Sheme shamayim* Ministering angels; Merkavah Shelsusim
3. *Zevul*   The Prince; Merkavah HLWYH
4. *ʻArafel*   The canopy of the Torah; Merkavah for the kings
5. *Shehaqim*   Jerusalem and the Temple; Merkavah Shelkeruv
6. *Makhon*   Treasure houses of snow and hail, punishment for the wicked and reward for the righteous
7. *ʻAravot*   Treasure houses of blessing, snow, peace, souls of the righteous, spirit of the souls to be created, punishment for the wicked and reward for the righteous; Merkavah ʻAv
8. *Kisse ha-kavod*   The hoofs of the (four) creatures and parts of their wings; Merkavah of fire and tempest; the wings of the creatures; the Holy One blessed be he

group with its "classical" sequence of heavens can be classified as "Babylonian." The close relationship of 3 Enoch and *SRdB* with *b. Hagigah* (not only with regard to the sequence of heavens but also to their inventories) makes it more likely that both belong to the Babylonian rather than to the Palestinian strand of tradition. The same is true for the netherworlds (see subsequent discussion): The *Re'uyot Yehezqel* and the *PRK/LevR* groups seem to be "Palestinian," whereas the *SRdB* group with its upside-down sequence is "Babylonian." Also, the texts enumerating the seven compartments of *Gehinnom* are clearly Babylonian, as is the Targumic Tosefta to Ezek. 1:1, which belongs to this literary complex.

[98] A rudimentary inventory is offered also in *Sefer ha-Razim*, but the text's main interest lies in the various angels present in the respective heavens.

Except for its idiosyncratic placement of the Merkavah in each heaven and the no less idiosyncratic addition of the canopy of the Torah in the heaven '*Arafel*, this inventory is strikingly similar to *b. Ḥagigah/SRdB*:

1. The heavenly bodies in *Raqia'* (first heaven in *RY*, second heaven in *b. Ḥagigah/SRdB*).
2. The Prince/Michael in *Zevul* (third heaven in *RY*, fourth heaven in *b. Ḥagigah/SRdB*). The Prince in *RY*, however, does not seem to be Michael: He is given a number of inexplicable *nomina barbara* names and is finally called Metatron (also the proof text Dan 7:9–10 seems to indicate that the Prince = Metatron is identified with the "Ancient of Days" = God in Daniel).[99]
3. Jerusalem and the Temple in *Sheḥaqim* (fifth heaven in *RY*, third heaven in *b. Ḥagigah/SRdB*), but only in *SRdB*! In *b. Ḥagigah*, Jerusalem and the Temple are located, together with Michael, in *Zevul*.
4. The treasure houses of snow and hail in *Makhon* (sixth heaven in both *RY* and in *b. Ḥagigah/SRdB*). The punishment for the wicked and the reward for the righteous are missing in *b. Ḥagigah/SRdB*, but repeated in *RY* in the seventh heaven '*Aravot*. It would make sense to have the punishment and the reward distributed between the sixth and the seventh heaven (together with the useful and the harmful elements of nature), but neither version follows this neat division.
5. The treasure houses of blessing and the souls of the righteous in '*Aravot* (seventh heaven in both *RY* and *b. Ḥagigah/SRdB*). But whereas *b. Ḥagigah/SRdB* follow with God on his Throne of Glory, surrounded by his heavenly court, *RY* has only the routine Merkavah in '*Aravot* and reserves the four creatures and God on his highest throne for the eighth heaven called *Kisse ha-kavod*.
6. The Ministering Angels are located in *RY* in *Sheme shamayim* (second heaven) and in *b. Ḥagigah/SRdB* in *Ma'on* (fifth heaven), which is altogether missing in *RY*.

There can be no doubt that *Re'uyot Yeḥezqel* and *b. Ḥagigah/SRdB* draw on the same repository of traditions about the heavenly realm, but it is highly unlikely that *Re'uyot Yeḥezqel* served as a direct source for the inventories in our third group.

---

[99] See Goldberg, "*Re'uyot Yeḥezqe'el*," 128, n. 131.

Earth(s) in the Classical Rabbinic Literature

Speculation about the earthly realm or the netherworld is less developed in the rabbinic literature than that about the heavenly realm. Nevertheless, several clusters of tradition can be isolated. The first is the simple statement that the earth (*eretz*) is called by several names:

GenR (13:12)	*Eretz*	*Tevel*	*Adamah*	*Arqa*						
AdRN[A][100]	*Eretz*	*Adamah*	*Arqa*	*Ḥaravah*	*Yabashah*	*Tevel*	*Ḥeled*			
AdRN[B][101]	*Adamah*	*Yabashah*	*Ḥaravah*	*Tevel*	*Ḥeled*	*Arqa*	*Reshit*	*Ge'*	*Sadeh*	*Eretz*
Midrash Proverbs 8[102]	*Eretz*	*Adamah*	*Ḥaravah*	*Yabashah*	*Arqa*	*Tevel*	*Ḥeled*	*Reshit*	*Ge'*	*Sadeh*

Genesis Rabbah has only four names of the earth because it equates these four names with the four seasons of the year; this has obviously nothing to do with any notion of the netherworld. *Avot de-Rabbi Nathan* (version A) presents the counterimage of the aforementioned seven heavens: Just as there are seven heavens with different names, so too is the earth called by seven names. Note, however, the carefully phrased difference between the heavens (in the plural) and the earth (in the singular): "R. Meir says: There are seven heavens (*reqi'in*), namely.... Accordingly, he called the earth by seven names, namely...." R. Meir seems to be reluctant to conclude that there are indeed seven earths; his dictum represents a transitional stage between the observation that the Hebrew language provides a variety of names for "earth" and the conclusion that there is, in fact, a number of different "earths" or "netherworlds" below the surface of our visible earth. The parallel in *Avot de-Rabbi Nathan* (version B) has the same careful formulation (this time anonymously): "'earth' [no article] is called by ten names ... " and gives a quite unique order of the seven earths known from *AdRN*[A], supplemented with three more. The same is true for *Midrash Proverbs*, which also insists that the earth is called by ten names.

[100] *AdRN*[A] 37 (Schechter, 110).
[101] *AdRN*[B] 43 (Schechter, 119).
[102] B. Visotzky, ed., *Midrash Mishle* (New York, 1990), 60.

The sequence follows the one in *AdRN*[A] (with some deviations), but at the end, the three earths known from *AdRN*[B] are added.

The next well-defined cluster of texts is the tradition about the seven compartments of *Gehinnom*. As has been argued, it seems probable that here again the Bavli serves as the source of *SRdB* (and the texts depending on it). *SRdB* makes use of a rather simple textual unit, providing seven names for *Gehinnom*, and integrates it into its own highly sophisticated scheme of seven earths.

The final step is the recognition that there are not just seven names for the earth or for *Gehinnom* but, in fact, seven "earths." The following chart summarizes the relevant texts:

RY[103]	Adamah: Num 16:31	Eretz: Num 16:32	Heled: Ps 49:2	Neshiyah: Ps 88:13	Dumah: Ps 115:17	She'ol: Num 16:33	Tit ha-yawen: Ps 40:3
PRK 23 (Mandelbaum)[104]	*Eretz*	*Adamah*	*Arqa*	*Ge'*	*Tziyah*	*Shetiyah*	*Tevel:* Ps 9:9
PRK 23 (Buber)[105]	*Eretz*	*Adamah*	*Arqa*	*Ge'*	*Tziyah*	*Neshiyah*	*Tevel:* Ps 9:9
LevR 29:11	*Eretz*	*Adamah*	*Arqa*	*Ge'*	*Tziyah*	*Neshiyah*	*Tevel*
Targumic Tosefta to Ezek 1:1[106]	*She'ol*	*Be'er shahat*	*Gehinnom*	*Dumah*	*Arqa*	*Tit ha-yawen*	*Avaddon le-'olam*
SRdB Vatican 288	*Heled*	*Tevel*	*Arqa*				*Eretz ha-tahtonah*
***SRdB* Oxford (§§741–766)**	*Heled*	*Tevel*	*Arqa*	*Yabashah*	*Haravah*	*Adamah*	*Eretz ha-tahtonah*
Midrash Konen[107]	*Heled*	*Tevel*	*Arqa*	*Yabashah*	*Haravah*	*Adamah*	*Eretz ha-tahtonah*

---

[103] Gruenwald, *Temirin*, 107–8; Goldberg, *"Re'uyot Yeḥezqe'el,"* 4.2 (p. 112).
[104] Mandelbaum, ed., *Pesikta de Rav Kahana*, 2:344.
[105] Buber, *Pesiqta*, 155a.
[106] Wertheimer, *Batei Midrashot*, 2:139.
[107] Jellinek, *Beit ha-Midrash*, 1:35–36.

All these texts are aware of a multiplicity of earths, with the stable number of seven (the only exception is *SRdB*, MS Vatican 288; see subsequent discussion). *Re'uyot Yeḥezqel* says explicitly, "And these are the seven lower compartments [*medorin*]," using the same word as *SRdB* for the seven compartments of *Gehinnom*. The same is true for the Targumic Tosefta to Ezek 1:1, which speaks of "seven compartments [*medorin*]," corresponding to its seven "upper compartments." *Pesiqta de-Rav Kahana* and *Leviticus Rabbah* merely follow the pattern of the seven heavens, adding that, among the earths, too, the seventh (*Tevel*) is the favorite. By contrast, *SRdB* and *Midrash Konen* explicitly enumerate – in addition to the "seven fountains [*ma'yanot*] above" and the "seven depths [*tehomot*] below" (§431 [§842]) – "seven dwelling places [*me'onot*] that are in heaven" and the corresponding "seven dwelling places [*me'onot*] that are on earth" (§743).

Like its version of the names of the seven/eight heavens, the names of the seven earths given in *Re'uyot Yeḥezqel* similarly stand out with a number of peculiarities. Only *Adamah, Eretz,* and *Ḥeled* correspond to the other lists; *Neshiyah* is attested to also in *Pesiqta de-Rav Kahana* (Buber) and in *Leviticus Rabbah,* and *Dumah* also in the Targumic Tosefta. *She'ol* and *Tit ha-yawen* are unique to *Re'uyot Yeḥezqel* and to the Targumic Tosefta, and it seems as if both did not "originally" belong to the list of the seven earths; rather, it appears that they filtered into it from the unit enumerating the seven compartments of *Gehinnom*.[108] The same is true for *Be'er Shaḥat, Gehinnom,* and *Avaddon le-'olam* in the Targumic Tosefta, which makes it likely that this list, in fact, belongs to the seven compartments of *Gehinnom*. This is supported by the narrative of the Targumic Tosefta, which talks about Nebuchadnezzar, who, in his idolatrous pride, tries to destroy the heavenly compartments and instead – thrown into the seven subterranean compartments – ends up in *Avaddon 'olam,* the lowest earth, from which he will never return. As we are told also in *SRdB,* the destroyers of both Temples are destined for eternal damnation.

The *Pesiqta de-Rav Kahana/Leviticus Rabbah* group seems to combine the four names of the earth from *Genesis Rabbah* (albeit in a different order) with three highly unusual names: *Ge', Tziyah,* and *Shetiyah/Neshiyah*. Of the latter, *Ge'* is attested to also in the list of ten names provided by *AdRN^B*, and

---

[108] *Dumah* is a special case: It is attested among the seven earths in *Re'uyot Yeḥezqel* and in the Targumic Tosefta, and among the seven compartments of *Gehinnom* only in *Midrash Konen.* As strange as it appears in the list of the earths, it is hard to imagine that it originated in the list of the seven compartments of *Gehinnom.*

Midrash Proverbs (whereas *Reshit* sounds suspiciously like *Shetiya*, and *Sadeh* like *Tziyah*). In any case, both lists clearly overlap and focus on the names of the earth(s). Finally, it is noteworthy that the *SRdB* and *Midrash Konen* group turns upside down the sequence of the group represented by *Genesis Rabbah*, *AdRN*, and *Midrash Proverbs* (best preserved in *AdRN*^{A}): *Eretz* becomes *Eretz ha-tahtonah* ("the lowest earth") and, accordingly, the other earths are listed in reversed order, with *Heled* as the topmost earth.[109]

Altogether, except for the *SRdB* group, the rabbinic traditions about the netherworld remain conspicuously colorless. They do not go much beyond listing the various names of the earth and, at most, conclude that there exist several earths just as several heavens exist. Certainly, none of the rabbinic texts outside *SRdB* provides an inventory of the seven earths: *Re'uyot Yehezqel* contents itself with enumerating the earths, and b. *Hagigah* does not even mention the seven earths at all (let alone their inventory). Moreover, and most importantly, none of the rabbinic texts – again with the sole exception of *SRdB* – gives the impression that the seven heavens and the seven earths are arranged in corresponding semicircles or hemispheres. In other words, the heavens and the earths seem to be piled up in both directions like a multistory building, not like semicircles meeting each other at a central axis (the surface of our inhabited earth).

This makes the innovation initiated by *SRdB* all the more remarkable. This late rabbinic or early geonic tractate is the first text in late antique Judaism that imagines the visible earth as surrounded by spheres that constitute heavens above and netherworlds below. To be sure, this is not yet the Ptolemaic model with its planets surrounding the earth. Yet, in adopting a similar picture of the cosmos, *SRdB* transforms the old biblical model into something quite new, which comes close to the Ptolemaic model. With its unique image of the seventh heaven and the seventh earth touching each other, it guarantees that God's physical presence is on the lowest earth just as it is in the highest heaven. God does not only govern the universe that we know from the Bible, but also the universe as we know it now – not through biblical exegesis but through the new astronomical science. *SRdB*, then, is the first Jewish text that attempts to reconcile the old universe with the new one.

---

[109] *SRdB* MS Vatican 228 with only four earths could have been influenced by the almost identical, albeit reversed, list in *Genesis Rabbah* (only *Adamah* is exchanged for *Heled*).

Hekhalot Literature

In conclusion, it is appropriate to venture a brief look at the Hekhalot literature proper, the companion of *ma'aseh bereshit* as expounded in *SRdB*. What is the cosmological structure, if any, of those texts that are concerned with *ma'aseh merkavah* and the ascent of the Merkavah mystic to the heavenly realm?[110]

The first observation, as might be expected, is that the Hekhalot literature, like the earlier biblical and apocalyptic tradition, is almost exclusively interested in the heavenly realm. The Merkavah mystic is imagined as ascending into heaven and not descending into the netherworld. Despite the perplexing terminology of *yarad* instead of *'alah*,[111] this literature makes no attempt to measure, let alone to describe, the netherworld. Not surprisingly, the only exception to this general tendency is 3 Enoch.[112] Here, we learn that the sweat of the four holy creatures (the *Ḥayyot*) is collected in the rivers of fire mentioned in Dan 7:10 and pours through the seven heavens[113] until it reaches the heads of the wicked in *Gehinnom*, somewhere below the lowest heaven *Shamayim* (§50). This tradition is known also from the Bavli (*b. Ḥagigah* 13b)[114] – further indication of the proximity of 3 Enoch to the rabbinic literature in general and to the Bavli in particular. In another, quite detailed chapter of 3, Enoch the angel Metatron shows R. Ishmael – very much in the style of the heavenly journey of the early Jewish apocalypses – the souls of the wicked being punished in the fire of *Gehinnom* and the souls of the "indifferent" [*benoniyyim*], which are able to be purified (§62).

The bulk of the Hekhalot literature, however, is concerned with the heavens, which are counted in most cases as seven. The so-called water test, which takes place in the sixth heaven, clearly presupposes a seventh heaven in which God is seated on his throne (§345, §408), and whether *Hekhalot Rabbati* hints at an eighth heaven from which God descends to sit down on his throne in

---

[110] I am dealing here with the classical Hekhalot texts, including 3 Enoch (although I discussed it within the context of rabbinical literature as well; see n. 83).

[111] See Schäfer, *Hidden and Manifest God*, 2–3, n. 4; A. Kuyt, *The 'Descent' to the Chariot: Towards a Description of the Terminology, Place, Function and Nature of the Yeridah in Hekhalot Literature* (TSAJ 45; Tübingen, 1995).

[112] §972 (a version of the *Shi'ur Qomah* macroform that is preserved only in MS Munich 40) casually mentions the inhabitants of *Tehom, Avaddon, Tziyah,* and *Tzalmawet,* who are frightened of God's name.

[113] Actually, it is only six heavens in 3 Enoch; see §50 and preceding discussion.

[114] It is probably hinted at in 2 Enoch 10:2; see also *Massekhet Gehinnom* 4 (Jellinek, *Beit ha-Midrash,* 1:149).

the seventh heaven[115] is doubtful (§§100–101). The technical term used for the seven heavens (hekhal, plural hekhalot; lit. "palaces" or "halls") is unique to the Hekhalot literature and refers to the context of the Temple liturgy: It is taken from the architecture of the Temple, in which it is used for the entrance hall to the Holiest of Holies [qodesh ha-qodashim]. Hence, the ascent of the Merkavah mystic through the six heavens to the seventh heaven is primarily a liturgical act and has little to do with the exploration of heavenly cosmology. Most Hekhalot texts use the term raqia' synonymously with the term hekhal,[116] or even combine hekhal with raqia'.[117] This linguistic usage is derived from the term for the seventh hekhal, the full name of which is 'Arevot raqia'.[118] Other than this designation for the seventh heaven, names for the seven heavens are rare in this literature[119]; they are mostly counted as the "first," "second," and so on, up to the seventh hekhal.[120]

Finally, the most striking observation regarding the physical structure of the heavenly world in the Hekhalot literature is that the seventh hekhal, 'Arevot, the desired goal of the Merkavah mystic, is not just a single open heaven, but is composed of hadarim (singular: heder), literally "rooms," "apartments," or "chambers." This term is completely unique to the Hekhalot literature.[121] The very beginning of Hekhalot Rabbati in all the manuscripts – after referring to the songs of praise, which are to be sung by the successful Merkavah mystic – mentions the angels who escort the mystic to the "chambers of the palace of 'Arevot raqia'" [hadre hekhal 'arevot raqia'], where they place him on the right side of the Throne of Glory (§81). There, in the seventh heaven, God dwells "in the chambers of the palace of pride" [be-hadre hekhal ge'avah] or "in the chambers of the palace of silence" [be-hadre hekhal demamah]. These and similar phrases are very frequent in the Hekhalot literature.[122] What precisely

---

[115] I. Gruenwald, Apocalyptic and Merkavah Mysticism (AGAJU 14; Leiden, 1980), 153–4.

[116] See §§179, 180, 201 (Hekhalot Rabbati), 664–670 (Merkavah Rabbah), 966 (Shi'ur Qomah), 15, 17, 21, 56 (3 Enoch).

[117] See, e.g., §595 (Ma'aseh Merkavah), where R. Aqiva sees from the "hekhal of the first raqia' to the seventh hekhal."

[118] See, e.g., §§81, 180, 182, 189, 244 (Hekhalot Rabbati), 10, 15, 17, 26 (3 Enoch).

[119] Most notably in §§966 (Shi'ur Qomah), 21, and 50 (3 Enoch).

[120] The classic example are the names of the guardian angels at the entrances to the seven hekhalot: §§207–212 (Hekhalot Rabbati).

[121] This may be a faint echo of the house within a house (in which the inner one is even bigger than the outer one) that Enoch sees in 1 Enoch 14.

[122] See, e.g., §§153, 157, 256, 320, 322 (Hekhalot Rabbati), 544 (Ma'aseh Merkavah); 653, 694 (Merkavah Rabbah); 976 (Shi'ur Qomah); and P. Schäfer, ed., Konkordanz zur Hekhalot-Literatur, 2 vols. (TSAJ 12–13; Tübingen, 1986, 1988).

do these phrases mean? Obviously, there are several of these *ḥadarim* in the *hekhal 'Aravot*; the texts sometimes speak of the "chambers of the chambers" [*ḥadre ḥadarim*][123] or the "chambers of the height" [*ḥadre marom*], in which God resides.[124] The number of these chambers within the seventh heaven is not communicated, but it is possible that, like the heavens, there are seven of them. There can be little doubt, however, that these chambers – whatever their number – are nested within each other and that God dwells in the innermost chamber. This seems to be the meaning of the enigmatic phrase in *Hekhalot Rabbati*: "R. Ishmael said: This is what R. Neḥunya b. Haqana said: In seven palaces [*hekhalot*] sits TWTRWSY'Y, the Lord, the God of Israel, chamber within chamber (*ḥeder betokh ḥeder*; §206)." Of course, God does not sit in all the seven palaces, but he dwells in the innermost chamber of the many chambers of the seventh palace.[125]

In other words, the chambers within the seventh heaven are arranged in concentric circles, and God sits in the innermost circle of the (seven?) circles. This is immediately reminiscent of the seven semicircles (or hemispheres) constituting the seven heavens and the seven earths in *SRdB*. Thus, whereas the structure of the seven heavens in the Hekhalot literature does not indicate any sign of influence of the Ptolemaic model (i.e., because the heavens seem to be piled up again like a multistory building), the chambers within the seventh heaven may well reflect a certain adoption of the Ptolemaic model along the lines previously described with regard to *SRdB*. In the Hekhalot model, however, God does not reside in the outermost layer of the system of "chambers" but in the innermost layer. Nevertheless, this makes perfect sense because the mystic has already reached the seventh and outermost heaven, and within this heaven he now turns inward, toward its very center. One might even go a step farther and argue that precisely this image of turning from outside toward inside, from the outer layer to the innermost center (like a kernel with several shells), created the strange phrase of the *yored merkavah*, of the mystic who descends (rather than ascends) to the Merkavah: After his ascent to the seventh heaven, the mystic finally descends to the very center

---

[123] For example, §§403 (*Hekhalot Zutarti*), 554, 559, 579 (*Ma'aseh Merkavah*).

[124] For example, §§544 (*Ma'aseh Merkavah*), 694 (*Merkavah Rabbah*).

[125] A late echo of this structure is preserved in 3 Enoch in which R. Ishmael says of himself (§1), "When I ascended to the height to behold the vision of the Merkavah, I entered six palaces, chamber within chamber." This seems to blur the originally distinct "palaces" (= heavens) and "chambers" (within the highest heaven).

of this heaven, to the innermost chamber with the Throne of Glory and God residing on his throne.[126]

In any case, whatever the solution of the enigmatic phrase *yeridah la-merkavah*, the Hekhalot literature seems to combine the old biblical model with its seven-story heaven and the new Ptolemaic model in a quite unprecedented manner. However, whereas in *SRdB* God becomes visible in all the heavens and all the earths – in the universe as it is revealed through the new astronomical science – in the Hekhalot literature he is hidden again, more than ever, in the innermost chamber of the seventh heaven. True, the Merkavah mystic ascends and descends to this hidden God and assures the community on earth that he is still there, in the chambers of chambers of the highest heaven. But this knowledge is clearly not meant to reconcile the traditional worldview with the new astronomical model. Rather, it is esoteric knowledge that can be enacted only through the liturgical ritual of the elite few.

---

[126] E. Wolfson (*"Yeridah la-Merkavah*: Typology of Ecstasy and Enthronement in Ancient Jewish Mysticism," in *Mystics of the Book: Themes, Topics, and Typologies*, ed. R. A. Herrera [New York, 1993], 13–44; see also idem, *Through a Speculum that Shines: Vision and Imagination in Medieval Jewish Mysticism* [Princeton, N. J., 1994], 82–5) proposes that the term *yeridah la-merkavah* does not refer to the whole process of ascent through the seven palaces, but to the final stage of the journey, only the "entry" of the mystic to the chariot of the seventh palace (and, accordingly, the term *'aliyyah* to the "exit" from the seventh palace). I agree that the sources suggest a two-stage journey, but I do not believe, mainly on philological grounds, that the enigma of the phrase *yeridah la-merkavah* can be solved by positing that *yeridah* means "entry" and *'aliyyah* "exit."

14

The Faces of the Moon: Cosmology, Genesis, and the *Mithras Liturgy*

Radcliffe G. Edmonds III

"D" o not invoke the self-manifesting image of Physis." The *Chaldaean Oracles* instruct the theurgist to avoid the face of the moon, as Proclus identifies the self-manifesting image of Physis [Nature]. "Do not look upon Physis!" says another *Oracle*, "For her name is like Fate."[1] In the so-called *Mithras Liturgy*, a spell for immortalization contained in the Great Paris Magical Papyrus,[2] the magician seems to heed the advice of the *Oracles*, for the ritual preparations are carefully timed to avoid the presence of the moon in the sky, and the magician does not see the moon during his ascent through the heavens to a meeting with the supreme god.[3] Why must the theurgist take such precautions and carefully bypass the power of the moon? By contrast, Emperor Julian's Selene shows a beneficent face to the sleeping world below: "Selene beholds the intelligible which is higher than the heavens and

I would like to thank Ra'anan Boustan, Annette Reed, and Peter Schäfer for organizing an excellent symposium and for encouraging me to proceed with further research into this topic. I would also like to thank Michael Williams and Sarah Johnston for their critiques and comments, although I need scarcely say that any infelicities, obscurities, or outright errors are wholly the products of my own ignorance, carelessness, or obstinacy.

[1] *Chaldaean Oracles* 101 = Psellus, *PG* 122, 1136 c12: μὴ φύσεως καλέσῃς αὐτόπτον ἄγαλμα; Proclus *In Remp.* 2.133.15–17: εἰς τὴν σεληνιακὴν…σφαῖραν, ἐν ᾗ τῆς γενέσεως αἰτίαι πάσης καὶ, ὡς φησίν τις ἱερὸς λόγος, τὸ "αὐτόπτον ἄγαλμα τῆς φύσεως" προσλάμπει; Proclus, *In Tim.* 3.69.15–16: σελήνη μεν αἰτία τοῖς θνητοῖς τῆς φύσεως, τὸ "αὐτόπτον ἄγαλμα" οὖσα τῆς πηγαίας φύσεως; *CO* 102 = Proclus, *Theol. Plat.* 317.29: Μὴ φύσιν ἐμβλέψῃς· εἱμαρμένον οὔνομα τῆσδε. Citations of the *Chaldaean Oracles* are according to the numbering of E. Des Places, ed., trans., and comm., *Oracles chaldaïques avec un choix de commentaires anciens* (Paris, 1971), adapted by R. Majercik, trans. and comm., *The Chaldean Oracles: Text, Translation, and Commentary* (SGRR 5; Leiden, 1989).

[2] The *Mithras Liturgy* consists of lines 475–834 of the so-called Great Paris Magical Papyrus (*PGM* IV), which is generally agreed to date to the third or early fourth century B.C.E.

[3] See my arguments in R. G. Edmonds, "At the Seizure of the Moon: The Absence of the Moon in the Mithras Liturgy," in *Prayer, Magic, and the Stars in the Ancient and Late Antique World*, ed. S. Noegel, J. Walker, and B. Wheeler (University Park, Penn., 2003), 194–204.

adorns with its forms the realm of matter that lies below her, and thus she does away with its savagery and confusion and disorder."[4] Likewise, Plutarch claims that the face in the moon is the face of the prophetic sibyl, and the moon is the necessary way station for the soul in Plutarch's myth of the soul's ascent in *De facie*.[5] The theurgists, however, are not the only testimony to the moon's terrifying face. Clement relates that Orpheus called the moon Gorgonian because of its terrifying face, a face like that which Odysseus feared Persephone would send up to him in the underworld when he was consulting the shades.[6] Plutarch too knows of this frightening face, which terrifies souls coming out of incarnation, although he rationalizes it as merely a cliff formation on the surface of the moon.[7] The moon shows different faces in these cosmologies, ranging from the most benevolent to the most terrifying.

In this essay, I locate these different faces of the moon and the cosmology of the *Mithras Liturgy* within the spectrum of cosmological systems in the first several centuries C.E. I argue that the *Oracles'* caution against the face of the moon and the Mithras Liturgist's avoidance of the moon stem from a particular set of cosmological choices within this spectrum, whereas Julian's and Plutarch's images of the moon stem from a different set of options. I focus on a limited set of elements within these cosmologies to make my comparisons. The first element is the role of the moon in the important divisions made within the cosmos, particularly the contrast between three realms and the seven planetary spheres as the significant division of the cosmos. The second element to be considered is the evaluation of the process of genesis, the soul's descent from the higher realms into matter. The final element is the nature of the intermediary powers that govern the boundaries between the divisions of the cosmos, particularly the entity who governs the border between the material and heavenly realms, the mistress of genesis. Different choices for each of these elements produce radically different cosmologies and suggest varying solutions for the problems of living within the cosmos.

The *Mithras Liturgy* represents one such solution, one way of living in the late antique world. Here, there is a tripartite division among earthly, heavenly, and hyperouranian realms, each governed by a luminary, rather than a focus on seven planetary spheres. The magician appeals to the highest powers in the realms beyond the material to bypass the power responsible for genesis

---

[4] Julian, *Or.* 4.150a.
[5] The sibyl's face: Plutarch, *Pyth. orac.* 398cd; *Sera* 566d. As a way station, cf. *Fac.* 943bc.
[6] Clement of Alexandria, *Strom.* 5.49 = *OF* 33; *Od.* 11.633–635.
[7] Plutarch, *Fac.* 944bc.

instead of calling on her aid. This bypassing suggests that the mistress of genesis is seen as hostile to souls trying to escape from genesis, rather than as a necessary intermediary for ascent. Although the moon is not depicted in the *Mithras Liturgy* itself, the depictions of the lunar goddess in other spells within the Great Paris Magical Papyrus indicate that the moon is a dangerous power, whose terrifying face should be avoided in a spell that seeks to bring the magician beyond her realm.

Cosmological Divisions

The basic division in any cosmology is between the familiar world of mortals, the material realm of earth, and elsewhere, the realms of divine or demonic powers and the dead. In the Hellenistic and late antique eras, the earth was most often postulated as the center of the cosmos, with other realms in spherical levels above it. Visible above the earth are the heavens, including the sun, moon, and stars, both the wandering stars (planets) and the fixed. These heavenly entities were often imagined in eight separate levels, starting with the moon and rising up to the highest sphere of the fixed stars. Beyond the visible cosmos, some philosophers postulated a hypercosmic realm, accessible only to the intellect, that was the true locus of real being, the perfect pleroma of the highest principles.[8] Following the metaphor in Plato's *Republic*, a hypercosmic sun dominated this highest realm, just as the cosmic sun did the lower realm.[9] The most significant cosmological divisions, therefore, were either tripartite, among the material, heavenly, and hypercosmic

[8] The image of the hyperouranian realm goes back to the myth in Plato's *Phaedrus*, but it was developed and modified by philosophers and theologians of various persuasions. Cf. M. Tardieu, "La Gnose Valentinienne et les Oracles Chaldaïques," in *The Rediscovery of Gnosticism*, Vol. 1: *The School of Valentinus*, ed. B. Layton (SHR 41; Leiden, 1980), 194–237, esp. 209, on the relation to the three fires of Stoicism; J. Dillon, *The Middle Platonists* (London, 1977), 30–3. J. Flamant prefers to see the three-level cosmos as an older model, deriving from the Orient, but picked up by Greek thinkers as early as Anaximander ("Sotériologie et systèmes planétaires," in *La Soteriologia dei Culti Orientali nell' Impero Romano*, ed. U. Bianchi and M. J. Vermaseren [EPRO 92; Leiden, 1982], 223–42). The idea of an eighth heaven, a hyperouranian realm beyond the seven planetary levels, appears in a number of cosmologies; e.g., the "gnostic" *Hypostasis of the Archons* 95.31–35 and *On the Origin of the World* 112.1–25 (NHC II 4, 5) or the Hermetic *Poimandres* (CH I 24–26). Cf. the one-upmanship of the Hermetic *Discourse on the Eighth and Ninth* (NHC VI 6) and the "gnostic" *Apocalypse of Paul* (NHC V 2, 24:1–9), which reveal a ninth and possibly tenth realm above the eighth, which is above the world.

[9] Plato *Resp.* 517bc; cf. Proclus, *In Tim.* 3.82.19–85.31; Plutarch, *Def. orac.* 433d; Philo, *Virt.* 104; *QG* 4.1; *In Exod.* 2.51; Julian, *Or.* 4.148a; Proclus, *Theol. Plat.* 2.43.12–51.19; 2.64.10–65.26; *In Crat.* 101; *In Parm.* 1043.30–1045.25.

realms, or sevenfold, among the seven planets.[10] Note that these two types of divisions are not mutually exclusive.[11] On the contrary, the division into seven planetary spheres implies a difference between heaven and earth and the realm beyond the planets, and the division into three realms can perfectly well acknowledge seven planetary spheres within the heavenly realm. The distinction lies in the relative importance placed on the different divisions within the cosmological system. In a tripartite system, the luminaries (the sun and the moon) tend to play a more important role than in sevenfold systems, in which they are grouped in among all the other planets.

The *Mithras Liturgy*, although it acknowledges the seven gods of the world in one invocation, operates within a primarily tripartite cosmos. The magician leaves the realm of earth and enters into the realm of wandering stars and other astral powers.[12] The boundary of this realm is the doors of the sun, beyond which lie the hypercosmic depths that are the realm of the highest god. The magician does not actually enter this realm, but waits at the doors of the sun for the epiphany of the supreme father.[13] The description of the magician's ascent is clearly divided into three sections – leaving earth, traversing the heavens, looking into the hyperouranian realm – rather than into seven

---

[10] Macrobius, *In Somn.* 1.11.4–9, divides the cosmologies of his predecessors into three basic groups. First, those who make a single division between the divine realm, which includes the fixed stars, the planets and the moon, and the earthly realm. Second, those who divide the universe according to the four elements, with a sequence of earth, water, air, and fire leading up to the moon, followed by a double sequence from earth to fire and fire to earth in the spheres of the planets and the fixed stars. Third, those who make the division between the fixed stars as the heavenly realm and all the planetary spheres and the earth as the lower realm. For the relation of Macrobius' account to his Middle and Neoplatonic sources, see J. Flamant, *Macrobe et le Néo-Platonism Latin à la Fin du IVe Siècle* (EPRO 58; Leiden, 1977), 525–65.

[11] Cf. the attempts of Proclus and Psellus to synthesize the tripartite and varying sevenfold (Platonic and Chaldaean) cosmological structures of their sources: Proclus, *In Tim.* 257d–259e and Psellus, *PG* 122, 1149c.

[12] *PGM* IV 545–550: "You will see the divine order of the skies: the presiding gods rising into heaven and others setting. Now the course of the visible gods will appear through the disk of god, my father." All citations to the *PGM* are to K. Preisendanz and A. Henrichs, eds., *Papyri Graecae Magicae: Die griechischen Zauber papyri,* 2 vols., 2nd ed. (Stuttgart, 1973–4). All translations of the *PGM* are from H. D. Betz, ed., *The Greek Magical Papyri in Translation, Including the Demotic Spells* (Chicago, 1986).

[13] *PGM* IV 624–629: "Then open your eyes, and you will see the doors open and the world of the gods which is within the doors, so that from the pleasure and joy of the sight, your spirit runs ahead and ascends. So stand still and at once draw breath [*pneuma*] from the divine into yourself, while you look intently." The hypercosmic realm of the highest father, in both the Mithras Liturgy and the Chaldaean Oracles, is described as the depths; cf. *PGM* IV 664; *CO* frs. 18 and 183.

sections, as, for example, is the ascent through the planetary archons or the Mithraic ladder described in Origen's *Against Celsus*.[14] Albrecht Dieterich, in his attempts to make the *Mithras Liturgy* fit in with the Mithraic ladder in Origen, divided the ascent into seven scenes, but even Dieterich's arbitrary seven sections do not correspond well to the seven planetary spheres. Although Franz Cumont rejected Dieterich's connection of the *Mithras Liturgy* with the Mithraic ladder, scholars such as Reinhold Merkelbach still explain the cosmology of the *Mithras Liturgy* as an ascent through the seven planetary spheres to the realm beyond the fixed stars.[15] Such a reading distorts the cosmology underlying the spell.

The Descent of the Soul Through the Divisions of the Cosmos

The importance of the significant divisions in the cosmological system lies in the descent of the soul into the material world during the process of genesis. Although the moon sits at the boundary of heavenly and material worlds, in a system that emphasizes the seven planetary spheres, the moon may be less important in the process of the soul's descent. In each of the realms through which the soul descends on its way to incarnation, it picks up some element of its mortal composition. If the planetary spheres are the primary division, the soul acquires some characteristic of the planetary ruler as she passes through its sphere of influence. The clearest description of this process comes from Macrobius:

> The soul, having started on its downward movement from the intersection of the zodiac and the Milky Way to the successive spheres lying beneath, as it passes through these spheres, not only takes on the aforementioned envelopment in each sphere by approaching a luminous body, but also acquires each of the attributes which it will exercise later, as follows: in the sphere of Saturn it obtains reason and understanding, called *logistikon* and *theoretikon*; in Jupiter's sphere, the power to act, called *praktikon*; in Mars' sphere, a bold spirit or *thymikon*; in the Sun's sphere, sense perception and imagination, *aisthetikon* and *phantastikon*;

---

14 Origen, *Cels.* 4.30–31 for the celestial "customs;" 4.22 for the Mithraic ladder. Cf. Paul's passage through the seven heavens with extra realms beyond in the Nag Hammadi *Apoc. Paul* (NHC V 2) 20:5–21:28, 24:1–9. Another elaborate set of seven planetary celestial customs may be found in the Mandaean Ginza (*GL* III 51; Lidzbarski 578–582).

15 A. Dieterich, *Eine Mithrasliturgie*, 3rd ed. (Teubner, 1923), 89. Cf. F. Cumont, *Textes et monuments figurés relatifs aux mystère de Mithra* (Bruxelles, 1899), 41; R. Merkelbach, "Immortality Rituals in Late Antiquity," *Diogenes* 42 (1994): 85–109; Festugière, *Révélation*, 1:305 n. 3, who describes the sun as in its customary fourth sphere, thus presuming the sevenfold division.

in Venus' sphere, the impulse of passion, *epithymetikon*; in Mercury's sphere, the ability to speak and interpret, *hermeneutikon*; and in the sphere of the moon, the power of sowing and growing bodies, *phytikon*.[16]

Although the characteristics in Macrobius' account are positive attributes, useful to a productive life, the Hermetic account in the *Poimandres* describes the negative characteristics that the soul sheds at each planetary station as it makes its way out of incarnation:

> Poimandres said: "First, in releasing the material body you give the body itself over to alteration, and the form that you used to have vanishes. To the demon you give over your temperament, now inactive. The body's senses rise up and flow back to their particular sources, becoming separate parts and mingling again with the energies. And feeling and longing go on toward irrational nature. Thence the human being rushes up through the cosmic framework, at the first zone surrendering the energy of increase and decrease; at the second evil machination, a device now inactive; at the third the illusion of longing; at the fourth the ruler's arrogance, now freed of excess; at the fifth unholy presumption and daring recklessness; at the sixth the evil impulses that come from wealth, now inactive; and at the seventh zone the deceit that lies in ambush. And then, stripped of the effects of the cosmic framework, the human enters the region of the ogdoad; he has his own proper power, and along with the blessed he hymns the father."[17]

Even if a process of physical descent is not described, the idea of acquiring planetary influences on the way to incarnation is often part of the process of genesis. In the *Pistis Sophia*, for example, each of the planetary archons contributes to the binding of the soul with its counterfeit spirit, causing it to become bound up in forgetfulness and the passions of the world.[18]

If the seven planetary spheres are not the primary cosmological division, the entity entering incarnation may still be imagined as acquiring parts of its being in its descent.[19] Indeed, the basic idea that the soul acquires a body as it passes into the material realm depends on the division of the heavenly and earthly realms. In a more elaborate conception of the human being as composed of mind, soul, and body, Plutarch describes how the sun provides

[16] Macrobius, *In Somn.* 1.12, trans. Stahl. Cf. Proclus, *In Tim.* 3.355.13; Servius, *In Aen.* 11.51; and the Hermetic excerpt in Stobaeus 1.5.14 (= Stobaeus, *Herm.* XXXIX)

[17] *CH* I 24–26. Translated in B. Copenhaver, *Hermetica: The Greek Corpus Hermeticum and the Latin Asclepius in a New English Translation* (Cambridge, 1992), 5–6.

[18] *Pistis Sophia* 131; cf. *CH* XVI 13–16.

[19] Cf. Porphyry, *Sent.* 14.12.

the mind, which acquires a soul at the moon, and a body when it reaches the earth.[20]

The moon thus becomes the portal to genesis, dividing the mortal from the immortal world.[21] Porphyry relates that the moon is the gate of the descending soul: "The theologians make the 'gates' of souls the sun and the moon, the ascent taking place through the sun and the descent through the moon."[22] Whether the stages of the soul's descent are imagined as two, three, or seven, the moon provides the lowest boundary before the earth.[23] As the final station in the soul's descent, the moon completes the process of the soul's incarnation.

Nevertheless, the role of the moon may be more significant in cosmologies with fewer divisions or those in which the moon is directly responsible for a greater portion of the soul's accretions – the whole physical body instead of just the faculty of growth. Firmicus Maternus describes her role thus:

> The whole essence of the earthly body is governed by the power of the moon. Since she is located in the lower regions of the heavens, because of her nearness she has been allotted power over the earth and all the bodies animated by the breath of the Divine Mind. She maintains her course with infinite variety and runs with speed through all the signs, joining herself to all the planets. From different elements she builds up the human body, once conceived, and dissolves it again into its elements.[24]

In these cosmologies, the moon is seen as the mistress of genesis, the power responsible for the incarnation of souls into bodily form, and the stranger in Plutarch's myth urges the narrator, "among the visible gods, to honor the moon especially, since she is most powerful over life."[25]

---

[20] Plutarch, *Fac.* 943a, 944ef, 945c. Cf. *De genio* 591b.

[21] Cf., e.g., *CH* XI 7; Macrobius, *In Somn.* 1.11.6; Ocellus Lucanus II, §2. The idea can be traced back to Aristotle (e.g., *De generatione* 1.6 and *Cael.* 1.3), but is probably older. Plutarch refers to the moon as the turning point of genesis (*Gen. Socr.* 591c 9), ἡ καμπὴ τῆς γενεσέως. She also is the physical mediator between earth and heaven in *Fac.* 938ef.

[22] Porphyry, *Antr. nymph.* 18.

[23] Cf. Proclus, *In Tim.* 3.65.17–19, which describes the moon as nearest the earth, having the title [*logos*] of Physis and mother of genesis: τὴν μὲν σελήνην πρώτην εἰς τὸν περὶ γῆν τόπον τετάχθαι λέγων, ὡς φύσεως ἔχουσαν λόγον καὶ μητρὸς πρὸς τὴν γένεσιν. Cf. 3.69.9 as the cause of all genesis and corruption: μονὰς μὲν ἡ σελήνη, πάσης αἰτία γενεσέως καὶ φθορᾶς.

[24] Firmicus 4.1.6.

[25] Plutarch, *Fac.* 942c.

The Evaluation of Genesis

What, then, determines which face the moon as mistress of genesis will wear? The role of the moon in a cosmology is often dependent on the evaluation of the material world and the process of genesis that brings the soul into it. If the moon is identified as the intermediary principle responsible for the fate of souls in the material world, then the way in which mortal life is regarded colors the nature of that intermediary principle. In all the cosmologies of Late Antiquity, the material world was acknowledged to be inferior to the realm of the gods, so all cosmological systems had to grapple with the question of why human beings should live in an inferior condition. As the Hermetic *Asclepius* expresses it, "But what need was there, Trismegistus, that man should be placed in this material world? Why might he not have dwelt in the region where God is, and there enjoyed perfect happiness?"[26] There existed a whole spectrum of possible attitudes toward genesis, ranging from the most positive Platonic celebrations of the beauty of the cosmos to the most negative rejections of the world as the prison and torture chamber of the evil archons. An optimistic attitude to incarnation would correspond to a more positive image for the power responsible for genesis, whereas a more pessimistic attitude to genesis would correspond to a more negative image, a more terrifying face if that power were identified with the moon.[27]

As Plotinus points out in his treatment of the question, interpreters in the Platonic tradition must start with the different, even contradictory, accounts given by Plato in the dialogues. The contrast between the imagery of the prison in the *Phaedo* or the fall of the soul in the *Phaedrus* and the description of the cosmos as good and beautiful in the *Timaeus* leaves open a wide range of interpretations of Plato's feelings about the process of genesis.[28]

[26] *Asclepius* 1.7c. Cf. J. Dillon, "The Descent of the Soul in Middle Platonic and Gnostic Thought," in *Rediscovery of Gnosticism*, 1:357–64, here 357: "Perhaps the chief problem that faces any religious or philosophical system which postulates, as does the Platonic, a primary state or entity of pure and unitary perfection, is that of explaining how from such a first principle anything further could have arisen." Arnobius puts it more crudely (*Adv. haer.* 2.37).

[27] Festugière's terminology of "optimistic" and "pessimistic" should be applied with caution and precision to specific facets of a cosmology, e.g., the evaluation of genesis, rather than to the cosmology as a whole. Any logos for living within the cosmos will describe the obstacles to living a happy life as well as providing for ways to get around these obstacles.

[28] Plotinus 4.8.1. Cf. Plato, *Phaed.* 67d, 62b; *Crat.* 400c; *Resp.* 514a–517b, 619d; *Phaedr.* 246c–247c; *Tim.* 34b.

Both Alcinous in the *Didaskalikos* and Iamblichus in his work *On the Soul* survey the answers of various philosophers to the problem of genesis, examining both the purposes of the descents into genesis postulated and the types of descent (voluntary or involuntary).[29] This typology of descents proves useful for understanding the accounts in other cosmologies as well, as accounts with both positive and negative evaluations of genesis may differ in the purposes for which they imagine that souls become incarnate in the material world. A further distinction may be observed. Some of these descriptions of the descent of the soul describe the descent of individual souls as they come into incarnation, whereas other narratives describe the original descent of Soul [Psyche] as representative of the movement of all souls from the higher realms to the realms below. Nevertheless, the reasons, positive or negative, for which the soul may descend are similar in both types of accounts.

The positive reasons for the descent of the soul are primarily derived from the *Timaeus*. Some argue that the soul descends into genesis to fill out the cosmos, bringing into existence every possible form of entity, whereas others emphasize the benefits that the descent of divine influence brings to the lower realms.[30] These benefits of the upper realms may take the form of care and administration, or the soul's purpose may be described as the purification, perfection, and salvation of the lower realms.[31] A positive effect on the soul that is tested and improved by its trials in the material realm is even suggested by some.[32] Thus, the positive views of genesis all imagine that, in some way, the cosmos, or certain parts of it, is brought nearer perfection by the descent of the soul into matter.

The negative reasons for genesis and the descent of the soul may, following Iamblichus, be divided into voluntary and involuntary descents. In some cosmologies, the soul (or, more often, Soul or some other primary feminine

---

[29] Cf. Dillon, *Descent of the Soul*, and Festugière, *Révélation*, for overviews of these treatments and comparisons with some other contemporary cosmologies.

[30] Cf. Plato, *Tim.* 39e and 41b. Iamblichus in Stobaeus 1.49.39.44–53 ascribes to the Platonists of the school of Taurus the idea of completing the universe and unspecified others the idea of manifesting the divine. This idea of divine self-manifestation was also employed by Christian Platonists; see S. Elm in this volume.

[31] *Asclepius* 1.8; Iamblichus quoted in Stobaeus 1.49.40.22–24. See S. I. Johnston in this volume for an account of the reincarnation of angelic souls for the purpose of helping and perfecting those in the lower world in the system of the *Chaldaean Oracles*.

[32] Iamblichus quoted in Stobaeus, 1.49.40.24–27; cf. Plotinus 4.8.5.

entity) abandons the heavenly realm through curiosity or some other form of willfulness. In various cosmologies described as "gnostic," the lowest entity in the heavenly pleroma precipitates the fall of the soul into matter by her curiosity about the Highest Father or her desire to create on her own.[33] In its most extreme form, the soul is depicted as a helpless maiden, who leaves her father's house and is raped and reduced to a life of prostitution in the evil world of matter.[34] In other systems, however, the fall is involuntary, either as a punishment for the same kind of willful behavior or for other crimes.[35] To suffer for her willfulness or crimes, the soul is fettered within the body as a prison, a prison that is built up out of the material elements or planetary influences through which she has passed.[36] Often this term of imprisonment is pictured as the "death" of the soul, her descent to the underworld and the torments of Hades.[37] Bodily passions become the torments of the underworld, inflicted by the daimones under the control of the ruler of this realm, who is, therefore, often identified with Hekate or Persephone.[38] This shift of the realm of death from chthonic to cosmic often corresponds to the identification of these traditional underworld goddesses with a celestial power such as the moon.

---

[33] Sophia in the Valentinian cosmologies described by Irenaeus (*Adv. haer.* 1.2.2–4) and Hippolytus (*Haer.* 5.25). Cf. also, e.g., the *Letter of Peter to Philip*, NHC VIII 2.135:10–28; *CH* I 12–14; Plotinus 4.3.12. On the problems of the familiar term "gnosticism" as a category, see M. A. Williams, *Rethinking "Gnosticism": An Argument for Dismantling a Dubious Category* (Princeton, N. J., 1999).

[34] Cf. *The Exegesis on the Soul*, NHC II 6.127.18–129.5. Cf. M. A. Williams, "Variety in Gnostic Perspectives on Gender," in *Images of the Feminine in Gnosticism*, ed. K. King (Philadelphia, 1988), 15.

[35] Origen, *Cels.* 8.53; cf. the Hermetic *Kore Kosmou* in Stobaeus, *Herm.* 23.24 = Stobaeus, I 49.44. The idea of the soul becoming incarnate for crimes such as oath-breaking or bloodshed goes back to Empedocles.

[36] For example, *Kore Kosmou*, in which souls are imprisoned in bodies made from the residue of previous creation mixed with water, to which the planets contribute their influences (Stobaeus, *Herm.* 23.26–30). The planetary daimons in *CH* XVI 13–16 govern mortals through the instrument of the body and irrational parts of the soul. Heimarmene is the name given to the whole system of government. Cf. also the creation of the body in Zosimus, *On the Letter Omega* 9–11, in which the body is formed from the four elements as a prison for the spiritual man, Phos.

[37] The basic idea that life is death and death is life appears in many places from as early as Empedocles, but later cosmologies elaborate on the paradox.

[38] Macrobius, *In Somn.* 1.10.9–17. Cf. H. Lewy, *Chaldaean Oracles and Theurgy: Mysticism, Magic and Neoplatonism in the Later Roman Empire*, 2nd ed. by M. Tardieu (Paris, 1978), 282 and sources in n. 90.

Feminine Intermediary Principles

The Moon, however, is not the only entity imagined as mediating between the higher and lower realms in these cosmologies. The identity of the mediating power and the boundary that she mediates may vary widely in different systems. The nature of this entity, moreover, is dependent on the positive or negative evaluation of the material world and the process of genesis over that she presides. As John Dillon has pointed out, these mediating principles are most often conceived of as feminine, not just grammatically, but also in their function as generating lower principles.[39] In Pythagorean and Platonic systems, for example, the Indefinite Dyad is the principle that expands the entities of the universe from the original One to multiplicity.[40] Within the philosophical traditions (including the Peripatetics and Stoics) that drew on Plato's *Timaeus* for cosmological imagery, the Soul (Psyche) of the world and the Receptacle of Being are both feminine entities that serve a mediating function between the designs of the higher powers and the realms below.[41] These abstract entities were often given names or attributes in more mythical cosmologies, such as Sige [Silence] or the Barbelo in certain "gnostic" systems. In some cosmologies, the rational principle that orders the lower world is called Providence (Pronoia or even Prometheia) or personified as the wisdom [Sophia] of the highest.[42] The Barbelo is described as the Perfect Forethought [Pronoia] of the Father, as well as a womb for the entirety, all of the entities that come into being after her.[43] The Hekate of the *Chaldaean*

---

[39] J. Dillon, "Female Principles in Platonism," *Itaca* 1 (1986): 107–23, esp. 107–8; repr. in idem, *The Golden Chain: Studies in the Development of Platonism and Christianity* (Hampshire, 1990).

[40] Cf. Aristotle, *Metaph.* 1.6 (987b20); cf. Dillon, "Female Principles," 108–10.

[41] Receptacle of Being in Plato, *Tim.* 48d–53c. World Soul in *Tim.* 34b–36d; *Leg.* 896de (in which passage later interpreters understood a differentiation between good and evil world souls). Cf. Dillon, "Female Principles," 110–23.

[42] Providence: e.g., *Ap. John* 27.1–14; *Orig. World* 113.5–9. Sophia: e.g., Irenaeus, *Adv. haer.* 1.1–4; *Soph. Jes. Chr.* (NHC III 3); *Eugnostos* (NHC III 4); *Hyp. Arch.* (NHC III 4); *1 Apoc. Jas.* (NHC V 3). For further examples and discussions, see most notably M. A. Williams, "Higher Providence, Lower Providences, and Fate in Gnosticism and Middle Platonism," in *Neoplatonism and Gnosticism*, ed. R. T. Wallis (Studies in Neoplatonism; Albany, N. Y., 1992), 483–507; and I. P. Culianu, "Feminine versus Masculine: The Sophia Myth and the Origins of Feminism," in *Struggles of Gods: Papers of the Groningen Work Group for the Study of the History of Religions*, ed. H. G. Kippenberg (Berlin, 1984), 65–98.

[43] Sige: e.g., in Irenaeus, *Adv. haer.* 1.1.1; *Eugnostos* (NHC III.4) 88:5–10. Barbelo: e.g., in *Ap. John* 4.26–27. Attributes of the Barbelo in *Ap. John* 5.5.

Oracles is the fount and womb, the life-giving mother for the lower realms.[44] This maternal aspect, which is present even in Plato's Receptacle, recurs in many different feminine principles within these cosmological systems.[45]

This feminine intermediary serves both to connect the higher with the lower and to mark the separation between them.[46] On the one hand, she represents the force that conveys the divine, supreme qualities of the higher beings to the lower, as Julian describes Providence [Prometheia] setting in order, correcting, and changing to the better all the dregs of the universe.[47] However, this principle can also be seen as the separating wall that marks the boundary. In the *Chaldaean Oracles*, Hekate is described as a kind of membrane that keeps apart the fires above and below that long to join together.[48] Plutarch combines both functions in the moon, but divides them into two different traditional names: "the moon both takes and gives and joins together and divides asunder in virtue of her different powers, of which the one that joins together is called Ilithyia and that which divides asunder Artemis."[49]

This tendency to separate the two functions of the intermediary leads to the multiplication of such intermediary entities in various cosmologies. The higher and the lower aspects of the intermediary are distributed to different entities, as Plutarch does with Ilithyia and Artemis.[50] These feminine

---

[44] CO fr. 30: πηγὴ τῶν πηγῶν, μήτρα συνέχουσα τὰ πάντα. Cf. CO fr. 32: τὸν ζωογόνον...Ἑκάτης κόλπον.

[45] ὑποδοχή described as τιθήνη at Plato, *Tim.* 49a. Cf., e.g., Philo's Sophia (*Det.* 116–117) as trophos, tithenikomos, mother of all things in the world; Plutarch's Isis in *Is. Os.* 372e; even Alcinous, *Didask.* 10.

[46] Tardieu, *Gnose Valentinienne*, 217, points out that different systems emphasized either the connective or the disjunctive function.

[47] Julian, *Or.* V 170d; cf. *Or.* IV 150a.

[48] CO fr. 6 (= Simplicius, *In Aristotelis de Caelo* 2.1) quotes this line to describe Atlas as the dividing connector, but the line is also found in Damascius (2.13, 29). Tardieu points to the similarities with the Valentinian Horos, who likewise divides the realms (*Gnose Valentinienne*, 208). See also S. I. Johnston, *Hekate Soteira: A Study of Hekate's Roles in the Chaldean Oracles and Related Literature* (ACS 21; Atlanta, Ga., 1990), 53–61.

[49] Plutarch, *Fac.* 945c. Cf. *Quaest. conv.* 658–659. Ilithyia is the goddess of childbirth, whereas Artemis is the divider, based on an etymologizing of her name as ἀερότομις (the one who cuts through the air) or perhaps ἀρταμεῖν. Cf. Porphyry *apud* Eusebius, *Praep. ev.* 3.11; Macrobius, *Sat.* 1.15.20.

[50] G. C. Stead, "The Valentinian Myth of Sophia," *JTS* 11 (1969): 75–104, distinguishes five types of Sophia in the Valentinian tradition. Sophia is given various other names in this tradition, however, that are specific to the particular type, e.g., Sige or Barbelo as god's consort; Achamoth as the lower Sophia; Eleleth. As Tardieu, *Gnose Valentinienne*, 211, notes, in complex triadic systems such as Valentinian gnosticism or the *Chaldaean Oracles*, the lowest entity of the higher triad can become the first entity of the lower triad.

mediating principles may be imagined either as personifications of abstract principles or identified with divine figures from the mythic tradition. Moreover, depending on the complexity of the system, traditional names may be distributed among multiple entities, each of which has a somewhat different function, or a single entity may be identified with a variety of names from the tradition. Once again, the evaluation of genesis in the cosmology determines the nature of these entities. Systems with an optimistic view of genesis emphasize the higher principles that convey the benefits of the divine to the world below, whereas more pessimistic systems may multiply the entities that separate mortals from the divine and emphasize their absolute domination of human life.

The principle that animates and brings generation to the cosmos can be seen as the World Soul (Psyche) or as the animate cosmos itself personified as Nature (Physis).[51] The different aspects of this feminine intermediary principle may be seen as separate entities, with different names and functions. Thus, as Lewy notes,

> Plotinus distinguished two aspects of the World-Soul, of which the above remains without relation to the sensible world, while the lower, directing itself towards this world, gives form to all things in which and through which it moves [Plotinus, V 1.2]. This lower aspect of the World-Soul was called by Plotinus Physis [Plotinus, III 8.4 *et passim*].[52]

The *Chaldaean Oracles* identified the Cosmic Soul with Hekate, to whom they attributed positive, even maternal characteristics, whereas they warned against the lower aspect, Physis, described as the mistress of daimones and connected with Destiny (Heimarmene).[53] In other cosmologies, too, Physis appears not as a benevolent Mother Nature but as a dangerous and highly sexualized entity, seducing higher spiritual principles into her material embrace.[54]

---

[51] As Tardieu, *Gnose Valentinienne*, 214, notes, both the Valentinians and the Manichaeans imagined Psyche as an intermediary power.

[52] Lewy, *Chaldaean Oracles*, 356.

[53] Johnston, *Hekate Soteira*, 136–9. Lewy, *Chaldaean Oracles*, 98, instead of distinguishing their roles, argues that Hecate was identified with the whole range of positive and negative intermediaries.

[54] Cf. *Paraph. Shem* (NHC VII 1). In some texts, the entity Physis seems to be imagined as *physis*, which can mean the female genitalia. Cf. such uses of the term in *PGM* IV 2305, 2594, and 2655.

These powers are often also identified with traditional mythic goddesses. Pronoia, the forethought of the Father, is often connected with Athena, who sprang motherless from the head of Zeus. Not only is Athena traditionally associated with thought and wisdom, but her Delphic epithet Pronaia is easily read as Pronoia to strengthen the identification.[55] Xenocrates seems to have identified the Indefinite Dyad with the Mother of the Gods, whereas Julian made a distinction between higher and lower Pronoias, whom he identified with Cybele and Athena, respectively.[56]

The multiplication of these entities within a given cosmology is common. Several Pronoias may exist at different levels of the cosmos, or the aspect more concerned with the lower world, Physis, may herself be divided into several levels of powers, such as Anagke [Necessity], Tyche [Fortune], and Heimarmene [Destiny], that order the worlds below them.[57] A Hermetic text, for example, assigns Pronoia to the rational, Anagke to the irrational, and Heimarmene to the somatic, whereas the *De fato* attributed to Plutarch describes three Pronoias that relate to Heimarmene in different ways.[58] These powers of fate might be identified with the Moirae (Fates) of the poetic tradition, and the three Moirae – Clotho, Atropos, and Lachesis – were distributed at different levels of the cosmos by different thinkers.[59] Indeed, philosophers and theologians meditating on the problems of fate and free will devised a vast number of different configurations of the relations of Physis to Pronoia, Anagke, Tyche, Heimarmene, and the Moirae, but all these powers are feminine principles that impose order on the lower world from their intermediary position.[60] Although divine Providence is generally positively evaluated, Necessity, Fortune, the Fates, and Destiny are more often negatively viewed by the mortals whose fates they determine. In particular, the lowest level of fate (whether called Heimarmene, Anagke, or another name) becomes, in a

---

[55] Julian, *Or.* 4.149bd; Macrobius, *Sat.* 1.17.55, 70.

[56] Xenocrates, fr. 15, makes Zeus the Monad and Mother of the Gods the Dyad; cf. Rhea as Dyad in Philolaus, fr. 20a; Julian, *Or.* 5.166a.

[57] Williams, "Higher Providence," discusses the different Providences and Fates in Middle Platonism and Gnosticism.

[58] Stobaeus, *Herm.* 8.7 = Stobaeus, I 4.8; Pseudo-Plutarch, *De fato* 572f–574b.

[59] Many Platonic philosophers, drawing on Plato's myth in *Resp.* 617c, make use of these figures. Cf., e.g., Plutarch's *Fac.* 945c 3 with the Moirae on sun, moon, and earth.

[60] For example, Pseudo-Plutarch, *De fato* 568ef; Apuleius, *De Plat.* 1.12; Chalcidius, *In Tim.* c. 142, 144, 148; Nemesius, *De nat. hom.* 38, 753b; Plutarch, *De procreat. anim.* 27.1 1026b; Atticus *apud* Eusebius, *Praep. ev.* 15.12.1; Plotinus 3.1.7; Proclus, *In Remp.* II 356.28. Cf. the wide range of selections in Stobaeus 1.4 (*peri Anagke*) and 1.5 (*peri Heimarmene*). Cf. Williams, "Higher Providence," and Dillon, "Female Principles."

cosmology with a pessimistic view of genesis, the power responsible for keeping souls imprisoned and miserable in matter.[61]

Again, the Moon could be imagined in this intermediary role, but her nature as benevolent or malevolent was dependent on the outlook of the cosmology on genesis. Among the more optimistic Platonists, Plutarch calls the World Soul and Receptacle Isis, whom he also identifies with Athena.[62] Plutarch, however, also identifies the feminine intermediary power, whether as Athena Pronoia or as Isis, with the Moon, making the Moon a benevolent, even salvific deity. He further describes the Moon as Hekate and Kore, since Kore/Persephone, as mistress of the underworld, is often identified with the Moon who receives souls departing from incarnation after death.[63] Hekate, of course, is identified with the Moon in many sources, but her aspect is not always as positive as it is in Plutarch.[64] In addition to being identified with the goddesses of death, the Moon can also be seen as the fate that controls the lower realm. Clement relates that Orpheus described the white-robed Moirae [Fates] as the phases of the moon.[65]

The Moon then could be identified with a range of these feminine intermediary principles, but her nature would thus depend on whether she were identified with the lower powers such as Physis or Anagke, who imposed order on the material world and divided the material from the celestial, or with a higher power, such as Isis or Athena, whose function was more to unite the lower with the higher.[66] In the *Mithras Liturgy*, the moon is avoided in the ascent and, therefore, not described, but the magician begins by invoking Pronoia and Psyche, clearly positive aspects of the higher feminine

---

[61] Cf. the creation of Fate by the evil archons in *Ap. John* (BG 72.2–12; CG II 11–32) to trap humans in the world and prevent them from remembering the realms above. The planets (the five of Heimarmene and the sun and moon) give the soul a cup of Lethe in *Pistis Sophia* 3.131; cf. *CH* XVI 13–16; Stobaeus *Herm.* XII = Stobaeus, 1.5.20.

[62] Plutarch, *Is. Or.* 372e; cf. 354c.

[63] Athena in *Fac.* 922a, 938b; Isis in *Is. Or.* 372d; Hekate in *Fac.* 937f, *Def. orac.* 416e; Persephone/Kore in *Fac.* 942de. For Isis as Persephone, cf. *Is. Or.* 361e. Porphyry, too, identifies Athena as the moon (*apud* Eusebius, *Praep. ev.* 3.11, 113c).

[64] Cf. Epicharmus, fr. B54 (= Ennius in Varro, *De Ling. Lat.* v 68); Porphyry *Antr. nymph.* 18; Iamblichus in Lydus, *De mens.* 4.149; Martianus Capella 2.161–162.

[65] Cf. Moon as Fortuna in Macrobius, *Sat.* 1.19.17.

[66] The *Chaldaean Oracle*'s Hekate provides an interesting case in this regard, as so many of Hekate's traditional attributes are negative. Nevertheless, as Johnston points out, Hekate's traditional kourotrophic functions as well as her connections with magic make her a positive figure within the *Chaldaean Oracle*'s cosmology (*Hekate Soteira*). In other cosmologies, however, such as that found in *PGM* IV as a whole, Hekate may not have been so beneficent.

intermediary.[67] In the Great Paris Magical Papyrus from which the *Mithras Liturgy* comes, moreover, there are a number of spells with elaborate invocations to and descriptions of a lunar goddess, Selene, who is identified with a number of different goddesses and powers, particularly Hekate, Persephone, Physis, and Anagke.[68] Although the cosmology of the *Mithras Liturgy* itself and the cosmology of the redactor who compiled the papyrus are by no means identical, they seem to share certain basic ideas, among which is the evaluation of the moon as a dangerous power. As I have argued elsewhere, the redactor divided the papyrus into sections, one of which contained spells appealing to solar powers and one of which contained spells appealing to lunar powers.[69] The *Mithras Liturgy*, which avoids the power of the moon, is placed in the solar section with other spells that appeal to the sun as a beneficent power connected with special knowledge. By contrast, all the spells that appeal to the moon do so for purposes connected with sex, death, or the underworld.[70] Although the *Mithras Liturgy* shuns the power of the moon, other spells in the papyrus invoke Selene as Anagke, Hekate, Persephone, and a host of other epithets, emphasizing her malevolent nature:

> "Hail, Holy Light, ruler of Tartaros, who strike with rays; hail, Holy Beam, who whirl up out of darkness and subvert all things with aimless plans... awesome destiny is ever subject to you ... e'er with sorrows fresh, wolf-formed, denounced as infamous, destructive, quick, grim-eyed, shrill-screaming." Or: "You whose womb is decked out with the scales of creeping things, with pois'nous rows of serpents down the back, bound down your backs with horrifying chains ... O you who bring death and destruction, and who feast on hearts, flesh-eater, who devour those dead untimely, and you who make grief resound and spread madness."[71]

Some invocations seem particularly suited to the moon as the ruler of genesis and the material world:

---

[67] *PGM* IV 475. The contrast between positive and negative aspects of the feminine intermediary thus supports the MS reading Psyche instead of Dieterich's suggestion of Tyche for this first line of the *Mithras Liturgy*.

[68] Physis: *PGM* IV 2830, 2913; Anagke and Moira: 2855 (cf. 2242 where Anagke is subject to the moon); Hekate and Persephone/Kore: 2241–2358, 2441–2621, 2708–2784, 2708, and 2785–2890.

[69] Cf. Edmonds, "Seizure," for more on the divisions of the papyrus.

[70] *PGM* IV 2441–2621, 2708–2784, 2891–2942, 2943–2966 are all erotic charms; 2241–2358, 2622–2707, 2785–2890 are designed to cause the goddess to wreak violent harm on someone.

[71] *PGM* IV 2241–2245, 2246, 2276–2278, 2802–2206, 2865–2869.

Mistress of night and chthonic realms, holy, black-clad, 'round whom the star-traversing nature of the world revolves whene'er you wax too great. You have established every worldly thing, for you engendered everything on earth and from the sea and every race in turn of winged birds who seek their nests again, Mother of all.[72]

The Moon shows her terrifying face as a dangerous goddess whose violence must be carefully channeled against someone else, a goddess whose control over sex and death reveals the darker aspects of the mistress of genesis.

Living in the World

The different cosmologies here surveyed offer a variety of solutions for interacting with the power that controls the material world, whether that power is imagined as an abstract astrological fate or a hostile and dangerous goddess. Vettius Valens, in keeping with Stoic theories of astrological fate, proclaimed, "No one is free; all are slaves of Destiny [Heimarmene]," whereas Manilius advised mortals to forget their worries in the knowledge that Fate predetermines all things.[73] The impersonal nature of astrological fate could be a reassuring idea in contrast to the idea of hostile goddess and her demonic cohorts, actively working for the detriment of mankind.

Philosophers who rejected, with Plato, the idea that gods could be moved by prayers, counseled that one should "submit to fate without unseemly wrangle" rather than rail against the situation,[74] but the majority of folk were often unwilling simply to accept their lot in life without trying to improve it in some way. Traditional Graeco–Roman religion would suggest that the divine powers that rule the world, however they are identified, be supplicated with prayers and sacrifices to win their favor. The so-called "Orphic Hymns" prescribe prayers and sacrifices not only for traditional deities such as Zeus, Dionysos, and Poseidon, but also for Tyche and Physis, who is identified variously as Fate [Aisa] and Life [Zoe] and Pronoia.[75] Many people turned to the various mystery cults available in order to get special treatment from the gods, but the cults of different deities made different claims. The salvific

---

[72] *PGM* IV 2550–2556.

[73] Vettius Valens 5.9; Manilius, *Astronomica* 4.12–16.

[74] Cf. Plotinus' comparison of two men, one who accepts his mortal life and the other who cries out against it (2.9.18).

[75] *Orphic Hymn* 10 to Physis; cf. 72 to Tyche. Others claim that the stars that control fate can be swayed by prayer, e.g., Nemesius 36.745.

deity in a mystery cult was often precisely the higher and beneficent aspect of the feminine intermediary power, whose mediation of the upper and lower worlds brought divine help to the world below. Isis, in Apuleius, plays this role, saving her worshipper from his sufferings at the hands of Fortuna, the higher intermediary trumping the powers of the lower.[76] In some of the "gnostic" tales, Sophia, or a similar figure, not only brings about the fall of soul into matter, but is also responsible for the soul's salvation, transmitting the understanding of the higher realms to humans trapped in the material world.[77]

However, others turned not to a feminine intermediary power, but to a masculine power from a higher level of the cosmic hierarchy. The Logos or Christ is sometimes substituted for Sophia as the savior in "gnostic" stories, and in other sources Christ brings salvation from the domination of astrological fate in particular.[78] In the *Pistis Sophia*, Christ ingeniously reverses the rotation of the planetary and astral spheres for part of the year, thus disrupting all the calculations of the astrologers and freeing humans from the domination of the planetary archons.[79] Christ was not the only such savior; Osiris and Serapis were seen by some as Egyptian alternatives superior even to Isis,[80] whereas Attis and Mithras were among the other figures to whom people turned for rescue from the domination of the rulers of the material world.[81]

---

[76] Apuleius, *Metam.* 11.15, in which Isis identifies herself not only with a number of traditional mythic deities but also with such entities as Pronoia. Cf. the whole genre of Isis aretalogies (texts collected in M. Totti, *Ausgewahlte Texte der Isis-und Sarapis-Religion* [Hildesheim, 1985]). Isis also plays a salvific role in the *Kore Kosmou* (Stobaeus, *Herm.* XXIII 64–69 = Stobaeus, I 44.492–532). Julian's identification of the higher Providence with Magna Mater (*Or.* 5.166a) links the savior cult with the philosophical descriptions of the feminine intermediary power. Perhaps some such idea underlies Plotinus' reference to gnostics who conjure the world soul (2.9.14).

[77] Cf., e.g., the discussion in Williams, "Higher Providence," 486, of the role of Barbelo/Pronoia, the higher feminine entity, in the recensions of *Ap. John.*

[78] Tatian, *ad Graecos* 10; John Chrysostom, *Homily* VI on Matthew 1; Clement of Alexandria, *Exc.* 74, 78.

[79] *Pist. Soph.* 1.18; cf. *Trim. Prot.* (NHC XIII 1) 43.13–26.

[80] Julian identifies Serapis with the Sun as the power that frees mortals from genesis (4.136b), and a papyrus fragment preserves Serapis' promise to a worshipper to alter his fate (D. L. Page, *Select Papyri* [Cambridge, Mass., 1962], 3:426); cf. this and other examples cited in R. Merkelbach and M. Totti, *Abrasax: ausgewählte Papyri religiösen und magischen Inhalts* (Opladen, 1990), 80–1. In the *Kore Kosmou* (Stobaeus, *Herm.* XXIII 64–69 = Stobaeus, I 44.492–532), Osiris is listed along with Isis as a deity sent to save mortals in incarnation. Note that Apuleius' Lucius must be initiated into the mysteries of Osiris even after he turns to Isis.

[81] Julian, *Or.* 5.162a, 165b, retells the myth of Attis.

Not only did mystery groups offer special connections with the gods, but individual practitioners performed rites that they claimed would alter adverse fate or help the soul free itself from the dominion of the rulers of this world. Magicians devised rituals for contact with the highest powers of the universe that would allow the magicians not only to change their fate but to perform a whole range of wonders in the material world, from resurrecting the dead to crossing the Nile on a crocodile.[82] Other spells, however, rather than appealing to a power beyond the cosmos, invoke the powers that govern this world, the astrological rulers of the day and hour, the planets and constellations, and even the mistress of genesis herself, Heimarmene, Physis, or Anagke.[83] The *Chaldaean Oracles* provided divine revelations from Hekate and other deities, whereas Platonic philosophers such as Iamblichus and Proclus practiced theurgy to help their spirits ascend free from mortal constraints.[84] Different cosmological perspectives permitted different ways of coping with the problems of the material world and living beneath the dominion of the mistress of genesis.

Conclusion

The magician in the *Mithras Liturgy* then must, as does the theurgist of the *Chaldaean Oracles*, avoid the face of the moon because the moon is imagined as a malevolent and dangerous mistress of genesis, allied, if not wholly identified, with the bitter and pressing Necessity the magician hopes to escape – if only for a while. By contrast, the benevolent face of the moon that shines in Plutarch is part of a cosmological system with an optimistic outlook on genesis, which identifies the feminine intermediary principle with beneficent deities like Athena and Isis and emphasizes her role as the one who connects the lower realms with the upper. In the *Mithras Liturgy*, these benevolent,

---

[82] Cf. the list of magic works in *PGM* XIII 235–340. Arnobius (2.13, 62) attacks those who promise through magic rites to climb to heaven or free themselves from death. Cf. Porphyry, *Philos. orac. apud* Eusebius, *Praep. ev.* 4.4.

[83] Rulers of the day, etc. Cf., e.g., *PGM* II 8–79; XIII 30, 58, 118, 230, 430; Psellus, *Quaenam sunt Graecorum opiniones de daemonibus* c. 7 (= J. Bidez and F. Cumont, *Les Mages Hellénisés* [Paris, 1938], 2:172.2). Heimarmene is seldom mentioned in the *PGM* (only *PGM* I 216 and XIII 635), but Anagke is often invoked (*PGM* III 120; IV 1175, 1399, 1456, 2056, 2062, 2196, 2241, 2855; VII 236, 302, 475; VIII 94–95; IX 11; XI 64; XV 10, 13; XIXa 11; XXXVI 342, 346; CI 1).

[84] Tardieu, *Gnose Valentinienne*, 223, draws the parallel between the theurgical and philosophic practices and the rituals of other groups, such as baptism, in escaping the domination of the mistress of genesis and fate.

higher aspects are perhaps mentioned as Pronoia and Psyche, but they play no role in the magician's ascent. The magician is enabled to rise out of the earthly sphere through the pneumatic rays of Mithras Helios, the salvific light that streams from the hypercosmic sun through the cosmic sun and down into the material world.[85] The feminine intermediary principle plays a more active role in the theurgy of the *Chaldaean Oracles*, as Hekate seems to be the primary deity invoked for help in the ascension rituals.[86] Nevertheless, the Chaldaean theurgist must always avoid Physis, the lower aspect of the World Soul, who may appear with her daimon dogs to drag the theurgist back into the "mortal covering of bitter matter," as the body is described.[87]

Magic, however, is a more flexible system for dealing with the world than any philosophical system. A magician who makes use of other spells in the Great Paris Magical Papyrus may at times find a way to interact with the power he avoids in the *Mithras Liturgy*. The magician invokes the moon to help him in a violent act, either stirring up her anger against someone and inciting her to violent revenge, or bringing to fruition a violent "love charm" in which the victim is compelled to go immediately to the magician or suffer excruciating torments.[88] These spells harness the dangerous power of the malevolent mistress of genesis, often involving an element of coercion of the hostile goddess to turn her power against another. There is, however, an element of danger should the magician himself become the target of her

---

[85] *PGM* IV 539–541. On the technique of inhaling the sun rays to ascend, see R. G. Edmonds, "Did the Mithraists Inhale? – A Technique for Theurgic Ascent in the *Mithras Liturgy*, the *Chaldaean Oracles*, and Some Mithraic Frescoes," *Ancient World* 32 (2000): 10–24; S. I. Johnston, "Rising to the Occasion: Theurgical Ascent in its Cultural Milieu," in *Envisioning Magic: A Princeton Seminar and Symposium*, ed. P. Schäfer and H. G. Kippenberg (SHR 75; Leiden, 1997), 165–94, esp. 181–3; Lewy, *Chaldaean Oracles*, 184–5, 209. Cf. Julian, *Or.* 5.172cd; *CO* 123, 124; *CH* XVI 16.

[86] Johnston, *Hekate Soteira*.

[87] *CO* 129. Psellus, *PG* 122, 1137 a1–10, describes the epiphany of Physis as preceded by deceptive daimones. Synesius, *Hymn* 5 (2) 52–53, describes Physis as mother of daimones. The nature of the moon herself is unclear in the *Chaldaean Oracles*, as she is nowhere in the extant fragments identified directly either with Hekate or with Physis. Lewy, *Chaldaean Oracles*, 144, suggested that the moon should be seen as the Material Teletarch, corresponding to the Intellectual and Intelligible Suns in the higher realms, but he admits that she is never so identified; cf. Majercik, *Chaldean Oracles*, 12 and 17. Although parallels with Plutarch and Julian make such an identification seem plausible, Proclus' identification of the image of Physis as the moon, along with the warnings against invoking or looking on the image of Physis, seems to suggest that the moon was identified instead with Physis.

[88] Cf. the so-called "slander spells" at *PGM* IV 2241–2358, 2441–2621, 2622–2707; charms of attraction at 1390–1495, 2441–2621, 2708–2784, 2943–2966. On these *agoge* spells, see C. A. Faraone, *Ancient Greek Love Magic* (Cambridge, Mass., 1999), 41, 133–46.

wrath. As one spell notes, "the goddess is accustomed to make airborne those who perform this rite unprotected by a charm and to hurl them from aloft down to the ground."[89]

Both the *Mithras Liturgy* and the spells to the moon in the Great Paris Magical Papyrus assume a cosmological system in which the moon, as the feminine principle that governs the boundary of the material world, is a dangerous and malevolent goddess. Although the moon may show another face in more optimistic cosmologies, such as those of Julian or Plutarch, the attitudes toward genesis and the material world that underlie the spells in the Great Paris Magical Papyrus are more pessimistic, showing a world presided over by the terrifying face of the moon.

[89] *PGM* IV 2507–2509; cf. 2627.

15

"O Paradoxical Fusion!": Gregory of Nazianzus on Baptism and Cosmology (*Orations* 38–40)

Susanna Elm

O new mixture! O paradoxical fusion!
> (Gregory of Nazianzus, *On the Nativity* 38.13)[1]

"I attest before God and the elected angels" that you will be baptized with this faith. If one has written in you something other than my sermon has set out, come here, so what has been written in you will be modified. I am not without talent to write that into you; I write what has been written into me.
> (Gregory of Nazianzus, *On Baptism* 40.44)

In thinking about the theme of this volume, it has been my principal interest to investigate how men who belonged to the Greek-speaking elites of the later Roman Empire, such as Gregory of Nazianzus, understood and expressed notions of "heavenly realms and earthly realities." Specifically, how did Gregory of Nazianzus conceptualize instances in which the two realms met, and how did he perceive his role in bringing about such "meetings"? The answer to these questions points to a larger issue: How did Gregory and others like him understand salvation and the mechanisms by which it was achieved? For Gregory, a proper understanding of the manner in which the imagined realms of the (Neo-)Platonic cosmic spheres could intersect with the material realm below them was essential for attaining salvation. Each individual could actualize this process of salvation within himself or herself, but only by fully comprehending the mystery exemplified in the unprecedented merging of the two realms in the Incarnation. Gregory, therefore, viewed the meeting of the heavenly and the material as a specific form of

[1] C. Moreschini, ed., *Grégoire de Nazianze: Discours 38–41*, trans. P. Gallay (SC 358; Paris, 1990). I would like to thank Peter Brown, Michael Maas, and Elaine Pagels for their many insights; Anthony Grafton for making my stay at the Davis Center and, thus, this research not only possible, but a great pleasure; and Peter Schäfer for inviting me to participate in the conference at which all these ideas were first discussed.

change: namely, as a change of cosmological affiliation. Salvation was predicated on the shift from one set of "imagined realms" to another.

Gregory's specific articulation of this shift emerged within the context of the most far-reaching intellectual project of his day: the integration of the account of creation in Genesis into a variety of Platonic and Neoplatonic cosmological traditions, which both permitted the identification of the divine sphere with the heavenly realm and produced differing ways of conceptualizing the individual and his participation in this cosmological drama. This process of adapting Scripture to existing cosmologies is well known as the battle between orthodoxy and heresy and, in particular, the controversies regarding the nature of the Trinity. As a result, Gregory's understanding of the meeting of "heaven and earth," his own role in this process of salvation, and the nature of the change developed in response to the fierce disputes regarding the meaning of baptism in late fourth-century Constantinople. These debates were, in turn, part and parcel of a conflict of even longer *durée*, namely that over whether the divine, or heavenly and "hypercosmic," realm could in fact interact with the material one and, if so, how. The various solutions to this problem, which centered on the possibility of the soul's descent into an incarnate body and, consequently, the degree to which a material entity such as a body could intermingle with an immaterial essence such as a soul, were thus also profoundly shaped by contemporary debates concerning the nature and efficacy of theurgy.[2]

The second citation in the opening epigrams, drawn from Gregory's sermon *On Baptism* (*Oration* 40), contains three of the notions just discussed: first, the heavenly realms (i.e., "God and the elected angels"); second, baptism; and, third, change or modification. However, this sentence also introduces a fourth and perhaps even more surprising notion, namely that of inscribing: "If one has written in you something other than my sermon has set out, come here, so what has been written in you will be modified." We are used to considering each of these notions separately. Heaven and earth, baptism, conversion, modification, and inscription can all be defined independently of each other, but here Gregory combined all of them in one sermon, in fact, in a single sentence. This chapter examines how Gregory of Nazianzus

---

[2] Also see the chapters by R. Edmonds, S. I. Johnston, and C. Faraone in this volume. As Johnston's chapter, e.g., makes clear, the idea that the material body could achieve association with the "divine" was antithetical to many (see her discussion of the aspiration to have one's soul "flying out of the heavy cycle"). Hence, Gregory's insistence on the uniqueness of the mixture, on which see the subsequent discussion.

fit these concepts together and, more important, why he did so precisely in this manner. In short, what did Gregory mean by "writing into you" and "modifying what has been written" in the context of baptism, and how did he relate both concepts to cosmology? And to what earthly realities did all of the preceding relate?

Gregory of Nazianzus' *Orations* 38, 39, and 40 form a set of three interrelated sermons, which he held on and around the Feast of the Nativity in 380/381.[3] At that time, Gregory had just been ordained bishop of Constantinople, essentially by imperial fiat and against intense competition by a number of different contenders, many of whom subscribed to an understanding of the Trinity polemically known as "Arianism."[4] *Orations* 39 and 40 were held on consecutive days, probably January 5 and 6, 381, and take their cue from Christ's baptism, whereas *Oration* 38, celebrating the Theophany or birth of Christ as well as the adoration of the Magi, was perhaps held as early as December 25, 380. Its central theme is Christ's Incarnation.[5]

Gregory's *Oration* 40, in particular, has frequently been discussed, although "mined" is perhaps the more appropriate expression. With few exceptions – for example, that of Claudio Moreschini – scholars have studied *Oration* 40 to gain insights into specific liturgical questions, such as the precise order in which baptism was celebrated in the Constantinopolitan church in the 380s[6]; whether or not confirmation and baptism were one or two separate

[3] The date is controversial; earlier scholarship favored 379/380 C.E., i.e., before Gregory's nomination as bishop, but the more recent consensus is 380/381; Moreschini, *Discours 38–41*, 16–22.

[4] J. F. Matthews, *Western Aristocracies and Imperial Court, A.D. 364–425* (Oxford, 1975), 120–4; N. McLynn, "Theodosius, Spain, and the Nicene Faith," in *Congreso Internacional La Hispania di Teodosio* (Segovia, 1997), 1:171–78; S. Elm, "A Programmatic Life: Gregory of Nazianzus' Orations 42 and 43 and the Constantinopolitan Elites," *Arethusa* 33 (2000): 411–27.

[5] By 380, two separate days of celebration surrounding Christ's birth appear to have been common in Constantinople: The earlier day was dedicated to the birth of Christ and the adoration of the Magi (perhaps celebrated on December 25) as evoked in Gregory's Or. 38. The second day was dedicated to Christ's epiphany and baptism, celebrated on January 6 and the occasion for Or. 39 and 40; Moreschini, *Discours 38–41*, 11–17; J. Mossay, *Les fêtes de Noël et d'Épiphanie d'après les sources littéraires cappadociennes du IVᵉ siècle* (Louvain, 1965), 34; J. Bernardi, *La prédication des pères cappadociens* (Paris, 1968), 205; H. Usener, *Das Weihnachtsfest* (Religionsgeschichtliche Untersuchungen 1; Bonn, 1911), 260–9.

[6] G. W. H. Lampe, *The Seal of the Spirit: A Study in the Doctrine of Baptism and Confirmation in the New Testament and the Fathers* (London, 1967); V. Saxer, *Les rites de l'initiation chrétienne du IIe au VIe siècle: Esquisse historique et signification d'après leurs principaux témoins* (Spoleto, 1988), 297–332.

ceremonies; what precise developments regarding penitential regulations might be gleaned from Gregory[7]; how catechumens were instructed[8]; to what degree Gregory's descriptions are representative of Syrian or Cappadocian practices; and whether or not the Roman festival calendar had already been adopted in Constantinople.[9]

Although much can and should be said about these and other questions raised by these three orations, I do not do so in this context. Instead, I consider the three sermons as a unit in order to elucidate Gregory's understanding of "inscriptions," "baptism," "change," and their relation to heavenly and earthly spheres. I argue that Gregory uses the vocabulary of "inscriptions" (e.g., marking, impressing, writing into; χαρακτήρ, σφραγίς, τύπος, γράμματα, πλάκαι, σκιαγράφοι) to describe a historically defined moment of change, which forms part of and initiates a lifelong process of transformation. Both, the moment and the process, are expressed through the vocabulary of baptism combined with the concept of *metanoia*, "change of heart and mind," frequently translated as "conversion" (and/or as "penitence").[10]

The red thread that holds baptism, change, inscriptions, heaven, and earth together is Gregory's understanding and use of illumination. In classic Platonic manner, illumination in Gregory's writing is "code" for cosmology. Illumination is, in essence, God. Baptism as illumination actualizes and makes personal for each individual two singular yet eternal cosmological events. The paradoxical fusion of which Gregory speaks (παραδόξα κρᾶσις) is the meeting of two utterly incommensurable essences: that of the unknown

---

[7] Representative is, for example, the study by H. M. Riley, *Christian Initiation: A Comparative Study of the Interpretation of the Baptismal Liturgy in the Mystagogical Writings of Cyril of Jerusalem, John Chrysostom, Theodore of Mopsuestia, and Ambrose of Milan* (Washington, D.C., 1974), who, however, omits Gregory entirely. For some of the historiographic reasons why so many authors on the subject of baptism omit Gregory' *Oration* 40 altogether, see Elm, "Programmatic Life," 411–15.

[8] E. Ferguson, ed., *Conversion, Catechumenate, and Baptism in the Early Church* (New York, 1993); M. Dujarier, *A History of the Catechumenate: The First Six Centuries*, trans. E. Haasl (New York, 1979).

[9] See the overview and critical remarks of P. F. Bradshaw, *The Search for the Origins of Christian Worship: Sources and Methods for the Study of Early Liturgy* (New York, 1992), 161–74, 202–4. G. Winkler, *Das armenische Initiationsrituale: Entwicklungsgeschichtliche und liturgievergleichende Untersuchungen der Quellen des 3. bis 10. Jahrhunderts* (OrChrAn 217; Rome, 1982), 100–75.

[10] These concepts are developed in greater detail in S. Elm, "Marking the Self in Late Antiquity: Inscriptions, Baptism, and the Conversion of Mimes," in *Stigmata*, ed. B. Menken and B. Vinken (forthcoming).

realm of the immaterial, intelligible, unchanging, illuminated, and divine with that of the material or human, which is capable of change.[11] According to Gregory, this "paradoxical fusion" occurred twice: once when God, or the supreme Light and Goodness, decided to create the sensible world and man, and a second time, when the *Logos* became flesh, the divine human, to save man from the consequences of his disobedience.

Baptism is the actualization of that formation of "one unique being formed out of two opposites" (*Or.* 38.13) in each human, the marker aligning the individual with this cosmological process. That is, baptism, too, is both a one-time historic event as well as an ongoing process intended to restore man to his original dignity, to his prelapsarian state as Adam. The act of inscription, of marking, symbolizes and makes vivid a similar tension that is inherent in the fusion of two incommensurable notions, that of a specific moment that is at the same time *à la longue durée*. For Gregory, Christ's Incarnation is thus the model event through which the underlying Platonic structure is personalized and transcended. In this concept, heaven is a state rather than a place, a temporal rather than geographic realm; in fact, Gregory spends almost no time on any elaboration, allegorical or otherwise, of the notion of Paradise (38.12). Inscription is an essential part of the entire baptismal ritual. It represents its culmination, thereby initiating the lifelong process of illumination and purification.

The notion of inscribing is such a central component of baptism for Gregory because at the time he wrote his orations the precise meaning of the baptismal formula had been debated for more than seventy years: What must one understand by the words "in the name of the Father, the Son, and the Holy Spirit" (*Or.* 40.45)? Each variation in the precise interpretation of these words, their meaning, and their resulting relation to each other corresponded to a different understanding of the underlying cosmology, which in turn prompted different views of what precisely baptism actualized: Christ's Incarnation, his resurrection, or his death? Hence, Gregory's insistence that the slate be cleaned first so that the correct wording could be written into each soul – a vital act precisely because Gregory's interpretation of baptism was neither the only nor the most favored one in Constantinople at that time.

---

[11] Κρᾶσις and μίξις are originally Stoic notions; Origen, *Princ.* 2.6.3. H. Althaus, *Die Heilslehre des heiligen Gregors von Nazianz* (Münster, 1972), 57–60.

However, before plunging more deeply into Gregory's texts describing baptism and illumination – that is, the fusion of heaven and earth – and before attempting to reconstruct some of the context that apparently prompted him to "divulge as much about our mysteries as is not forbidden to the ears of the many" (*Or.* 40.45), I would like to step back for a moment and briefly discuss notions of "conversion" and "inscriptions" and their relevance to Gregory's orations on baptism.

Conversions and Inscriptions

"By conversion we mean the reorientation of the soul of an individual, his deliberate turning from indifference or from an earlier form of piety to another, a turning which implies a consciousness that a great change is involved, that the old was wrong and the new is right."[12] Arthur Darby Nock's classic definition, formulated in 1933, is still the paradigmatic understanding of "conversion." However, the recent studies by Peter Brown, Paula Fredriksen, and Karl Morrison of one of the classic narratives of "conversion," Augustine's *Confessions*, have challenged at least one component part of "conversion" implicit in Nock's definition: that of a "turning point," a decisive moment of dramatic change from A to B.[13] Morrison, for example, stressed instead that Augustine used the term *conversion* sparingly in his *Confessions* "to denote a sequence of action and response... [at times] stretched out over years," arguing that for Augustine conversion was "the unfolding of a supernatural process, initiated and sustained by God... and distinct from its formal signs... (which include baptism)."[14]

Much the same is true for Gregory of Nazianzus. Here, too, the most important aspect of changing one's affiliation from one "imagined realm" to another one is that of process. But Gregory signals the historical moment of change in "religious" status through a different choice of vocabulary, a

---

[12] A. D. Nock, *Conversion: The Old and the New Religion from Alexander the Great to Augustine of Hippo* (London, 1933), 7 and 2–3.

[13] P. Fredriksen, "Paul and Augustine: Conversion Narratives, Orthodox Traditions, and the Retrospective Self," *JTS* 37 (1986): 3–34; K. F. Morrison, *Understanding Conversion* (Charlottesville, Va., 1992); P. Brown, "Conversion and Christianization in Late Antiquity: The Case of Augustine," in *The World of Late Antiquity: The Challenge of New Historiography*, ed. R. Lim and C. Straw (Berkeley, Calif., forthcoming).

[14] K. F. Morrison, *Conversion and Text: The Cases of Augustine of Hippo, Herman-Judah, and Constantine Tsatsos* (Charlottesville, Va., 1992), viii–x.

different set of signifiers: It is not the "conversion" described in the Lukan and Augustinian narratives as "flash of insight"[15] but an inscription.[16] This might seem strange, as inscriptions by their very nature appear to represent the opposite of change: fixation, *status quo*, stability. However, in Gregory's case, the act of writing does precisely what he needs it to do.[17] Inscriptions do indeed mark a historic moment – that is, the moment of writing something into stone, onto a tablet, into a forehead or a soul; yet, the moment carries within it the intention of making the inscribed last, ideally for eternity.[18] Hence, the many inscriptions that inform their readers that they, the inscriptions, will still be there when the reader is long gone or the many attempts by the authors of inscriptions to regulate their posterity – for example, by cursing those who might want to alter the inscribed.[19] For everyone also knew that inscriptions, although meant to last, could be changed. Simply the erasure of a small part could alter the content profoundly.[20] Equally to the point, although a clean slate was preferable, a palimpsest could also do. A modified writing could be as effective as one that had been carved into a clean surface. In a different register, the inscription of a person into the "roll of citizens" immediately changed one's social status and, as a result, one's entire way of life. Thus, the vocabulary of inscribing, writing into, and impressing conveyed Gregory's message: It marked a moment with

---

[15] "Not in rioting and drunkenness, not in chambering and wantonness, not in contention and envy; but put ye on the Lord Jesus Christ....I had no wish to read any further, and no need. For in that instance, with the very ending of the sentence, it was as though a light of utter confidence shone in all my heart, and all the darkness of uncertainty vanished away" (*Conf.* 8.12.29). P. Brown, *Augustine of Hippo: A Biography* (Berkeley, Calif., 1967), 113, already described Augustine's conversion as "an astonishingly tranquil process," a crisis of will rather than a flash of insight. See now the 2000 edition with a new epilogue.

[16] Gregory does use very little Pauline baptismal language; for potential reasons, see E. Pagels, "Ritual in the *Gospel of Phillip*," in *The Nag Hammadi Library after Fifty Years: Proceedings of the 1995 Society of Biblical Literature Commemoration*, ed. J. D. Turner and A. McGuire (Nag Hammadi and Manichaean Studies 44; Leiden, 1997), 280–91.

[17] Morrison, *Understanding Conversion*, 1–27, on conversion and metaphor.

[18] For other related aspects of inscriptions, see S. Elm, "'Sklave Gottes' – *Stigmata*, Bischöfe, und anti-häretische Propaganda im vierten Jahrhundert n.C.," *Historische Anthropologie* 8 (1999): 415–63.

[19] Cf. e.g., J. Ma, "The Epigraphy of Hellenistic Asia Minor," *AJA* 104 (2000): 95–121.

[20] In addition to all kinds of erasures on inscriptions (in stone), wax tablets and other writing tablets used in a classroom context also come to mind; Gregory specifically evokes a teaching context in *Or.* 40.45. A. C. Dionisotti, "From Ausonius' Schooldays? A Schoolbook and Its Relations," *JRS* 72 (1982): 83–125; R. A. Kaster, *Guardians of Language: The Grammarian and Society in Late Antiquity* (The Transformation of the Classical Heritage 11; Berkeley, Calif., 1988), 77–8.

long-term consequences. And, as is shown in the following section, so did Christ's Incarnation.

Incarnation

"Christ is born, give praise, Christ has come from the heavens, go out to meet him, Christ is on earth, lift yourselves upward" – thus, Gregory's opening, and the theme of *Oration* 38. The divine has become human, the Word flesh, and this event required the most exalted celebration. Such a celebration could not replicate the "material feast" as performed by "the Greeks" – instead, the celebration of the Word required words, and naturally, the most appropriately festive words were those of Gregory (38.4–6).

Because the sermon was about the *Logos*, it was, according to Gregory, about God. Indeed, most of the remaining *Oration* 38 is devoted, first, to Gregory's interpretation of the nature of the divinity (i.e., *theologia*) and, second and in even greater detail, to the interaction of the divine with its opposite, the cosmos and man (i.e., *oikonomia*). The lion's share of *Oration 38* is devoted to the unfolding and expansion of the divine and, most important, to the mystery of its mixture with things "entirely alien to its nature" (38.10). Thus Gregory opens the entire cycle of his three orations on the nativity, illumination, and baptism with his exposition and exegesis of Plato's cosmology through Genesis and Luke's account of the nativity.[21]

Gregory begins by stating that "God is" – that is, that "he possesses being without beginning and end, like an ocean of being" (38.7).[22] God is timeless, a being without beginning and end, "without limit and hence difficult to contemplate." This aspect of the divine alone is easy to grasp for humans: namely, that God is timeless and limitless. Although this may lead one to believe that God's nature is, therefore, simple (ἁπλῆς), this is not so. According to Gregory, neither simplicity nor composition completely comprise the nature of the divine. Rather, Gregory asserts that by "saying God, I intend to say Father, Son, and Holy Spirit" (38.8–9). Although the divinity does not extend beyond those three to form more divine persons, it is neither constricted into a monad or a construct of subordinate beings. Instead, it is an infinite cohesion of three limitless beings.[23] However, this cohesion,

---

[21] C. Moreschini, "Influenze di Origine su Gregorio di Nazianzo," in *Atti dell'Academia Toscana di Science e Lettere La Columbaria* 44 (1979): 35–57.

[22] Exod 3:10; Plato, *Symp.* 210d.

[23] Cf., e.g., *Or.* 39.11; 40.41.

despite the fact that the Son has taken his origin from the Father, must not be understood as a sequence of time or cause. The Son as well as the Spirit has "proceeded" from the Father (ἐκπορεύεσθαι)[24] in seamless expansion. Such a "procession" left the divine "nature" unchanged. All that changed in the resulting formation of the Son and the Spirit were their properties (ἰδίτητας). Thus, the Father is the beginning of two other beings, but they are not inferior or different in nature. The nature of all three remains one and the same, even if there are three different *hypostaseis* (39.11).

Having made that point – which he will elaborate on further in each of the two subsequent sermons – Gregory focuses on the manner in which this supreme divinity, God, created the universe (*Or.* 38.9). Not content to contemplate itself, the supreme Good, in an act of divine euergetism, expanded itself: "Thus the second splendors were created, of service to the first." The creation of the intelligible universe (κόσμος νοητός) led to that of the sensible one, in part because God wanted "to show not only his own nature, but also his capacity to create a nature utterly alien to his own" (38.10). This moment, according to Gregory, was the first instance of a great fusion of two incommensurable entities: the mysterious commingling of intelligible and sensible elements, which led to the creation of the sensible world and First Man, the "initiate into the visible world." This "visible world" was a second universe, itself a mixture of invisible and visible natures (38.11).

At this juncture, Gregory begins his exegesis of Genesis, which he situates entirely within the structure of the Platonic cosmology he has employed thus far. "This being (i.e., First Man or the first fusion or κρᾶμα of two incommensurables) God placed into the Paradise – what was then the Paradise." This half sentence comprises the sum total of Gregory's discussion of the subject "Paradise," thereby downplaying the concept of Paradise as "space" in favor of the "divine sphere" and further emphasizing Plato's master narrative, the presence of Genesis notwithstanding. For Gregory, heaven was a "divine sphere," a state of being rather than a geographic location (*Or.* 38.12).

First Man, thus created as the perfect mixture of divine and sensible elements, was given free will and agency "so that the good would be the labor

---

[24] Moreschini, *Discours 38–41*, 41–42; K. Holl, *Amphilochius von Ikonium in seinem Verhältnis zu den grossen Kappadoziern*, repr. ed. (Darmstadt, 1969), 160–70.

of him who chooses it."[25] Choice implied the possibility to disagree, and disobedience led to the Fall, which in turn caused sin.[26] Disobedience and sin led to continuous decline and, finally (after some failed divine attempts at prior warning), to the second even more spectacular fusion of two incommensurable natures: the incarnation of the *Logos* for the salvation of humankind. "God came forth with that which he has assumed, unique being out of two opposites: flesh and spirit, one makes divine, the other is made divine. O new mixture! O paradoxical fusion!" (*Or.* 38.13).

The Incarnation was the central event and, according to Gregory, the *raison d'être* not only for all three sermons but for baptism itself: the extraordinary mixing, the formation of a unique being out of two opposites, the paradoxical fusion of the divine splendid light with sensible matter. It was a historic event that was at the same time of eternal and timeless significance. It resulted from a "process," yet was crystallized in a moment; thus, it was also the fusion of moment and process. The agent that permitted this extraordinary fusion to occur was, according to Gregory, illumination, the theme of *Oration 39*.

Illumination

Gregory's "terminology of light" was foundational to his entire cosmological construct, going back to his first orations composed in 362/363.[27] Accordingly, God is light, a light that surpasses that of all other entities in purity.[28]

---

[25] Gregory Nazianzus, *Poem.* 1.1.8 vv. 100–102; Plato, *Resp.* 617e.

[26] This raises, of course, the thorny issues of sin and the origins of evil, which Gregory, relying on Plato, solved in the tradition of Clement, *Protr.* 117.1; *Strom.* 6.96.1. Gregory's interpretation of the fall is both pedagogical and "external": God intended man to be able to contemplate him but not without labor. Man needed to prove through the potential and then the actuality of sin that he was capable of choosing the good. First Man's disobedience was thus the cause of sin yet suggested by a jealous demon, the "external" aspect (Gregory Nazianzus, *Poem.* 1.1.7.64–66; *Or.* 36.5); cf. J. M. Szymusiak, "Grégoire de Nazianze et le péché," *StPatr* 9 (1966): 288–305; Althaus, *Die Heilslehre*, 130; F. X. Portmann, *Die göttliche Paidagogia bei Gregor von Nazianz* (St. Ottilien, 1954), 68–78. For the ramifications of Gregory's thought on original sin, especially for Augustine, see B. Altaner, "Augustinus und Gregor von Nazianz, Gregor von Nyssa," in *Kleine Patristische Schriften*, ed. G. Glockmann (Berlin, 1967), 277–85; P. F. Beatrice, *Tradux peccati: Alle fonti della dottrina agostiniana del peccato originale* (Milan, 1978), 115–16, 200–1.

[27] Gregory Nazianzus, *Or.* 2.5. "Terminology of light" is Claudio Moreschini's very apt expression ("Luce e purificazione nella dottrina di Gregorio Nazianzeno," *Augustinianum* 13 [1973]: 535–49).

Indeed, "light" [φῶς], illumination, is Gregory's foundational metaphor in explicating Genesis and Exodus: "The first commandment given to the first man was also light.... The written law provides a commensurate prototype of the light [φῶς τυπικὸν καί σύμμετριον], foreshadowing (σκιαγραφῶν; lit. "painting in shadows") the truth and the mystery of the light..." (Or. 40.6). But even though this divine light is in essence inaccessible – because it is God – it does not elude man entirely because man originally participated in it.[29] In fact, human beings are linked to the divine, and this link between man and God (ὁμόιωσις Θεῷ) is light itself, expressed through the sun, which therefore indicates the way in which man may return to the divine splendor.[30] Provided the human soul is properly purified, it too may be illuminated. Illumination, therefore, requires purification. The higher the degree of purification, the greater that of illumination and the closer, therefore, the link between man and the divine. The logical consequence, according to Gregory, is that illumination *is* purification and vice versa; they are synonymous. But Gregory took this notion a step further: Illumination (φῶτισμός) is not only purification; it is also baptism (φῶτισμός).[31] Illumination, purification, and baptism are mutual preconditions as well as synonyms.[32] God demands purity but also *is* purity; he demands illumination and *is* illumination.[33] Likewise, baptism both demands purification and illumination (φῶτισμός) and *is* also both. All three are necessary first conditions for contemplating the divine, but all three also make such contemplation possible through their potential to restore man to his original dignity.[34]

Baptism

Christians, in Gregory's opinion, thus have many reasons to celebrate baptism. It represents their passage from darkness to light, from ignorance to the

---

[28] Gregory Nazianzus, Or. 36.5; 39.1; 40.5. Moreschini, *Discours 38–41*, 62–70.

[29] Plato, *Resp.* 508c; *Tim.* 45b–c; also Plotinus, *Enn.* 5.3.8, Origen, and numerous others; cf. C. Moreschini, "Il platonismo cristiano di Gregorio Nazianzeno," *Annali della Scuola Normale Superiore di Pisa* 3:4 (1974): 1347–92; J. Daniélou, *Platonisme et théologie mystique: Doctrine spirituelle de Saint Grégoire de Nysse*, 2nd. ed. (Paris, 1954).

[30] H. Pinault, *Le platonisme de saint Grégoire de Nazianze* (La-Roche-sur-Yon, 1925), 52.

[31] A traditional word denoting baptism. J. Ysebaert, *Greek Baptismal Terminology: Its Origins and Early Development* (Nijmegen, 1962), 167–74.

[32] Gregory Nazianzus, Or. 21.1; 28.30; 40.5, 37; 44.3, 9, 17.

[33] Gregory Nazianzus, Or. 2.5; 30.20.

[34] Plato, *Phaidon*, 67b; Gregory Nazianzus, Or. 7.17; 27.3; 40.5; 31.15, 21; 38.7.

knowledge of truth, from paganism to Christianity (*Or.* 39.3–6) and, as such, is a journey between two utterly incommensurable states of being. More to the point, baptism actualizes in each individual the two great moments of fusion – especially, however, the second great mingling of two incommensurables: namely, the Incarnation. And, like the Incarnation, a historic event of timeless consequence, baptism too is a moment and a process, illumination and purification, initiating and manifesting man's restoration to his original nature – that is, his salvation.

Oration 40 begins again where *Oration* 39 left off: by restating the central identity of illumination, purification, and baptism (40.5–7). Now, however, Gregory proceeds "to philosophize" about how, when, and by whom baptism, now properly introduced (and hopefully understood), should be administered and who should receive it. None of these issues was obvious, not least because "Christ, who gave this gift, is called by multiple and various names, so is his gift, baptism" (40.4).[35] Historically, there had been five types of baptism, and so Gregory traces the history of salvation (39.17): Moses had baptized but only figuratively (τυπικῶς) – that is, in water – by guiding his people through the Red Sea. John the Baptist had also baptized but no longer "in the Jewish manner" – that is, not solely in water. He had already adduced a spiritual baptism by demanding *metanoia*, a "change of heart and mind," or penitence. Jesus, then, baptized purely in the spirit; "that was perfection." Christ himself then received the fourth baptism: the baptism of blood, the baptism of the martyrs. Gregory, "being human and, therefore, a changeable being of instable nature," had received baptism in the fifth manner: namely, the baptism "of tears, but it is even harder" (39.17–18). "I accept this baptism with an open heart; I venerate him who gave it to me; I transmit it to others."

This "baptism of tears" is the baptism for the rest of humankind, and it is the one Gregory will now transmit to his catechumens. Accordingly, he devotes the remainder of his – very long – *Oration* 40 to the precise mechanism according to which this "transmission" ought to unfold. Following Jesus' example, baptism should be administered when one is around the age of thirty, while one is in the fullness of reason yet has time to lead a life of continuing purification (40.29). Therefore, one "should not postpone baptism too close

---

[35] Gregory uses approximately twenty-one expressions for baptism; those referring to light and purity predominate followed by those denoting "marking." Rebirth is used very rarely: Moreschini, *Discours*, 31–41, 357; cf. n. 38.

to death. What kind of dignity is exhibited by a baptism where the priest has to fight with the physicians and the lawyers at the bedside?" (40.11).[36] Child baptism is permitted, but only if death seems imminent. Marking the child with the seal of baptism will be its "greatest and most beautiful talisman [φυλακτήριον]" (40.17, 28).

Equal in significance to the time of baptism were Gregory's following points: baptism - Gregory stresses this at least seven times in *Oration* 40 alone - is not a rite reserved for the elites, but is also intended and necessary for the poor.[37] Baptism does not require the attendance of family, friends, and retinue. Nor should one insist on being baptized by a metropolitan bishop or a *Pneumatikos*, an unmarried bishop (40.25, 26). Other bishops and priests can also baptize.

This was the case because in baptism "all the old *characteres* (i.e., letters or external markers) disappear. Christ will have been imposed on all in one form [μιᾷ μορφῇ]" (40.27). How did such an erasure and reimpression occur in practice? In this context, Gregory likens baptism to rebirth.[38] Resorting to Platonic as well as scriptural notions, Gregory identifies three types of the "elect": namely, slaves, mercenaries, and sons, allegorically represented by matter, sense, and intellect/*logos* (40.2, 13). Hence, all three aspects are present in each human being, and all three must, therefore, be reborn - that is, purified. Thus, the entire process of baptism requires three "stages": a stage of purification (exorcism and washing), a second one in which that which has been purified is now "prepared" and protected through anointing and sealing, and a third stage in which the new "faith" is written onto the cleansed and prepared surface. Expressed through this tripartite preparation is the "dual" nature of baptism as purification and illumination, which, however, are a single act. Thus, exorcism and washing *purify*, whereas anointing, sealing, and especially writing *illuminate*. Here, writing should ideally be performed on a clean slate, but in Gregory's hands, it is powerful enough even to modify earlier faulty writings by erasing parts or the whole of old inscriptions (*Or.* 40.2-3, 5-8, 31-38, and 44-45). Thus, baptism, as a triple

---

[36] For the rarity of delayed baptism in North Africa, for example, see É. Rebillard, "Le figure du catéchumène et le problème du délai du baptême dans la pastorale de saint Augustin," in *Augustin Prédicateur (395–411)*, ed. G. Madec (Paris, 1998), 285-92.

[37] Gregory Nazianzus, *Or.* 32.22; 40.8, 10, 25-27.

[38] Gregory Nazianzus, *Or.* 40.2, 8; 39.2 and 6 are brief allusions to the widespread notion of baptism as rebirth following John 3:5-6. This notion plays a truly minimal role in Gregory's conceptualization, *pace* Saxer, *Rites*, 304.

yet single act, reenacts and actualizes the fusion of two incommensurable natures, hence the Incarnation.

All three acts are powerful. Washing accomplishes purification. Sealing protects the newly purified against the continuous and even intensifying attacks of demons – which now home in on the newly cleaned space with particular ferocity[39] – but at the same time also marks the intimacy of fusing two opposing "essences," the seal and the flesh/soul. Finally, writing continues this process of fusion, further enhancing it through its transformative powers. Gregory claims that, by writing the characters of the formulation of faith into the catechumen's soul, he writes into it "with the fingers of God a new covenant, a summary of salvation. . . . In the name of the Father and the Son and the Holy Ghost." Written into the tablet of the soul and the memory (like a teacher onto those of a pupil), the writing thus makes the fusion indelible: It signals the assumption of a new *character*, the new letter of the one form in Christ (*Or.* 40.27, 44–45).

In Gregory's interpretation, all the "actualizers" or markers of baptism demand human choice and agency because all are part of an ongoing process of purification. Tears had to be shed day and night because demons and sins did not cease. All thoughts, senses, and limbs had to be cleansed continually though fasting, vigils, tears, compassion toward the needy, and the sharing of one's possessions.[40] The "impression" of baptism aids in maintaining such purity and in its recuperation if lost through negligence, but daily actualization was called for to restore the purity of the "first birth" (*Or.* 40.31, 38). The "signs" actualize and mark the potential. They initiate a process of purification, for which the signs and markers in turn provide support and strength.

Thus, it all forms a coherent whole: The nature of the divine essence "causes" the "paradoxical" fusion of the divine and the material. This profound mixture is the Incarnation, which baptism actualizes in each individual, and thus provides the model for and guarantor of salvation – if properly carried out. Thus, baptism is a moment and a process, in which all its parts,

---

[39] Gregory Nazianzus, *Or.* 40.10, 35, 36. Note also Gregory's use of baptism as purifying fire in *Or.* 40.36; Gregory's poetry also contains frequent use of apotropaic language, also in the context of baptism (Gregory Nazianzus, *Poem.* 1.2.1. v. 162; cf. Lampe, *Seal of the Spirit*, 261–96). An example of the widespread use of such language is Emperor Julian's remark: "The whole sum of Christian philosophy consist in two things, whistling to keep away the demons and making the sign of the cross on their foreheads" (*Ep.* 79).

[40] Gregory also uses medical language denoting the unclogging of pores that will permit illumination to flow unhindered (*Or.* 38; 40).

heaven, earth, change, fusion, inscription, are brought into a coherent whole: The "now" of baptism is not a determined moment, but it is the all of "moment" that this "now" indicates" (*Or.* 40.13).

Rival Cosmologies, Rival Baptisms

Why did Gregory – after all, the bishop of Constantinople – feel it necessary to elaborate to such an extent on baptism? Three sermons, one of which, namely, *Oration* 40 in its present form as revised for publication, is Gregory's second longest?[41] Why reveal these mysteries to such a degree to uninitiated ears (40.45)? The reasons are clear. Gregory's interpretation of baptism was neither the only, nor necessarily the most widely favored, one in Constantinople at that time. In fact, he appears to have represented the minority opinion. As his own sermons show, there were other ways in which Platonic cosmology could be reinterpreted, other emphases placed on divine essence and activity, resulting in seemingly similar but structurally very different accounts of cosmology, fusion, and baptism.[42] And, these competing interpretations of all aspects of baptism and its cosmological implications enjoyed great favor, especially among those who counted most and whose favor Gregory, like his competitors, had to win: namely, the members of the Constantinopolitan elite.[43]

As Gregory himself implied, baptism itself, the rite that marks the "belonging to Christ," was an intensely elite event. Of course, one not only had to be baptized with one's full retinue present, but also by a person who represented and, therefore, possessed the highest power and could thus administer the powerful rite of baptism most appropriately, without either contaminating the catechumen or, even worse, misdirecting the enormous potency of the act (*Or.* 40.26). And, there were many who presented themselves as powerful initiators. Thus, according to Gregory, Constantinopolitans preferred to be baptized by a metropolitan[44] or by a *Pneumatikos*. There were "Arians," "Sabellians," and "Novatians"; there were the "acerbic calculators of the

---

[41] Moreschini, *Discours 38–41*, 17; only *Or.* 4 (*Against Julian*) and 43 (*In Praise of Basil*) are slightly longer.

[42] Gregory Nazianzus, *Or.* 40.22 and 44; 39.18–19.

[43] Thus, his explicit recommendation of baptism as essential for those engaged in public office (*Or.* 40.19).

[44] Gregory Nazianzus, *Or.* 40.26; e.g., by the metropolitan from Jerusalem, whereas the local metropolitan at that time was still resident in Heraclea; Dagron, *Naissance*, 446, 459.

divinity" (38.14), those who denied the divinity of the Spirit, those who misunderstood the nature of Christ's fusion, and those who misconstrued baptism's power to purify.[45]

Behind Gregory's labels and allusions stood influential men. For example, Demophilus, for twenty years the "Arian" bishop of Constantinople, had been dispatched to the suburbs by imperial order on November 26, 380, only a few months before the occasion of Gregory's sermons. There, he continued to celebrate mass.[46] Eunomius, foremost among those whom Gregory derided as "calculators of Christ," was at that moment the toast of the town, drawing crowds, which included some of the most influential court eunuchs to his estate in nearby Chalcedon.[47] A significant number of people who belonged to *la crème de la crème* of the Constantinopolitan ascetics denied the divinity of the Spirit, continuing the tradition of Bishop Macedonius, Demophilus' precursor. They counted among their supporters men of great influence at court.[48] Others, like Isaac, another prominent ascetic who had just then been offered housing for himself and his followers on the suburban estates of not one but two powerful courtiers, Saturnius and Victor, attracted vast numbers of faithful who sought them out on a daily basis.[49] Each and every single one of these men and their supporters promoted different interpretations of the meaning and function of baptism and its theological–cosmological significance.

Thus, the so-called "Novatians," who were very popular among the elites, preferred baptism late in life, considering it a one-time act of complete purification. They rejected all notion of penitence, indeed, the possibility of sin after baptism, and punished the lapsed draconically – in diametric opposition to Gregory's point of view, which was clearly intended to win over "Novatians" by offering them inclusion without rebaptism. In their case, it sufficed to "modify what had been written into" them.[50]

---

[45] H. Dörrie, "Die Epiphanias-Predigt des Gregor von Nazianz (Hom. 39) und ihre geistesgeschichtliche Bedeutung," in *Kyriakon: Festschrift Johannes Quasten*, ed. P. Granfield and J. A. Jungmann (Münster, 1970), 409–23.

[46] Socrates, *Hist. eccl.* 5.7; Sozomen, *Hist. eccl.* 7.5.5–7. Matthews, *Western Aristocracies*, 122.

[47] Sozomen, *Hist. eccl.* 7.17.7; 7.6.2; cf. Socrates, *Hist. eccl.* 5.20.

[48] Socrates, *Hist. eccl.* 5.8; Holl, *Amphilochius*, 160–170. Cf. P. Rousseau, *Basil of Caesarea* (The Transformation of the Classical Heritage 20; Berkeley, Calif., 1994), 245–69.

[49] D. Caner, *Wandering, Begging Monks: Spiritual Authority and the Promotion of Monasticism in Late Antiquity* (The Transformation of the Classical Heritage 33; Berkeley, Calif., 2001), 190–9.

[50] Gregory Nazianzus, *Or.* 39, 18–19; *Can. Laod.* 7; Basil, *Ep.* 188. M. Wallraff, "Die Geschichte des Novatianismus seit dem vierten Jahrhundert im Osten," *JAC* 1 (1997): 251–79, esp. 257–63.

Controversies regarding the divinity of the Holy Spirit had been on Gregory's mind for quite some time.[51] That many of the city's ascetic stars, also known as *Pneumtatikoi* or "the Poor," doubted that the Spirit was divine presented a true challenge. Moreover, a significant portion of these ascetic and pneumatic "poor" were of the opinion that their daily regime of "tears and groaning," combined with fasting and constant prayer, made baptism as such entirely superfluous since they had direct access to the divine through their life of continuous purification.[52] Hence, Gregory's insistence that baptism was also necessary for the "poor."[53] On the one hand, he sought to emphasize that baptism was not reserved for the social elite alone, but encompassed nearly all strata on the social scale.[54] Therefore, he stressed repeatedly that one should not feel humiliated when baptized next to a vendor, a debtor, or even a slave: "do not refuse to be baptized with the poor, you who are rich, or you, the noble, with a low-class person, or you, the master, with your own slave . . . Christ himself took on the form of a slave" (*Or.* 40.25, 27).[55] On the other hand, such remarks also polemicized against competing *Pneumatikoi*, the ascetic "poor," who deemed baptism superfluous, at least for themselves, and who were frequently identical with those who rejected the divinity of the Spirit. In one fell swoop, Gregory further argued against those who denied the full mixture of divine and human, who rejected Christ's full assumption of humanity: Christ had not only become fully human – he had even taken on the form of a slave.

Wrong teachings regarding the "fusion" – that is, the relationship between Father and Son, and hence its mixture with the human in the Incarnation – could have devastating consequences. Some erred, according to Gregory, because they unduly reduced Father and Son into one ("like the Jews"); others separated them too rigidly, thereby introducing subordination or, even worse, the multiplicity of divinities of "paganism," and yet others denied

---

[51] Basil, *De Spirit.* 9.22–23.

[52] Cf. Adelphius' "confession" that "there is no benefit from baptism for those who receive it for only continuous prayer can drive out the indwelling demon," at the "anti-Messalian" synod of Antioch in the early 380's; Photius, *Bib.* 52; Theodotus, *Hist. eccl.* 4.11.7; Caner, *Wandering*, 90–3.

[53] A year earlier, while he was in the process of baptizing, ascetics and the "poor" had "stoned" Gregory (Gregory Nazianzus, *Ep.* 77.1–3; 78.1–4).

[54] R. Lim, "Converting the Unchristianizable," Davis Center Paper, on the continuing exclusion of actors and other infamous social types.

[55] P. Brown, *Poverty and Leadership in the Later Roman Empire* (The Menahem Stern Jerusalem Lectures 2000; Hanover, N.H., 2002).

the thoroughness of Christ's mixture with the humble aspects of mankind, to wit, "Sabellians," "Arians," and "Apollinarists" (*Or.* 38.8, 14–15; 39.12; 40.11, 20–21).[56]

The consequences of such different notions for baptism become perhaps most clearly apparent in the thought of Eunomius. Eunomius and a significant proportion of Eastern Christians propagated a baptism neither in Christ's Incarnation, as proposed by Gregory, nor in his resurrection, but "into the death of Christ."[57] Eunomius' interpretation of divine essence and agency, prompted in part by a difference in his understanding of Aristotelian language theory, led him to formulate a seemingly similar yet structurally very different Christian exegesis of Platonic cosmology.[58] Following Aristotle's dictum that "essence does not admit of degree,"[59] Eunomius explained the relationship between Father and Son as one of difference in essence. Thus, he maintained that, despite the fact that God was immaterial and hence without spatial limits, he was not boundless. This understanding, which was diametrically opposed to Gregory's concept of a progress of the divine essence, resulted in the *hypostasis* of the Son and the Spirit.[60] Such epistemological differences had cosmological implications. Because essence here implied difference, Son and Father differed. Hence, the Son began his journey of salvation from the Father's throne and proceeded on through the history of Israel to achieve genuine incarnation (without the mixing in of a soul), after which he ascended to return.[61] This resulted in a different understanding of heaven and earth, a different understanding of the personalization of the cosmological evolution, and, as a consequence, a notion of the Incarnation quite different from Gregory's concept of complete fusion. Eunomius' popularity among the classically trained elites of Constantinople is easily explained if we consider that his view of the incarnate Christ was predicated on the inherent difference between the divine and

---

[56] Dörrie, "Epiphaniaspredigt," 409–23; B. Pruche, trans., *Basile de Césarée: Traité du Saint-Esprit* (SC 17; Paris, 1947), 88.

[57] Philostorgius described this as the practice of his own church in Constantinople, *Hist. eccl.* 10.4; Socrates, *Hist. eccl.* 6.26.2, Sozomen, *Hist. eccl.* 6.26.4; Theodotus, *Haer.* 4.3; Basil, *De Spirit.* 12.28.1–7.

[58] See also S. Elm, "Orthodoxy and the True Philosophical Life: Julian and Gregory of Nazianzus," *StPatr* 37 (2001): 69–85.

[59] Aristotle, *Cat.* 5.3.33–37.

[60] Eunomius, *Apol.* 23.4–10.

[61] Eunomius, *Expos. Fidei* 3.33–42; cf. Basil, *Eun.* 2.22.27–32. See R. Vaggione, *Eunomius of Cyzicus and the Nicene Revolution* (Oxford, 2000), 328–29.

the material: after all, the inherent inferiority of matter implicit in his cosmology reverberated much more strongly with the traditional Neoplatonic cosmologies, no friend of matter.[62] Indeed, Gregory too was fully aware of the fact that matter was the complete opposite of all that is divine: For him, however, this was precisely the precondition that made the Incarnation so powerful – this was the paradox of the fusion. Baptism, of course, reflected these underlying differences, as shown by the following quotation from the *Apostolic Constitutions*:

> Baptism, after all, is administered into the Son's death: the water is instead of burial, the seal instead of the cross; the chrism is the confirmation of the confession. The Father is mentioned because he is the source and the sender; the Spirit is included because he is the witness. The immersion (singular) is the dying with Christ, the ascent the rising with him.[63]

Hence, the reasons that Gregory had to expend so much effort demonstrating that baptism was both moment and process, actualization of a perfect fusion yet requiring continuous purification, application of a seal on a cleansed slate yet also an inscription that could be modified. Gregory needed to demonstrate that he was a *Pneumatikos*, that he possessed the power to write, inscribe, stamp, impress, and rewrite correctly, because the appropriate had been written into him. His constant recourse to the exegesis of the most powerful cosmologies of the day, Plato through Scripture, his virtuoso mixing of these two worlds, marked him as capable of initiating correctly into the mystery of baptism. Even more so, in his orations Gregory places himself squarely at the nexus between heaven and earth. Both because his life as priest and ascetic had provided him with a more perfect understanding of the mysterious nature [*physis*] of the divine and because he could demonstrate this perfect understanding through the shape and form of his own body [*physis*] as a *xenos*, a "poor" countryman without a court (38.6), he could also administer the appropriate form of illumination. Moreover, he

---

[62] Gregory Nazianzus, *Or.* 38.2. See R. Edmonds in this volume; S. I. Johnston, "Rising to the Occasion: Theurgical Ascent in Its Cultural Milieu," in *Envisioning Magic: A Princeton Seminar and Symposium*, ed. P. Schäfer and H. G. Kippenberg (SHR 75; Leiden, 1997), 165–94.

[63] *Const. App.* 3.16.20–17.10; reflecting the alterations of the fourth-century editor, cf. *Didasc.* 3.12.3. In fact, the "Eunomian" circles appear to have altered their baptismal ritual in the early 380s, probably around 383/384. M. Wiles, "Triple and Single Immersion: Baptism in the Arian Controversy," *StPatr* 30 (1997): 337–49; Vaggione, *Eunomius*, 324–42; R. Williams, "Baptism and the Arian Controversy," in *Arianism after Arius: Essays on the Development of the Fourth Century Trinitarian Conflicts* (Edinburgh, 1993), 170.

could overwrite the false inscriptions of others. The power to correct faulty initiations was power indeed, because to be baptized wrongly signified the utter corruption of the entire salvation history – and hence precluded the return to the original, perfect, and heavenly state. Thus, although interesting for modern scholars, such concerns were vital for Gregory as bishop of Constantinople: His entire concept of baptism was developed in response to others whom he considered not only wrong, but a direct threat to the salvation of all in his care. Gregory's celebration of the Word through his words proved successful. On January 10, 381, Emperor Theodosius issued a law banning the heretical teachings of the "Arians" and the "Eunomians," but not those of the "Novatians."[64]

---

[64] *Corpus Theodosianum* 16.5.6.

Select Bibliography

Abusch, R. S. "Seven-fold Hymns in the *Songs of the Sabbath Sacrifice* and the Hekhalot Literature: Formalism, Hierarchy and the Limits of Human Participation," in *The Dead Sea Scrolls as Background to Post-Biblical Judaism and Early Christianity*, ed. J. Davila. STDJ 46. Leiden, 2002, 228–32.

Amat, J. *Songes et visions: L'au-delà dans la littérature latine tardive.* Paris, 1985.

Ameling, W., ed., *Märtyrer und Märtyrerakten.* Stuttgart, 2002.

Ankarloo, B. and Clark, S., eds., *Witchcraft and Magic in Europe: Ancient Greece and Rome.* Philadelphia, 1999.

Aune, D. E. *Revelation*, 2 vols. Dallas, Tex., 1997–8.

Avery-Peck, A. J. and Neusner, J., eds., *Judaism in Late Antiquity*; part 4, *Death, Life-After-Death, Resurrection and the World to Come in the Judaisms of Antiquity.* Leiden, 2000.

Barton, T. *Ancient Astrology.* London, 1994.
  Power and Knowledge: Astrology, Physiognomics, and Medicine Under the Roman Empire. Ann Arbor, Mich., 1994.

Becker, A. H. and Reed, A. Y., eds., *The Ways That Never Parted: Jews and Christians in Late Antiquity and the Early Middle Ages.* TSAJ 95. Tübingen, 2003.

Beirnaert, L. "Le symbolisme ascensionnel dans la liturgie et la mystique chrétiennes," *Eranos-Jahrbuch* 19 (1950): 41–63.

Berger, K. *Die Auferstehung des Propheten und die Erhöhung des Menschensohnes.* Göttingen, 1976.

Bernstein, A. E. *The Formation of Hell: Death and Retribution in the Ancient and Early Christian Worlds.* London, 1993.

Betz, H. D., ed., *The Greek Magical Papyri in Translation, Including the Demotic Spells*, 2nd ed. Chicago, 1992.

Bianchi, U. and Vermaseren, M. J., eds., *La Soteriologia dei Culti Orientali nell' Impero Romano.* Etudes préliminaires aux religions orientales dans l'empire romain 92. Leiden, 1982.

Bockmuehl, M. *Revelation and Mystery in Ancient Judaism and Pauline Christianity.* Tübingen, 1990.

Boll, F., Bezold, C., and Gundel, W. *Sternglaube und Sterndeutung: Die Geschichte und das Wesen der Astrologie*, 5th ed. Darmstadt, 1966.

Select Bibliography

Borgeaud, P., ed., *Orphisme et Orphée: En l'honneur de Jean Rudhardt.* Geneva, 1991.

Bouché-Leclercq, A. *L'Astrologie grecque.* Paris, 1899.

Boyarin, D. *Dying for God: Martyrdom and the Making of Christianity and Judaism.* Stanford, Calif., 1999.

Bradshaw, P. F. *The Search for the Origins of Christian Worship: Sources and Methods for the Study of Early Liturgy.* New York, 1992.

Brashear, W. "The Greek Magical Papyri: An Introduction and Survey; Annotated Bibliography (1928–1994)," *ANRW* II 18.5 (1995): 3380–684.

Bremmer, J. N. *The Rise and Fall of the Afterlife: The 1995 Read-Tuckwell Lectures at the University of Bristol.* London, 2001.

  The Early Greek Concept of the Soul. Princeton, N.J., 1983.

Brock, S. *Studies in Syriac Christianity.* Brookfield, Vt., 1992.

Brown, P. R. L. *Power and Persuasion in Late Antiquity: Towards a Christian Empire.* Madison, Wisc., 1992.

  The Making of Late Antiquity. Cambridge, Mass., 1978.

Burkert, W. *Griechische Religion der archaischen und klassischen Epoche.* Die Religionen der Menschheit 15. Stuttgart, 1977. English edition: *Greek Religion: Archaic and Classical,* trans. J. Raffan. Cambridge, Mass., 1985.

Carpenter, T. and Faraone, C. A., eds., *Masks of Dionysus.* Ithaca, N.Y., 1993.

Charlesworth, J. H., ed., *The Old Testament Pseudepigrapha,* 2 vols. Garden City, N.Y., 1983–5.

Chernus, I. *Mysticism in Rabbinic Judaism.* Berlin, 1982.

Collins, A. Y. *Cosmology and Eschatology in Jewish and Christian Apocalypticism.* SJSJ 50. Leiden, 1996.

  Crisis and Catharsis: The Power of the Apocalypse. Philadelphia, 1984.

Collins, J. J. *The Apocalyptic Imagination: An Introduction to Jewish Apocalyptic Literature,* 2nd rev. ed. Grand Rapids, Mich., 1998.

Copenhaver, B. P., trans., *Hermetica: The Greek Corpus Hermeticum and the Latin Asclepius in a New English Translation.* Cambridge, 1992.

Cramer, F. H. *Astrology in Roman Law and Politics.* Philadelphia, 1954.

Cumont, F. V. M. *Lux perpetua.* Paris, 1949.

  Astrology and Religion Among the Greeks and Romans. American Lectures on the History of Religions, 1911–1912. New York, 1912.

Daniélou, J. *Platonisme et théologie mystique: Doctrine spirituelle de Saint Grégoire de Nysse.* 2nd ed. Paris, 1954.

Davila, J. R. "The Macrocosmic Temple, Scriptural Exegesis, and the Songs of the Sabbath Sacrifice," *DSD* 9 (2002): 1–19.

Des Places, E., ed., trans. and comm., *Oracles chaldaïques avec un choix de commentaires anciens.* Paris, 1971.

  ed., trans. and comm., *Jamblique: Les mystères d'Égypte.* Paris, 1966.

Dieterich, A. *Eine Mithrasliturgie,* 3rd ed. Teubner, 1923.

Dillon, J. *The Golden Chain: Studies in the Development of Platonism and Christianity.* Hampshire, 1990.

  The Middle Platonists. London, 1977.

Dinzelbacher, P. *Die Jenseitsbrücke im Mittelalter*. Vienna, 1973.

Edmonds, R. G. "Did the Mithraists Inhale? – A Technique for Theurgic Ascent in the *Mithras Liturgy*, the *Chaldaean Oracles*, and Some Mithraic Frescoes," *Ancient World* 32 (2000): 10–24.

Eitrem, S. *Orakel und Mysterien am Ausgang der Antike*. Zürich, 1947.

Eliade, M. *Le chamanisme et les techniques archaïques de l'extase*. Paris, 1951. Revised English edition: *Shamanism: Ancient Techniques of Ecstasy*, trans. W. R. Trask. New York, 1964.

Elliott, J. K., ed., *Apocryphal New Testament: A Collection of Apocryphal Christian Literature in an English translation*. Oxford, 1993.

Faraone, C. A. *Ancient Greek Love Magic*. Cambridge, Mass., 1999.

Faraone, C. A. and Obbink, D., eds., *Magika Hiera: Ancient Greek Magic and Religion*. New York, 1997.

Festugière, A. J. *La Révélation d'Hermès Trismégiste*, 4 vols. Paris, 1950.

Finamore, J. *Iamblichus and the Theory of the Vehicle of the Soul*. American Classical Studies 14. Chico, Calif., 1985.

Fowden, G. *The Egyptian Hermes: A Historical Approach to the Late Pagan Mind*. Princeton, N.J., 1986.

Frankfurter, D. *Elijah in Upper Egypt*. Minneapolis, Minn., 1993.

Friesen, S. J. *Imperial Cults and the Apocalypse of John: Reading Revelation in the Ruins*. New York, 2001.

Geudtner, O. *Die Seelenlehre der Chaldischen Orakel*. Meisenheim am Glan, 1971.

Goldberg, A. *Gesammelte Studien*, Vol. 1, *Mystik und Theologie des rabbinischen Judentums*, eds. M. Schlüter and P. Schäfer. TSAJ 61. Tübingen, 1997.

Graf, F. *Magie dans l'antiquité gréco-romaine: Idéologie et pratique*. Paris, 1994. English edition: *Magic in the Ancient World*, trans. F. Philip. Revealing Antiquity 10. Cambridge, Mass., 1997.

 Eleusis und die orphische Dichtung Athens in vorhellenisticher Zeit. Religionsgeschichtliche Versuche und Vorarbeiten 33. Berlin, 1974.

Grötzinger, K. E. *Musik und Gesang in der Theologie der frühen jüdischen Literatur*. TSAJ 3. Tübingen, 1982.

Gruenwald, I. *Apocalyptic and Merkavah Mysticism*. AGAJU 14. Leiden, 1980.

Gundel, W. and Gundel, H. G. *Astrologumena: Die astrologische Literatur in der Antike und ihre Geschichte*. Wiesbaden, 1966.

Halperin, D. J. *The Merkabah in Rabbinic Literature*. New Haven, Conn., 1980.

Hanson, P., ed., *Visionaries and Their Apocalypses*. IRT 4. Philadelphia, 1983.

Heck, C. *L'Échelle céleste dans l'art du Moyen Âge: Une image de la quête du ciel*. Paris, 1997.

Hengel, M. "Die Throngemeinschaft des Lammes mit Gott in der Johannesapokalypse," *ThBeitr* 96 (1996): 159–75.

Herrera, R. A., ed., *Mystics of the Book: Themes, Topics, and Typologies*. New York, 1993.

Hill, C. *Regnum caelorum: Patterns of Millennial Thought in Early Christianity*, 2nd ed. Grand Rapids, Mich., 2001.

Himmelfarb, M. *Ascent to Heaven in Jewish and Christian Apocalypses*. New York, 1993.

 Tours of Hell: An Apocalyptic Form in Jewish and Christian Literature. Philadelphia, 1983.

Hübner, W. "Manilius als Astrologe und Dichter," *ANRW* II 32.1 (1984): 126–320.

Hultgård, A. "Das Paradies: vom Park des Perserkönigs zum Ort der Seligen," in *La cité de dieu = Die Stadt Gottes*, eds. M. Hengel, S. Mittmann, and A. M. Schwemmer. Tübingen, 2000, 1–43.

Jellinek, A., ed., *Beit ha-Midrash*, 6 vols., 3rd ed. Jerusalem, 1967.

Johnston, S. I. *Restless Dead: Encounters Between the Living and the Dead in Ancient Greece.* Berkeley, Calif., 1999.

    Hekate Soteira: A Study of Hekate's Roles in the Chaldean Oracles and Related Literature. ACS 21. Atlanta, Ga., 1990.

Jordan, D. R., Montgomery, H., and Thomassen, E., eds., *The World of Ancient Magic: Papers from the First International Samson Eitrem Seminar at the Norwegian Institute at Athens, 4–8 May 1997.* Papers from the Norwegian Institute at Athens 4. Bergen, 1999.

Kingsley, P. *Ancient Philosophy, Mystery and Magic: Empedocles and Pythagorean Tradition.* Oxford, 1995.

Kühnel, B. *From the Earthly to the Heavenly Jerusalem: Representations of the Holy City in Christian Art of the First Millennium.* Rome, 1987.

Kuyt, A. *The 'Descent' to the Chariot: Towards a Description of the Terminology, Place, Function and Nature of the Yeridah in Hekhalot Literature.* TSAJ 45. Tübingen, 1995.

Lang, B. and McDannell, C. *Heaven: A History*, 2nd ed. New Haven, Conn., 2001.

Levenson, J. D. "The Jerusalem Temple in Devotional and Visionary Experience," in *Jewish Spirituality I: From the Bible Through the Middle Ages*, ed. A. Green. New York, 1985, 32–61.

Lewy, H. *Chaldaean Oracles and Theurgy: Mysticism, Magic and Neoplatonism in the Later Roman Empire*, 2nd ed. by Michel Tardieu. Paris, 1978.

Lumpe, A. and Bietenhard, H. "Himmel," *RAC* 15 (1991): 173–212.

Luttikhuizen, G. P., ed., *Paradise Interpreted.* Leiden, 1999.

MacRae, G. W. "Heavenly Temple and Eschatology in the Letter to the Hebrews," *Semeia* 12 (1978): 179–99.

Maier, J. "Serienbildung und 'numinoser' Eindruckseffekt in den poetischen Stücken der Hekhalot-Literatur," *Semitics* 3 (1973): 36–66.

Majercik, R., trans. and comm., *The Chaldean Oracles: Text, Translation and Commentary.* SGRR 5. Leiden, 1989.

Malina, B. J. *On the Genre and Message of Revelation: Star Visions and Sky Journeys.* Peabody, Mass., 1995.

Marshall, J. W. *Parables of War: Reading John's Jewish Apocalypse.* Waterloo, Ont., 2001.

Merkelbach, R. "Immortality Rituals in Late Antiquity," *Diogenes* 42 (1994): 85–109.

    Mithras. Koenigstein, 1984.

Meyer, M. and Mirecki, P., eds., *Ancient Magic and Ritual Power.* RGRW 129. Leiden, 1995.

Miller, P. C. *Dreams in Late Antiquity: Studies in the Imagination of a Culture.* Princeton, N.J., 1994.

Musurillo, H. *The Acts of the Christian Martyrs.* Oxford, 1972.

Nasemann, B. *Theurgie und Philosophie in Jamblichs de Mysteriis.* Beiträge zur Altertumskunde 11. Stuttgart, 1991.

Newsom, C. A. *Songs of the Sabbath Sacrifice: A Critical Edition.* HSS 27. Atlanta, Ga., 1985.

Nickelsburg, G. W. E. *1 Enoch 1: A Commentary on the Book of 1 Enoch 1–36; 81–108.* Hermeneia. Minneapolis, Minn., 2001.

Nitzan, B. *Qumran Prayer and Religious Poetry.* Leiden, 1994.

Nock, A. D. *Conversion: The Old and the New Religion from Alexander the Great to Augustine of Hippo.* London, 1933.

Noegel, S., Walker, J., and Wheeler, B., eds., *Prayer, Magic, and the Stars in the Ancient and Late Antique World.* University Park, Penn., 2003.

Pagels, E. "Ritual in the *Gospel of Phillip*," in *The Nag Hammadi Library After Fifty Years: Proceedings of the 1995 Society of Biblical Literature Commemoration*, ed. J. D. Turner and A. McGuire. Nag Hammadi and Manichaean Studies 44. Leiden, 1997, 280–91.

Parke, H. W. *The Oracles of Apollo in Asia Minor.* London, 1985.

Preisendanz, K. and Henrichs, A., eds., *Papyri Graecae Magicae: Die griechischen Zauberpapyri*, 2 vols., 2nd ed. Stuttgart, 1973–4.

Price, S. R. F. *Rituals and Power: The Roman Imperial Cult in Asia Minor.* Cambridge, 1984.

Recheis, A. *Engel, Tod und Seelenreise: Das Wirken der Geister beim Heimgang des Menschen in der Lehre der alexandrinischen und kappadokischen Väter.* Rome, 1958.

Rowland, C. *The Open Heaven: A Study of Apocalyptic in Judaism and Early Christianity.* London, 1982.

Russell, J. B. *A History of Heaven: The Singing Silence.* Princeton, N.J., 1997.

Schäfer, P. *Hekhalot-Studien.* TSAJ 19. Tübingen, 1988.

 ed., *Konkordanz zur Hekhalot-Literatur*, 2 vols. TSAJ 12–13. Tübingen, 1986–8.

Der verborgene und offenbare Gott: Hauptthemen der frühen jüdischen Mystik. Tübingen, 1981. English edition: *The Hidden and Manifest God: Some Major Themes in Early Jewish Mysticism*, trans. A. Pomerance. Albany, N.Y., 1992.

 ed., with M. Schlüter and H. G. von Mutius. *Synopse zur Hekhalot-Literatur.* TSAJ 2. Tübingen, 1981.

Rivalität zwischen Engeln und Menschen: Untersuchungen zur rabbinischen Engelvorstellung. SJ 8. Berlin, 1975.

Schäfer, P. and Kippenberg, H. G., eds., *Envisioning Magic: A Princeton Seminar and Symposium.* Studies in the History of Religions 75. Leiden, 1997.

Schimanowski, G. *Die himmlische Liturgie in der Apokalypse des Johannes: Die frühjüdischen Traditionen in Offenbarung 4–5 unter Einschluß der Hekhalotliteratur.* WUNT 2,154. Tübingen, 2002.

Scholem, G. *Jewish Gnosticism, Merkabah Mysticism, and Talmudic Tradition.* New York, 1965.

Major Trends in Jewish Mysticism. New York, 1941.

Sed, N. *La mystique cosmologique juive.* Paris: Mouton, 1981.

Segal, A. F. "Heavenly Ascent in Hellenistic Judaism, Early Christianity, and Their Environment," *ANRW* II 23.2 (1980): 1333–94.

Select Bibliography

Shaw, G. *Theurgy and the Soul: The Neoplatonism of Iamblichus.* University Park, Penn., 1995.

Shepkaru, S. "To Die for God: Martyrs' Heaven in Hebrew and Latin Crusade Narratives," *Speculum* 77 (2002): 311–41.

Smith, J. Z. *Map Is Not Territory: Studies in the History of Religion.* Chicago, 1978.

Solomon, J. ed., *Apollo: Origins and Influences.* Tucson, Ariz., 1994.

Sourvinou-Inwood, C. *"Reading" Greek Death: To the End of the Classical Period.* Oxford, 1995.

Stone, M. E. "Enoch, Aramaic Levi and Sectarian Origins," *JSJ* 19 (1988): 159–70.

"Lists of Revealed Things in the Apocalyptic Literature," in *Magnalia Dei: The Mighty Acts of God: Essays on the Bible and Archaeology in Memory of G. Ernest Wright*, eds. F. M. Cross, W. Lemke, and P. D. Miller. Garden City, N.J., 1976, 426–41.

Stuckenbruck, L. *Angel Veneration and Christology: A Study in Early Judaism and in the Christology of the Apocalypse of John.* Tübingen, 1995.

Sullivan, L. E. ed., *Death, Afterlife and the Soul.* New York, 1987.

Tardieu, M. "La Gnose Valentinienne et les Oracles Chaldaïques," in *The Rediscovery of Gnosticism*, Vol. 1: *The School of Valentinus*, ed. B. Layton. SHR 41. Leiden, 1980, 194–237.

VanderKam, J. *Enoch and the Growth of the Apocalyptic Tradition.* Washington, D.C., 1984.

VanderKam, J. and Adler, W., eds., *Jewish Apocalyptic Heritage in Early Christianity.* Assen, 1996.

Volk, K. "Pious and Impious Approaches to Cosmology in Manilius," *Materiali e discussioni per l'analisi dei testi classici* 47 (2001): 85–117.

Wallis, R. T., ed., *Neoplatonism and Gnosticism.* Studies in Neoplatonism 6. Albany, N.Y., 1992.

Wertheimer, S. A., ed., *Batei Midrashot*, 2 vols., 2nd ed. by A. J. Wertheimer. Jerusalem, 1950–3.

Williams, M. A. *Rethinking "Gnosticism": An Argument for Dismantling a Dubious Category.* Princeton, N.J., 1999.

Wright, J. E. *The Early History of Heaven.* New York, 2000.

Index

Index

Brock, Sebastian, 189
Brown, Peter, 2, 9, 301, 302

Cain, 176
Carthage, 160, 162, 166, 168
Cause of the Foundation of the Schools: asceticism and scholasticism in, 183; content, genre, and provenance of, 174; exegesis of Genesis in, 177; heavenly classroom in, 175; pedagogical imagery in, 177–179; and scholastic culture of East Syrian Christianity, 182–185; Theodore of Mopsuestia's influence on, 174, 177–179, 191
Chalcedon, 311
Chaldaean Oracles: conception of afterlife in, 88, 91, 94; date and provenance of, 87; Hekate in, 285–290, 293, 294; *Mithras Liturgy* and, 275–276, 278, 285–290, 293; the moon in, 275, 293, 294, 295; reincarnation of souls in, 283. *See also* theurgy
chariot: of God, 201, 210, 211, 265; in the Mishnah, 234. *See also Maʿaseh Merkavah*; Merkavah mysticism
Charon, 19, 23, 25, 26, 143. *See also* ferryman
Cherubim. *See Keruvim*
Christ. *See* Jesus
Christianity: conceptions of heaven in, 159–160, 186–190, 259–261; diversity of, 9; East Syrian, 174, 178–185, 186–190; in North Africa, 160; and book of Revelation, 124–125; heavenly Jerusalem in, 23, 143, 158
chthonic realms: archaic and classical Greek conception of, 213–214; as distinct from celestial realm, 213, 221, 224; in later Roman period, 216–217, 225, 231–232; as source of oracular knowledge, 214. *See also* Hades; hell; underworld
Cicero, 23–25, 27
City of Christ, 85, 157; monastery as model for, 143–144, 153–154; rivers around, 154. *See also Apocalypse of Paul*
City of David, 157
city: heavenly, 12, 143–144, 152–158; as model for cosmos or heaven, 11
Claros: oracle of Apollo at, 217, 221, 223–224
classroom. *See* school
Clement of Alexandria, 276, 289

Collins, Adele Yarbro, 260
Collins, John J., 52–53
Constantine, 143
Constantinople, 15, 297–299, 300, 310–311, 313–315
constellations, 216, 293. *See also* planets; stars; zodiac
conversion, 301–303
Copeland, Kirsti B., 12, 23, 185
Corpus Hermeticum, 40, 42; on ascent of soul, 91; aversion to incarnation of soul in, 95, 280, 282; on descent of soul, 280–281, 284; Neoplatonic background of, 91; and theurgy, 91. *See also* specific titles
cosmology, in Enochic literature, 47, 49, 56–57; Gregory of Nazianzus' conception of, 35–36, 298, 299–300, 303–304, 310, 313; in Manilius, 35–6; in *Mithras Liturgy*, 14; Platonic, 303–304, 310, 313
cosmos: "pagan" views of, 14; rabbinic Jewish views of, 14; Stoic views of, 35–36
court. *See* tribunal
creation: in *The Cause of the Foundation of the Schools*, 175–177, 184; in 1 Enoch, 56, 65; in *Genesis Rabbah*, 235; in Revelation, 70–71, 73, 77–79; in *Seder Rabbah di-Bereshit*, 238; and theurgy, 97–98
Crusades, 164
Culianu, Ioan, 21
cult: in heaven, 12; in Jerusalem Temple, 13, 103, 104, 122, 203, 206–207. *See also* sacrifice
Cumont, Franz, 20, 29, 279
Cyprian (bishop): on afterlife as garden, 166; as character in *Passion of Saints Marian and Jacob*, 161, 163–164, 169; as confessor, 163; influence on martyrological literature, 162–164, 172. *See also Life of Cyprian*

Damascus Document, 116
Daniel (biblical book), 7, 47, 57, 127, 129; resurrection in, 257
Dante, 19, 26, 143
Daphne: laurel tree and maiden sacred to Apollo, 220, 225
David (biblical figure), 129, 157, 158
Davila, James R., 197, 200
Dead Sea Scrolls, 5, 6–7, 107; 4QBerakhot, 198, 206; 4QMMT, 103, 106–107; *Songs of the Maskil* (4Q510, 4Q511), 198. *See also*

325

Index

Index

Hebrew Bible, 5, 125, 141, 150, 212; creation in, 235; model of universe in, 260. *See also* specific book titles

Hekate: in *Chaldaean Oracles*, 284, 285–290, 293, 294; as underworld deity, 41. *See also* moon

Hekhalot literature, 7–8, 262; angelic duty to praise God in, 94; angelic hymns in, 74; on mystics as messengers from God, 93; and rabbinic literature, 187; and Revelation, 73–74, 76, 211; rivers of fire in, 94; and *Songs of the Sabbath Sacrifice*, 195, 202, 211

Hekhalot Rabbati, 1, 74, 76, 252, 271–274

Helios: Apollo equated with, 219, 221, 223–224, 227–228, 231; in *Mithras Liturgy*, 294

hell, 14, 19, 23, 28, 259; in the *Book of Watchers*, 254–255; in pre-Rabbinic Judaism, 253–261. *See also* Hades, chthonic realms, underworld

Hengel, Martin, 1, 76

Hera, 41

Heracles, 93

heresy, 6, 8

Hermas, 7

Hermes: as underworld deity, 214, 216, 225, 232

Hermeticism: cosmology in, 280; on descent of soul into matter, 280–281, 284; spiritual ascent in, 37, 280–281. *See also Corpus Hermeticum*

Herod, 154

Himmelfarb, Martha, 11, 50, 57, 91, 145, 146, 199, 212, 256, 259

History of the Franks. See Gregory of Tours

History of the Monks in Egypt, 152, 155

hole in the ground: as passageway to underworld, 19

Holy of Holies, 145, 151

Homer, 19, 27, 85, 182, 215–216, 226; *Odyssey*, 165, 215, 231

Horace, 167

Horus, 215, 223

Housman, Alfred E., 35, 38, 43

humankind, 35, 69, 176, 244, 245, 250, 251, 256, 288

hybridity, cultural, 5, 129

hymns: to Apollo, 214–217, 221, 224; heaven and earth bridged by, 11, 67–69, 71, 80–81;

in Hekhalot literature, 74; to Helios, 227–228, 231; in *Songs of the Sabbath Sacrifice*, 195, 197. *See also* liturgy; praise; worship

Ḥayyot (angelic creatures), 76, 242, 245, 264

Iamblichus, 87, 88, 89, 97, 283–284, 293

Iao: as celestial deity, 219; Apollo equated with, 224, 226. *See also* Adonai; Yahweh

incarnation: of Christ, 297–298, 300–301, 303–304, 307, 309–310, 312–314; in Graeco-Roman religions, 14; of soul in Neoplatonism and theurgy, 279–284. *See also* reincarnation

incense: contrasted with blood sacrifice, 121–122; in meal offering, 110; as offering in heavenly cult, 12; in *Jubilees*, 118–121. *See also* aroma

Irenaeus of Lyons, 147–149, 284

Isaac (biblical figure): in *Aramaic Levi*, 103, 104, 105–114, 116, 121; in *Jubilees*, 116; as priest, 116

Isaiah (biblical book): Irenaeus' use of, 147; restoration of Jerusalem in, 144–145; trisagion in, 68, 70

Isaiah (biblical figure), 91, 203

Isis, 286, 289, 292

Islam, 1

Israel, land of, 144. *See also* Palestine

Israel, people of, 146, 181, 313; oppressors of, 249

Jacob (biblical figure): dream of, 20, 30, 32; ladder of, 20, 30, 32, 41; as priest in *Jubilees*, 116, 119

Jacob of Serug, 188

Jerome: dream of, 25, 26; on monks of Egypt, 152

Jerusalem, 123, 128, 204; as Aelia Capitolina, 148, 151, 158; ascent to heaven of, 145; in *Book of Watchers*, 254; destruction of, 146; as heavenly or celestial city, 12, 28–29, 83, 143–149, 245, 249, 264, 265, 266; Jesus' entry into, 31; in rabbinic Jewish thought, 149; relationship between heavenly and earthly, 144–152; restoration of, 144–149; Rome and, 132–133; Temple in, 13, 79, 83

Jesus, 31, 92, 140, 150, 159, 163, 292; baptism of, 298, 307; as beautiful youth, 162; and beast in Revelation, 76–77, 81; crucifixion

328

Index

Macrobius, 278, 280

magic, magicians, 49, 54; modern scholarship on, 2-3, 6-7; in mystery groups, 259, 278, 292-294

Maier, Johann, 196, 198

Manilius, 10, 34-45; astrological worldview of, 291; *Astronomica* of, 10, 34, 38; as didactic poet, 35, 38, 40, 45; on Fate, 45, 59-60; influence of Stoic philosophy on, 35; poetic style of, 37, 39-40; on zodiac, 43, 93

manna, 245, 249, 264

Marian (martyr), 12, 160-173. *See also* under *Passion of Saints Marian and Jacob*

Mark, Gospel of, 31

Marshall, John W., 12, 76, 81, 83, 147

martyrdom, 2, 12; cup as symbol of, 169-171; of Cyprian, 160, 162-164; of Marian, 160-173; as motif in Revelation, 76; as path to heaven, 172; of Perpetua, 31-32, 172; of Quartillosia, 170

martyrological literature, 6, 12-13; visions of heaven in, 31-32, 160-173. *See also specific titles*

martyrs: ascent of, 162, 164; as recipients of visions of heaven, 31-32, 160-173. *See also specific names*

Masada, 197, 198

Massekhet Hekhalot, 234

Matthew, Gospel of, 11, 26, 92

Menander Rhetor, 214, 221, 224

Merkavah mysticism, 234-235, 271-272. *See also* chariot

Merkelbach, Reinhold, 279

Mesopotamia, 19, 214, 231; contacts between Jews and Christians in, 13, 185; and origin of astrology, 34

Metatron (angel), 92, 94, 266, 271

Methodius, 168

Michael (angel), 23, 134, 226, 264, 266; in *Seder Rabbah di-Bereshit*, 245, 246, 249, 257, 264, 266

Michael Psellus, 87

Midrash Konen, 269, 270

Midrash Proverbs, 267, 270

Midrash, 149, 238

Mishnah: depiction of sacrificial cult in, 105; on bloodied priestly vestments, 107; on *Ma'aseh Bereshit* and *ha-Merkavah*, 234, 245; on order of sacrifice, 110

Mithraism, 10, 41; ladder of ascent in, 20, 41, 279; and *Mithras Liturgy*, 279

Mithras Liturgy, and *Chaldaean Oracles*, 275-276, 278, 285-286; cosmology of, 278-279, 290-295; moon absent from, 14, 275-277, 290-295; place within Great Paris Magical Papyrus, 290

Mithras, 215, 292

Molenberg, Corrie, 57

monastery: as model for heaven, 12, 152-158, 185; of St. Benedict, 30; of Wenlock, 27

monasticism, 22, 30; East Syrian, 182, 183; Egyptian, 152-158

monks, 22, 27; as angels, 12; *Apocalypse of Paul* on post-mortem fate of, 153-157

Montanism, 148-149

moon, 24, 33, 44, 55-56, 126, 166-167, 215, 245, 250, 251, 264, 265, 275; absent from *Mithras Liturgy*, 14, 275-277, 290-295; as intermediary principle responsible for fate, 275, 282; in *Chaldaean Oracles*, 275-276, 293, 294, 295

Moreschini, Claudio, 298, 305

Morray-Jones, Christopher, 198, 200

Morrison, Karl, 301

Moses (biblical figure), 176, 177, 307

Muses, 218, 222-223, 227

mysticism, 2; and Manilius, 35, 37; and *Songs of the Sabbath Sacrifice*, 195, 196. *See also* Merkavah mysticism

myth: of angelic descent, 49-50, 53-54, 59-61; of Apollo and Branchus, 222-223, 224, 225; of Apollo and Daphne, 220, 225; of Er, 25-26, 93, 94

Nag Hammadi Library, 8-9. *See also specific titles*

Narsai, 184-185, 188

Nebuchadnezzar, 269

necromancy: celestial and chthonic elements in, 213, 214-217, 231; rituals of, 213-214, 224-232

Neoplatonism: and astrology, 291-292; on descent of soul into matter, 279-284; in East-Syrian Christianity, 185; influence on Gregory of Nazianzus, 297, 314; spiritual ascent in, 37; and theurgy, 87, 90

Nero, 129, 135, 140

netherworld. *See* chthonic realms; hell

New Prophecy. *See* Montanism

Index

Index

Suetonius, 12, 129, 130, 131, 134, 137, 138

sun, 7, 24, 44, 86, 126, 131, 140, 156, 166–167, 188, 224, 245, 250, 251, 264, 265, 306; Apollo equated with various gods of, 13–14, 214–224, 227–230, 231–232; illicit knowledge about, 55–57; in *Mithras Liturgy*, 278–279, 290, 294; in Neoplatonic cosmologies, 277, 279, 289, 292, 294; in *Seder Rabbah di-Bereshit*, 251

Sunniulf of Randan, 22–26

Sybilline Oracles, 167

syncretism, 214–217, 218–219

Syriac Christian literature, 174, 179–185

Tacitus (historian), 12, 123, 126, 133, 134, 135, 139, 140

Talmud: Babylonian, 185, 191, 234, 237, 246, 249, 268, 271; and East-Syrian Christian literature, 185–187, 191; heaven as academy in, 185–187

Tantalus, 85

Tartarus, 24

Temple Scroll, 103, 105, 111

Temple, Jewish: in *Aramaic Levi*, 103–104; in Ezekiel, 201, 202, 204; in heaven, 12, 196, 199, 200–203, 206, 208, 210, 212, 245, 264, 265; heavenly and earthly, 121–122, 144–146; images of angels in, 197, 206; importance in pre-Rabbinic Judaism, 103; in 1 Kings, 204; punishment for enemies of, 248, 249; in Revelation, 79, 132–133; Second, 11, 79–80, 145, 203, 205, 206

Tertullian, 32; as editor of Perpetua's diary, 32; on heaven as garden, 166; as Montanist, 148; on New Jerusalem, 148–149

Testament of Levi, 67, 76, 259; on bloodless sacrificial offering in heaven, 121; heaven as Temple in, 146. *See also Aramaic Levi*

Theodore of Mopsuestia: as authority in East-Syrian tradition, 179–185; on exegesis of Genesis 1, 177–179; as influence on *Cause of the Foundation of the Schools*, 174, 177–179, 191; Narsai influenced by, 184–185; on notion of divine *Paideia*, 174, 178; school of, 177

Theodosius, 157

theurgy, 11, 297; as combining locative and utopian worldviews, 98; conception of afterlife in, 88–89, 90–91; and Hekhalot literature, 93–94; and *Hermetica*, 91; *Mithras Liturgy* and, 275–276, 285–290, 292–293; moon as malevolent power in, 293, 294, 295; Platonic influences on, 96–99; reincarnation of souls in, 88–89; Socratic ideal city-state as model for cosmos in, 96. *See also Chaldaean Oracles*; Neoplatonism

throne, 1303; of glory, 12, 242, 251; of God, 234, 254, 255, 264, 271, 313

Titus, 123–124, 126, 134

Tnugdal. *See Vision of Tnugdal*

Torah (Pentateuch), 56, 245; *Jubilees* relatively faithful to, 117; on meal offering, 110–112; on order of sacrifice, 108–110; prescriptions for cultic practice in, 107; on weights and measures for sacrificial offerings, 112–115; on washing, 107; on wood for altar, 108. *See also specific book titles*

Tower of Babel, 258

tribunal, heavenly, 28, 161–164

Trinity, 303–304, 312–314

trisagion, 52, 67, 68, 77–80, 199. *See also under* Isaiah; Revelation

Tritopatores: ancestral spirits worshipped by Greeks, 93

Vespasian, 123–124, 126, 134, 140

Vettius Valens, 291

Virgil, 19, 23, 24, 25, 26, 28, 33

virtue, 11. *See also* righteous

Vision of Tnugdal, 29

visions: of Baruch, 146–147; of Cyprian, 162–164; didactic purpose of, 22, 26; of Enoch, 48, 63; of Er, 25–26; of Ezekiel, 144–145; of Ezra, 146–147; of heaven as garden, 164–171; of heaven as throne-room, 12, 69–71, 79–80, 82, 128–129; of hell and Paradise, 23; of Isaiah, 144–145; of Jerusalem restored, 144–145; of John of Patmos, 69–71, 80, 83, 127, 128–129; of martyrs, 29, 31–32, 160–173; of Marian, 160–173; of monk of Wenlock, 27–29; of Paradise, 22–23, 28, 164, 166–167; of Paul, 23, 24, 154–157, 165; of Salvius of Albi, 24;

Index

of Tnugdal, 29; of tribunal in heaven, 28, 161–164. *See also* dreams
Volk, Katharina, 10, 20

Watchers (angelic creatures): as fathers of Giants, 49, 54, 59–60, 65; rebuke and punishments of, 50, 53; sexual sins of, 54, 55, 59; teachings of, 49–55, 57, 65
Wisdom literature: attitudes toward knowledge in, 57–59; as produced in priestly and scribal circles, 58–59; relationship to apocalyptic literature, 57–58. *See also* Qohelet; Wisdom of ben Sira
Wisdom of ben Sira, 57–58, 79
Wolfson, Elliot R., 196
Wright, J. Edward, 259–261

Yadin, Yigael, 197
Yahweh: as celestial deity, 216; Apollo equated with, 224, 226, 231. *See also* Iao
yeshivah. *See* school
Yoḥanan ben Zakkai, 234

Zechariah (biblical figure), 132, 167
Zeus, 90, 148, 288, 291; as celestial or solar deity, 213, 219, 226; as underworld deity, 216
Zion, 135. *See also* Jerusalem
zodiac: Manilius' discussion of, 10, 37, 38, 43–45; in Neoplatonic thought, 279. *See also* astrology; astronomy; constellations; planets
Zoroastrians, 176, 181, 190

335